INTERNATIONAL COOKING
for the
KOSHER HOME

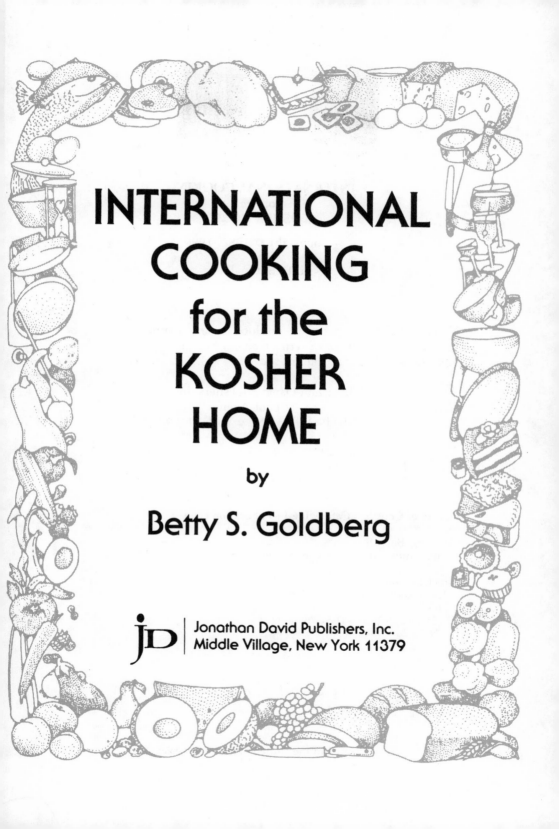

INTERNATIONAL COOKING for the KOSHER HOME

by

Betty S. Goldberg

jD | Jonathan David Publishers, Inc.
Middle Village, New York 11379

INTERNATIONAL COOKING
for the
KOSHER HOME

Copyright © 1988, 1990
by
Betty S. Goldberg

Jonathan David Publishers, Inc.
68-22 Eliot Avenue
Middle Village, New York 11379

1994
10 9 8 7 6 5 4 3 2

Library of Congress Cataloging-in-Publication Data

Goldberg, Betty S.
  International cooking for the kosher home.

  Includes index.
  1. Cookery, Jewish. 2. Cookery, International.
I. Title.
TX724.G6525 1987 641.5′676 86-32813
ISBN 0-8246-0346-X

Layout by Arlene Schleifer Goldberg

Printed in the United States of America

To my Grandmas

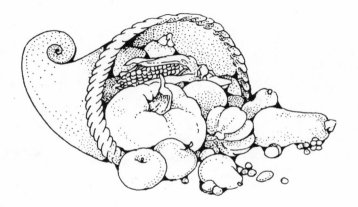

Acknowledgments

For the special help and support I received in writing this book, I would like to thank the following:

My publisher, Rabbi Alfred J. Kolatch, for having confidence in me again; my editor, David Kolatch, for helping me shape the idea and for showing me how to turn the pedantic into the inviting; Carol Smith for her encouragement after an early reading; Lois Levine for reading the complete manuscript and being gracious as always; my sister, Anne Feldman, for not complaining about being edited out a second time; my husband, Josh, for his unwavering enthusiasm, and our children, Aaron, Michael, Benjamin, and Nancy, for sharing the adventure of eating in an international kitchen.

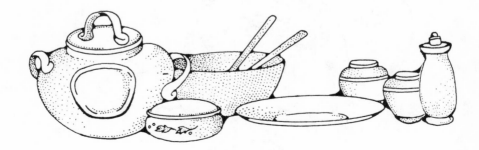

Contents

Preface 9

Introduction 11
    Adaptations for the Kosher Home 11
    Selecting Ingredients 12

1. **Europe**
    Introduction 35
    Appetizers and Soups 47
    Condiments and Sauces 63
    Main Dishes 66
    Side Dishes 89
    Desserts 102

2. **The Middle East**
    Introduction 123
    Appetizers and Soups 128
    Condiments and Sauces 136
    Main Dishes 141
    Side Dishes 164
    Desserts 170

3. **Asia and the Pacific Islands**
    Introduction 179
    Appetizers and Soups 187
    Condiments and Sauces 200
    Main Dishes 211
    Side Dishes 245
    Desserts 259

4. The Americas

Introduction 267
Appetizers and Soups 276
Condiments and Sauces 289
Main Dishes 295
Side Dishes 318
Desserts 329

Index 341

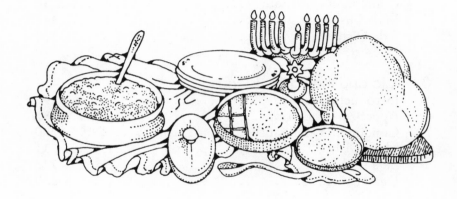

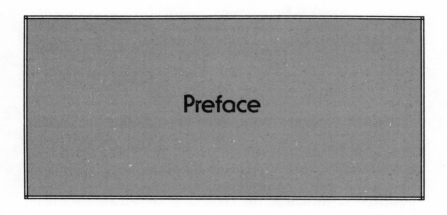

Preface

Welcome to an adventure in exotic kosher cooking. The idea for this book began early in 1985, when an Asian Indian high school student became part of our family for five months. Like any other teenager he missed his mother's cooking, and because I enjoy experimenting with foreign cuisines, I promised him one Indian meal a week. Before long I realized I had a most wonderful opportunity to learn about authentic Indian cuisine. Here was a knowledgeable, appreciative, yet critical audience who could tell me how close my meals came to Indian home cooking.

Does this taste like your mother's rice? Is my homemade yogurt okay? Is the beef curry missing any important spices? Did I buy the right hot peppers this time? As I cooked, asked questions, and listened to his comments, it became apparent that not only was I learning to prepare Indian meals with some authenticity, I was also gathering recipes and information for a cookbook.

I knew from my experience developing recipes for my last book, *Chinese Kosher Cooking*, that well-known Chinese dishes such as shrimp toast, sweet-and-sour pork, and lobster Cantonese could be turned into delicious kosher preparations. My weekly experiments with Indian meals made it apparent that the spicy meat-and-yogurt combinations of India could be adapted to the kosher kitchen as well. But why stop with India? With international cooking as a hobby, I was already familiar with many foreign cuisines—Greek, Italian, French, and Mexican (my son took two homemade *enchiladas* for lunch every day for several years)—and I was eager to acquaint myself with other cuisines.

And so began many months of researching, testing, and

retesting. Our kitchen shelves were stocked with *udon* and *somen* (Japanese noodles), *couscous* (semolina grain), chickpeas and sesame seeds, countless spices, and many different kinds of soy sauce. Hungry teenagers opened the refrigerator to find leeks and lemon grass, fresh herbs, breadfruit, cassava, and papayas. During our "coconut phase" there were fresh coconuts all over the kitchen, waiting to be turned into milk and cream for Thai curries and Hawaiian desserts.

My family members were reasonably enthusiastic about our experimental meals, and they helped me establish guidelines for the recipes to include in this cookbook. "When are we having that French veal stew again?" was a definite indication that Blanquette de Veau was a must for the book, whereas "I guess I'm not too hungry tonight" gave a different message. The results are representatives of the best of the cuisines of the world, tested and enjoyed in Woodbridge, Connecticut, and presented for you to prepare and enjoy in your own home.

B.S.G.

Woodbridge, Connecticut

Introduction

Close your eyes and imagine yourself removing an unusually aromatic Indian chicken preparation from your oven. Can you smell the spices? Or picture an exquisite Tahitian fish wrapped in tropical leaves or a hearty Brazilian dish of black beans with tomatoes.

International Cooking for the Kosher Home contains a range of enticing specialties from all over the world, including the United States. Each of the four chapters represents a geographic area, with an underlying eye toward culinary similarities. Thus, although Iran is an Asian country and Morocco is located west of the area generally considered Middle Eastern, because their cuisines are related to the cooking of the Mideast, Iran and Morocco are presented in the chapter "The Middle East." Recipes were selected on the basis of interest, appeal, and of course taste, with particular attention to preparations not usually found in kosher cookbooks.

Adaptations for the Kosher Home

How can the classic, festive, and everyday dishes of unusual foreign cuisines be turned into recipes that meet the strict Jewish dietary laws? For meat-and-dairy combinations, sometimes it is possible to turn one recipe into two. In this way, a meat-and-cheese pizza becomes a meat-and-tomato pizza (Pepperoni Pizza, page 77) and a cheese-and-tomato pizza (Variation, page 79); a traditional Greek moussaka becomes a meat-and-eggplant moussaka and a cheese moussaka (page 160); and so on. For Indian dishes that combine meat and yogurt, by omitting the yogurt but selecting the appropriate spices, we can retain the essence of the original preparations. Using veal broth instead of cream in "cream" sauces (Swedish Meatballs, page 74) and substituting vegetarian broth for chicken or beef broth in cream soups (Cream of Mushroom Soup, page 58) are other ways of making preparations kosher.

In kosher cooking it is contrary to tradition to mix meat and fish in the same dish. In exotic meat-and-fish dishes chicken can easily take the place of the fish. A rich vegetarian broth (page 55) is a good substitute for chicken broth in recipes where fish is cooked in broth.

Nonkosher foods such as pork and shellfish can be replaced by beef (Pepperoni, page 76), veal (Veal with Apples and Prunes, page 70), or fish having fins and scales (Tempura, page 237). Chicken livers require special handling to make them kosher, for they must be broiled to extract as much blood as possible. Broiled chicken livers can successfully be used for Hawaiian Rumaki (page 193) even though the livers are broiled twice, because the pastrami in which they are wrapped for the second broiling protects the livers from being overcooked.

Many unusual and tasty international preparations require no kosher adaptations at all. While this book tries not to duplicate recipes commonly found in other cookbooks, when a dish is so enticing, delicious, and representative of a cuisine that it deserves attention, it is included.

Selecting Ingredients

You may be surprised at how many ingredients used in foreign dishes are available in ordinary groceries and supermarkets. Check the produce section carefully, as well as the shelves where international foods are stocked. Gourmet food stores, health food stores, specialty shops, and food co-ops often have or can order unusual ingredients. International food stores—Chinese, Japanese, general Asian, Indian, Spanish, Greek, or Middle Eastern, for example—carry the specialty items needed for all the recipes in this cookbook.

The Yellow Pages is helpful in locating appropriate food

stores. Check the heading "Grocers-Retail" and scan individual listings for Spanish, Middle Eastern, and Indian markets. Chinese and Japanese food stores are usually listed under "Oriental Foods" or "Food-Oriental." "Gourmet Shops" and "Health Food Stores" are other common listings. Cultural centers in universities and ethnic restaurants are also good places to call for sources of ingredients. Many people will be delighted that you are taking an interest in their cuisine and will help you locate the ingredients you need.

The following section describes special ingredients called for in the recipes presented here. Some are ingredients used in everyday cooking, but they are listed here because in this book they are used in more than one form (ground cinnamon and stick cinnamon, for example) or because they might be confused with another ingredient (parsley with Chinese parsley, for example).

Allspice

Although allspice tastes and smells like a blend of cloves, nutmeg, and other spices, it is actually not a spice mixture but the dried berry of a tropical American tree. The berry, which is used whole or ground, is stored as any other spice, at room temperature in a tightly covered jar.

Annatto (Achiote)

These dried magenta-red seeds of the tropical annatto tree are used to color and flavor Philippine and Mexican preparations. Hard and irregularly shaped, annatto seeds are approximately ⅛ inch long. Available in the Spanish or Mexican section of supermarkets and in Latin American groceries, the seeds may be stored indefinitely at room temperature in a tightly covered jar.

Banana Leaves

In Asia and the Pacific Islands, the large green leathery, inedible leaves of the banana plant are used for wrapping foods. The wrapped foods are then cooked, and while the leaves may become charred, the food inside does not burn. Banana leaves flavor food delicately with a taste similar to lettuce leaves. Available in Asian groceries, banana leaves will keep for a few days in the refrigerator and can be frozen for months.

Basil

There are numerous varieties of the basil plant, whose aromatic leaves have more than a hint of a licorice scent. Used fresh or dried in many cuisines, basil leaves are particularly well known in Italian preparations. The dried version is sold as "sweet basil," referring to a variety of basil plant, while gardeners cultivate both bush basil and sweet basil to use as a fresh herb. Purple and lemon basils have different flavors from the bush and sweet varieties and may change the flavor of a recipe.

Bay Leaves

The pungent and aromatic leaves of the laurel plant, commonly known as bay leaves, are sold dried and are used sparingly to flavor soups and stews. While most often used whole and removed before serving, for some recipes the leaves are crushed and incorporated into the preparations.

Black Beans

Known also as turtle beans and *frijoles negros*, these ⅜-inch-long dried beans used in soups and main dishes are available in one-pound packages in supermarkets. Do not confuse them with the semisoft fermented black beans used in Chinese cooking.

Black Pepper

The dried black berrylike fruit of the woody vine *Piper nigrum*, known as a peppercorn, can be used whole or ground. Ground peppercorns are the seasoning commonly referred to as pepper. When recipes in this book call for ground pepper, black pepper, or salt and pepper, the commonly used black pepper is what is meant.

Boniatos *See* Potatoes

Breadcrumbs

When breadcrumbs or soft breadcrumbs are called for as an ingredient in a recipe in this book, they refer to breadcrumbs made at home by pulverizing white bread in a food processor or blender. One slice of white bread yields about half a cup of breadcrumbs. To use French or Italian bread, first remove the crusts.

Breadfruit

The edible starchy fruit of the breadfruit tree is available in supermarkets featuring tropical fruits. Breadfruits are baked or boiled before they are eaten, and the taste of cooked breadfruit is reminiscent of whole-grain bread. The fruit is oblong, with a brown skin and yellowish-brown interior. Buy breadfruit when slightly soft, and store in the refrigerator for up to ten days.

Burghul (Bulghur, Bulgur)

This coarse, irregularly shaped grain is wheat that has been boiled, sun-dried, then cracked. The cracked wheat is used all over the Middle East in *pilafs*, salads, and lamb mixtures. Sold here in Middle Eastern groceries and natural or health food stores, *burghul* can be stored for many months at room temperature in a tightly covered jar.

Capsicum

Capsicum is the scientific name for the podlike fruits we know as peppers. Included in the *Capsicum* family are sweet bell peppers, hot cayenne peppers, the peppers from which paprika is made, and all chili peppers, from mild to hot. The common black peppercorns that yield ground black pepper are not in the *Capsicum* family.

Cardamom

This spice can be purchased either ground or in pod form. When a recipe uses the seeds from a pod, open the pod with your fingers or a knife, and use the seeds only. Tasting somewhat like cloves but sweeter, cardamom is used in many Indian and Middle Eastern preparations. In Europe and the United States it is used to flavor baked goods. For Middle Eastern meals, crush a cardamom pod with the side of a heavy knife or cleaver and place the seeds in a cup of tea.

Cassava

A starchy white Brazilian root that is used to make tapioca, cassava is popular in South American countries. The tuber looks like a thick piece of horseradish with a rough dark brown skin and a white interior. When boiled or fried, cassava is an unusual potato substitute, tasting a little like a winter squash but sweeter and more starchy. If the cassava is already cut so you can see the interior, purchase those pieces that are moist and uncracked. The skin should be unbroken and the exterior should not appear excessively dry and shriveled.

Cayenne Pepper

A red-hot pepper, widely available in ground form, cayenne is used often in the cooking of Texas and New Orleans. Use cayenne sparingly, for as little as a quarter-teaspoon of this bright red pepper can make an entire preparation fiery.

Cellophane Noodles

Made of mung beans, these long white brittle, dry noodles are used in Asian cuisines. They are available in Asian groceries and will keep for a very long time at room temperature. Unless they are to be fried, cellophane noodles must be soaked in water before they are cooked. Upon soaking, they become soft and transparent.

Chickpea Flour

This fine-grained flour, yellow in color, is made from ground uncooked chickpeas. Used in Indian cooking, chickpea flour can be purchased in Indian groceries and some natural or health food stores. All-purpose flour is an acceptable substitute.

Chili Peppers

Red, green, and yellow peppers of the *Capsicum* family range from mild to hot, but the fresh chili peppers used in this book are always hot. Chili peppers, which are used in many cuisines, are native to Mexico, where they are used extensively.

Dried chili peppers range from mild to hot, but the ones commonly available in supermarkets, natural or health food stores, gourmet food shops, and Asian groceries, are all hot.

Chili Powder

When used in this book, the term "chili powder" always refers to a purchased blend of spices made of hot chili peppers, oregano, cumin, and garlic. The proportions of the spices vary from manufacturer to manufacturer, so you might want to do a bit of experimenting until you find a brand you especially like.

Chilies, Peeled Green

These canned peppers used in Mexican cooking are available in supermarkets that feature foreign foods. They range from mild to hot, so check the label carefully before buying.

Chinese Cabbage

Three kinds of Chinese cabbage are widely available in Asian groceries and in some American supermarkets. *Bok choy,* most commonly used by the Chinese, has long, smooth white stalks and dark green leaves; it looks like Swiss chard but is sold in a bunch like celery. *Celery cabbage* has broad white stalks that shade to a medium green where the stalk blends smoothly into the leaf. *Nappa* is similar in appearance to celery cabbage, but the leaves are broader, whiter, and more crinkly, and the head more stout. Neither regular green cabbage nor celery is an adequate substitute for any of the Chinese cabbages. Store in the refrigerator.

Chinese Hot Turnip   *See* Hot Turnip and Hot Radish

Chinese Mushrooms, Dried   *See* Dried Chinese Mushrooms

Cinnamon

This well-known spice, the dried bark of a tropical Asian tree commonly known as the cinnamon tree, is used in solid form (stick cinnamon) or ground. Most often used in baking in European countries and the United States, cinnamon is a main dish seasoning in Indian, Moroccan, and other Asian and Middle Eastern cuisines.

Clarified Butter   *See also* Ghee

When butter is melted and all of the milky residue is removed, the result is clarified butter. To make clarified butter, cut the butter into small bits, then cook over moderate heat until the butter foams. Skim off the foam, immediately reduce the heat to low so the butter does not brown, and cook for a few minutes. To remove all the solids, pour the liquid through a strainer lined with slightly dampened cheesecloth or muslin. The strained milky residue is discarded. One stick (½ cup) of butter yields about six tablespoons of clarified butter.

Coriander (Chinese Parsley, Cilantro)

The leaves of the coriander plant resemble parsley in appearance, but they have a more distinctive, acrid taste with a sharp aftertaste. Because even a small amount of coriander will affect the final flavor of a preparation, I strongly recommend that you taste fresh coriander and find out if you like it before using it in a recipe. Fresh coriander is available in the produce section of some supermarkets and in Asian, Spanish, Middle Eastern, and Indian groceries.

The dried small round seeds of the coriander plant are used whole, crushed, or ground. They are aromatic but not nearly as acrid as the fresh leaves of the plant. Ground coriander is usually an ingredient in prepared curry powders. Although ground coriander is widely available, you may enjoy grinding your own.

Couscous

This coarse yellow grain made of tiny round pellets of semolina is available in natural or health food stores and Middle Eastern groceries. It will keep well at room temperature in a tightly covered jar. *Couscous* refers to a particular preparation as well as to the mildly flavored grain itself.

Crushed Dried Red Pepper

When crushed dried red pepper is called for in a recipe, the term refers to the widely available round flat flakes of hot pepper typically sprinkled on Italian foods but used in many other cuisines.

Cumin (Comino)

A widely available spice popular in many cuisines, cumin seed is used whole, crushed, or ground. Cumin is an ingredient in both chili and curry powders, and has a smell and taste reminiscent of caraway seeds.

Curry Paste

A mixture of herbs and spices used in Thai preparations, curry pastes are identified by color. They are usually red or green, but may be yellow or orange, depending on the ingredients used. Although freshly-prepared curry pastes are fiery hot, when combined with coconut milk in Thai recipes, their hotness is considerably diminished.

Curry Powder *See also* Masala

Curry powder is a Western version of a prepared mixture of spices used in Indian cooking. I recommend that you make your own spice mixture (see Index listing under *masala*), or buy a mixture from an Indian food store. The authentic Indian mixtures are likely to be more fresh and tastier than national brands available in supermarkets.

Dashi

The Japanese soup base made of dried seaweed and dried bonito flakes, *dashi* is sweet and smoky with more of a vegetable than a fish flavor. Prepackaged *dashi* mixes are available in Asian groceries and some natural food stores. A recipe for homemade *dashi* appears in this book.

Dill

The fresh leaves of the dill plant, sometimes called dill weed, are dark green and feathery in appearance, aromatic and distinctive in taste. Fresh dill is available in many supermarkets, where it is usually located near the fresh parsley. Dried dill may be substituted in a recipe only if specified. When a dried herb is used in place of the fresh leaves, only about one-third the amount is needed. Dill seed is not a substitute for fresh dill.

Dried Chili Peppers *See* Chili Peppers

Dried Chinese Mushrooms

Unlike fresh mushrooms, these are chewy, with an earthy, slightly smoky taste. They are soaked in boiling water and softened, and the tough stems are removed before using the mushrooms in a recipe. Although expensive, dried Chinese mushrooms are used sparingly in most dishes, and they keep well at room temperature in a tightly covered jar.

Fenugreek

These small mildly pungent yellow-orange seeds are used whole or ground in Indian cuisine. With a sweet, smoky aroma and a slightly bitter but pleasant taste somewhat like a mixture of ground cumin and mustard, a pinch of fenugreek adds a

subtle flavor to Indian preparations. Available in Indian groceries and some natural or health food stores, fenugreek should
not be confused with the more widely known licorice-flavored
fennel seeds.

Fermented Black Beans (Salted Black Beans)

These soft, slightly chewy, very salty small black beans are
sold prepackaged in Asian groceries. Used sparingly to season
Chinese and Vietnamese preparations, fermented black beans
can be soaked before cooking to reduce the saltiness. They will
keep for years in a tightly covered jar at room temperature.

Filé Powder

Made of ground sassafras leaves, this green powder is used
in place of okra to thicken and flavor some Louisiana gumbos. It
is available in spice shops and some gourmet food stores. Be
careful when you use filé powder, because if you add the
powder to a lovely smooth gravy and then allow the mixture to
come to the boil, the gravy will turn unpleasantly stringy.

Garam Masala

Literally "hot mixture," this blend of ground cardamom,
cloves, black pepper, cumin, coriander, and cinnamon makes a
spicy mixture that is used as a seasoning in preparing Indian
dishes. *Garam masala* is usually added during the last few minutes of cooking so the spices will retain their strength. It is
tastiest when prepared from freshly ground spices.

Ghee *See also* Clarified Butter

The clarified butter of India, *ghee* is important in Indian
cuisine both because it does not burn at high cooking tempera-
tures and because it will keep for months at room temperature
without becoming rancid. *Ghee* is prepared like clarified butter,
but the cooking time over low heat is increased to 45 minutes,
and the butter is strained through a triple layer of cheesecloth
so that every speck of solid material is removed.

Ginger, Ground

The powdered, dried root of the ginger plant is not as
aromatic as fresh ginger root, but there are times when ground
ginger is the preferred form in a recipe. Many Moroccan recipes

use ground ginger. Do not use fresh ginger root and ground ginger interchangeably in the recipes in this book.

Ginger Root, Fresh

Fresh ginger root, pungent and tangy, is used most often in Chinese, Indian, and Japanese preparations. It looks like a gnarled tree root and can be found in the produce section of supermarkets and in Asian food stores. Look for a thin, light brown skin. Store unpeeled ginger root unwrapped in the vegetable compartment of the refrigerator, where it will keep for a few days to several weeks. Any cut ends that become moldy may be sliced off. For longer storage, peel the ginger root and either freeze it or place it in a small jar of sherry or white wine and store in the refrigerator.

Glutinous Rice

Glutinous rice is one of the rices commonly used in China, Japan, Thailand, and Vietnam. This chewy stubby starchy rice is also called "sticky rice" because it becomes sticky when cooked and "sweet rice" because it is used in desserts. It is used to make puddings, stuffings, and the *congees* (porridgelike soups) of China. Purchase glutinous rice in Asian groceries, and store as any other rice.

Golden Needles *See* Tiger Lily Buds

Green Peppers

When a recipe in this book lists green peppers as an ingredient, use common green bell peppers.

Hoisin Sauce

This thick, smooth purplish-brown sauce has a soybean base with added flavorings of sugar, vinegar, garlic, and chili. Used in Chinese cooking, it is available in cans in Asian groceries. Refrigerate for several weeks in a tightly closed jar, or freeze for long-term storage. *Hoisin* sauce does not freeze solidly, so it can be used directly from the freezer without thawing.

Hot Turnip and Hot Radish

Also known as Szechwan turnip and Szechwan radish, these two spicy vegetable preparations are sold in small to medium-size cans in Asian groceries. Once opened, transfer the turnip or radish to a small jar with a good lid, and store in the refrigerator, where the vegetable will keep for many weeks.

Laos

This root, related to ginger but neither as pungent nor as aromatic, is sold in Asian food stores in dried or powdered form. It is used in the cooking of Thailand and Indonesia.

Leeks

Onions, leeks, chives, garlic, and scallions—all members of the *Allium* family—are pungent when raw and mellow when cooked. The leek, a root vegetable that looks like a thick scallion, is sweet and subtle. When cooked, it has more of a green vegetable flavor than cooked onions. Enjoyed as both a vege-table and a seasoning in soups throughout Europe, leeks are also well known in Middle Eastern cuisines. Because leeks trap soil in between their leaves as they grow, they must be cleaned well before using. The tough dark green tops of leeks are not used in cooking.

Lemon Grass

Aromatic and lemony, appearing similar to a dried scallion, lemon grass is used in Thai, Indonesian, and Vietnamese prepa-rations. It is available in Asian groceries either fresh or dried. Store fresh lemon grass in the refrigerator, and always soak the dried version before using.

Lentils

The round flattened seeds found in the pods of the *Lens culinaris,* a leguminous plant, lentils are a major protein source in India, where dozens of varieties are grown. Brown and red lentils are well known in the Middle East and Europe. When lentils are called for as an ingredient in this cookbook, use the brown lentils commonly available in one-pound packages in supermarkets.

Masa Harina

This specially prepared corn flour used in making tortillas is available in packages in some supermarkets and in Mexican groceries. The more commonly available corn meal is more coarse than *masa harina*, although it may be used in the preparation of tortillas if used in combination with other flours.

Masala

A blend of spices used in Indian preparations, *masala* is made of cumin, coriander, and turmeric as basic ingredients, with a selection of smaller amounts of cardamom, cloves, hot red peppers, cinnamon, fenugreek, mustard seeds, and other spices added to change the flavor and spiciness of the mixture. Different mixtures of spices are used for each dish. Because ground spices lose flavor rapidly, *masalas* are best when prepared from whole spices that are freshly ground and mixed as necessary. Leftover *masalas* will retain their potency for several weeks at room temperature in a tightly closed jar.

Mint

The aromatic and strongly flavored leaves of the mint plant are used to perk up tea and other beverages, salads, and marinades. Use fresh spearmint leaves for recipes in this book, or dried mint leaves where specified.

Mirin *See also* Rice Wine

The sweetened rice wine of Japan, *mirin* contributes a delicate flavor to marinades and rice dishes. It is available in Asian groceries.

Miso

A salty bean paste used to thicken, flavor, and color Japanese soups, *miso* comes in colors ranging from yellow to deep red. The bean paste is available in packages or jars in Asian groceries and some natural or health food stores. Chinese red bean paste is not a substitute.

Mushrooms, Dried *See* Dried Chinese Mushrooms

Mustard

Pungent yellow or black seeds from the mustard plant are used whole or ground. The ground yellow seeds are used to make the spicy condiment commonly referred to as "prepared mustard" or simply "mustard." When recipes call for ground mustard or dry mustard powder, use a plain dry mustard that is not premixed with any other ingredients, or grind the powder from the yellow seeds. The smaller black mustard seeds are often used in Indian cooking, but the more readily available yellow mustard seeds are an acceptable alternative.

Navy Beans

Also known as "pea beans," these are the small oval white beans used in preparing New England Baked Beans.

Oil, Vegetable *See* Vegetable Oils

Okra

A tall plant that yields tender ribbed green pods, okra is grown in hot regions—India, the Middle East, Africa, and the southern United States. The pods are used as a cooked vegetable and in soups and stews. Bruised okra will reveal a saplike liquid that is responsible for thickening gravies and stews. Whole okra that is overcooked will develop a slimy consistency that is not to everyone's liking. When okra is sliced crosswise, the pieces look like tiny wagon wheels. Select unbruised, bright green okra, and store fresh pods in the refrigerator.

Olive Oil

Olive oil is the cooking oil of the Middle East, Spain, Portugal, and southern Italy. Because there are many different brands available with markedly different tastes (some have a lovely delicacy, others are so heavy that they overpower, still others taste rancid when fresh), buy olive oil in small quantities until you find one you like.

Panir

Panir is a kind of cheese. When used in this book, the term refers to a curd cheese of India made from yogurt and milk.

Paprika

Made from small red peppers that are dried and then ground into a powder, this spice adds color and piquancy to soups, stews, and gravies. Both hot and mild paprikas are available, but whenever paprika is listed as an ingredient in this book, use a mild one, preferably a sweet Hungarian paprika.

Parsley

Use either curly leaf or flat leaf (Italian) parsley. Do not substitute dried parsley flakes unless specified. With dried parsley flakes, use one-third the amount of the fresh parsley, since dried herbs are stronger than the fresh leaves. Parsley sprigs refer to branches of parsley—leaves and stems included.

Parsley, Chinese *See* Coriander

Pea Beans *See* Navy Beans

Pepper, Black *See* Black Pepper

Peppers, Chili *See* Chili Peppers

Peppers, Sweet Red or Green

These are the commonly available large bell peppers.

Phyllo Dough

Paper-thin leaves of pastry sold as strudel leaves or phyllo dough are available in one-half and one-pound packages in Greek markets or in the refrigerator or frozen food cases of supermarkets. Follow package directions for thawing frozen phyllo, and read the recipes carefully before using the fresh or frozen dough. Because frozen phyllo dough may crack or become sticky, it is often more difficult to use than the more pliable fresh leaves. Therefore, fresh phyllo is recommended.

Pilaf

Originally a Turkish rice dish, the term *pilaf* now refers to rice or cracked wheat preparations that use broth as the cooking liquid and may include bits of meats, fruits, and vegetables.

Pine Nuts

These small white ovals are the seeds of any of several varieties of pine trees. Although expensive, they are usually used in small quantities. Also known as pignolia nuts, the seeds are available in Middle Eastern groceries, natural or health food stores, and often in the Italian section of supermarkets.

Pink Beans

Available in one-pound packages in supermarkets, dry pink beans may be used interchangeably with pinto beans for recipes in this book.

Pinto Beans

Dry pinto beans are available in one-pound packages in supermarkets. Although a mottled pinkish-tan when uncooked, boiled pinto beans turn a solid, deep red and color the cooking liquid attractively as well. Pink beans are a good substitute for pinto beans, since they look and taste about the same when cooked.

Potatoes

The common white potato *(Solanum tuberosum)*, a descendant of white- or yellow-fleshed Peruvian potatoes, is unrelated to the sweet potato *(Ipomoea batata)*, which may also have white flesh. True yams (genus *Dioscorea*) are not in the same family as sweet potatoes, and most "yams" commonly available in the United States are actually a variety of sweet potato.

When potatoes or white potatoes are called for in a recipe, they always refer to common white potatoes, sold everywhere simply as "potatoes." When sweet potatoes or yams are called for, use the widely available orange-fleshed potatoes sold as "sweet potatoes" or "yams." For South American sweet potatoes (which are in the same family as the orange-fleshed potatoes but are more likely to have white flesh), purchase *batatas* or *boniatos* in Latin American groceries and some supermarkets. *Batata* is the general name for the South American sweet potato, and *boniato* is a specific kind of sweet potato.

Rice Noodles

Rice noodles, made of rice flour, are similar to cellophane noodles in appearance and texture but have a more distinctive flavor when cooked. The brittle, dry noodles become soft when soaked in warm water, and they puff up when deep-fried in hot oil. Do not soak rice noodles that are to be deep-fried. Available in Asian groceries, rice noodles are used in the cooking of China, Thailand, Indonesia, and other Asian countries. They will keep indefinitely at room temperature. Rice noodles come in various thicknesses, from very thin to the ¼-inch-wide rice sticks.

Rice Wine *See also* Mirin

A tablespoon or two of Chinese rice wine is used in Cantonese marinades; dry sherry is an acceptable substitute. *Sake,* the rice wine of Japan, is consumed as a beverage. *Mirin,* a sweetened Japanese rice wine, is used in cooking only.

Saffron

Saffron threads are the dried stigmas of the plant *Crocus sativus.* It takes thousands of threads to make but one ounce of saffron, and the spice is sold in fractions of an ounce. Saffron is expensive, but fortunately most recipes call for a very small amount. In Indian and Middle Eastern preparations, the spice is used for its orange-red color and for its delicate, faintly burnt taste. It can be purchased in spice and other specialty shops, some natural or health food stores, and in Indian and Middle Eastern groceries.

Salted Fermented Black Beans *See* Fermented Black Beans

Scallions (Green Onions, Spring Onions)

A scallion is an immature onion with a long, thick green stem and a small white bulb at the root end. For most recipes, both the white and the green parts are used. Onions, scallions, and leeks are all related, but because there are subtle differences in taste, substitutions are not recommended. Store scallions in the refrigerator; discard the tops if they become very soft.

Seaweed, Dried

This vegetable product, used in Asian cuisines, is available in Oriental groceries. It is sold in packages of thin brittle dark greenish-brown sheets. When softened in boiling water, dried seaweed takes on a rubbery consistency and tastes more like fish than vegetable. It is used to make *dashi,* imparting a sweet, smoky taste to the boiling water. Dried seaweed may be stored at room temperature for many months.

Sesame Oil

Asian sesame oil, a golden brown oil made from roasted sesame seeds, is aromatic, with a strong, nutty, smoky taste. It is usually used to flavor dishes after they have been cooked, and it will affect the taste of the entire preparation. Asian sesame oil is more concentrated and darker than the Middle Eastern version. Buy a good quality sesame oil in an Asian grocery. Sesame oil will keep at room temperature for months.

Sesame Seeds

The small flat seeds of the plant *Sesamum indicum* are eaten whole or ground into a paste, or they may be used to make oil. To bring out the flavor of whole sesame seeds, toast them lightly in an ungreased skillet. Although both black and white sesame seeds are available, the more easily obtained white seeds were used in testing the recipes in this book.

Shallots

Shallots are edible bulbs that look somewhat like garlic but have a brown skin instead of the white or purple skin of garlic bulbs. More delicate in taste than both garlic and onions but resembling both, shallots are used in European and Vietnamese cuisines. Shallots are easy to grow in the garden and can be purchased in the produce department of many supermarkets.

Shoyu *See* Soy Sauce

Somen

This very thin, white Japanese noodle is available in Asian groceries. Packaged in small bunches, *somen* will keep at room temperature as long as any dried noodle.

Sour Cream

When sour cream is called for as an ingredient, it refers to the thick dairy sour cream produced by companies such as Breakstone's, not to light or heavy cream that has soured.

Soy Sauce

Soy sauce, a major seasoning in many Asian cuisines, is used for its saltiness, slightly fermented taste, and dark brown color.

There are many different kinds of soy sauce, and although soy sauce tasting has not reached the popularity of wine tasting, a knowledgeable person can distinguish the country of origin of a particular soy. Indonesian soys, for example, are sweetened; Japanese *shoyu* has a more fermented flavor; and China uses a range of soys, from thin and light to thick, dark, and robust.

Squash Blossoms

The large bright orange blossoms of pumpkins and gourds add a delicate taste and a splash of color to Spanish and Mexican soups and stews. Smaller yellow zucchini blossoms are fried and eaten as a vegetable in Italy. Available in Spanish, Mexican, and sometimes Italian groceries, squash blossoms dry out rapidly and should be refrigerated and used shortly after they are purchased. When picking the blossoms fresh from the garden, use immediately.

Sweet Potatoes *See* Potatoes

Ti Leaves *See also* Banana Leaves

In the Pacific Islands, long tapered leaves of the tropical ti plant are used to wrap foods for steaming or baking. It is possible to grow ti leaves from ti logs sold through garden catalogs, and some florists will order ti leaves for you. The more readily available banana leaves are an alternative, and aluminum foil is an acceptable, although not exotic, substitute.

Tiger Lily Buds (Golden Needles)

Tiger lily buds are purchased dried in packages in Asian food stores. They are brittle when dry, but when soaked in hot water they soften and become chewy with a woodsy flavor. They are about three inches long, less than ⅛ inch wide, and orange to golden brown in color. They will keep almost indefinitely at room temperature in a covered jar, although they darken after several years.

Tofu

Although *tofu* may look like farmer cheese, it is a pure vegetable product. High in protein and low in cost, *tofu*, also known as fresh bean curd, is made from pressed soybeans.

Fresh *tofu* is creamy white, with the consistency of custard pie. It has little flavor of its own, but it picks up the flavors of other ingredients.

A mainstay of many Chinese, Japanese, and Korean diets, *tofu* is available in Asian groceries, natural or health food stores, and in the produce section of many supermarkets. *Tofu* comes in small square cakes or in one-pound blocks. Firm *tofu* will hold up better than soft *tofu* for the recipes in this book. Store *tofu* covered with water in the refrigerator, where it will keep for at least a week if you change the water every day. Drained *tofu* can be frozen, although it will freeze like a block of ice and will take some time to thaw. Gently squeeze excess water from thawed *tofu* before using.

Tomatillo

This very small, round Mexican green tomato is enclosed by a paperlike husk that is removed before the tomato is used. Sweeter than regular (unripe) green tomatoes, *tomatillos* are available fresh in Mexican food stores and in the produce section of some supermarkets. They are also sold in cans.

Tree Ears (Wood Ears)

These dried charcoal-black irregular-shaped pieces of fungus are sold in various weight packages in Asian groceries and some specialty shops. They must be soaked in hot or boiling water before they are used. When soaked they swell considerably, and their texture changes from brittle to rubbery. Tree ears, used in Chinese and Vietnamese cooking, will keep almost indefinitely at room temperature in a tightly closed jar.

Turmeric

The bright orange powdered root of a plant that grows in India, turmeric is used mainly for its color. It is an ingredient in prepared curry powders. The harsh taste of turmeric can be made pleasant by cooking the turmeric in a little butter, margarine, or oil in the beginning of a recipe instead of adding it directly to something that is already cooking.

Vegetable Oils

For most recipes in this book, the kind of oil to use for sautéing or frying is not specified. With the exception of olive oil and sesame oil, which have strong flavors, whatever oil you usually use for salads or cooking is acceptable. Pure soybean, sunflower, or safflower oils have the least taste of their own. While both corn and peanut oils have characteristic tastes, they are not so strong that they will dominate a preparation. Blended oils are also satisfactory.

Wasabi Paste

Wasabi paste is made from a horseradishlike root and is easily as potent as horseradish, although it has a slightly different taste. This Japanese condiment is available in small tubes in Asian groceries. Don't be surprised by the green color—it's not spoiled, it is supposed to be a lovely light green.

Water Chestnuts

Fresh water chestnuts are sweet and delicately flavored, but the much more readily available canned water chestnuts are an acceptable substitute for the recipes in this book.

Wonton Wrappers

Sold fresh or frozen in one-pound packages in Asian groceries and some supermarkets, *wonton* wrappers are made from flour, water, and egg. A homemade *kreplach* dough is a fine alternative. Egg roll wrappers cut into four squares each can also be substituted for the precut *wonton* wrappers.

Yogurt

Yogurt is a thickened milk product with a custardlike consistency and a tart flavor. It is prepared from milk that has been coagulated by bacteria.

1
EUROPE

Introduction

Geography and climate always shape an area's cuisine: fish is important in the diets of seacoast communities; cattle are raised where there is good pastureland, goats and sheep in rockier areas; root crops are grown in cold regions, tomatoes and eggplant in warmer ones. But conditions of nature aren't the only determinants of a country's cuisine. In Europe, for example, a "holy alliance" of sorts—the marriage of Italy's Catherine de' Medici to the future King Henri II of France—was inadvertently responsible for changing the entire direction of continental (or western) cooking. Food historians agree that until Catherine brought her expert cooks to France in 1533, French cooking was relatively unsophisticated, far from the world-famous *haute cuisine* that would develop. From Italy came pastries and cakes, vegetables unknown to the French, and an attitude toward food preparation and presentation that transformed eating into dining—first in France then in other European countries.

ITALY

Now if you are wondering how the leap was made from spaghetti to classical French cuisine, you should know that there is more to Italian cooking than pasta and pizza. Americans are generally familiar with the cooking of southern Italy—with its pasta, pizza, garlic, olive oil, and tomatoes—because most Italians who emigrated to the United States were from the South. Although pasta *is* eaten in northern Italian cities, tasty rice preparations are also enjoyed in the North, along with delicate veal dishes, buttery sauces, and a sophisticated approach to cooking that was in part a result of the Italian Renaissance.

While Italian cuisine was influencing French cooking in the sixteenth century, ingredients from the New World were being introduced into the Italian kitchen. Italians took tiny yellow tomatoes from Mexico and from them, over the next two hundred years, developed big red varieties that they began to use in cooking and for salads. Corn was turned into *polenta,* a yellow porridge served as a side dish, and some of the beans of Mexico found their way into Italian soups.

Obviously Italy's climate was suitable for growing tomatoes, corn, and beans, but Italy's geography has also played a significant role in molding its eating patterns. With so much of the country surrounded by water, seafood is very important in Italian cooking. Mountains and hills covering 75 percent of the country—the Apennines traverse the entire length of Italy— led to the evolution of distinct regions of cooking within the country (in addition to northern and southern differences). Milan, Bologna, Venice, Rome, and Naples all have their own styles of cooking, and many an Italian preparation is so closely identified with a particular city that *alla milanese* or *alla bolognese,* for example, is part of its name.

Still, there are unifying elements in Italian cuisine. The shapes may change, the sauces may differ, but pasta is pasta all over Italy, and it is served daily. Cheese is another basic ingredient in Italian cooking. Again, the kind of cheese may vary (Parmesan is a northern cheese, and mozzarella is the most famous cheese of southern Italy), but any of over a hundred Italian cheeses may appear at any course of an Italian meal, from appetizer through dessert. Wines—Chianti is but one of hundreds—are consumed during meals all over Italy.

Meal patterns are similar throughout the country. Appetizers, known to us as *antipasti,* sometimes begin an Italian dinner, particularly on a Sunday or holiday, whether at home or in a restaurant. A first course is a must. This will be a soup or a pasta or other starch that may be dressed with the same sauce used in the second (main) course. Meat, poultry, fish, or eggs make up the main course, but in poorer families the meal will be heavy on the pasta with little or no meat. The second course includes or is followed by one or more cooked fresh vegetable often dressed simply with lemon juice and olive oil (if this dressing sounds Greek, that's because it is), and served warm or cold. Salad, if served, will follow the second course, and unlike the tossed green salads of France it will include tomatoes and other vegetables along with salad greens. The meal ends with cheese or fruit or both. The elaborate Italian pastries that became a part of French cuisine are reserved for special occasions and restaurant meals.

SPAIN

Because Spain is separated from the rest of Europe by the Pyrenees, Spanish cuisine sees little influence from its European neighbors. Moorish invasions beginning in the 700s were responsible for the introduction of olive oil to Spain, and oranges were also brought by the Moors. As in Italy, mountain ranges and variations in climate and geography resulted in distinct regions of cooking within the country. The sun-scorched southern province of Andalusia is the home of *gazpacho* (page 60); *paella* (page 80) originated as a seafood and rice preparation in the coastal city of Valencia; and from Madrid comes *cocido*, a hearty stew that warms the body during the long, harsh winters of central Spain. Seafood reigns supreme in Catalonia on the northeast coast, and in the northern Basque provinces the men are so protective of the fish they catch that they do not allow the women to do the cooking. The Basque region, home of all-male cooking societies, is known for its near-legendary eaters, who can consume more food each day than the people of any other region in Spain.

Despite the differences in cooking styles from one region of Spain to another, there is a central theme underlying Spanish cuisine: simplicity. Even the most ornate Spanish preparation, *paella*, is at heart a peasant dish, and *paella* is often cooked and served at picnics. Tomatoes, garlic, and parsley are important in Spanish cookery, but sauces and highly spiced foods are uncharacteristic. Freshness is a must. Fresh seafood is eaten daily by inhabitants near enough to coastal areas; fresh fruit including figs, dates, strawberries, oranges, lemons, and other citrus are grown and eaten year-round in warm areas and only seasonally elsewhere. Vineyards abound. Local sherries and the red wine and fruit preparation known as *sangria* are the beverage hallmarks of the country.

Meal patterns throughout Spain are unlike those of the rest of Europe, but if you are familiar with the way teenagers snack, then you are also familiar with an important aspect of Spanish eating patterns: a quick breakfast of rolls and hot chocolate or coffee, a substantial multicourse afternoon meal corresponding to dinner in the United States, and a late supper are interspersed with considerable between-meal snacking throughout the day. And that evening supper, although light, may start at ten and go on until midnight or into the morning hours.

PORTUGAL

Although Spain and Portugal share a common border, the separation of the two countries by mountains coupled with the rugged individualism of the seafaring Portuguese resulted in the development of different cuisines. While Portuguese cooking, like that of Spain, is a cuisine of the people, simple and usually unsauced, it tends to be spicier—more garlic, pungent fresh coriander often appearing in place of regular parsley, and lemon juice sprinkled over many preparations. Fresh-caught fish and dried salt cod (caught in Newfoundland, dried in Portugal) are eaten throughout Portugal, and potatoes, kale, and turnips are enjoyed along with tomatoes and sweet peppers. The olive oil of Portugal is stronger than Spain's (some call it rancid). The wine of Portugal, of course, is port; coffee is the other beverage of note.

FRANCE

France also has a cuisine of the people. An *hors d'oeuvre* served at the table begins the main midday meal. It may be plain or elegant, but it will be light, a teaser meant to prepare the palate for what is to come. The main course—meat, fish, or poultry—is next, followed by a vegetable dish. If the *hors d'oeuvre* was a vegetable, a salad of tossed greens lightly dressed with vinegar and oil will take the place of the vegetable dish. As in Italy, wine is relished during the meal, and cheese and fruit end the typical family meal. Crusty bread, purchased daily in local bakeries, remains on the table throughout the meal, the last slices to be enjoyed with the dessert cheese. Coffee follows the meal. Supper is likely to be soup, maybe also an omelet, a vegetable, again the crusty bread, and a light dessert.

This all sounds very nice but not very fancy, and perhaps not what you think of as French cuisine. That is because it is a description of the cuisine of provincial France, the cooking of the people. There is a mighty difference between provincial cooking and classical French cuisine, the cooking of the finest French chefs in the finest French restaurants. Provincial cooking is earthy and delicious; it is meant to provide pleasure, not merely sustenance; and it is full of the most wonderful soups and stews, soufflés, quiches, fresh vegetables, and regional specialties. Classical French cooking, on the other hand, strives for perfection, with meticulous attention to detail—from the selection of menus and ingredients through precise cooking and elegant service. The difference between home cooking and *haute cuisine* is the difference between a lovely cheese soufflé served at supper and a frozen Grand Marnier soufflé surrounded by magnificent glazed berries, the crowning glory to a grand repast. Recently there have been modifications. Some of today's French chefs, aware of the health concerns of their clientele, have moved away from the rich, creamy sauces of the past and turned to the lighter cuisine, especially emphasizing fresh vegetables and fruits.

The French are proud of all of their cooking, and justifiably so, for French food is satisfying but not heavy; sauced, herbed, and tasty but not overspiced. While the French are passionate about their food, the food itself tends to be subtle and delicate. When you have eaten fine French food, you leave the table knowing what an exquisite meal is.

GERMANY

France's neighbor to the northeast, Germany, is not subtle in its language, its history, or its food. By and large, when you've finished a German meal, you know you have eaten something substantial. *Sauerbraten* (page 67), dumplings of all kinds, sausages, and sauerkraut—these are the kinds of foods we associate with German cooking. Like many other European countries, Germany has a multitude of regional cuisines, with some preparations characteristic of particular provinces or cities and other dishes more generally described as northern, central, or southern. Partly because of Germany's fluid borders in the past, regional cooking near Germany's boundaries shows the influence of neighboring cuisines. For example, where Germany borders Poland, gravies are enriched with sour cream. The *haute cuisine* of Germany is established in the southwestern region near France. And *spätzle* (page 95) are especially popular in southern Germany, near the Austrian border.

German cuisine features many nonkosher foods, including the eel, very popular in northern regions, ham from Westphalia, many different kinds of pork sausages (there's that famous sausage from Frankfurt), and meat and dairy combinations. Bacon and lard are used in general cooking and seasoning. For some of these foods we have well-known alternatives: we are all familiar with kosher frankfurters. Other German preparations that can be used in the kosher home without making changes include veal dishes, roast goose, most dumplings, potato pancakes, and a variety of German pastries served at the coffee hour in the afternoon.

Although meal patterns in Germany have changed, five meals are traditionally served—an early breakfast followed later in the morning by a second breakfast, a heavy midday dinner, *kaffee* (coffee), and a relatively light supper (by German standards). The traditional supper gives us our "delicatessen" (delicate eating), the name given to the assortment of cold cuts, sausages, and cheeses eaten on bread to make up this "light" meal. In present-day Germany, there is a shift toward eating the heavy meal in the evening.

Although beer is considered the national beverage, the vineyards of the Rhine and Moselle Rivers in western and southern Germany produce some lovely light wines that are consumed daily in Germany and exported as well. Coffee is another important beverage, and the afternoon coffee is a special social event and a time for good eating. Pastries served at *kaffee* time range from doughnuts, pound cakes, honey cakes, gingerbread, and many different varieties of butter cookies to the rich kirsch-laced Black Forest cherry cake of southern Germany.

AUSTRIA

While many German pastries and cookies have become very popular in the United States, it is to Austria that we look for the tortes, strudels, and multilayered cakes that represent the quintessence of European pastries. The Viennese dessert tables presented at some Bar Mitzvah receptions are based on the lavish assortment of rich pastries that is one of the legacies of the Austro-Hungarian Empire. With Austria and Hungary at the core, the Empire was extended by the ruling Hapsburg family through marriage and diplomacy until it reached as far north as Poland and as far east as Russia, including Yugoslavia, Czechoslovakia, and part of Romania. Although present-day Austria is but a shadow of the glorious Empire in size, the elegant, sophisticated cuisine that grew out of the cultured and affluent capital of Vienna remains.

There are striking similarities between the meal patterns of Germany and Austria: an early breakfast followed by a second breakfast, a large midday dinner, rich pastries and coffee in the afternoon, and an evening supper. But in general the cuisine of Austria is more refined, the cooking of Germany more earthy. Austria's most famous veal dish, *weiner schnitzel*, is a thin, delicate breaded veal cutlet that is simple and light. The most popular main dish is a slowly simmered beef—brisket is among the many cuts used by Austrians—cooked with leeks, carrots, celery, and onions (page 69). The resulting stock is strained and served with dumplings as a first course, and the meat is served with horseradish or applesauce and browned boiled potatoes. Lettuce or cold vegetable salads are served with Austrian meals, and everyone looks forward to sweet desserts to conclude the meal.

With such close historical ties until the Austro-Hungarian Empire broke up in 1918, Austria and Hungary share many culinary treasures. Identical recipes for dumplings appear in Viennese and Hungarian cookbooks, and strudels are part of the dessert repertoire in both countries. However, Austria has more of an international cuisine than its neighbor to the east. The ruling class set the tone for Austrian cooking, so while Austrian cooking is cosmopolitan, Hungarian cooking is nationalistic, homey.

HUNGARY

Hungary's most famous dish is *gulyas,* or goulash, a simple stew of beef, onions, green peppers, and tomatoes, flavored with caraway seeds and seasoned lavishly with sweet red paprika, which also colors the stew vibrantly. Caraway seeds and the abundant use of Hungarian paprika—sometimes hot, sometimes sweet—characterize many Hungarian preparations, and sour cream is frequently used to thicken and flavor soups and gravies. The word "paprikash" in the name of a Hungarian recipe means that there is sour cream in the preparation. Soups and vegetables (and delicious vegetable soups) are important in Hungarian cuisine. Cabbage is used inventively in strudels and for stuffing. Savory stuffed cabbage—cooked on a bed of sauerkraut that tastes very much like my mother's marvelous stuffed cabbage—is Hungarian (although my mother is not).

Hungarian meals end with something sweet—a custard, a thin *blintz*-like pancake (*palacsinta*) stuffed with jam and nuts, a pice of strudel, (*rétes* to Hungarians), or perhaps an elaborate fancy cake. Probably the best-known Hungarian dessert, named the Dobostorte after its creator, is a multilayered sponge cake filled with a creamy chocolate filling and topped with caramel (page 113). One of the more unusual but representative Hungarian desserts is much more simple and less sweet: buttered noodles are mixed with poppy seeds or walnuts and then sprinkled with sugar and eaten hot. Other noodle dessert preparations made with sour cream and eggs look (to me) remarkably like main dish dairy *kugels.*

POLAND

To the north of Hungary but separated by Czechoslovakia is Poland, a country that has held fast to its food traditions through wars, conquests, and partitions. Poland was erased from the map for a time but the Polish spirit could not be wiped out. Sandwiched between Germany on the west and Russia on the east (sometimes crushed between the two), Poland has a cuisine influenced by both countries. Sauerkraut and dumplings from Germany, and borscht, sour cream, and black bread from Russia are all part of daily Polish meals. But the national dish, called *bigos* or hunter's stew, is Poland's own. The reward of the hunt, a traditional Polish sport, *bigos* is a concoction of game, sausage, and sauerkraut cooked in a huge cauldron. More typical everyday fare includes cabbage, barley, and other hefty soups enjoyed during the long, cold winters; buckwheat groats (kasha); and the previously mentioned sauerkraut and sour cream. Dill is a favorite herb for soups and sauces, and strongly flavored wild mushrooms (picked rather than purchased) appear in many preparations. Sweets are enjoyed, especially the most famous of the Polish cakes, *babka*.

UNION OF SOVIET SOCIALIST REPUBLICS

Proceeding from Poland to the vast USSR (Russia is but one of fifteen republics) is a little like picturing Pinocchio next to Monstro the Whale. Spanning the continents of both Europe and Asia, the Soviet Union is the world's largest and third most heavily populated country (after China and India). Without question there are culinary differences among the republics, but we will concentrate on Russia, the most populous of the republics and the cultural center of the Soviet Union, and on the Ukraine, located south of Russia.

There are two cuisines of Russia: one is the legacy of the aristocracy of Czarist Russia; the other, the cuisine of the people of the contemporary Russian republic. From the aristocracy come the majestic dishes: *koulebiaka*, a puff pastry filled with fresh salmon and eggs; beef stroganoff, a dish of tender beef, mushrooms, onions, and sour cream created for a Russian count in the nineteenth century; and chicken kiev (page 83), a deep-fried chicken cutlet specialty originating in the Ukraine but enjoyed by the well-to-do Russians. From the wealthy class also comes *zakuska*, or appetizers. Originally a creation of the nobility, lavish *zakuska* tables—featuring caviar and herring, cold meats, and vegetable preparations—traditionally were presented to guests at country homes to tide them over until dinner.

Kasha, cabbage, borscht, sour cream, black bread, mushrooms, dill—the peasant foods of Poland—are the same foods sustaining the people of Russia today. Curd cheeses such as cottage and pot cheese are popular; fruit soups and compotes are enjoyed; and meats are served more in satisfying main dish soups than as roasts. A Russian favorite is *shchi*, a hearty cabbage and beef soup with a sweet-and-sour taste. Vodka and tea are the national beverages, as they were in the days of the Czars. A more modest selection of *zakuska* remains a part of Russian cuisine. *Bliny*, not to be confused with *blintzes*, are buckwheat pancakes made of a yeast batter. Neither rolled nor filled, the pancakes are topped simply with sour cream or butter or for special occasions and affairs of state topped more ornately with salmon or caviar. Stuffed pastries known as *pirozhki* (page 49) make wonderful *zakuski*.

Because many Ukrainian Jews emigrated to the United States in the late 1800s (the result of religious persecution), numerous dishes that we now think of as Jewish had their origins as Ukrainian preparations. Borscht originated in the Ukraine, the dumplings known as *varenyky* are Ukrainian, and so are stuffed cabbages, noodle puddings, and honey cakes. Owing to its rich, black soil, making it one of the best areas in Europe for growing grains, the Ukraine became known as the breadbasket of Europe. The repertoire of Ukrainian breads includes dark rye and pumpernickel breads and ring-shaped rolls that look suspiciously like bagels.

SWEDEN

The more elaborate *zakuska* tables of Russia's past bear a remarkable resemblance to the smorgasbords of Sweden, one of the Scandinavian countries. This is not so surprising, considering that Sweden has historical ties to the Russian Empire and is separated from the Soviet Union only by Finland and the Baltic Sea. As in Russia, the famous Swedish spreads apparently arose from the gathering of guests in country homes. In Sweden, where homes were far apart and travel was long and difficult, guests might stay for weeks at a time. When a gathering occurred, the guests each brought a favorite dish, and the foods were all placed on the table to be shared. (Sounds to me like a pot-luck supper.)

For today's smorgasbords, there is a definite order to be followed. First come the herrings. (The plural is deliberate. Herring is a staple food in all Scandinavian countries, and whole cookbooks could be written about herring alone. Pickled, salted, dried, smoked, marinated, and sauced in numerous ways, a large variety of herring dishes may appear as part of a smorgasbord.) Next is a selection of other fish dishes, followed by cold meats and salads, hot preparations (such as Swedish meatballs, page 74), and cheeses. Aquavit, a strong, clear liquor distilled from potatoes or grain and flavored with caraway seeds, is the beverage served with the smorgasbord. Swedes also enjoy pastries and desserts, especially their light crisp pancakes, served with homemake jams and preserves.

DENMARK

The most famous of the Scandinavian pastries are from Denmark. To the Danes, however, the rich, flaky baked goods we call Danish pastries are *Wienerbröd*—Viennese bread—for it was from the pastry chefs of Vienna that the people of Denmark learned the art of making these buttery breakfast pastries. For its size—it is a country of just over five million—Denmark has had a disproportionate but deserved impact on world cuisines. In addition to its pastries, the smorgasbord of Denmark, *smörrebröd*, is a world-famous bounty of artistically arranged open-faced sandwiches served on thin slices of well-buttered bread at lunchtime. *Smörrebröd* must not just taste good, the sandwiches must be beautiful as well.

Owing to a common cultural history, Denmark is considered one of the Scandinavian countries even though it is not on the same peninsula as Sweden, Norway, and Finland. The meal patterns of Denmark are similar to those of the other Scandinavian countries, with the main, heavier meal being served in the evening. Baltic herring and other fish are important in Danish cuisine, but unlike the other Scandinavian countries Denmark is mostly low-lying and agricultural, ideal for raising livestock and poultry. The Danes love their butter and cream, and dairy cattle are more important than cattle raised for beef. While beef is eaten, pork is the primary meat, and pork and fruit combinations are popular. Fruits are more important than vegetables in all Scandinavian cuisines, because except for root vegetables, the climate and topography are better suited to orchards than vegetable gardens. Scandinavian children don't hear "Eat your green vegetables" too often. Instead, colorful fruit soups and salads and sweet fruit desserts, cakes, tarts, and compotes are enjoyed.

While the foods and meal patterns of Denmark are related to those of Sweden, the whole attitude toward food is less Spartan among Danes. Like other people in Western Europe, Danes do not just eat, they love to eat. Danes look forward to their breakfast pastries as much as the French relish their morning croissants, and they are as proud of the sheer numbers of sandwiches they have artfully constructed as Italians are of their myriad pastas. In looking at actual recipes and food combinations, though, Denmark appears to have more in common with the Netherlands (popularly known as Holland) than other Western European countries.

THE NETHERLANDS

Like the Danes, the Dutch love herring and fancy meat and fruit combinations. And a thick and meaty split pea soup (page 59) featured on winter menus in the Netherlands is quite similar to a soup that warms and fills the Danish people during the winter. The Netherlands is low compared to the rest of Europe, with a fair part of the country lying below sea level. Dairying is important to the economy. The world-famous Gouda and Edam cheeses are Dutch in origin.

It is tempting to compare the lavish *rijsttafel* (rice table, see page 184) of the Netherlands with the Swedish smorgasbord because each has its profusion of foods. But while the smorgasbord is an outgrowth of hospitality, the *rijsttafel* came to the Netherlands by way of the Dutch colony of Indonesia—and by no means do Indonesians consider the Dutch adaptation of the rice table flattering. The Dutch also brought back spices from the Orient; and cloves, cinnamon, and nutmeg are used in the Netherlands as well as many other countries of Europe. The hot curries that are served as part of the *rijsttafel* are not part of other European cuisines.

Appetizers and Soups

Tapas (Spanish appetizers) parties or dinners, a dining phenomenon of the eighties, are an indication that Americans are discovering what Spaniards have known all along: appetizers are enticing between-meal snacks, they take the edge off the appetite before late meals, and they are simply wonderful as complete meals. Portuguese also enjoy appetizers as late-night snacks, while other Europeans serve appetizers early in the evening. Some cuisines feature such an impressive array of appetizers that they would be whole meals to us. The Swedish smorgasbord, for example, is actually meant to precede a meal. And while an Italian antipasto typically comes "before the pasta," it can be expanded to make a light meal.

The peasant soups of Europe serve more basic needs: they fill the tummy and they help keep people warm during harsh winters. When thick and full of vegetables (and meat for those who can afford it), soups double as whole meals, to be enjoyed with dark breads. A soup course always begins the main meal of the day in Spain and Portugal, ranging from simple bread or garlic soups to rich bean and meat soups that are almost stews. Portuguese soups may be light with interesting touches such as lemon juice, fresh mint, or fresh coriander; or they may be more substantial—meals in themselves. Some of the clear broths of Austria are vehicles for one of the many different kinds of dumplings that are a part of the cuisine. In fact, Austrian soups are named by the type of dumpling served in the soup. French restaurants feature creamy vegetable soups and rich consommés with carefully sliced vegetables. Even when classic French soups are simple, there will be subtleties, and often luxurious touches.

ROASTED SWEET RED PEPPERS
Pimientos Asado, Peperoni Arrosto

Spain, Italy

Serves 6

Tapas cafes in Spain may offer as many as fifty selections in one evening, from toasted almonds, roast peppers with garlic, and marinated vegetables through more elaborate seafood or meat preparations. As a Spanish appetizer these roast peppers are simply served in a bowl along with bowls of other *tapas*. For an Italian meal the peppers make a nice first course when arranged on a bed of lettuce and garnished with anchovies and hard-cooked egg slices.

> **3 large sweet red peppers**
> **Olive oil**
> **2 large cloves garlic, sliced into thin rounds**

To roast the peppers under a broiler, place the peppers on a sheet of foil within an inch of a preheated broiler. Cook the peppers until they blacken all over, turning as necessary. The skin of the peppers will become charred, and the meat inside will soften but will not become discolored. Remove the peppers and set aside until cool.

To roast the peppers over a gas flame, working with one pepper at a time use a long kitchen fork to spear the pepper through the core. Carefully hold the pepper close to the flame, turning as necessary until the skin is blackened all over. Repeat with the remaining peppers.

When the roast peppers are cool enough to handle, use your fingers to peel off the skin. Cut the peppers in half, remove and discard the core and seeds, then slice the peppers into quarters, strips, or even-size chunks. Place in a bowl, sprinkle liberally with olive oil, and scatter the garlic over the peppers. Toss lightly. Leave the peppers at room temperature for an hour, then cover and refrigerate until serving time. The peppers can be prepared up to two days in advance but should be stirred from time to time. If desired, remove the garlic slices before serving.

PIROZHKI

Russia, Poland

Makes 12

My grandmother used to make pastry by working in the shortening with her fingers, so I love to make the dough for these filled pastries, because I automatically think of Grandma when I work in the butter. The dough is light and flaky, the filling seasoned delicately with herbs. The word for these small pastries is derived from *pir*, meaning "feast," and one taste of these mushroom *pirozhki* encased by a tender sour cream dough will confirm that you are feasting.

The Filling:

> 1 tablespoon unsalted butter
> ½ cup minced onion
> 1¼ cups chopped fresh mushrooms
> 2 tablespoons chopped fresh parsley
> 2 teaspoons chopped fresh dill or 1 teaspoon (scant) dried dill
> Salt and freshly ground black pepper

The Dough:

> 1½ cups unsifted all-purpose flour
> ¼ cup (½ stick) unsalted butter
> ¾ cup sour cream
> 1 egg yolk beaten with 1 teaspoon water

For the filling, in an 8-inch skillet melt the tablespoon of butter over moderate heat. Add the onion, sauté for 2 minutes, then add the mushrooms and cook for an additional 3 minutes. Mix in the parsley and dill, sprinkle with salt and plenty of pepper, and mix well. Transfer to a bowl and allow the filling to cool while you prepare the dough.

In a medium-size mixing bowl, measure the flour and the ¼ cup of butter. Use your fingers to break up the butter into small bits and distribute it evenly throughout the dough. Now use a fork to mix in ¼ cup of sour cream at a time. After all the sour cream

Recipe continues on the following page . . .

is added, work the dough with your fingers to make a smooth ball.

Divide the dough evenly into 12 pieces, and roll each piece into a smooth ball. On a 12 x 12-inch sheet of wax paper, place 4 balls of dough, leaving 2 inches of space between the balls. Flatten each ball with your palm to make a 3-inch circle. Now cover the wax paper with another sheet, and use a rolling pin to gently roll the dough into a 4-inch circle. This will not take much rolling. Carefully peel off the top sheet of wax paper, replace it, and flip over the 2 sheets of wax paper. Now peel off the top sheet of wax paper (which a moment ago was the bottom). What you are doing is making sure the dough doesn't stick to the wax paper.

Drain the liquid from the mushroom filling. Place a level table-spoon of filling on the center of each round of dough, then shape the filling so it is roughly 1½ x 2 inches. Fold the top of the dough over the filling, fold in the sides, then fold up the bottom, pressing to make a tight package. Transfer the filled pastry to a lightly buttered baking sheet or a piece of wax paper set on a plate. Repeat with the remaining dough and filling. Refrigerate, lightly covered with wax paper, until ready to bake (up to 4 hours).

To bake, preheat the oven to 400 degrees F. Place the *pirozhki* seam side down on a lightly buttered baking sheet. Brush the tops thoroughly with the beaten egg yolk. Bake for 25 minutes, until a beautiful golden brown.

HERBED MUSHROOMS
Champignons aux Herbes

France

Serves 4 to 6

Mushrooms, a favorite vegetable in Europe, are an appropriate substitute for the mussels, eels, and snails prepared in herbed butter sauces in France and Belgium. Mushrooms are soft but chewy, and their taste is not so strong that it interferes with the herbs and seasonings. If you prefer, omit the bread-crumbs and final broiling, and serve this as a first course, with French bread for dipping.

2 tablespoons unsalted butter or margarine
2 tablespoons vegetable oil
1 teaspoon fresh lemon juice
2 tablespoons chopped shallots
4 tablespoons chopped scallions (white and
    crisp green parts)
1 teaspoon minced garlic
½ pound small fresh mushrooms, cleaned
⅓ cup chopped fresh parsley
1 teaspoon dried tarragon
Salt and freshly ground black pepper
2 tablespoons unsalted butter or margarine
2 tablespoons vegetable oil
3 slices white bread, pulverized into crumbs
    in a food processor or a blender (1½ cups,
    approximately)
Additional melted butter or margarine, if
    desired

In an 8-inch skillet, heat the 2 tablespoons of butter or marga-rine with the 2 tablespoons of vegetable oil over moderate heat. When the butter has melted, stir in the lemon juice, then the shallots, scallions, and garlic. Sauté for half a minute, then add the mushrooms, stirring them to coat with the butter-and-oil mixture. Cook for about 4 minutes, stirring often, until the mushrooms are just barely tender. Sprinkle on the parsley and tarragon and the salt and pepper to taste. Toss lightly. Now add the remaining 2 tablespoons each of butter or margarine and oil, and when the butter has melted, mix in the breadcrumbs. Taste and add more butter or margarine if the mixture seems dry.

Turn into a heatproof casserole (a 1-quart Corning Ware is the right size). The mushrooms may be prepared as long as an hour in advance up to this point. Just before serving, place the casse-role a few inches under a hot broiler, and broil until the bread-crumbs are light brown.

MARINATED MUSHROOMS
Funghi Marinati

Italy

Serves 6

These are not only the easiest marinated mushrooms I know of, they are also the best. They came from a Jewish-Italian friend of mine who knows all the secrets of both cuisines. Her secret with these mushrooms is to *not* cook them first. Just pour about a cup of your favorite Italian vinegar-and-oil dressing on the mushrooms (or use the recipe below), and allow them to marinate in the refrigerator up to a week or at room temperature for two to four days, depending on the temperature of the room. You only need to remember to turn them several times a day.

We have served many pounds of these mushrooms as part of a giant salad bar at all our home Bar/Bat Mitzvah receptions, and every last one gets eaten. They are also perfect for an Italian antipasto.

> **1 pound small whole mushrooms**
> **½ cup olive oil (part salad oil, to taste)**
> **¼ cup distilled white vinegar**
> **2 tablespoons water**
> **1 clove garlic, crushed then minced**
> **½ teaspoon sugar**
> **¼ teaspoon salt**
> **¼ teaspoon dried parsley flakes**
> **¼ teaspoon dried oregano**

Cut off any brown ends from the mushroom stems; clean the mushrooms. In a 2-cup jar with a good lid, combine all the ingredients for the dressing. Shake well. Place the mushrooms in a bowl in which they fit comfortably. Pour on the dressing and mix gently but thoroughly. The dressing will not completely cover the mushrooms, so you will need to stir them every few hours in the beginning, less often as they marinate. Cover the mushrooms with plastic wrap.

If you are in a hurry, leave the mushrooms at room temperature. In about 2 days they will appear cooked—they will be darkened and softened and permeated by the dressing. Refrigerate before they soften too much. They will keep an additional 2 days in the refrigerator. To "cook" the mushrooms in the refrigerator, mix the mushrooms and dressing and refrigerate immediately. Don't forget to stir the mushrooms at least 3 times a day, more often in the beginning. They will be "cooked" after 4 to 7 days in the refrigerator. Drain off the liquid before serving.

SPANISH SAUSAGE MEATBALLS
Chorizo Albondigas

Spain

Makes 24 meatballs

The spicy Spanish sausage known as *chorizo* can be used to make wonderful meatballs to serve as a *tapas* or in soups.

1 pound Chorizo (page 79)

Shape the meat mixture into twenty-four 1¼-inch compact balls. For appetizers, either bake or fry the meatballs. To bake, preheat the oven to 400 degrees F. Place the meatballs in a baking pan or on a cookie sheet with sides, and bake for 10 or 15 minutes, until brown and cooked through. To fry, place the meatballs in an ungreased skillet and cook over moderate heat. Shake the pan often to keep the meat from sticking. Cook until the meatballs are brown all over and cooked through, turning as necessary. Serve plain or with green tomato sauce (page 291), uncooked red sauce (page 292), or a purchased taco sauce.

For soup, drop the meatballs into the broth and cook for about 10 minutes.

FISH WITH GARLIC AND SHERRY
Pescado Al Ajillo y Jerez

Spain

Serves 6

Seafood baked or broiled in small earthenware dishes are popular *tapas*. Garlic, olive oil, and parsley—staples of Spanish cuisine—combine with sherry for a simple marinade that doubles as a light sauce. In this recipe fish fillets or steaks substitute for the shrimp traditionally eaten in Spain. Individual ramekins or shells are ideal for cooking and serving, but a one-quart baking dish can be used.

>   **1 pound bluefish fillets or cod fillets or**
>   **steaks**
>   **¼ cup olive oil**
>   **¼ cup dry sherry**
>   **4 cloves garlic, sliced in half**
>   **1 tablespoon minced fresh parsley**

Cut the fish into ¾-inch squares.

In a medium-size mixing bowl or a 1-quart ovenproof baking dish combine all the ingredients. Marinate in the refrigerator for 2 to 3 hours, stirring the fish occasionally.

Remove the garlic, then divide the fish among individual ramekins or shells, spooning some of the marinade over each portion. Or leave the fish in the 1-quart baking dish. Place the fish under a preheated broiler 4 inches from the heat, and broil for 6 to 8 minutes, until the fish is lightly browned and cooked through. Serve immediately.

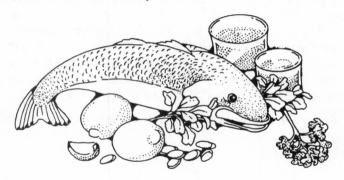

VEGETARIAN BROTH

General Europe

Makes 1 quart

There are two things to remember about making a vegetarian broth: (1) Wash the vegetables well, especially the unpared ones, and (2) use the onion skins. From there, it is a matter of gathering together uncooked parings, scraps, or fresh vegetables, covering them with water, and then cooking and straining. Why the onion skins? Because they will turn the broth a rich golden brown, and the lovely color makes the broth more inviting. The simplified version has fewer calories and is considerably easier to prepare, while the sautéed version is a bit more flavorful.

Simplified Version:

> 4 carrots, unpeeled, sliced
> 2 large onions, unpeeled, cut into quarters
> 1 wedge (¼ pound) green cabbage or 2 stalks Chinese cabbage
> 4 celery tops (leaves plus 2 inches of the stalks)
> 4 cloves garlic, crushed
> 1 leek (discard tough green parts), washed well then cut into 1-inch pieces; or 4 scallions (white and crisp green parts), cut up
> Handful of snipped fresh chives (optional)
> 1 piece (1 inch) fresh ginger root, peeled
> ½ cup cubed turnip or sweet potato
> Uncooked vegetable peelings and scraps
> Onion skins
> 3 sprigs fresh parsley
> 1 tablespoon chopped fresh dill (optional)
> Salt

Fill a 4-quart pot halfway with the uncooked vegetables, peelings, and scraps, using all the ingredients above except the parsley, dill, and salt. Add enough water to just barely cover the vegetables. Bring to the boil over high heat, reduce to a gentle boil, cover, and cook for 1 hour. Add the parsley and dill, and cook for an additional 5 minutes, then add salt to taste. Cook 5 minutes longer. Turn off the heat, allowing the vegetables to remain in the pot on the turned-off burner for an additional 15 minutes.

Remove the vegetables with a slotted spoon, and strain the broth through paper towels. Use immediately or refrigerate or freeze, leaving an inch of headspace. Do not freeze soup in glass containers.

Sautéed Version:

> 2 tablespoons unsalted butter or margarine
> 1 tablespoon vegetable oil
> 1 cup chopped peeled carrots
> 1 cup chopped peeled onion
> ½ cup chopped celery
> 4 cloves garlic, chopped
> 1 wedge (¼ pound) green cabbage or 2 stalks
>   Chinese cabbage, shredded
> 4 tablespoons chopped celery leaves
> 1 leek (discard tough green parts), washed
>   well then cut into 1-inch pieces; or 4 scal-
>   lions (white and crisp green parts), sliced
> Handful of snipped fresh chives (optional)
> 1 piece (1 inch) fresh ginger root, peeled
> ½ cup cubed turnip or sweet potato
> Uncooked vegetable peelings and scraps
> Onion skins
> 3 sprigs fresh parsley
> 1 tablespoon chopped fresh dill (optional)
> Salt

In a 4-quart pot, heat the butter or margarine and oil until the butter is sizzling but not browned. Add the chopped carrots, onion, celery, and garlic. Cook, stirring occasionally, for 10 to 15 minutes, until the vegetables are softened and just beginning to brown lightly. Add the remaining ingredients except the parsley, dill, and salt. Mix well. Add enough water to just barely cover the vegetables. Continue cooking as directed in the simplified version.

ONION SOUP

Soupe à l'Oignon

France

Serves 4

A rich vegetarian broth provides a wonderful base for onion soup, taking the place of the beef broth that is usually used. The soup is served in the traditional manner, with grated cheese. Slow cooking over moderately low heat makes the onions soft and sweet.

> **5 cups sliced onions (¼-inch-thick rounds)**
> **¼ cup (½ stick) unsalted butter**
> **2 cups Vegetarian Broth (preceding recipe)**
> **4 slices (1-inch-thick) French bread**
> **Butter or vegetable oil for the bread**
> **½ cup grated Swiss cheese, approximately**

If the onion rounds are more than 3 inches in diameter, cut them in half. In a 2-quart pot, melt the butter over moderately low heat. Add the onion rounds, and cook them until they are light brown, stirring often. This may take as long as half an hour. Add the vegetarian broth and bring to the boil. Reduce the heat and simmer for 1 minute.

A few minutes before serving, toast the bread in a 300-degree F. oven until it is light brown on both sides. If you like, before toasting, lightly butter the bread or brush it on both sides with vegetable oil.

Pour the onion soup into 4 heatproof crocks or small casseroles. Put a slice of toasted bread in each serving, sprinkle lavishly with the grated cheese, and place under the broiler until the cheese is melted, bubbly, and barely browned.

CREAM OF MUSHROOM SOUP

Gomba Krem Leves

Hungary

Makes 2 quarts

This is a typical Hungarian soup, although it may not be the kind of cream soup you expect, because sour cream is used instead of sweet cream or milk. Hungarians enjoy all kinds of vegetable soups, including those made with cauliflower, kohlrabi, and green beans. These soups are often prepared exactly like this mushroom soup: they are seasoned with sweet paprika, thickened with flour, and finished off with sour cream. The result is a creamy soup with an orange-red hue, tasting of and textured by the vegetable with which it is prepared.

> **2 tablespoons vegetable oil**
> **½ cup finely chopped onion**
> **1 teaspoon sweet Hungarian paprika**
> **¾ pound fresh mushrooms, cleaned and coarsely chopped**
> **1 quart Vegetarian Broth (page 55)**
> **2 tablespoons vegetable oil**
> **3 tablespoons unsifted all-purpose flour**
> **2 tablespoons chopped fresh parsley**
> **½ cup sour cream**

In a 2- or 3-quart pot, heat the 2 tablespoons of oil over moderately low heat for a minute, then add the chopped onion. The oil must not be too hot or the onion will brown, and Hungarians do not allow their onions to brown. Cook, stirring often, until the onions are softened. Sprinkle the paprika over the onions, then add the mushrooms and cook, stirring constantly, until the mushrooms darken and soften. This will take only a few minutes. Stir in the broth, and adjust the heat so the broth boils gently for 5 minutes, uncovered. Give the soup an occasional stir.

In another 2-quart pot, heat the other 2 tablespoons of oil over moderate heat. Add the flour, stirring constantly and rapidly. Cook the flour and oil mixture until it is smooth and bubbly but not brown, stirring all the while. It should cook for at least a minute so the flour will not have a starchy taste. Mix in the parsley, then blend in the mushroom soup a cup at a time, stirring with a spoon after each addition until the mixture is smooth. Bring to the boil over high heat, stirring often, then reduce the heat so the soup cooks gently for 5 to 10 minutes. The soup may be prepared up to this point and refrigerated overnight.

To complete the cooking, reheat the soup to the boiling point, then reduce the heat so the soup no longer boils. In a medium- to large-size heatproof bowl, stir the sour cream with a fork or a whisk. *Very gradually* add at least half the soup to the sour cream, stirring constantly, then stir this mixture back into the soup pot. Blend well. Keep the soup warm, but do not allow it to boil or the sour cream will curdle.

SPLIT PEA SOUP
Erwtensoep

The Netherlands

Serves 8 as a first course,
4 as a main dish

Holland in the spring is warm enough to produce the world's most gorgeous tulips, and it is cold enough during the winter to bring forth this thick, meaty split pea soup. In this recipe, tongue replaces the pork products used by the Dutch, giving the soup a smoky taste and providing plenty of meat. To enjoy as a soup course alone, you may want to serve the soup without the tongue, reserving the meat for another meal. Or, serve the meat as the second course.

> **1 pound dried split green peas, picked**
> **through and rinsed**
> **1 smoked beef tongue (3 to 4 pounds), rinsed**
> **3 quarts water**

Recipe continues on the following page . . .

2 cups cubed potatoes (¼-inch cubes)
1 stalk celery, including leaves, diced
4 medium-size leeks (discard tough green
parts), washed well then chopped

In an 8-quart pot, place the split peas, the tongue, and the water. Add water if necessary to cover the tongue. Bring to the boil over high heat. Reduce the heat so the liquid boils moderately, then cover the pot and cook for 2½ to 3 hours, until the tongue is tender when pierced with a fork. From time to time, stir up the peas to make sure they are not sticking, and turn the tongue over occasionally.

Remove the cooked tongue and add the potatoes, celery, and leeks. Raise the heat to again bring the liquid to the boil, then reduce the heat to a gentle boil and cook, uncovered, over moderate heat until everything is tender, stirring from time to time. The split peas must be nice and soft. Meanwhile, remove the skin from the tongue while it is still warm. Keep the tongue warm by wrapping it in foil until you are ready to serve the soup.

The soup should be thick. If it is watery, raise the heat to boil off some of the liquid, stirring often. To serve the tongue right in the soup, slice it and then cut it into chunks. To serve as a separate course, slice the tongue and keep it warm.

This soup is excellent reheated, and it can be frozen.

GAZPACHO

Spain

Serves 4 to 6

You don't have to be Spanish to serve *gazpacho* at Bar Mitzvah receptions. Three out of four of ours were during tomato season, and we increased this marvelous recipe to serve about a hundred people. It is a family favorite at any time. The recipe here departs from other *gazpachos* in two ways: the vegetables are left in small pieces instead of being mashed or puréed, so every spoonful offers both the taste and the touch of each vegetable. And there are no croutons to detract from the fresh vegetable taste.

You will notice that the amounts of vinegar, oil, salt, and pepper are flexible, and you will have to taste the *gazpacho* to adjust the seasonings. Be very careful when you do this—I have found gazpacho to be near addictive. You may even end up doubling the recipe as I do, so there will be enough for the family after the tastes. Never seem to be able to get that seasoning just right!

> **1 clove garlic, cut in half**
> **3 pounds very ripe red tomatoes**
> **2 medium-to-large (6- to 8-inch) cucumbers**
> **½ cup minced green pepper**
> **½ cup minced onion**
> **2 cups tomato juice**
> **3 tablespoons red wine vinegar, or to taste**
> **2 tablespoons olive oil, or to taste**
> **Salt and freshly ground black pepper**
> **Dash of liquid red pepper sauce (Tabasco**
> **sauce), optional**

Rub a soup tureen or an attractive 3-quart serving bowl with the cut surface of the garlic clove. Using a vegetable peeler (see note below), skin the tomatoes. Cut out the cores, then cut the tomatoes into ⅜-inch cubes. Do not use a food processor for the chopping. Add the tomatoes, with their juice, to the serving bowl.

Peel the cucumbers, slice them in half lengthwise, and scoop out the seeds. Chop the cucumbers into ¼-inch pieces, and mix them with the tomatoes along with the minced green pepper and onion. Stir in the tomato juice, the vinegar, oil, and seasonings. Taste and correct seasoning. Chill. Serve the *gazpacho* cold. It will keep in the refrigerator for 2 days, but it cannot be frozen.

Note: One way to peel tomatoes is to dip them into boiling water for 10 or 15 seconds, then plunge them into cold water and peel the loosened skin with a sharp knife. For *gazpacho*, in which the very ripe tomatoes are not cooked, I recommend using a vegetable peeler so there is no chance of accidentally softening the tomatoes.

GREEN SOUP
Caldo Verde

Portugal

Serves 6

Cooked kale is delicate and sweet (much more so than cooked spinach). Kale swells considerably when cooked, so even finely shredded kale will yield sizeable cooked pieces. Mashed potatoes act as a thickener in the soup, and olive oil is always used for flavor. This is a bland soup, and we prefer it with a chicken soup base instead of the plain water used by Portuguese. You will taste the olive oil (to my surprise more than the kale), so select the olive oil carefully.

The Portuguese like to flavor this classic soup with a garlic sausage. If you do not have *chorizo* made up, kosher hot dogs, although not Portuguese, are a nice addition.

> **1 pound potatoes**
> **6 cups chicken broth**
> **½ pound fresh kale**
> **¼ cup olive oil**
> **½ pound Chorizo (page 79), shaped into**
>   **meatballs**
> **Salt and freshly ground black pepper**
> **Garlic Croutons (page 94)**

Peel the potatoes and cut them into 1-inch cubes. In a 4-quart pot, bring the chicken broth to the boil. Add the potatoes, reduce the heat to a gentle boil, cover the pot, and cook the potatoes for about 15 minutes, until tender.
Meanwhile, wash the kale and cut the leaves from the stems. Discard the stems and shred the leaves into the thinnest strips possible. Set aside.

When the potatoes are tender, use a slotted spoon to transfer the cooked potatoes to a bowl. Mash the potatoes with a fork or a potato masher until they are smooth, then stir them back into the chicken broth along with the olive oil. Bring the broth back to the boil, then drop the *chorizo* meatballs into the soup. Cook, covered, for 5 minutes. Now add the shredded kale, pushing the greens gently under the liquid. Simmer, uncovered, for 3 or 4 minutes, until the kale is tender. Taste for seasoning, adding salt and pepper as necessary. Simmer for another minute. Pass around the garlic croutons separately.

Condiments and Sauces

When my daughter was studying mythology and I learned all about Tantalus, I realized that "Condiments and Sauces" in the European section would be one of the most tantalizing parts of this book. Tantalus' eternal punishment for his offenses was to be surrounded by water that receded whenever he tried to drink of it, and luscious fruits that withdrew as he reached for them. Now let me assure you that in no way is this section designed to be a punishment. But it will be tantalizing in a sense, because I will describe some of the condiments and sauces important to the cuisines of European countries without presenting the recipes. Happily, the recipes are not really out of reach, because they are standard, as close as the cookbook section of your local library. The sauce base known as *sofrito* is presented here because *sofrito* recipes are not often found in cookbooks.

Italian sauces used to dress pasta may be spaghetti sauce to us, but there are hundreds of ways of saucing pastas with meat, a variety of cheeses, or vegetables. One unusual vegetable accompaniment for pasta appears on page 98, in the Side Dishes section of this chapter.

Most sauces in Spanish cooking are based on gravies, the liquids accumulated from the foods being cooked. Notable exceptions include Spain's *ali-oli,* a mayonnaiselike blend of garlic, oil, lemon juice; a parsley sauce; and the *sofrito.* The tomato-based sauce familiar to Americans as Spanish omelette sauce is known in Spain as *salsa portuguesa* or sometimes *salsa americana!* Portugal is even less a country of sauces than Spain, though olive oil, lemon juice, tomatoes, parsley, the more acrid fresh coriander, and garlic are used in cooking foods and in seasoning cooked foods.

French cuisine has a host of notable sauces, including mayonnaise made simply of egg yolks, lemon juice or vinegar, and oil; white sauces such as *veloutés* (thickened veal, fish, or chicken stock); *béchamel* (cream sauce); *Mornay* (cream sauce enriched with cheese); and *hollandaise* (a thick, rich sauce made of butter, egg yolks, and lemon juice); and lovely brown glazes and wine sauces (such as *bordelaise*) to go with meats. Dijon mustard from the province of Burgundy appears on the table as a condiment all over France.

For Russian and Polish meals, you can't go wrong with sour cream, mixed with chopped fresh dill if you like, as a standard condiment with dairy meals. In Hungary, a dollop of sour cream to complete a dairy soup or gravy is always in order. A favorite Viennese condiment is horseradish, one accompaniment to the boiled beef that is the most popular meat in Austria. Applesauce (page 99) is enjoyed with Austrian meals, and thick fruit sauces are served in Germany and Russia as well, both with main dishes and as desserts.

SAUCE BASE
Sofrito

Spain

Makes 1 cup

Garlic and onions sautéed in olive oil make up the most elementary sauce base in Spanish cooking. Fresh tomatoes are typically (but not necessarily) part of the base. Sweet red or green peppers may be added, and some cooks like to add ground almonds or sieved hard-cooked egg yolks as well as chopped fresh parsley. The result is a combination that characterizes many Spanish preparations.

Sofrito is used as a basic sauce to which other ingredients are added. Eggs are baked on top of a *sofrito*, fish is poached in it, rice cooks in a *sofrito*, and so on. Unlike smooth canned tomato sauces, *sofrito* is a textured blend of fine bits of vegetables.

> **2 tablespoons olive oil**
> **½ cup finely chopped onion**
> **2 large cloves garlic, minced**
> **¼ cup finely chopped sweet red or green
>   pepper**
> **1 pound ripe red tomatoes, peeled and
>   chopped fine**
> **1 tablespoon minced fresh parsley**
> **Salt and freshly ground black pepper**

In a 2-quart pot or an 8-inch skillet, heat the oil over moderate heat. The oil should not be smoking. Add the onion, cook for a minute, then add the garlic and continue to cook for another 2 minutes, stirring often. Regulate the heat so the onion and garlic soften and turn golden, but do not brown. Mix in the red or green pepper, and continue to cook, stirring often, until the vegetables are tender. Add the tomatoes and parsley and salt and pepper to taste. Cook for another 5 minutes, stirring occasionally, until the mixture is thickened and blended. Add a little water if necessary to keep the vegetables from sticking. Refrigerate leftovers.

Main Dishes

Veal, beef, pork, lamb, chicken, goose, pheasant, duck, rabbit, fish—you name it, somewhere in Europe it is a specialty. Veal is favored in Italy and parts of France, and the French have wonderful ways with baby lamb. Beef is the preferred meat in Austria, where butchers take pride in knowing over forty different cuts of beef. In Denmark and Germany, pork products are most often available. What cannot be eaten "as is" is often turned into sausage. Germany is a leader in sausage production, with numerous "wursts" of beef, pork, veal, and liver, ground with spices and stuffed into casings.

Because meat is enjoyed but not always affordable, thrifty Europeans have devised delicious ways of "stretching" meats. In Sweden, while fish is there for the taking, meat is at a premium. So when a pound of chopped meat can be made into seventy tasty Swedish meatballs, it is understandable that this dish will become famous (see page 74). The French *cassoulet* does use several meats, but beans are also a major ingredient, so the preparation can serve many people. Germans also enjoy a meat and bean combination that includes fruit as well. Succulent stews such as Hungary's goulash are served over *spätzle* (page 95), both to absorb the gravy and to make the meat go a little further, and main dish soups are known throughout Europe.

In Spain and Portugal, main dishes can be considered major events. Hearty meat and dried bean stews, meat and fresh vegetable combinations, substantial fish stews with numerous fresh-caught seafood in one pot, and preparations with more than one kind of meat are common. When something like plain broiled fish is served, it is likely to be one course during the main meal of the day, but not the main dish.

One of Spain's best-known one-pot preparations, *cocido*, was originally prepared by Jews as a stew of chickpeas, meats, and vegetables. During the Inquisition, pork was added to prove a commitment to Christianity. So if you see a recipe for *cocido* in a Spanish cookbook, omit the pork and your "kosher adaptation" will be as authentic as can be.

Eastern European Jews who emigrated to the United States brought with them the technique of slowly simmering tough cuts of meat, such as brisket, flanken, and breast of veal, to make them tender. So tasty are these preparations that what used to be the cheaper cuts of meat have become desirable and more expensive.

Dairy products and eggs are major ingredients in important main dishes in European cuisines, especially those prepared for lighter meals. Italy, France, the Netherlands, and Denmark are major cheese producers (and consumers). Sour cream is not only a favorite condiment but an important source of protein for Russians, Poles, and Hungarians. Eggs are eggs everywhere, but when transformed by the French into tender omelets and airy soufflés, they become choice main dishes for the evening meal. Spanish cuisine features a thick vegetable omelet (page 87) that is also eaten at the lighter evening meal.

SAUERBRATEN

Germany

Serves 6

Probably the best-known meat preparation of Germany, *sauerbraten* is simply a pot roast that has marinated for days in a mixture of vinegar and spices. The effect is to tenderize the meat and give the gravy a pleasant tartness. In this recipe, red wine is used as well as vinegar, making the gravy a little more tasty and less sharp. Flour is used as a thickener, replacing the sour cream that is often added at the end to make the gravy creamy. *Spätzle* (page 95) or boiled potatoes and cooked shredded red cabbage are appropriate accompaniments.

Recipe continues on the following page . . .

4 pounds boneless chuck roast or brisket
1½ cups red wine vinegar
¾ cup dry red wine
1 cup sliced onion
3 bay leaves
1 teaspoon whole black peppercorns
¼ cup vegetable oil
Half a lemon, sliced into rounds
¼ teaspoon powdered ginger
¼ teaspoon freshly ground black pepper
3 tablespoons vegetable oil, approximately
3 tablespoons unsifted all-purpose flour

In a bowl large enough to hold the meat comfortably, place the chuck roast or brisket. Add the wine vinegar, red wine, onion, bay leaves, and whole black peppercorns. Add enough water to just cover the meat. Cover the bowl with foil and refrigerate for 2 to 5 days. Twice a day, turn over the meat.

To cook, in a heavy pot in which the meat will just fit, heat the ¼ cup of oil over moderate heat. Remove the meat from the marinade, reserving the marinade. Pat the meat dry. Brown the meat on both sides, then pour the reserved marinade over the meat, adding the lemon slices, powdered ginger, and ground pepper. Cook, covered, for 3 hours, until the meat is tender when pierced with a fork. Regulate the heat so the meat cooks gently, and turn the meat over every half-hour. The meat can be cooled and refrigerated in the gravy at this point.

To thicken the gravy, reheat the meat and gravy until heated through. Remove the meat from the pot. Strain the gravy into a bowl, skim off the fat, and measure the liquid. For each cup of liquid, heat 1 tablespoon of vegetable oil over moderate heat in the same pot in which the meat cooked. For each tablespoon of oil, add 1 tablespoon of flour, stirring until bubbly. (If you have 2½ cups of liquid, you'll use 2½ tablespoons of oil and 2½ tablespoons of flour.) Continue to cook and stir for a minute, then gradually blend 1 cup of the gravy at a time back into the pot, stirring until smooth and thickened. Boil for 1 minute after all the gravy has been added, then reduce the heat, return the meat to the pot, and cook until the meat is heated through. Or slice the *sauerbraten* first and add the sliced meat to the gravy. Leftovers may be refrigerated or frozen and reheated.

BOILED BEEF
Wiener Tafelspitz

Austria

Serves 6 to 8

We all have our favorite way of cooking fresh brisket of beef, and if you are Austrian, this is probably yours. The meat cooks slowly along with a selection of soup vegetables, making a tender brisket and a tasty broth that is served with small dumplings as a first course. Serve the brisket as the Austrians do, with applesauce (see page 99) or horseradish.

1 whole fresh brisket of beef, well trimmed (6 or 7 pounds after trimming)
3 pounds beef bones or chicken wings, backs, and necks
2 tablespoons vegetable oil
2 cups sliced onion
2 parsnips, peeled and sliced into 1-inch rounds
4 medium-size carrots, peeled and sliced into 1-inch rounds
2 celery ribs, cut into 1-inch pieces
2 leeks (discard tough green parts), washed well and sliced into ½-inch pieces
½ cup coarsely chopped fresh parsley
Salt and freshly ground black pepper

In a 10- to 12-quart pot, place the brisket and beef bones or chicken parts with enough water to cover. Bring to the boil over high heat, and immediately reduce the heat to a gentle boil. Skim off any scum that rises to the surface.

Meanwhile, in a 10-inch skillet heat the oil over moderate heat. Add the onion, parsnips, carrots, celery, and leeks, and cook the vegetables for about 5 minutes, stirring often, until the onion just begins to brown. Add the vegetables to the brisket along with the parsley and salt and pepper to taste. Cover and cook over low heat so the liquid continues to boil gently. Cook for 2½ to 3 hours, until the brisket is tender when pierced by a fork. From time to time turn the meat over.

Recipe continues on the following page . . .

When the meat is tender, remove it from the cooking stock. Taste the broth, add salt if necessary, and cook for another minute or two. Skim off all fat. Strain the broth, discarding the vegetables. Serve the broth with noodles or dumplings, then slice the meat and serve. It is traditional to serve the boiled beef with small browned potatoes. The brisket can be prepared ahead of time and refrigerated or frozen.

VEAL WITH APPLES AND PRUNES
Helstegt Morbrad Med Svesker

Denmark

Serves 4

Meat and apple combinations are common in the cooking of the Netherlands, Denmark, Germany, and other European countries. Here is a roast enjoyed in Denmark for Sunday dinner. Veal breast (taking the place of the pork eaten in Denmark) is stuffed with both prunes and apples. The dish is as uncomplicated as that, and part of its attractiveness lies in its simplicity, because the tastes of the fruits are not masked by any spices. Serve with *spätzle* (page 95) and the rich, sweet gravy that accumulates.

> **1 cup pitted prunes**
> **Boiling water**
> **4 to 5 pounds breast of veal, cut with a**
> **   pocket for stuffing**
> **Salt and freshly ground black pepper**
> **2 tablespoons vegetable oil**
> **4 medium-size cooking apples (1½ pounds)**
> **1 cup chicken broth**
> **2 tablespoons vegetable oil or chicken fat**
> **2 tablespoons unsifted all-purpose flour**

In a heatproof bowl, place the prunes with enough boiling water to cover them by 2 inches. Allow the prunes to soak for 15 minutes.

Meanwhile, rub the veal with salt and pepper. In a 5- to 6-quart pot, heat 2 tablespoons of oil over moderate heat. Brown the veal on both sides, then remove the pot from the heat and take out the veal.

Peel and core the apples, then slice them into thin wedges (16 wedges each). Drain the prunes, then mix them with the apples. When the veal is cool enough to handle, stuff the veal pocket with the prunes and apples. (This is a generous amount of stuffing, and if you stuff the veal before browning, much of the stuffing will fall out when you turn the meat over.)

Return the veal to the pot, add the broth, then cover and cook the veal over moderate heat for 1½ hours, until it is tender. The broth should be boiling gently all the while.

To thicken the gravy, transfer the veal to a serving platter. Pour the gravy into a heatproof cup or bowl. Skim off the fat. In the pot in which the veal cooked, heat the 2 tablespoons of oil or chicken fat over moderate heat. (Or, if you like, use 2 table-spoons of the fat skimmed from the gravy.) Stir in the flour and cook, stirring constantly, for a minute. The flour mixture should be sizzling and bubbly but not brown. Gradually mix in the gravy, stirring constantly until the mixture is smooth and thickened. Cook for one minute after the gravy comes to the boil. Slice the veal into ribs, keeping the stuffing intact, and pass the gravy around separately.

VEAL STEW
Blanquette de Veau

France

Serves 6

Although *blanquette* does not translate to blanket, I think of this as a lovely combination of veal, mushrooms, and small whole onions blanketed by a creamy sauce. The veal, mush-rooms, and onions are each cooked separately and are combined at the end. The seasonings are delicate, and the interest of the

Recipe continues on the following page . . .

stew comes from the individual tastes and the three different textures of the principal ingredients.

> **3 pounds boneless veal shoulder, cut into 1½-inch cubes**
> **Water**
> **1 large carrot, peeled and cut into chunks**
> **2 medium-size onions, peeled but left whole**
> **1 small stalk celery, leaves included**
> **1 medium-size leek (discard tough green parts), washed well**
> **3 sprigs parsley**
> **1 small bay leaf**
> **1 quart chicken broth**
> **Salt**
> **18 small white boiling onions (1 inch diameter), peeled**
> **½ pound small whole mushrooms, cleaned**
> **2 teaspoons lemon juice**
> **3 tablespoons vegetable oil**
> **3 tablespoons unsifted all-purpose flour**
> **2 egg yolks (from eggs graded large or extra-large)**

In a 4-quart pot, cover the veal with water by an inch. Bring to a full boil, then turn off the heat. Allow the veal to remain on the turned-off burner for half a minute, then drain the veal into a colander, run cold water over the meat to wash away any accumulated scum, and clean the pot.

Return the veal to the pot along with the carrot, medium-size onions, celery, the leek, parsley, and bay leaf. Add the chicken broth and enough water (or additional broth) to just cover the ingredients. Bring to the boil, reduce the heat to moderately low, and cook, partially covered, for 1½ hours, until the veal is tender. Adjust the heat so the liquid boils gently throughout the cooking time. Taste the broth after an hour, and add salt to taste. When the veal is tender, turn off the burner, and leave the veal on the turned-off burner.

Meanwhile, use a sharp knife to cut an "x" ¼ inch deep in one end of each of the 18 small white onions; this will help keep the onions whole. In a 2-quart pot or a skillet in which the onions will just fit in one layer, place the onions. After the veal has cooked for an hour, take ¾ cup of the liquid from the veal, and pour it into the pot with the onions. Bring to the boil, cover, and reduce the heat to a gentle boil. Cook for 20 to 30 minutes, until the onions are tender. Use a slotted spoon to remove the onions to a bowl.

Add the mushrooms and 2 teaspoons lemon juice to the liquid in which the onions cooked. Bring to the boil, reduce the heat to a gentle boil, and cook, uncovered, for 5 minutes, tossing the mushrooms around occasionally. Use a slotted spoon to transfer the mushrooms to a bowl, reserving the liquid.

After the veal has cooked for 1½ hours and rested for ½ hour, it is time to complete the cooking. Drain the veal into a colander set over a large heatproof bowl. Transfer the pieces of veal to a heatproof top-of-range casserole, and add the mushrooms and onions. Stir the cooking liquid from the mushrooms and onions into the veal casserole.

For the sauce, in a 2-quart pot heat 3 tablespoons of oil over moderate heat. Mix in the flour and cook, stirring constantly, for a minute. The *roux*, as it is called, should be smooth and bubbly. Do not allow it to brown. Remove the pot from the heat, then gradually add a cup of the broth from the veal casserole to the *roux*, stirring rapidly and constantly as you do. Add another ½ cup liquid, setting the pot over the heat again. Blend in 2 cups more of the broth, stirring all the while. Cook for 5 minutes. Pour the sauce over the veal and vegetables in the casserole. The veal can be prepared up to this point and refrigerated, covered, when cool.

To complete the cooking, heat the casserole until the veal, vegetables, and sauce are all hot. In a 2-cup heatproof glass measuring cup, beat the egg yolks well with a fork. Pour in about ¼ cup of the hot, thickened broth, beating constantly. Add another ¼ cup and continue beating. Add a total of 2 cups, beating all the time. Now pour this mixture back into the remaining sauce in the veal casserole, stirring gently all the while. Bring just to the boil, turn off the heat, and serve.

SWEDISH MEATBALLS
Köttbullar

Sweden

Makes seventy-five 1-inch meatballs

Light and tender meatballs are one of the hot dishes served at smorgasbords in Sweden, and in the United States they are a popular *hors d'oeuvre*. What distinguishes Swedish meatballs from other meatballs? They combine two or three ground meats with onion and a lot of breadcrumbs; they are very lightly seasoned so as not to mask the meat taste; and they are usually made with cream and served in a cream sauce. In this version, beef and veal are the meats, and a delicate veal broth is used in place of cream.

The Veal Broth:

> 2 tablespoons vegetable oil
> ½ cup each chopped onion, carrot, and celery
> 1 pound veal bones
> Salt and freshly ground black pepper
> 3 cups water

In a 2-quart pot, heat the oil over moderate heat. Add the vegetables and sauté for 5 minutes, stirring occasionally, until they soften. Regulate the heat so the vegetables do not brown. Rub the veal bones with salt and pepper, and stir the bones into the pot, mixing them with the vegetables. Now add 3 cups of water, bring to the boil, reduce the heat to a gentle boil, and cook, partially covered, for about 45 minutes. Taste the broth and add salt and pepper if you like, then strain the broth. Reserve for use in making the meatballs.

The Meatballs:

> 1 cup soft breadcrumbs
> 1 cup veal broth from above
> 1 pound extra-lean ground beef
> ½ pound lean veal, ground

½ cup minced onion
½ teaspoon salt
1 egg (graded large), beaten
2 tablespoons vegetable oil
1 cup veal broth from above
Optional, to thicken the gravy: 1 tablespoon
    vegetable oil and 1 tablespoon unsifted all-
    purpose flour

In a medium-size bowl, soak the breadcrumbs in a cup of veal broth for 10 minutes. On a clean work surface, use your hands to mix together the ground beef and veal, onion, and salt. Mix in the soaked breadcrumbs and the beaten egg. Using your hands, knead the mixture for about 5 minutes. The meat mixture may be too soft to shape. If so, refrigerate it until it is firm enough to shape into balls.

Shape the meat mixture into compact 1-to 1¼-inch balls. In a 10-inch skillet, heat the 2 tablespoons of oil over moderate heat. Add a third of the meatballs. Occasionally turn them gently, and shake the skillet from time to time so they do not stick. Brown the meatballs all over, then use a slotted spoon to transfer them to a bowl. Then brown another third of the meatballs. Continue until all the meatballs are browned.

Return all of the browned meatballs to the skillet, cover the skillet, and cook for 15 minutes. Now, with a slotted spoon remove the meatballs from the skillet, and pour off any accumulated fat. Stir the second cup of veal broth into the skillet, scraping up any bits of meat. Return the meatballs to the skillet, stir them to coat with the veal broth, cover the skillet, and cook gently for 30 minutes.

If you want to thicken the gravy, use a slotted spoon to again transfer the meatballs to a bowl. Pour the gravy into a heat-proof bowl or cup. In the same 10-inch skillet, heat the remaining tablespoon of oil over medium heat, then stir in the flour. Cook, stirring constantly, for one minute. Gradually stir the gravy back into the skillet. Cook, stirring constantly, until the liquid boils and thickens. Cook for one more minute, then return the meatballs to the skillet. Serve immediately or refrigerate or freeze for later use.

PEPPERONI

Italy

Makes two 10-inch sticks

Pepperoni is commonly known as a spicy *dried* sausage that is a favorite topping for pizza. Because it is impractical for most people to set aside a cool, dry area for drying out the pepperoni for two months, this recipe is for a fresh all-beef pepperoni that is ready to be used after only a day or two of drying. While it may not taste exactly like the dried version, it is an excellent sausage to use for pizza, sausage and peppers, and other Italian dishes. (You will notice a smell of garlic in your refrigerator when the pepperoni is placed there unwrapped. You may want to cover the pepperoni and cook it as a fresh sausage that will be softer than the slightly dried sticks.)

> **1 pound well-trimmed stewing beef, cut into**
> **1-inch cubes**
> **1 teaspoon kosher salt**
> **½ teaspoon sugar**
> **½ teaspoon ground cayenne pepper**
> **1 teaspoon sweet paprika**
> **1 medium clove garlic, minced**

Grind the beef in a meat grinder, or mince with the chopping blade of a food processor. Be careful not to turn the meat into a paste. Transfer the meat to a clean work surface, flatten it out, and sprinkle the remaining ingredients over the meat. Use your hands to thoroughly combine all the ingredients.

Shape into 2 long thin rolls, 1 x 10 inches each. Place the pepperoni sticks on a sheet of foil or wax paper, and leave *uncovered* in the refrigerator or in a cold (40-degree F.) room. Turn over the pepperoni sticks every 8 hours. Use after a day or two, or freeze for later use.

For thin slices of pepperoni, first freeze the sticks for about an hour, until they are partially frozen but can still be sliced. Then, use a very sharp knife to make ¼ inch slices. To use for pizza, see the following recipe.

PEPPERONI PIZZA

Italy

Makes 2 large pizzas

Take a piece of extra bread dough, flatten it out, spread it with a layer of surplus garden tomatoes, sprinkle with basil from the garden, bake until crisp, and there you have the original Italian pizza, a peasant preparation that makes excellent use of ingredients at hand. With a pound of purchased frozen bread dough and a cup of tomato sauce for each pizza, it is easy to make pizza at home. If you have the time, however, it is best to prepare the homemade dough below and top it with fresh tomatoes and homemade pepperoni.

For a dairy meal, you can omit the pepperoni and turn this into a cheese pizza. See the variations following the recipe. When you read the cottage cheese variation, bear in mind that when I taught a cooking course in religious school, the fourth and fifth graders were appalled at the idea of a cottage cheese pizza until they tasted it.

> **6 cups unsifted all-purpose flour or 2 pounds**
> **frozen bread dough, thawed**
> **1 package active dry yeast**
> **1 tablespoon sugar**
> **1 teaspoon salt**
> **2 cups hot (120 to 130 degrees F.) water**
> **2 tablespoons olive oil or other vegetable oil**
> **3 pounds ripe red tomatoes or 2 cups**
> **(16 ounces) tomato sauce**
> **2 tablespoons olive oil**
> **¼ cup chopped fresh parsley**
> **2 tablespoons chopped fresh basil leaves or 2**
> **teaspoons dried basil**
> **1 teaspoon dried oregano**
> **2 pepperoni sticks (see previous recipe)**
> **Optional toppings: chopped green pepper,**
> **chopped onion, canned or slightly sautéed**
> **sliced fresh mushrooms**

If you are using frozen bread dough, you will not need the flour,

Recipe continues on the following page . . .

yeast, sugar, salt, water, or the first 2 tablespoons of oil.

In a large mixing bowl, mix 2 cups of the flour with the yeast, sugar, and salt. Stir in the hot water and 2 tablespoons of oil. Beat with a large spoon (or use the dough hook of a heavy-duty electric mixer) for 2 minutes. Beat in 3 more cups of flour 1 cup at a time. Spread the last cup of flour on a clean work surface, turn out the dough onto the floured surface, and knead for 6 to 8 minutes, until all the flour has been worked in. Press a finger into the dough. If the indentation does not remain, the dough is ready to use.

Place the homemade dough in a clean bowl that will be large enough to accommodate the dough when double in bulk. (Purchased bread dough does not need to rise before being shaped into pizza crust.) Cover the top of the bowl with plastic wrap, and allow the dough to rise in a warm place (80 to 85 degrees F.). A warm room, a gas oven with a pilot light, or an oven with a hot pan of water on the bottom shelf and the bowl of dough on the shelf above will do. It will take the dough about an hour to rise in a warm place, longer if the room is cool. To slow down the rising, place the bowl of dough in the refrigerator. To test the dough to see if it has risen enough, press your finger into it; if the dough is ready, the indentation will remain.

Punch down the dough and knead it a few times in the bowl, until it is smooth again. Divide the dough into 2 equal pieces. Shape each piece into a smooth ball.

Preheat the oven to 450 degrees F. Grease 2 large cookie sheets. Take one ball of dough and flatten it between your hands, then stretch it gently into a flat circle. When it becomes too difficult to do this midair, or if the dough begins to tear, put it in the center of the cookie sheet. Now, using your fingers, gently push and stretch the dough, working from the center to the outside, until you have a large circle or rectangle. (Our pizzas are usually 13 x 16 inches). If the dough tears or you have difficulty pushing it, let it rest for a few minutes while you begin the other piece. You may patch tears using thicker parts of the dough. When the pizza is the size you want it, pinch up the edges. Repeat with the second ball of dough.

For the topping, spread each pizza with half the chopped tomatoes or a cup of tomato sauce (or use both if you want a saucy pizza with the texture of chopped tomatoes). Sprinkle each pizza with a tablespoon of olive oil, then sprinkle each with half the parsley, basil, and oregano. Slice the pepperoni into ¼-inch rounds, and distribute the pepperoni on the pizza. Sprinkle with any of the optional toppings.

Bake the pizzas in the preheated oven for 15 to 20 minutes, until they are hot and the pepperoni is sizzling and cooked through. Halfway through the baking period, reverse the cookie sheets top to bottom and front to back to ensure even browning. Slice the cooked pizzas into wedges or rectangles. Serve with a tossed green salad.

Variations:

For cheese pizza, omit the pepperoni. Sprinkle each pizza with ¼ cup grated Parmesan cheese and 2 cups (½ pound) shredded mozzarella cheese. Scatter with anchovies if you like.

Or top the pizzas with small spoonfuls of cottage cheese, spreading the cottage cheese gently with the back of a spoon. Use ½ pound per pizza. The cottage cheese will not cover the pizza completely, but it will melt into the pizza, making numerous islands of cheese.

CHORIZO

Spain

Makes 2 cups

The essence of this spicy Spanish sausage, featured in Mexican as well as Spanish cooking, is in the seasonings. Therefore, when ground beef is substituted for pork, the authentic taste is retained. This is a simplified sausage recipe, as the meat is neither smoked nor stuffed into a casing.

Chorizo is not eaten as a main dish itself, but is used as an appetizer (page 53) or as an ingredient—sometimes more as a seasoning than a meat—in other preparations. One-half to one cup of uncooked *chorizo* can be added to a *sofrito* (page 65), for example, before chicken or rice is cooked in the mixture. *Chorizo*

Recipe continues on the following page . . .

is the perfect meat for *tacos* and *tostadas*, and leftovers are a good filling for *empanaditas* (page 281). One pound fills six to eight tacos or tops four *tostadas* lavishly. The recipe can be prepared in quantity for convenience—just double, triple, or quadruple all ingredients. Freeze uncooked *chorizo* in one-cup (half-pound) packages.

> **1 pound extra-lean ground beef**
> **1 large clove garlic, minced**
> **½ teaspoon salt**
> **1 teaspoon dried oregano**
> **2 tablespoons chili powder**
> **2 tablespoons distilled white vinegar**

Flatten out the beef on a clean work surface. Sprinkle with the garlic, salt, oregano, chili powder, and vinegar. Use your hands to combine everything very well. Place the mixture in a bowl, and allow it to stand at room temperature for 1 hour, then cook, refrigerate, or freeze. The uncooked mixture will keep for a few days in the refrigerator.

To cook, put the meat in an ungreased skillet or pot. Turn the heat to medium-high and fry, uncovered, until the *chorizo* is cooked through. From time to time, use a large fork or the side of a spoon to break up any clumps of meat.

PAELLA

Spain

Serves 4 to 6

Whether a glorious restaurant preparation or a family picnic meal, *paella* is a rice dish. Born on the Mediterranean coast of Spain where rice is the staple, authentic *paella* is made with any combination of seafood, chicken, *chorizo*, and vegetables, but it will always have rice and saffron as its base. The name comes not from its ingredients but from the large heavy flat-bottomed pan—a *paellera*—in which the ingredients are cooked. Traditionally the *paella* pan is set on the center of the dining room table, and all the diners help themselves. Although *paella* is cooked uncovered in Spain, I prefer to cover it during part of the cooking to be sure the rice is tender.

> **1 large frying chicken (4 pounds) or 4 pounds
> mixed chicken parts (legs, thighs, breasts)
> Salt and paprika
> ¼ to ½ cup olive oil
> 1 cup finely chopped onion
> 1 large clove garlic, minced
> 1 pound Chorizo (page 79)
> 2 cups short or medium-grain white rice
> 1 quart chicken broth
> Salt and freshly ground black pepper
> ¼ teaspoon saffron
> 1 cup fresh peas or thawed frozen peas**

Cut the chickens or chicken parts into pieces. Cut each breast half in half again. If you have a chopping cleaver, cut the thighs in half through the bones. Sprinkle the chicken pieces with salt and paprika.

In a 14-inch *paella* pan or a 12-inch skillet, heat ¼ cup of the oil over moderate heat. Brown the chicken pieces well, turning as necessary. This will take 15 to 20 minutes. Remove the chicken to a bowl; set aside. Pour the accumulated fat into a heatproof measuring cup, and either pour ¼ cup back into the skillet or start with new oil.

Sauté the onion and garlic in the oil until the onion is softened but not browned. Add the *chorizo*, raising the heat if necessary to brown the *chorizo*. Use a large fork or spoon to break up any clumps of meat—the *chorizo* should be in small, separate pieces. Add the rice to the pan and cook for a minute or two, stirring to keep the rice from sticking or burning. Meanwhile, in a 2-quart pot bring the quart of chicken broth to the boil, adding salt and pepper to taste.

Sprinkle the saffron evenly over the rice, then pour the boiling broth into the pan. Scatter the peas in the pan. Place the browned chicken pieces on top of the rice and peas, and regulate the heat so the liquid just boils gently. Cook uncovered for 10 minutes, then cover the skillet or *paella* pan with a lid or foil and cook for an additional 15 minutes, until the liquid is absorbed.

Recipe continues on the following page . . .

Turn off the heat and let the *paella* rest, covered, for 10 minutes before serving. Serve directly from the pan, with a salad on the side.

CHICKEN PAPRIKA
Pörkölt Csirke

Hungary

Serves 4

Sweet Hungarian paprika is used abundantly to color and flavor this chicken. In this recipe the rich sauce, full of onion, green pepper, and tomato, is made without the traditional sour cream. When sour cream is used by Hungarians, the name of the preparation changes to *paprikas csirke*. Serve the chicken with an egg dumpling such as *spätzle* (page 95) or with noodles or rice.

> **1 large frying chicken (4 pounds)**
> **¼ cup vegetable oil**
> **2 cups chopped onion**
> **1 cup chicken broth**
> **1½ tablespoons sweet Hungarian paprika**
> **1 cup sliced green pepper strips**
> **½ pound ripe red tomatoes, peeled and sliced**
> **into thin wedges**
> **Salt**

Cut the chicken into serving-size pieces. Set aside. In a 5-quart pot, heat the oil over moderate heat. Add the chopped onion and cook for a few minutes, until the onion is wilted but not brown. Now add the chicken pieces skin side down. Cook for just a few minutes, until the chicken is coated and warmed by the oil but not browned or crusty, turning once to coat both sides. Remove the chicken to a bowl, then stir ½ cup of the chicken broth and the paprika into the pan drippings. Return the chicken to the pot, add the remaining chicken broth, and scatter the green pepper strips and tomato wedges over the chicken.

Bring the liquid to the boil, reduce the heat so the liquid boils gently, then cover the pot and cook the chicken for 30 to 45 minutes, until tender. Occasionally turn over the chicken pieces. Toward the end of the cooking time add salt to taste. The chicken can be prepared in advance and reheated, but freezing is not recommended because the consistency of the vegetables may change.

CHICKEN KIEV
Kievskie Kotlety

Ukraine

Serves 4

From the days of the Czars comes this classical Ukrainian preparation in which pounded chicken breasts are rolled around unseasoned fingers of butter, coated with breadcrumbs, then deep-fried. This updated version uses herbs for additional flavor, and of course margarine is substituted for the butter. The rolled and breaded chicken must be refrigerated for at least two hours prior to cooking so that the "butter" will be firm and the coating will be cold enough to brown slowly, ensuring thorough cooking of the chicken.

> **4 whole chicken breasts (1 pound each) or 8
>   chicken cutlets (2 pounds)**
> **¼ pound (1 stick) pareve margarine, softened**
> **1 tablespoon chopped fresh parsley**
> **1 tablespoon chopped fresh dill**
> **½ cup unsifted all-purpose flour**
> **2 eggs (graded large)**
> **1½ cups fine dry breadcrumbs made from ends
>   or crusts of bread**
> **½ teaspoon salt**
> **Freshly ground black pepper**
> **Oil for frying**

Remove and discard the skin from the whole chicken breasts. Cut the breasts in half through the breastbone, then bone the

Recipe continues on the following page . . .

chicken, making sure to keep the cutlets whole. You should have 8 cutlets.

Place the cutlets between two sheets of wax paper and pound the chicken as thin as possible, flipping the wax paper over several times during the pounding so both sides of the chicken are pounded. Set aside.

For the filling, in a small bowl use a fork to mash the margarine until it is soft, then mix in the chopped parsley and dill. Divide the margarine into 8 equal portions, and use your fingers to shape each portion into a thin "finger" about ½ x 3½ inches. Place one finger of seasoned margarine down the length of each chicken cutlet. There should be enough room on either end to fold the chicken over the margarine.

To wrap the chicken around the filling, first fold the two ends over the margarine, then roll the cutlet up tightly, completely enclosing the finger of margarine.

Place the flour in a bowl that will be big enough to accommodate one chicken roll at a time. Beat the eggs in a second bowl. Combine the breadcrumbs with the salt and pepper to taste in a third bowl. Dip each chicken roll into the flour, covering it completely (including the ends) with a light coating of flour. Now roll the floured chicken in the beaten egg, then in the seasoned breadcrumbs. The breadcrumbs must cover the chicken completely, even the ends. Refrigerate for 2 to 4 hours.

In a 12-inch skillet, heat ½ inch of oil to 375 degrees F. The oil will be hot but not yet smoking, and a drop of water will spatter instantly. Carefully place the chicken rolls in the hot oil seam side down. Fry for 5 to 7 minutes on one side until a rich brown, then use a large spoon to carefully turn the chicken over. Brown the other side for 5 to 7 minutes. Remove the chicken with a slotted spoon, drain on paper towels, and serve immediately.

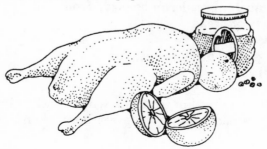

FRESH FISH STEW
Caldeirada

Portugal

*Serves 4 as a main dish,
6 to 8 as a first course*

If you really want to prepare this light, delicate soup-stew correctly, you will need to rent a boat, catch the fish, and cook your catch on board before returning to shore. The key word in Portuguese fish stew is fresh, and if you do not have access to really fresh fish, I suggest you skip this recipe. (Or, come to Connecticut to Temple Emanuel's annual Goods and Services Auction and bid on a one-day fishing excursion with Sherwin Fischman.)

For *caldeirada*, select four or five different kinds of fillets, choosing from such fish as cod, flounder, halibut, pollock, and red snapper. Serve as a soup course or as a main dish with hot bread and a big salad.

> 1 large onion, sliced into rounds
> 1 tablespoon minced garlic
> 3 medium-size white potatoes (1 pound total), peeled and sliced into thin rounds
> 1 pound fresh or canned tomatoes (drained if canned), chopped
> ¼ cup finely chopped fresh parsley
> Salt and freshly ground black pepper
> 6 cups water or fish broth
> ½ cup dry white wine (optional)
> Juice of ½ lemon
> 2 pounds mixed fish fillets, cut into 1½-inch squares
> Garlic Croutons (page 94)

In a 4- or 5-quart pot, place the onion rounds. Sprinkle them with the garlic, then scatter the potatoes, tomatoes, and parsley on top. Sprinkle with salt and pepper. Add the water or fish broth, the optional white wine, and the lemon juice. Bring to the boil over high heat, reduce the heat to a gentle boil, cover the pot, and cook for about 15 minutes, until the potatoes are

Recipe continues on the following page . . .

tender when pierced with a fork. Without stirring, add the fish fillets, gently pushing them under the liquid. Cover and cook for about 5 minutes longer, until the fish turns white and flakes easily when poked with a fork. Taste the broth, and add more salt and pepper to taste. Serve in soup bowls and pass garlic croutons separately.

FILETS DE SOLE À LA MEUNIÈRE

France

Serves 4

The miller's wife *(meunière)* knew how to cook fish with a delicate touch. Lightly floured, sautéed in butter, sauced with additional butter, then topped with a sprinkling of fresh lemon juice and chopped parsley, fish *à la meunière* is easy to prepare and attractive when served. Small whole trout (one-half pound each) are often cooked this way, and salmon fillets are also very good *à la meunière*.

> 1½ to 2 pounds fillets of sole or flounder
> Salt (optional)
> Unsifted all-purpose flour for dusting the
>   fish
> 3 tablespoons unsalted butter
> 1 tablespoon vegetable oil
> ½ cup (1 stick) unsalted butter
> 2 tablespoons freshly squeezed lemon juice
> ¼ cup chopped fresh parsley
> Lemon wedges for garnish

Sprinkle the fish with salt if desired. Place about ½ cup of flour in a bowl, or spread the flour on a plate. Dip each fish fillet into the flour, then shake off excess flour. In a large skillet, heat the 3 tablespoons of butter with the oil over moderate heat. The butter will foam, and just as the foaming subsides, add as many fish fillets as will fit in the skillet in one layer. Sauté the fish until it is light brown on one side, carefully turn with a large spoon or a pancake turner, and cook until the other side is light brown. Transfer to a platter, cover with foil to keep warm, and sauté the remaining fillets, adding a little more butter if necessary.

Just before the fish is done, in a small skillet melt the ½ cup of butter over moderate heat. Cook until the butter is just beginning to brown. Transfer the remaining fish to the serving platter. Pour the melted butter over the fish, sprinkle with the lemon juice then the chopped parsley, and garnish with lemon wedges. Serve immediately.

Variation:

For Sole Aux Amandes brown ½ cup blanched slivered almonds in the ½ cup of butter that will be poured over the fish, then strew the browned almonds over the cooked fish.

SPANISH OMELET
Tortilla de Español

Spain

Serves 1 or 2

My husband usually cooks breakfast on weekends, and one of his specialties is *matzo brei* which he makes to order as a big, thick pancake. His *matzo brei* never falls apart because he uses a cast-iron skillet and cooks one side until it is brown, holds a plate over the skillet, then flips the skillet and plate upside-down rapidly so the *matzo brei* falls onto the plate. Next he slides the uncooked surface back into the skillet, and when that is brown, he turns the *matzo brei* out onto a serving plate. And that is the technique to use for a Spanish omelet, known in Spain as a *tortilla*. (The Mexican *tortilla* is a flat bread. See page 319.)

The Spanish omelet of American cookbooks—a plain egg pancake sauced with a thick tomato, green pepper, and onion mixture—is not the omelet cooked in Spanish kitchens. Thick potato omelets like the one in this recipe are eaten daily in Spain, usually at the late evening meal. Tomatoes, onions, sweet peppers, and other vegetables are common additions.

1 small potato, 2 inches in diameter
½ cup olive oil

Recipe continues on the following page . . .

Salt and freshly ground black pepper
2 eggs (graded large), beaten

Peel the potato if you like and slice it into ⅛-inch rounds. In a 5-
or 6-inch cast-iron skillet, heat the olive oil until it just begins
to smoke. Carefully drop in one layer of potato slices, and cook
the potatoes until they just begin to become tender inside and
crisp and brown on the outside. Turn as necessary. Remove
them with a slotted spoon, and drain well on paper towels.
Repeat with the remaining potatoes. Sprinkle all the potatoes
well with salt and pepper.

Pour off the oil, then put the potatoes back into the same skillet
in which they fried. Pour the beaten eggs over the potatoes,
reduce the heat to moderately low, cover the skillet, and allow
the eggs to set. When the omelet is golden brown on the bottom
and moist but cooked on top, loosen the edges with a narrow
metal spatula, and flip the omelet as described in the introduction. Cook the other side until it is golden, then turn out onto a
plate and serve. The omelet can be served cold as well—good
picnic fare.

Note: A 4-egg omelet in an 8-inch skillet can be flipped and
cooked on both sides, but larger omelets in larger skillets are
more cumbersome. For omelets that are 10 or 12 inches, cook
the omelet on one side only. Cover the skillet during the last
minute of cooking until the top surface is no longer moist. Cut
the *tortilla* into wedges and serve directly from the skillet.

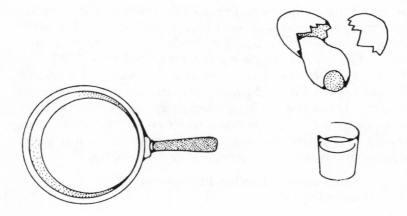

Side Dishes

Vegetables, fruit sauces, potatoes, rice and other starches—all are served to complement the main dish in European meals. Because bread is always on the table, two tempting bread recipes are included in this section of side dishes, along with a recipe for making croutons out of leftover bread. Even if you have never baked before, you will be able to follow the step-by-step directions for a marvelous dark bread from Russia and a sweet, light whole-grain bread (pages 90 and 93).

In addition to breads, European countries are known for their dumplings. Russia, Poland, Hungary, and Austria all feature dumplings in their cuisines, and Germans cook enough dumplings of flour, potatoes, and farina to fill a book, with a range that goes from soup through dessert dumplings. The dumplings of northern Italy, *gnocchi,* are often made of potatoes and served with tomato sauce, and Italians also specialize in ricotta-and-spinach *gnocchi.*

From this impressive array of European dumplings, the little light flour-and-egg dumplings known as *spätzle* stand out. Well known in the kitchens of Germany, Austria, and Hungary, *spätzle* are typically served in soups and with main dishes that have a lot of gravy. You may enjoy substituting *spätzle* for pasta and serving them with butter and cheese or with your favorite spaghetti sauce. A second substitute for pasta (or potatoes) appearing in this section is a rice dish, *risotto* (page 97), which is eaten often in northern Italy but not often seen in kosher cookbooks.

Imaginative vegetable preparations also appear on European tables. The French approach vegetables with the same tender loving care that they give to all foods, cooking them just until done and perhaps glazing them but not disguising them with heavy sauces. A favorite German vegetable dish, sweet-and-sour red cabbage, reflects that country's more vigorous approach to food. In northern areas where cabbages, turnips, and beets grow well, soups, salads, and other side dishes using these vegetables are popular. Mushrooms are a favorite vegetable among many Europeans, especially when they can be picked wild, and several mushroom preparations appear in the Appetizers and Soups section, beginning on page 47.

As we have seen, in some European countries, fruits are more important side dish accompaniments than vegetables, and a recipe for applesauce, which can be a side dish or a dessert, appears on page 99. Although applesauce is standard fare in the United States as well as Europe, one dish of a rosy home-made applesauce will convince you that even applesauce can be a special treat. Another recipe featuring apples combines the fruit with dried beans and fresh vegetables (see page 100).

One of the nicest things you can do to a vegetable is to use it for a pasta sauce, and the broccoli recipe in this section (page 98) may be enjoyed as a side dish or a pasta accompaniment. If you like it (and I think you will), experiment on your own with cauliflower or green beans (I think you'll like that also).

BLACK BREAD
Chornyi Khlyeb

Russia, Ukraine

Makes 2 round loaves

Dark, coarse, heavy, and chewy, this peasant bread is for all of us for whom wimpy white breads are unappealing. Black bread is found all over the USSR, and it can be found in your own kitchen as well. Dark or pumpernickel rye flour will make a more coarse loaf than the more readily available medium rye flour. Black bread is as easy to bake as any bread, but save time for eating, because you will not want to rush through the thick, hearty slices. If you enjoy meals of soup, bread, and cheese, here is the perfect bread.

4 cups unsifted medium, dark, or pumpernickel rye flour
4 cups unsifted all-purpose flour,
approximately
1 cup wheat bran (*not* cereal)
2 packages active dry yeast
2 tablespoons caraway seeds
1 tablespoon instant coffee powder or instant
espresso
1 tablespoon salt
1 tablespoon sugar
2½ cups water
¼ cup distilled white vinegar
¼ cup molasses
¼ cup solid vegetable shortening or ¼ cup (½
stick) unsalted butter or margarine
1 ounce (1 square) unsweetened baking
chocolate
Glaze: ½ cup cold water and 1 tablespoon
cornstarch

In a large mixing bowl, combine 1 cup of each of the flours, the bran, yeast, caraway seeds, instant coffee, salt, and sugar.

In a 2-quart pot, mix together the water, vinegar, molasses, shortening or butter or margarine, and the baking chocolate. Heat over moderately low heat, stirring from time to time. As soon as the shortening and chocolate melt but before the liquid becomes hot (130 degrees F.), remove the pot from the heat.

Blend the liquid into the dry ingredients, and beat for 2 minutes, either in a heavy-duty electric mixer equipped with a dough hook or with a big kitchen spoon and a strong arm. Now add 1 cup each of the white and rye flours, beat for another minute, then add another cup of each of the flours and continue beating. At this point, switch to hand-beating so you do not stress your mixer. (Your sore arm will heal.) Mix in the final cup of rye flour. Now take the last cup of white flour, and spread it on a clean, smooth work surface. Turn the dough out onto the counter, cover it with the mixing bowl, and allow it to rest for 15 minutes while you wash your hands and rest your arm.

Knead the dough for 8 to 10 minutes, adding sprinklings of

Recipe continues on the following page . . .

white flour if the dough becomes sticky. The dough is ready when it is springy and not at all sticky.

Place the dough in a bowl large enough to accommodate it when double in bulk. Cover the bowl tightly with plastic wrap, and set it to rise in a warm place (80 to 85 degrees F.) until the dough has doubled. A warm room, a gas oven with a pilot light, or an oven with a pan of hot water on the bottom shelf and the bowl of dough on the shelf above will do. To test the dough to see if it has risen enough, press your finger into it. The indentation will remain and the dough will not be sticky. Rising may take anywhere from 1½ hours to as long as 3 or 4 hours, depending on the temperature where the dough is rising.

Punch down the dough, turn it out onto a clean work surface, and knead 4 or 5 times, until it is a smooth ball. Using a sharp knife, divide the dough evenly into two pieces. Shape each piece into a ball, and place each ball on opposite ends of a large greased baking sheet. Cover the loaves with wax paper and allow them to rise in the warm place for 45 minutes.

Preheat the oven to 350 degrees F. Bake the loaves for 1 hour. There are two ways to check to see if the loaves are done. Take a metal cake tester or a toothpick and stick it through the center of a loaf (from the bottom so it doesn't show). It should come out clean and dry. Or, pick up a loaf and thump the bottom with your fingers. The thump should be loud and clear, not muffled.

Just before the bread is done, in a 1-quart pot mix the corn-starch and cold water. Stirring frequently, bring to the boil over medium heat, then boil for 5 to 10 seconds, stirring constantly. Quickly brush the loaves completely with the cornstarch glaze, return the loaves to the oven, turn off the heat, and allow the loaves to remain in the oven for 2 minutes, then transfer them to a wire rack to cool. Serve the bread warm or at room temperature—it is delicious both ways.

To freeze the loaves, wait until they are completely cool, then wrap well in heavy-duty foil or freezer wrap.

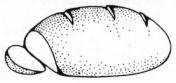

SMÖRREBRÖD BREAD

Denmark

Makes 2 round loaves

If Dagwood had tasted this sweet, earthy, whole-grain bread, his legendary gigantic sandwiches probably wouldn't exist, because he would not want to cover up the taste of the bread too much. This is an ideal bread for *smörrebröd*, the open-faced sandwiches of Denmark, for if you want a yummy sandwich, start with a yummy bread. It is particularly good with egg salad, cheese, and tuna fish, complementing these foods because while it is delicious itself, it is not too heavy or chewy, nor does it have strong or unusual flavors.

> **2 cups unsifted medium rye flour**
> **1 package active dry yeast**
> **¼ cup firmly packed dark brown sugar**
> **¼ cup granulated sugar**
> **2 teaspoons salt**
> **2 tablespoons solid vegetable shortening**
> **1½ cups hot water (120 to 130 degrees F.)**
> **2½ cups unsifted whole wheat flour,**
> **approximately**

In a large mixing bowl, stir together the rye flour, yeast, sugars, and salt. Add the shortening, then blend in the water. Beat with a large spoon for 2 minutes. Mix in a cup of the whole wheat flour, then a second cup. Work the dough with your fingers if it is too stiff for the spoon.

On a clean work surface, spread the remaining ½ cup of whole wheat flour. Turn out the dough onto the flour. Cover the dough with the bowl and allow it to rest for 10 minutes. Knead the dough for about 8 minutes, working in sprinkles of additional whole wheat flour or white flour. The dough should be smooth, springy, and hold together well, and it should lose all its stickiness.

Place the dough in a bowl large enough to accommodate it when double in bulk. Cover the bowl tightly with plastic wrap, and set it to rise in a warm place (80 to 85 degrees F.) until the dough has

Recipe continues on the following page . . .

doubled. A warm room, a gas oven with a pilot light, or an oven with a pan of hot water on the bottom shelf and the bowl of dough on the shelf above will do. To test the dough to see if it has risen enough, press your finger into it. The indentation should remain and the dough should not be sticky. Rising may take anywhere from 1½ hours to as long as 3 or 4 hours, depending on the temperature where the dough is rising.

Punch down the dough, turn it out onto a clean work surface, and knead 4 or 5 times until it is a smooth ball. Using a sharp knife, divide the dough evenly into two pieces. Shape each piece into a ball, and place each ball on opposite ends of a large greased baking sheet. Cover the loaves with wax paper and allow them to rise in the warm place for 1 hour.

Preheat the oven to 375 degrees F. Bake for 35 minutes, until a cake tester poked in from the bottom comes out clean. Or, pick up a loaf and thump the bottom with your fingers. The thump should be loud and clear, not muffled. Allow the bread to cool on a wire rack before slicing. Serve warm as a dinner bread, at room temperature as a sandwich bread. To freeze the loaves, wait until they are completely cool, then wrap well in heavy-duty foil or freezer wrap.

GARLIC CROUTONS
Migas

Spain

Makes 4 cups

Migas—bits of bread fried in olive oil—are the antecedents of croutons. They probably began as a way of using leftover bread: not wanting to waste even a slice, the Spanish housewife would tear leftover bread into small pieces and drop them into the cooking pot. *Migas* became a dish in itself, and *tapas* restaurants feature bread fried in garlic and olive oil, sometimes mixed with ham or anchovies.

This recipe is for the square croutons available in packages, but you will find that homemade croutons have a much better flavor than the ones that comes in boxes. Because the crusts are trimmed, regular white, whole-wheat, or rye breads are recommended. Crusty leftover French and Italian breads can be used to make more informal *migas* (simply tear the bread into small pieces and fry in garlic and olive oil).

8 slices white, whole wheat, or rye bread
½ cup olive oil (half vegetable oil if desired)
6 large cloves garlic, sliced

Preheat the oven to 300 degrees F. Trim the crusts from the bread, and cut the bread into ½-inch cubes. Spread out on a baking sheet and bake for 15 minutes, then carefully stir the bread cubes around and bake for another 5 or 10 minutes, until they are toasted all over.

Meanwhile, in a 2-quart pot heat the oil over *low* heat and add the garlic. Cook for a few minutes, until the garlic is sizzling and light brown. Turn off the heat.

Place the hot, toasted bread cubes in a large mixing bowl. Remove the garlic from the oil with a slotted spoon. Slowly pour the oil over the bread cubes, tossing the bread with a spoon as you pour. Continue tossing the bread around for a minute after all the oil has been added. Allow the croutons to cool, and when they are at room temperature, transfer to a plastic bag or a covered container. The croutons will keep for a few days at room temperature, and they freeze well.

SPÄTZLE

Germany, Austria, Hungary

Serves 6

Whether they are called *spätzle* (by Germans and Austrians), *galuska* (by Hungarians), or one of the other names given to dumplings by Europeans (*nockerl* and *knedliky*, for example), these are lovely little odd-shaped dumplings, yellow in color, that are

Recipe continues on the following page . . .

formed by passing a flour-and-egg batter through the holes of a colander and into boiling water. Once you discover the fun of making your own *spätzle* (without a mix, no less), you may even be motivated to buy a special *spätzle*-maker, making it even easier to produce these dumplings. Serve *spätzle* in soup, with butter and grated cheese, or with any stew or meat that has a nice gravy.

> 3½ cups unsifted all-purpose flour
> 1 teaspoon salt
> 6 eggs (graded large or extra-large)
> ½ to ¾ cup water

In a large mixing bowl, mix the flour and salt. Make a well in the center, and add the eggs and ½ cup water. Beat with a large spoon or the cake beater attachment of a heavy-duty mixer until the batter is smooth and begins to develop air bubbles on top. This will take a minute or two with an electric mixer, and 5 to 10 minutes by hand. Add a little more water if the dough is stiff. It will be thicker than cake batter but must be fluid enough to go through the holes of your colander or *spätzle*-maker.

In an 8-quart pot, bring 4 quarts of water to the boil. Pour the *spätzle* batter into the colander and use the back of a large kitchen spoon to push the batter through, into the boiling water. *The bottom of the colander must be at least two inches above the surface of the water.* When all the batter is pushed through, stir the *spätzle* with a clean spoon, and cook for an addition 3 or 4 minutes, until tender and cooked through. Taste for tenderness.

While the *spätzle* are cooking, wash the colander. Drain the tender *spätzle* in the colander. Mix the cooked *spätzle* with butter or oil to keep them from sticking, or rinse them well under cold water.

If you will not be serving the *spätzle* shortly after they are cooked, run cold water over them to cool them completely and keep them from sticking together. Refrigerate to store. Reheat the *spätzle* by steaming, or sauté in a little oil, butter, or margarine.

Note: For *spätzle* for 4, use 2⅓ cups flour, ½ teaspoon salt, 4 eggs, and ⅓ to ½ cup water.

RISOTTO

Italy

Serves 4

Rice dishes are as popular in northern Italy as pasta is in the South, and northern Italians have an unusual way of preparing their rice. First they sauté it in butter and olive oil, usually with onions. A little white wine is added, and when that is absorbed, only part of the cooking liquid—a seasoned broth—is stirred in at a time. The rice cooks until each addition is absorbed. The result is a creamy, flavorful rice, soft outside, with a little firmness at the core. Saffron is added for color and a subtle taste. Vegetables, cheese, or meats are often added.

> **2 tablespoons pareve margarine**
> **2 tablespoons olive oil**
> **½ cup minced onion**
> **1½ cups long-grain rice**
> **¼ cup dry white wine (optional)**
> **1 quart (4 cups) hot chicken broth**
> **Salt**
> **2 tablespoons chopped parsley**
> **⅛ teaspoon saffron, soaked in 3 tablespoons**
> **hot water (optional)**

In a 4-quart pot, melt the margarine with the olive oil over moderate heat. Add the onion and cook, stirring occasionally, until the onion is soft but not browned. Stir in the rice. Cook, stirring often for an additional 2 to 3 minutes. Now stir in the optional white wine, which will be absorbed almost immediately. Stir in ½ cup of the chicken broth, and cook, stirring often, until the broth is absorbed. Keep on adding ½ cup of broth at a time, stirring after each addition and cooking until the broth is absorbed. Push any rice that sticks to the spoon back into the pot so the grains will cook. Stir the pot often so no rice sticks to the bottom.

If the rice is not tender when all the broth has been added, add ½ cup more broth or water, cover the pot, turn the heat to low, and cook for 10 minutes, until the rice is as tender as you like it.

Recipe continues on the following page . . .

Add salt to taste. Stir in the parsley and the optional saffron and saffron water. Turn off the heat, cover the pot, and allow the rice to remain on the turned-off burner for 5 to 10 minutes.

Variation:

For a dairy meal serve *risotto alla milanese.* Use butter or margarine, and substitute a vegetarian broth for the chicken broth. Just before serving, mix in 6 tablespoons of grated Parmesan cheese.

BROCCOLI WITH GARLIC SAUCE
Broccoli Aglio

Italy

Serves 6

Let's play a word association game where you fill in the blank. I say "Spaghetti and ——." Did you say meatballs, meat sauce, or tomato sauce? I'd like to tell you about a "spaghetti and ——" that has neither meatballs nor meat sauce, nor tomato sauce, but is mainly broccoli. As authentic an Italian sauce as any, broccoli seasoned in a garlic and olive oil-and-butter sauce is made to serve with pasta. Of course you must like broccoli to appreciate the sauce, because even though you will taste the garlic, the broccoli is not the least bit disguised. Serve as a pasta sauce or as a vegetable side dish if you prefer.

> **1 medium-size bunch broccoli (1 pound)**
> **1 pound spaghetti or other pasta**
> **3 tablespoons unsalted butter or margarine**
> **3 tablespoons olive oil**
> **3 cloves garlic, crushed then minced**
> **Salt**
> **Grated Parmesan cheese (optional)**

Cut the broccoli florets from the stems; cut the large florets in half so the pieces are about the same size. Set aside. Peel the stems, then cut an inch or two of the stems into pieces of uniform size, about 1 inch long and ⅜ inch wide.

In a 4-quart pot, bring 3 quarts of water to the boil. Add the broccoli stems, cook for 5 minutes, then drop in the florets and cook the florets with the stems for an additional 5 minutes. Drain in a colander. If you like crisp broccoli, rinse with cold water until the broccoli is cool. If you prefer the vegetable soft, do not rinse; the broccoli will continue to cook from its own heat.

Cook the pasta as you usually do. A few minutes before serving, in a 10-inch skillet melt the butter or margarine with the olive oil until the butter sizzles but is not brown. Add the garlic, stirring for 2 or 3 minutes to cook the garlic without browning it. Mix in the cooked broccoli, carefully tossing it with the sauce. Add salt to taste. Mix together the cooked pasta and broccoli, or mix the pasta with a little oil or melted butter or margarine, place on a platter, and top with the broccoli sauce. For a dairy meal, sprinkle the broccoli-topped pasta with cheese if you like. To serve the broccoli as a vegetable, omit the pasta and cheese.

APPLESAUCE
Apfelsosse

Austria, Germany, Russia

Makes 1½ quarts

Homemade applesauce is easy to make, and so much better than store-bought. Apples are cut up and cooked with plums for a rosy color, then strained through a food mill. A little sugar? Not necessary—the natural sugars in the fruit will sweeten the sauce. Peaches, pears, and any kind of plum can be cooked with the apples. Serve the applesauce warm as a side dish or chilled for dessert.

> **3 pounds McIntosh apples or other red cook-
>   ing apples
> 6 fresh prune plums, pits removed
> Dash of ground cinnamon (optional)**

Wash the unpeeled apples, cut them into quarters, and place

Recipe continues on the following page . . .

them in a 5- or 6-quart pot with the pitted plums and about half an inch of water. Bring to the boil over high heat, then reduce to a gentle boil or you will have burned apples and a black-bottomed pot. Cook, covered, for 15 to 20 minutes, until the apples are tender, stirring a few times. When the fruit is nice and soft, stir again, then run through a food mill or use the back of a spoon to push through a strainer. Stir in cinnamon if you like. Serve warm or chilled with any meal, meat or dairy. Refrigerate leftovers, or freeze in a freezer container.

DRIED BEAN, FRESH VEGETABLE, AND FRUIT CASSEROLE
Blindhuhn

Germany

Serves 4 to 6

This Westphalian specialty must have begun as a harvest dish, for some recipes suggest enormous quantities of a variety of fresh fruits and vegetables. Even when reduced from a cauldron-size recipe to a manageable household preparation, it is a substantial side dish.

The dominant taste is of the fruit. While the apples and pears become very soft during the cooking, the green beans and carrots remain firm enough to give the preparation a contrasting texture. The authentic *blindhuhn* uses bacon and bacon fat for seasoning. In this recipe we use sugar and vinegar to create an enticing sweet-and-sour flavor that is typical of German vegetable dishes.

> 1 cup dried lima, navy, or other white beans, picked through and rinsed
> 1 quart water
> ½ teaspoon salt
> ½ pound fresh green beans (blossom end removed and discarded) sliced into 1½-inch pieces
> 2 medium-size carrots, peeled and cut into ¼-inch rounds

2 medium-size potatoes, peeled and cut into
½-inch cubes
1 pound firm ripe pears
1 pound Golden Delicious or McIntosh apples
¼ cup granulated sugar
½ cup distilled white vinegar
Salt and freshly ground black pepper

In a 4- or 5-quart pot, place the dried beans and the quart of water. Bring to the boil over high heat. Boil for 2 minutes, then turn off the heat, cover the pot, and allow the beans to soak for 1 hour. Bring the beans back to the boil and add the ½ teaspoon salt. Reduce the heat to a gentle boil, cover the pot, and cook the dried beans for 45 minutes to an hour, until barely tender.

Meanwhile, in a 2-quart pot bring 2 cups of water to the boil. Cook the fresh green beans and carrots for 5 to 7 minutes, then add the potatoes and cook for another 15 minutes or until the vegetables are tender but not overdone. Drain and rinse with cold water to cool the vegetables and prevent further cooking.

A few minutes before the dried beans are tender, peel and core the pears and apples. Cut the fruit into ½-inch wedges. Mix the fresh vegetables in with the cooked dried beans, then add the fruit. Cook, covered, over low heat for about 10 minutes, until the fruit softens somewhat. Stir the contents of the pot to mix in the fruit, then sprinkle on the sugar and vinegar. Cook, covered, for 5 minutes, then stir the vegetables and fruit gently to blend in the sugar and vinegar. Cook, covered, for an additional 5 minutes. The liquid must be boiling to dissolve the sugar and eliminate the harsh taste of the vinegar. Add salt and pepper to taste and cook an additional minute or two. The fruit should be nice and soft, but not cooked to a pulp. Serve hot. Refrigerate leftovers, but do not freeze.

Desserts

Ah, desserts. From France, raspberry mousses and custard-filled napoleons; from Italy, luscious cheesecakes and crisp *cannoli* (page 111); from Germany, butter cookies and gingerbread houses; from Russia and Poland, coffeecakes laden with fruits and nuts; Danish pastries that melt in the mouth; Swedish pancakes; chocolates from the Netherlands; Viennese tortes and Hungarian strudels; and from Spain and Portugal, caramel-topped *flan* (page 104) and sweet rice puddings. Some of the most exciting taste sensations of Europe come at the end of the meal.

This section covers a range of desserts, from refreshing fruit ices through spectacular tortes.

FRESH STRAWBERRY ICES
Granita di Fragole

Italy

Serves 4

When she didn't like someone, my grandmother used to say, "He gives me ice in the winter." These natural strawberry ices are so fruity and refreshing, you will enjoy having "ice in the winter." No special equipment is necessary, because fresh strawberries are simply mixed with a sugar syrup, frozen, and stirred every half hour during the freezing period. The ices have the texture of a semi-frozen slush, with the strawberries adding a lovely even texture of their own. For ices more like the shaved ice of Italian ices, the mixture is frozen solid then crushed using an ice crusher.

1 pint fresh strawberries
⅓ cup granulated sugar
1 cup water
1 tablespoon fresh lemon juice
1 tablespoon fresh orange juice

Wash and hull the strawberries, place them in a bowl, and mash them with a fork. Set aside.

In a 1-quart pot, place the sugar. Add the water and stir. Bring to the boil over high heat, stirring often until the sugar is dissolved. Boil uncovered for about 4 minutes. Do not boil the syrup too rapidly or you will boil away too much of the liquid. Remove the pot from the heat.

Cool to lukewarm—you should be able to touch the bottom of the pot without burning your hand. Stir in the lemon and orange juices, then stir in the strawberries and mix well. If you have an ice crusher that can be cleaned, freeze the mixture in an ice cube tray. Just before serving, remove the cubes and crush them in the ice crusher. This will give the ices the coarse texture of shaved ice.

Or pour the mixture into a 1-quart serving dish about 7 inches square. (Corning Ware is a good size.) Place uncovered in the freezer. Every 30 minutes stir the ices from the edge of the dish inward, scraping the ice particles that have formed around the edges. In 3 to 4 hours (depending on the freezer) the ices will be slushy and can be served. The longer the ices are frozen, the firmer they will become. If you will not be serving the ices after 4 hours, you will still need to stir them every half hour or they will freeze into a solid block.

If the ices are frozen overnight without being stirred they will become very firm and difficult to serve. You will then need to scrape the ices with the side of a spoon or a melon baller. Or dip the serving dish into a pan of hot water, loosen the edges with a warm metal spatula, and turn the ices out. The ices can then be shaved with a vegetable peeler or a sharp knife, or carefully broken up with a chisel or ice pick.

Recipe continues on the following page . . .

Variation:

For orange ices use 1½ cups water and ½ cup sugar. After the mixture has boiled and cooled to lukewarm, stir in 1 cup of fresh orange juice and 2 tablespoons of fresh lemon juice. Freeze and stir as directed above.

FLAN

Spain, Portugal

Serves 6

Baked custard topped with caramelized sugar, Spain's most famous dessert, is popular in Portugal and Mexico as well. Some recipes use heavy cream and egg yolks, but to cut down on the excessive richness this recipe uses milk and whole eggs. It is smooth, not too sweet, and plenty rich.

> **6 tablespoons granulated sugar**
> **3 eggs (graded large)**
> **⅓ cup granulated sugar**
> **1 teaspoon vanilla extract**
> **2½ cups hot milk (130 degrees F.)**

Have a 6- to 7-inch square baking dish at hand. A 1- or 1½-quart square Corning Ware dish is ideal.

To caramelize the sugar, in a heavy 5- to 6-inch skillet heat the 6 tablespoons of sugar over moderately low heat. Shake the skillet often so the sugar doesn't burn. As the sugar begins to melt, regulate the heat so it melts without becoming charred, and stir often. The heat has to be high enough to melt the sugar, but not so high that the sugar burns. As the sugar begins to melt, it may form lumps, but these will dissolve. When the sugar is completely melted, *immediately* pour it evenly into the bottom of the baking dish.

Preheat the oven to 350 degrees F. For the custard, in a medium-size mixing bowl beat the eggs with a fork or spoon. Stir in the ⅓ cup sugar, the vanilla extract, and the hot milk. Pour this mixture over the caramelized sugar. Fill a 9 x 13 x

2-inch baking pan almost halfway with very hot or boiling water, and carefully place this pan on the middle shelf in the oven. Now set the dish of custard in the center of the baking pan, being careful not to burn yourself. (An alternate method is to place the 9 x 13 x 2-inch pan in the oven, set the dish of custard in the pan, then pour an inch of water into the 9 x 13-inch pan. Special care must be taken so you do not splash any water into the custard.)

Bake the custard for 45 minutes. The top of the custard should be brown, and if you touch the top lightly it should not be liquid and your fingerprint should not remain. A knife inserted into the custard an inch from the edge should come out clean. Remove the dish of custard from the water and allow the custard to cool to room temperature.

Refrigerate until serving time. To serve, use a knife to go all around the outside of the custard, loosening it. Place a large flat plate on top of the custard, and quickly invert so the plate is on the bottom and the custard dish on top. The custard will come out in one piece, and the caramelized sugar will be on top. Refrigerate leftovers.

SOUFFLÉ DE GRAND MARNIER

France

Serves 4

Light and airy with a hint of orange liqueur, this soufflé is baked and served in individual dishes. Although it must be served directly from the oven, much of the preparation can be done in advance, and the individual soufflés take only twenty minutes to bake, making them practical to serve for company. Individual soufflés do not collapse quite as quickly as one large soufflé, and there is something special about presenting each diner with his or her own crusty, puffy dessert.

> **Soft unsalted butter or pareve margarine for coating the soufflé dishes**
> **Granulated sugar for coating**

Recipe continues on the following page . . .

4 eggs (graded large), separated
¼ cup granulated sugar
¼ cup Grand Marnier or other orange liqueur
2 teaspoons grated orange peel
¼ teaspoon cream of tartar
Sifted confectioners' sugar for dusting

Coat the bottoms and halfway up the sides of 4 individual soufflé dishes (2- to 2½-cup size) with softened butter or margarine. Sprinkle in granulated sugar, shaking the dishes so the sugar sticks evenly to the sides as well as the bottom. This can be done well in advance.

Place the egg whites in a large clean, dry mixing bowl and the yolks in another large mixing bowl. The eggs can be separated in advance and refrigerated, but remove them from the refrigerator an hour before they are to be used.

Preheat the oven to 375 degrees F. Place the oven shelf in the lower two-thirds of the oven, and make sure there is no shelf above it.

Beat the egg yolks with an electric mixer on high speed for 2 minutes, then add the sugar and continue beating 3 minutes longer. The egg yolks will become very thick and light in color. Stir in the Grand Marnier and the orange peel.

Using a whisk or clean, dry beaters, beat the egg whites until foamy, then add the cream of tartar and continue beating until the whites hold stiff peaks. Using a large rubber spatula fold about ¼ cup of the egg whites into the thickened yolks, then continue to gently fold the beaten whites into the yolks ½ cup at a time. The mixture should be uniform but still fluffy. Spoon the mixture into the prepared soufflé dishes, gently level off the tops, and bake immediately for 18 to 20 minutes. Quickly open the oven after the minimum baking time, and if the soufflés are puffed and golden brown, they are ready. Remove from the oven, sprinkle with the sifted confectioners' sugar, and serve at once.

Note: For 6 soufflés, use 6 eggs, 6 tablespoons sugar, 6 tablespoons Grand Marnier, 1 tablespoon grated orange peel, and ¼ teaspoon cream of tartar.

MOUSSE AU CHOCOLAT

France

Serves 4

Mousse—literally "froth" or "foam"—becomes firm when chilled but is still lighter than a cooked cornstarch pudding. Although mousse traditionally uses both whipped egg whites and heavy cream, this recipe does not use cream and the dessert can be served after any meal, meat or dairy. This mousse is dark and rich, and particularly easy to prepare.

> **1 cup (6 ounces) semisweet chocolate pieces**
> **⅓ cup boiling water**
> **4 eggs (graded large), separated**
> **1 tablespoon apricot or peach brandy (or 2**
> **teaspoons vanilla extract)**

Place the chocolate pieces in the container of an electric blender and blend on high speed for about 5 seconds. Turn off the blender and use a spatula to scrape down the chocolate from the sides. Turn on the blender, add the boiling water and blend on high speed for 10 seconds. Now add the egg yolks and the brandy or vanilla extract and blend for another 3 or 4 seconds.

In a medium-size or large mixing bowl, beat the egg whites until they hold stiff peaks. Gradually fold the chocolate mixture into the beaten egg whites, folding gently with a large rubber spatula so the egg whites do not collapse. Spoon the mixture into individual dessert dishes (parfait glasses are nice) or a serving bowl. Refrigerate for a minimum of 2 hours before serving. The dessert may be made up to a day in advance.

Note: If you do not have a blender, in a 1-quart pot melt the semisweet chocolate with the water over low heat. Set aside. In a small mixing bowl, with an electric mixer or a whisk beat the egg yolks until thickened. Mix in the brandy or vanilla extract, then gradually blend in the melted chocolate. Proceed with the egg whites as directed above.

LADYFINGERS
Biscuits à la Cuiller, Bizcocho Genovesa

France, Spain

Makes about 20

Dainty sponge cake fingers generously topped with confectioners' sugar are popular in France and Spain. They are used to line frozen mousses, to prepare the classic *charlotte russe* (see page 109), and they are traditionally served with a soft Spanish custard *(natillas)*. No special equipment is needed to form the ladyfingers, as the batter spreads only slightly during baking.

> **2 eggs (graded large), separated**
> **¼ cup granulated sugar**
> **½ teaspoon vanilla extract**
> **½ cup unsifted all-purpose flour**
> **¾ cup sifted confectioners' sugar**

Preheat the oven to 300 degrees F. Lightly grease a large baking sheet and set aside.

Place the egg whites in a clean, dry medium-size mixing bowl. Place the yolks in another medium-size bowl. Beat the egg whites with a whisk or an electric mixer using clean, dry beaters. When the whites become foamy, add 1 tablespoon of the granulated sugar and beat until the whites hold stiff peaks.

Now beat the egg yolks for a minute, until they become thick and light in color, then beat in the remaining 3 tablespoons of granulated sugar. Continue beating for a few minutes, until the egg yolks appear to be very thick, light yellow, and a ribbon forms when the beaters are lifted. Beat in the vanilla extract, then add the flour ¼ cup at a time, beating after each addition. The yolks will be very thick and difficult to mix. Turn off the mixer and scrape down the beaters.

Using a rubber spatula fold about ¼ cup of the egg whites into the egg yolk mixture. Gently fold in the remaining egg whites about ½ cup at a time. The whites should be incorporated into the yolks but the mixture should remain light and fluffy.

If you have a pastry bag and a round tube about ⅝ inch in

diameter, spoon the batter into the pastry bag. Onto the greased baking sheet pipe a line of batter about 2 inches long. Pipe a second line of batter right next to the first. The two lines of batter should touch to make one finger. (With a 1-inch tube you will only need to pipe one line for each finger.) Or use a large spoon to form even lines of batter 1¼ inches wide x 2 inches long. Leave about an inch between ladyfingers.

Hold a strainer or sifter over the ladyfingers, and resift the confectioners' sugar over the fingers, covering them lavishly. Don't worry about the extra sugar that falls between the fingers.

Bake the ladyfingers for 18 to 20 minutes, until they are set and pale golden but not brown. Remove from the baking sheet immediately and cool on a wire rack. Store the ladyfingers in a plastic bag for a day or two at room temperature, or freeze for later use.

SIMPLIFIED CHARLOTTE RUSSE

France

Serves 10 to 12

The traditional *charlotte russe*, a Bavarian cream piled into a mold lined with ladyfingers, is a French creation that sometimes appears in Russian cookbooks because it was served to Czar Alexander I by his French chef. The cream itself is made from a custard base combined with beaten egg whites, whipped cream, gelatin, and flavorings. The simplified version here uses a rich and creamy raspberry-and-whipped cream mixture that can be prepared well in advance and frozen.

> **1 recipe Ladyfingers (page 108)**
> **2 cups fresh raspberries or unsweetened frozen raspberries, thawed**
> **½ cup granulated sugar**
> **1 tablespoon fresh lemon juice**
> **1 tablespoon (1 envelope) kosher gelatin**
> **¼ cup cold water**

Recipe continues on the following page . . .

2 cups heavy or whipping cream
½ cup sifted confectioners' sugar
1 teaspoon vanilla extract

Chill a large mixing bowl and beaters or a whisk for whipping the cream.

In a 2-quart pot, mix together the raspberries, granulated sugar, and lemon juice. Bring to the boil over moderate heat, stirring often. Cook for 10 to 15 seconds after the mixture boils, then remove from the heat. Meanwhile, sprinkle the gelatin over the top of the cold water and allow it to dissolve. Blend the softened gelatin into the warm raspberry mixture. Cool to room temperature, stirring occasionally. The mixture must be cool when it is combined with the cream, but it should not be chilled in the refrigerator at this point.

When the raspberry mixture has cooled to room temperature, place the cream, confectioners' sugar, and the vanilla in the chilled bowl. Whip until the cream holds stiff peaks, taking care not to overbeat. Fold the raspberry mixture into the whipped cream. Blend well but do not beat the mixture.

Line the inside of a 9-inch spring-form pan with ladyfingers, placing the rounded side of the ladyfingers against the side of the pan. Pour the raspberry cream mixture into the pan and use a spatula to level off the top. Cover the spring-form pan with foil and refrigerate for a minimum of 3 hours, until firm. The filling must be firm before the *charlotte russe* is unmolded.

Before unmolding, use a small sharp knife to trim the lady-fingers so they come just to the top of the filling. Remove the outside of the spring-form pan. Cover the *charlotte* with a large serving plate, and invert the plate and the pan. Run a long, sharp knife or a metal spatula between the bottom of the spring-form pan and the top of the *charlotte russe*, taking care not to puncture the filling. The pan can now be easily removed.

Serve the dessert immediately or refrigerate for later use. Or freeze the *charlotte* uncovered, then wrap it well as soon as it is frozen. When served directly from the freezer, the mixture tastes like raspberry ice cream. When thawed, the filling returns to its original creamy consistency.

CANNOLI

Italy

Makes 1 dozen

Cannoli are crisp cinnamon-flavored shells traditionally filled with creamed ricotta cheese. These Sicilian pastries are named after the *canna* (bamboo cane), for they were originally fried while wrapped around pieces of cane. Modern-day *cannoli* are wrapped around aluminum tubes 1 x 6 inches, but you can make disposable tubes by wrapping aluminum foil around a broomstick handle.

The Shells:

> 1¾ cups unsifted all-purpose flour
> 1 tablespoon granulated sugar
> 1 teaspoon ground cinnamon
> 3 tablespoons wine vinegar
> 3 tablespoons water
> 1 egg (graded large)
> 2 tablespoons unsalted butter or margarine,
>   softened
> Oil for frying
> Beaten egg white for sealing

In a medium-size mixing bowl, mix together 1 cup of the flour with the sugar and cinnamon. Using a large spoon, beat in the vinegar, water, and the egg, then the butter. The ingredients should be mixed well but not necessarily fluffy. Mix in ¼ cup of the remaining flour, then work in another ¼ cup. Spread the remaining ¼ cup on a clean work surface, and turn the dough out onto the flour. Knead for 6 to 8 minutes, sprinkling on additional flour if the dough is sticky.

Divide the dough into 12 equal pieces, and shape each piece into a ball. Refrigerate the dough while you make the foil tubes. (If you have *cannoli* tubes, you may shape the dough immediately or refrigerate the dough for up to 24 hours.)

To make foil tubes, cut twelve 6-inch squares out of foil. Using the end of a broomstick that is about an inch in diameter, wrap

Recipe continues on the following page . . .

one piece of foil around the tube to make a 1 x 6-inch cylinder. Slide the cylinder off the tube, and turn in the top and bottom edges of the foil, crimping the foil so it holds together. Repeat with the other aluminum squares. Set aside.

In an 8-inch skillet or a 2-quart pot, place about ½ inch of oil. Heat the oil to 350 to 375 degrees F. The oil should not be below or above this range. If it is too cool, the shells will absorb too much oil before browning; too hot and they will puff and open up.

To shape the *cannoli*, flatten a ball of dough between 2 sheets of wax paper. Using a rolling pin, roll the ball to a very thin oval (about ¹/₁₆ inch) that is 4½ x 6 inches. From time to time peel the wax paper on one side, then the other, to make sure the dough is not sticking. Wrap the oval of dough lengthwise around a foil or *cannoli* tube, sealing the overlapping edge with beaten egg white. Place on a sheet of wax paper while you make up a second pastry. Place the two *cannoli* in the oil seam side down, and fry until they are golden brown all over, turning as necessary. Drain well on paper towels. When they are cool enough to handle, carefully slide the *cannoli* off the tubes. While the first *cannoli* are frying, shape two more. Repeat with the remaining *cannoli*, wrapping and frying until they are all cooked. It is not a good idea to wrap all at once as the dough is very thin and may stick to the wax paper. When the shells are cool, store them in a plastic bag or covered container until ready to fill. The unfilled shells will keep for a few days at room temperature, or they may be frozen.

The Filling:

> 2 cups (1 pound) ricotta cheese
> ½ cup granulated sugar
> 1 ounce (1 square) semisweet chocolate, grated
> ½ teaspoon ground cinnamon
> 1 tablespoon chopped pistachio nuts, for garnish
> Sifted confectioners' sugar for dusting

In a medium-size mixing bowl, beat the ricotta cheese with an electric mixer for about 3 minutes, until it is smooth and creamy. Add the granulated sugar and continue to beat for another 2 minutes. Mix in the grated semisweet chocolate and the cinnamon. Refrigerate until ready to fill the *cannoli*.

Using a small spoon, fill the *cannoli* from both ends, making sure the filling reaches the middle. When all the *cannoli* are filled, sprinkle the ends lightly with pistachio nuts. Dust the tops with confectioners' sugar. Serve immediately or refrigerate for up to 4 hours.

DOBOSTORTE

Hungary

Serves 12

The unique topping on this chocolate-buttercream-filled sponge cake is no doubt responsible for the fame of Chef Joseph Dobos' torte. Multiple layers and a rich chocolate filling were not uncommon creations among the pastry chefs of Austria and Hungary in the nineteenth century. However, a cake whose crunchy caramel-coated top layer had to be sliced *before* positioning it on the cake was unusual. The cake keeps well in the refrigerator and can be made a day or two in advance.

The Cake:

>6 eggs (graded extra-large), separated
>½ cup granulated sugar
>1 teaspoon vanilla extract
>1 cup unsifted all-purpose flour

First prepare the baking sheets. Because the batter does not change its shape during baking, no cake pans are needed. Instead, the batter is spread on greased wax paper, making it easy both to spread evenly and to remove when baked. Trace an 8-inch round on a sheet of wax paper. Cut out the round and make 6 more wax paper rounds. Place 2 rounds on a large baking sheet and lightly grease the wax paper (use softened butter or margarine or a solid white shortening). If you have another large baking sheet, prepare 2 more rounds.

Recipe continues on the following page . . .

Preheat the oven to 375 degrees F. Place an oven rack in the middle of the oven.

Place the egg whites in a large mixing bowl and the yolks in another large mixing bowl. Using an electric mixer at high speed, beat the yolks for 2 minutes then add ¼ cup of the sugar and continue beating 3 minutes longer. The yolks will be very thick and light in color. Beat in the vanilla. Now add the flour ¼ cup at a time, beating well after each addition. The mixture will be very thick.

Using clean, dry beaters, beat the egg whites until they are foamy. Add the remaining ¼ cup sugar and continue beating the whites until they hold stiff peaks. Fold about half a cup of the beaten egg whites into the yolk mixture, then gently fold the remaining whites into the yolks one cup at a time. The whites should be incorporated into the yolks but the mixture should remain fluffy.

Spread one-seventh (about 1 cup) of the batter evenly on one greased round of wax paper, covering the paper completely. The layer will be thin (less than half an inch thick). Repeat with a second round on the same baking sheet. Bake the layers for about 6 minutes, until they are lightly browned and set. Meanwhile, if you have another baking sheet, make up more layers ready to be baked. Turn the baked layers over onto wire racks and immediately remove the wax paper. Bake the second set of layers. Cool the first baking sheet by waving it in the air, and make up another round of layers. Repeat for the seventh layer.

The layers cool quickly and can be stacked while the filling is made, or they may be frozen for later use. When you are ready to assemble the cake, select the most even, unblemished layer for the top and set aside.

The Buttercream:

>   1 cup granulated sugar
>   ¼ cup water
>   6 egg yolks (from eggs graded large)
>   ½ cup unsweetened cocoa
>   1 teaspoon vanilla extract
>   1 cup (2 sticks) unsalted butter, softened

In a 1-quart pot, combine the sugar and water. Bring to the boil over high heat, stirring occasionally. Reduce the heat to moderate and cover the pot to help dissolve any crystals that have formed on the sides of the pot. Cook uncovered for about 5 minutes, until the syrup spins a 2-inch thread when dropped from a spoon (about 234 degrees F.).

Meanwhile, in the medium-size bowl of an electric mixer beat the egg yolks for about 3 minutes, until they are thick and light in color. Beating constantly, pour the hot syrup into the beaten egg yolks in a slow, steady stream. Continue beating for about 5 minutes, until the mixture cools to room temperature. The egg yolk mixture should be thick and creamy. Beat in the cocoa, then the vanilla extract. Now beat in the butter a tablespoon at a time, beating well after each addition so the filling will be smooth. Refrigerate the buttercream filling while preparing the caramelized sugar for the top layer.

The Caramel Topping:

> ¾ cup granulated sugar
> 2 tablespoons water

Have the top layer of the cake ready and at hand, because the caramel hardens almost immediately after it is removed from the heat. Set the layer on a large baking sheet or in a jelly roll pan. Have a metal spatula available.

In a small skillet or pot, mix the water with the sugar. The addition of a little water will make it a little easier to caramelize the sugar. Bring to the boil over moderate heat, stirring occasionally. Continue to boil until the syrup thickens, watching carefully. The syrup will turn very light brown and then golden brown. As soon as the syrup is caramel color, remove it from the heat, pour it over the single layer, and spread rapidly with a metal spatula to cover the layer completely. When the caramel has hardened slightly but is still warm, use a buttered knife or metal spatula to cut 12 equal wedges through the caramel. It will not be possible to cut through the caramel once it hardens, and these wedges will mark the slices of cake. It is okay to cut completely through the layer as long as you put the wedges back in order when you transfer them to the cake.

Recipe continues on the following page . . .

To assemble the cake, place one layer on a serving plate. With a metal spatula spread about ⅓ cup of filling on the layer. The buttercream filling should be about ⅛ inch thick and evenly spread. Top with another layer, spread with filling, and repeat until all layers except the caramel-topped layer are used. Now frost the side of the cake. Save any remaining filling for piping. Set the caramelized layer on top of the cake (move it in individual wedges if this is easiest). Pipe a border of buttercream around the top edge if desired. Refrigerate until serving.

LINZERTORTE

Austria

Makes one 9-inch torte

Viennese pastries are always rich and buttery and often very time-consuming to prepare. *Linzertorte* scores high on rich and buttery, but fortunately it is easy to put together. A lightly spiced butter-and-almond dough is mixed with the hands and patted into a spring-form cake pan. Raspberry jam covers the dough, and a lattice top completes the torte. It is sweet, fruity, crunchy, and it tastes heavenly. A most elegant dessert.

> 1½ cups unsifted all-purpose flour
> 1 cup ground unblanched almonds
> ½ cup granulated sugar
> ¼ teaspoon ground cinnamon
> ⅛ teaspoon ground cloves
> ¼ teaspoon grated lemon rind
> 1 cup (2 sticks) unsalted butter, at room
>   temperature
> 2 egg yolks (from eggs graded large)
> 1 cup seedless raspberry jam
> Sifted confectioners' sugar

Preheat the oven to 350 degrees F. In a large mixing bowl, combine the flour, almonds, granulated sugar, cinnamon, cloves, and lemon rind. Mix well with a fork. Using your fingers, blend in the butter by rubbing the butter and dry ingredients between your fingers over and over. The dough will be crumbly and won't quite hold together. Add the egg yolks one at a time, working them into the dough. Round the dough into a compact ball, and break off ¼ of the dough. Set aside this piece and work with the other ¾ of the dough.

Place the dough on the bottom of a 9-inch spring-form pan. Press the dough evenly to cover the bottom of the pan, and press it about ¾ of an inch up the sides. Spread the jam over the dough.

Between 2 sheets of wax paper, roll the remaining ¼ of the dough into a 9-inch circle. The dough is pliable, and if the edges aren't smooth you can bend them over to smooth them out. Peel off the top sheet of wax paper, replace it, flip over the dough between the 2 sheets of wax paper, and peel off what is now the top sheet.

Using a sharp knife, cut the dough into 10 even-size strips, each

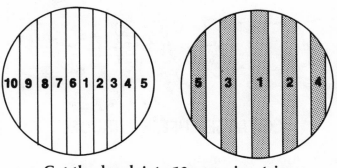

Cut the dough into 10 even-size strips.

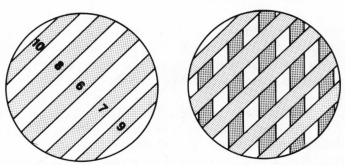

Place the strips over the jam, creating a lattice look.

Recipe continues on the following page . . .

just under an inch wide. Take one of the long middle strips and place it on top of the jam, down the middle of the torte. Take the next smallest size strip (2 in the diagram) and place it to the right of the first strip, leaving a little space between. Take the next smallest size strip (3) and place it to the left of the center strip. Strips 4 and 5 go toward the outside of the circle.

Now take the remaining strips and place them on a 45-degree angle over the first strips, again the longest strip in the center, the shortest near the edges. Press the ends of all the strips into the raised edge of the dough.

Bake at 350 degrees F. for 40 to 45 minutes, until a lovely golden brown. Place the pan on a wire rack, carefully remove the outside of the spring-form, and cool the cake for 15 minutes. Dust lavishly with sifted confectioners' sugar. Ideally, only the dough is covered with the sugar so the jam peeks through. Cool before serving.

COTTAGE CHEESE "STRUDEL"

Hungary, Austria, Germany

Makes 24 pieces

This pastry is marvelous. The dough is flaky and tender, and the filling, made of jam, raisins, and nuts, is fruity and sweet. My friend Bev Cedarbaum gave me the recipe, a treasure from her mother, Ida Seicol, who makes just about the best pie crusts I ever tasted.

Although as flaky as the classic hand-stretched strudel dough, it is not nearly the major production of most strudels. The dough is rolled out with a rolling pin, then filled and rolled like strudel. It also differs from European strudels in that cottage cheese is used in the *dough*, not the filling. If you like the recipe, you can show your appreciation by saving the crisp ends for Bev's husband, Harvey.

 1 cup unsifted all-purpose flour
 ¼ pound (½ cup) small curd cottage cheese
 ½ cup (1 stick) unsalted butter or margarine,
    softened
 2 tablespoons granulated sugar
 ½ teaspoon ground cinnamon
 1 cup dark raisins
 1 cup chopped walnuts or pecans
 ½ cup chunky damson plum jam and ½ cup
    chunky apricot preserves or the fruit pre-
    serves of your choice
 1 egg (graded large), separated

In a medium-size mixing bowl, place the flour and stir in the cottage cheese. Work in the butter or margarine with your fingers. It will be crumbly at first, but as you work in the butter the dough will become smooth. Form the dough into a ball, then flatten it, wrap in plastic wrap or wax paper, and allow it to rest in the refrigerator for 30 minutes.

In a small bowl, mix together the sugar and cinnamon, raisins, and nuts. In a separate bowl, mix together the plum jam and apricot preserves or the fruit preserves of your choice.

Grease a large baking sheet. Set aside. Preheat the oven to 375 degrees F.

Divide the chilled dough in half. Work with one piece at a time, keeping the remaining dough in the refrigerator. On a clean well-floured work surface, pat out the dough to a rectangle about 3 x 5 inches. Sprinkle the top of the dough with flour, then use a rolling pin to roll the dough into a rectangle approximately 10 x 15 inches. Let the dough rest occasionally between rollings and it will be easier to roll.

Brush the surface of the dough with half the jam mixture (½ cup) and sprinkle with half the raisin-nut mixture (1 cup). Roll the dough lengthwise into a tight log. Pinch together the ends of the log and turn them under to seal them. Beat the egg white lightly, and brush the long seam with the beaten egg white. Pinch the seam to seal it against the dough. Place the pastry,

Recipe continues on the following page . . .

seam side down, on the greased baking sheet. Repeat with the remaining ball of dough.

Beat the egg yolk with a teaspoon of water. Brush the pastry with the beaten yolk. Bake for 20 to 25 minutes, until a lovely brown. Place the baking sheet on a wire rack to cool, but do not attempt to transfer the pastry to the rack. While the pastry is still warm, but not hot, cut into 12 slices per roll, about 1¼ inches per slice.

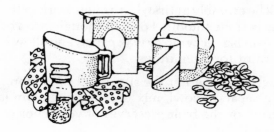

2

THE
MIDDLE
EAST

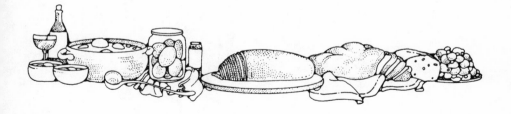

2

THE
MIDDLE
EAST

Introduction

The cuisines of the Middle Eastern countries were shaped measurably by wars and conquests. Our view of the Middle East is a broad one—part cultural, part geographic, part culinary—stretching from Morocco to the West to Iran to the East. It includes Greece, Turkey, and Armenia because of the close historical and culinary ties between these nations and the other countries in this area. It becomes apparent that centuries of Arab and Turkish invasions had lasting influence on the types of foods prepared in the different parts of the region. Moroccans, for example, were introduced to certain Iranian spices and food combinations by Arabs invading from the east. Striking similarities in the foods of Turkey, Greece, and Armenia are explained in part by hundreds of years of Turkish occupation. Certainly nowhere do these influences come together more than in the cuisine of Israel. This interplay of history and food will be considered as we look at the cuisines of the countries in this area.

ARMENIA

All that remains of Armenia is a small geographic area within the Soviet Union. Nevertheless, Armenians, like Jews, have maintained their identity from ancient times to the present. And, like Jews, one of the factors that has contributed to their survival as a people is their culinary heritage.

Originally located between the Black and Caspian Seas, Armenia, the land of Mount Ararat (now a part of Turkey), has had a stormy history. It was the victim of successive conquests by numerous kingdoms or nations, including the Ottoman Turks. Owing to the four-hundred-year Turkish occupation of Armenia, today many classic dishes are identified both as Armenian and as Turkish. Identical recipes for wheat *pilaf* (page 167), yogurt-and-cucumber soup (page 134), and apricot parfait (page 174), for example, are found in Armenian *and* Turkish cookbooks. Other foods, including Armenian string cheese and Armenian bread, have become identified with the Armenian cuisine alone.

Armenian cooking uses numerous herbs and spices in moderation, so that the food beckons rather than cries out. Mint, parsley, paprika, onions, tomatoes, pine nuts, walnuts, and almonds are ingredients frequently seen in Armenian recipes. Breakfasts and lunches are likely to be light—bread and cheese for breakfast, bread and yogurt or cheese for lunch. But dinners are lavish, consisting of several appetizers, a soup, a meat course (usually lamb) served with rice or cracked wheat *(burghul)* and at least one vegetable, but more often two: a hot stuffed vegetable and a cold one. Dessert is fresh fruit at most meals, with rich butter-and-nut pastries served on special occasions. Tea or coffee follows the meal.

GREECE

The cuisine of Greece—that warm, sunny southern European country on the Mediterranean—has much in common with the cuisine of Armenia. A Greek dinner might consist of a number of appetizers, a soup, meat (again, usually lamb), a hot stuffed vegetable, a cold stuffed vegetable, and dessert.

As the cuisines of Armenia and Greece are similar, so are those of Greece and Turkey. This is because Greece shares a small common border with Turkey and also because the Turkish conquests included Greece. An item served at a Turkish meal as a Turkish preparation might be served at a Greek meal as a famous Greek preparation (*baklava* comes to mind). Roman invasions left their mark on Greek dinner tables as well, and you are therefore likely to find a pasta course on your Greek menu.

Also identified with Greek cuisine are the tart, salty, crumbly *feta* cheese, made from goat's milk, and tart, salty Greek olives. With much of Greece surrounded by water, fresh fish is also important in Greek cookery.

TURKEY

Turkey, a Moslem but not Arab country that lies east of Greece, spans Europe and Asia, and its conquests involved both continents and extended as far as northern Africa. The Turkish invaders left an imprint on the cuisines of the nations they conquered. One of the most famous preparations they brought with them was *shish kebob,* or roasted skewered chunks of lamb. Born out of the availability of lamb coupled with the need for the armies of the Ottoman Empire to eat quickly, *shish kebob* was originally cooked on the soldiers' swords.

The Turkish armies were also responsible for introducing the peoples they conquered to coffee as a social beverage. Although coffee is native to Ethiopia, it was the Turks who made the drink a symbol of hospitality throughout the Middle East. Today, sweetened coffee, along with yogurt diluted with water, is still the favored Turkish beverage.

If there is one vegetable most associated with Turkey it is eggplant. The eggplant may be served fried, stuffed, puréed, braised, broiled, roasted, stewed, or sautéed and may be enjoyed as an appetizer, salad, vegetable, or main dish. Just as the Turkish eggplant preparations are varied, so is the larger cuisine. Garlic, tomatoes, parsley, walnuts, *burghul,* and olive oil are among the ingredients used to create tastes that are rich but subdued.

If you have a very sweet tooth, you will love Turkish pastries and desserts of fruits, nuts, whipped cream, honey, and sugar, often made by layering or rolling paper-thin sheets of phyllo pastry. These treats are anything but subdued.

IRAN

Turkey's eastern border meets Iran in the northwest, so it is not surprising that there are similarities between the two cuisines. Like the dishes of Turkey, Iranian preparations are likely to be spiced but subtle. Parsley, coriander leaves, dill, and mint are popular in both cuisines, although these herbs are used more lavishly by Iranians. Both peoples use fruits and nuts, but the cooks of Iran tend toward more elaborate preparations, and in Iran fruit is used imaginatively in combinations with meats to create rich sauces called *khoreshes* (page 144), which are designed to be served with the basic Iranian food, rice. Apples, quinces, pomegranates, apricots, and prunes are combined with vegetables and lamb or poultry, yielding exquisite gravies that are naturally sweet and fruity. Sweetened tea is the national beverage of Iran, with yogurt soups and drinks also popular.

MOROCCO

Arab invasions that swept through the Middle East in the seventh and eighth centuries—long before the Turkish reign—are responsible for bringing some of the secrets of Iranian cooking as far west as Morocco. This North African country, located south of Spain on the western end of the Mediterranean, shares with Iran a rich cuisine that comes from combining meats with fruit, mellow spice mixtures, and an abundance of fresh herbs. Morocco also sees a considerable culinary influence from Spain and France, again due to conquests and occupations, and the result is a "blended cuisine" with dishes found nowhere else in the world, such as chicken with preserved lemons and olives (page 154). Mint tea is enjoyed as the social beverage in Morocco.

EGYPT

At the other end of the Mediterranean but also in northern Africa is Egypt, which has a few curious culinary ties with Morocco. In Egypt one finds stuffed pigeons; in Morocco, pigeon pies. *Couscous,* Morocco's national dish, is a popular Egyptian dessert. But Egypt has more in common with the cuisines of its immediate neighbors.

The basic bread of Egypt is the Arab bread of Lebanon and Syria, variously sold all over the United States as Mideast, pocket, or *pita* bread. As in other countries of the region, in

Egypt olive oil and lemon juice are the seasonings for cold vegetables and salads, *burghul* is a common grain, and okra is one of the most popular vegetables. All kinds of dried legumes are an important protein source all over the Middle East, but Egypt has its own special bean dish called *ful medames*, which is served at snack stands and in Egyptian homes for breakfast, lunch, and occasionally dinner. Made of Egyptian brown beans, *ful medames* is seasoned with olive oil, lemon juice, and sometimes garlic.

SYRIA AND LEBANON

A more famous and widespread legume preparation of the Middle East, especially popular in Syria and Lebanon, is *hummus,* a purée of chickpeas combined with garlic, lemon juice, and *tahini* sauce (sesame seed sauce, page 137) and topped with a sprinkling of olive oil. As their national dish, Syria and Lebanon share *kibbe,* a ground lamb and *burghul* mixture known throughout the region. Lamb, *burghul,* eggplant, yogurt, and olive oil— these are basic ingredients in Syrian and Lebanese cuisines, and they are also basic to the cooking of other Middle Eastern nations.

ISRAEL

Considering the interaction that has taken place in the Middle East over the centuries, it is no wonder that today's Israeli cuisine includes so many dishes that originated in neighboring nations. But as a melting pot country, with its population coming from Europe, the Americas, and other parts of the world, Israel has a cuisine that is more diverse than other Middle Eastern cuisines. Starting with a broader base and taking advantage of local ingredients, especially fresh fruits and vegetables, enough indigenous dishes have evolved so that the Israeli cuisine now goes beyond *hummus, tahini, felafel* (page 162), and other preparations common to Israel's Arab neighbors. While the cooking of Israel is no less noteworthy than that of any other country, I have chosen not to duplicate the work of other cookbook authors and to refer you to the many Israeli cookbooks available.

Appetizers and Soups

Picture yourself seated before an array of marvelous snacks—olives, cheeses, stuffed grape leaves, salted nuts, flaky turnovers, chickpea dips, eggplant purées—and you can be sure you're at a table enjoying *mezze*, or appetizers. If you are not familiar with Middle Eastern dining protocol, you might think that the entire meal will consist of these savory tidbits (perhaps the Mideast counterpart of a Chinese *dim sum* luncheon), but be assured that dinner will follow. For a home meal, *mezze* may simply be a bowl of nuts or a salad, but when a guest is present the selection will be expanded and the host will serve an assortment of stuffed vegetables and pastries, dips, and other enticing morsels. Sometimes appetizers are small portions of dinner fare, so it is possible to take many main dish recipes and turn them into *mezze* if you like.

Soups are important in cuisines of the Middle East. While on festive occasions we traditionally serve chicken soup garnished with *kreplach* or *knaidlach*, many soups of the area—especially soups associated with religious or festive occasions—are made with lamb and lamb bones. For Turkish and Armenian weddings, a creamy lamb soup is enriched with egg yolks and lemon juice, like the well-known Greek *avgolemono* soup. Rich lentil, chickpea, and vegetable soups are often served as main dishes for everyday meals.

HERBED YOGURT CHEESE
<u>Labni</u>

Lebanon

Makes about 1¼ cups

Yogurt cheese is made simply by allowing the yogurt liquid to drip through cheesecloth overnight at room temperature. The cheese is not quite as sour as regular yogurt, and of course it is considerably more firm. In this version the yogurt cheese is mixed with fresh parsley, mint, and chives. A typical Lebanese breakfast consists of yogurt cheese spread on top of Mideast pocket bread *(pita)*, sprinkled with olive oil, often served with olives and a salad. It makes an unusual dip for an appetizer, and you may want to try it with whole wheat *pita* for a light summer lunch.

> **2 cups plain yogurt**
> **Cheesecloth (available in supermarkets and**
>   **housewares stores)**
> **¼ cup chopped fresh parsley**
> **¼ cup chopped fresh mint**
> **¼ cup chopped fresh chives**
> **Salt**
> **1 teaspoon olive oil**

Line a colander or a large strainer with a double layer of cheesecloth, then set the colander or strainer over a large bowl. Place the yogurt in the cheesecloth-lined colander or strainer and let the yogurt liquid drip through the cloth for a minimum of 10 hours. The longer the yogurt drains, the firmer it becomes. The yogurt cheese is what is left in the cheesecloth after the liquid drains through. Carefully transfer the yogurt cheese to a mixing bowl, mix with the herbs, and add salt to taste. Now transfer to a serving bowl, drizzle with the olive oil, and serve immediately, or refrigerate until ready to serve. The yogurt cheese will keep in the refrigerator for several days. Serve it as a dip with crackers or pieces of *pita*, as a sauce for *felafel* (page 162), or as a light main course with a salad and *pita*.

CHEESE TRIANGLES
Tyropitta

Armenia, Greece, Turkey

Makes 36 triangles

What is crisp and flaky, buttery, melts in your mouth, and will establish your reputation as a cook with one bite? These cheese-filled phyllo pastries meet all the above criteria, and once you get the knack of using the thin sheets of phyllo, you'll make them often. Best of all, they can be prepared in advance and frozen. Cottage cheese may be substituted for the *feta* cheese of Greece and Turkey because cottage cheese is easy to obtain, and if you're like me, you are likely to have it on hand. Although *tyropitta* are typically filled with *feta* cheese alone, Muenster and Swiss cheeses are tasty additions.

Note that phyllo dough is pliable when a fresh package is opened, but the thin sheets of dough rapidly become dry and brittle. Therefore, it is necessary to have all ingredients ready and at hand when working with phyllo. Work quickly, and always keep the unused portions of dough completely covered with a clean kitchen towel until ready for use.

> **1 cup (½ pound) feta cheese or cottage cheese**
> **½ cup shredded Muenster cheese**
> **½ cup shredded Swiss cheese**
> **2 tablespoons chopped fresh parsley**
> **1 egg (graded large or extra-large), beaten**
> **12 sheets phyllo dough (about ½ pound)**
> **½ cup (1 stick) unsalted butter, melted**

Butter a 10 x 15-inch baking sheet, preferably one with raised sides. Set aside.

In a small mixing bowl, combine the cheeses, sprinkle on the parsley, and mix in the beaten egg. Have the melted butter close at hand. Leaving the 12 sheets of phyllo dough stacked, cut the phyllo lengthwise into 3 strips. You now have 3 long stacks of dough, 12 strips in each. To prevent the phyllo from drying out, cover 2 stacks of dough completely with a slightly damp (but not wet) kitchen towel.

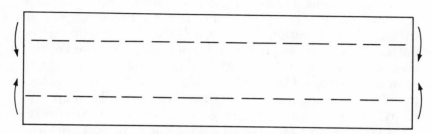

1. Fold each strip of dough lengthwise to meet in the middle.

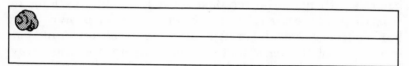

2. Place a heaping teaspoonful of filling at one end of the folded strip of dough.

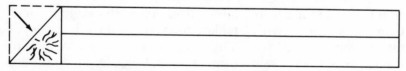

3. Fold the dough over the filling to make a triangle.

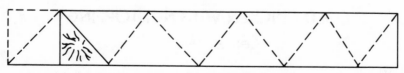

4. Continue folding the dough to enclose the filling, keeping the triangle shape.

Recipe continues on the following page . . .

Working on a clean, smooth surface with one stack of dough, carefully peel off one layer of phyllo. Cover the remaining stack of 11 strips. Using a pastry brush, brush the dough thoroughly with melted butter. Now fold the strip lengthwise to meet in the middle **(illustration 1),** and brush the surface with melted butter. Place a heaping teaspoonful of filling at one end of this long, narrow strip of dough **(2).** Fold the dough over the filling to make a triangle **(3).** Continue folding the dough to enclose the filling, keeping the triangle shape **(4).** You will end up with many layers of pastry enclosing the filling. Place the cheese-filled triangle on the buttered baking sheet. Repeat with the remaining strips of dough. The pastries may be wrapped and frozen at this point.

Preheat the oven to 400 degrees F. Brush the tops of the pastries with melted butter. Bake for 10 to 15 minutes (longer if frozen), until the triangles are a beautiful golden brown. Serve hot. To freeze after the pastries are baked, bake only until pale brown. Cool the *tyropittas* to room temperature, then tray-freeze. Brush the top of the pastries with additional melted butter before reheating.

Variation:

For meat-filled triangles, use a food processor or a meat grinder to mince ¾ pound lean lamb or beef cubes almost to a paste. Combine the meat with 2 tablespoons chopped fresh parsley; 1 tablespoon chopped fresh dill; 1 teaspoon chopped fresh mint leaves; ½ teaspoon salt (optional); and 1 egg (graded large or extra-large), beaten. Use in place of the cheese filling. Substitute ⅓ cup olive oil for the melted butter.

COLD CHICKEN WITH NUT TOPPING
Çerkes Tavuğu

Turkey

Serves 12 as part of a buffet

How do you get one medium-size chicken to serve twelve people? You make something that is so rich, only small portions are served. This famous Turkish buffet dish combines shredded chicken with a very thick sauce that looks like whipped cream but is actually a purée of nuts and chicken broth. Although walnuts are traditionally used in making *çerkes tavuğu,* almonds contribute a sweeter, more pleasant taste to the preparation and are therefore recommended.

> **1 frying chicken (3½ to 4 pounds), quartered**
> **1 carrot, quartered**
> **1 rib celery, cut into 4 pieces**
> **1 medium-size onion, quartered**
> **2 sprigs fresh parsley**
> **½ teaspoon salt**
> **Freshly ground black pepper to taste**
> **6 cups water**
> **2 cups blanched whole almonds**
> **1 small onion, chopped**
> **1 large clove garlic, minced**
> **3 slices white bread, crusts removed**
> **Salt and freshly ground black pepper**
> **2 tablespoons vegetable oil**
> **2 teaspoons paprika**

In a 4-quart pot, place the chicken, carrot, celery, onion, parsley, salt, and pepper. Add the water, which should just cover the chicken pieces. Bring to the boil over high heat. Reduce the heat to a gentle boil, cover the pot, and cook for the chicken for 30 minutes. Turn off the heat, leaving the chicken in the pot for an additional 15 minutes. Transfer the chicken to a plate or bowl, and allow it to cool until it can be handled. Strain the broth, reserving 1¼ cups for later use.

Using a food processor, blender, or a mortar and pestle, grind the almonds to a paste. Blend in the chopped onion and minced garlic until they are part of the purée. Tear the bread into small pieces and incorporate the bread into the paste. Gradually beat in the reserved broth, adding about a cup, enough to make a very thick sauce. The almond-broth mixture will turn white as it thickens. Season to taste with salt and pepper.

Use your fingers to remove the cooled chicken from the bones. Discard the bones and skin, then cut the chicken into match-stick-size strips, 1½ to 2 inches long. Mix ½ cup of the almond

Recipe continues on the following page . . .

sauce with the chicken, mound the chicken on a plate, then spread the remaining almond mixture over the chicken, covering completely. Refrigerate until serving, but remove the chicken from the refrigerator 1 hour before serving.

Just before serving, combine the oil and paprika and drizzle the mixture over the chicken.

CUCUMBER-YOGURT SOUP
Cacik

Turkey, Armenia

Serves 4

Different versions of this refreshing chilled soup (it is so thick it is sometimes served as a salad) are known throughout the Middle East and in the Balkans. Embellishments on the basic ingredients of chopped cucumbers and yogurt include fresh dill and mint leaves, parsley, scallions, walnuts, and hard-cooked egg yolks. If you have an herb garden (or friendly neighbors like mine), you'll enjoy experimenting with varying combinations of mint, dill, and parsley. *Cacik* makes a nice dairy lunch on a hot day, or serve it as a dip with small pieces of *pita* or Russian black bread (page 90).

> 1 cucumber (½ pound)
> 2 cups plain yogurt
> 1 teaspoon olive oil
> 1 tablespoon distilled white vinegar
> 1 tablespoon chopped fresh parsley
> 1 tablespoon chopped fresh dill
> 1 tablespoon chopped fresh mint
> Salt
> Garnishes: additional chopped fresh parsley,
>   dill, and/or mint; chopped chives or scal-
>   lions; chopped walnuts; yolks of 2 hard-
>   cooked eggs, chopped

Peel the cucumber, cut it in half lengthwise, and scoop out and discard the seeds. Grate the cucumber, or cut it into ¼-inch cubes.

In a medium-size bowl, stir the yogurt with a fork until it is smooth. Stir in the oil and vinegar, the cucumber, and the herbs. Add salt to taste. Chill for 2 hours or longer. Serve the soup with desired garnishes, and place an ice cube in each bowl if you like.

LENTIL SOUP
Shorabat Adas

General Middle East

*Serves 4 as a main dish,
6 to 8 as a first course*

Lentil soup seasoned with herbs is commonly eaten throughout the Middle East. To make this delicate version into a spicier Moroccan preparation, briefly cook one-half teaspoon each of ground turmeric, cinnamon, and ginger in two tablespoons olive oil, then proceed with the recipe. This recipe makes a thick soup with coarse but tender pieces of lentil throughout. For the vegetarian version, a dollop of yogurt or sour cream in each serving is a nice addition.

> **2 quarts lamb, chicken, or vegetarian broth**
> **1 pound brown lentils, picked through and
>   rinsed**
> **1 cup chopped onion**
> **2 cloves garlic, minced**
> **1 large ripe red tomato (½ pound), chopped,
>   or 2 tablespoons tomato paste**
> **3 tablespoons chopped fresh parsley or
>   1 tablespoon dried parsley flakes**
> **1 tablespoon chopped fresh dill or 1 teaspoon
>   dried dill**

Recipe continues on the following page . . .

Salt and freshly ground black pepper
1 tablespoon lemon juice
Garnishes: chopped fresh parsley, dill, and
   tomatoes

In a 4-quart pot, combine the broth and the lentils. Bring to the boil over high heat, reduce to a gentle boil, cover the pot, and cook for 45 minutes. Stir in the onion, garlic, and tomato or tomato paste; if you are using dried parsley and dill, add them now. Continue cooking, covered, for another 30 minutes. If you are using the fresh herbs, add them after the 30 minutes, and continue cooking for another 15 minutes. The lentils should be very soft and the soup very thick. Add salt and pepper to taste. Stir in the lemon juice, cook for another minute or two, and serve. Garnish as desired. This soup can be prepared a day or two ahead and refrigerated, and it freezes well. (Use freezer containers—not glass—and allow an inch headspace for expansion.)

Condiments and Sauces

Yogurt offers a way of preserving milk that would otherwise spoil, and the warm climate of the Middle East is ideal for the growth of the yogurt culture. Consequently, yogurt plays an important role in Middle Eastern cuisine: it appears in appetizers, soups, salads, sauces, as a side dish, a cheese (page 129), in desserts, and in diluted form as a beverage throughout the day.

Because yogurt is a dairy product, in recipes where it would be used as a sauce for meat dishes, an alternative is needed in the kosher home. There is a wonderful sauce already enjoyed in countries of the Middle East, the sesame sauce known as *tahini* or *tahina* sauce (page 137). A second alternative is *avgolemono* sauce, the smooth lemon-egg yolk sauce of Armenia, Greece, and Turkey. This sauce (page 138) is especially useful because it is nondairy and can be made without meat as well, so that it can be served with any meal.

Olives and lemons do well with the winter rains and summer droughts of the Mediterranean, so it is no wonder that olive oil and lemon juice are widely used. You'll see lemon juice in soups and main dishes, salads, sauces, and desserts, and lemons are preserved in a unique Moroccan preparation (page 139). Olive oil is always the choice for dressing cold vegetables and dips. Lamb fat and preserved butter are used regularly in cooking, but the Jews of the Middle East are more likely to cook with olive oil and corn oil, both of which can be used with either meat or dairy dishes.

A mixture of cayenne and paprika is often sprinkled on Turkish and Armenian cold foods or mixed in with meat dishes, adding a little spice and color. If you're looking for color, do what the Iranians do and decorate your table with a bowl of herbs—chopped parsley, coriander, and dill, for example—and they must be fresh. Sprinkle them on your eggs, soups, Friday night chicken, vegetables, and rice. If you're looking to decrease your salt intake, a bowl of herbs may be the answer.

TAHINI

General Middle East

Makes about 1 cup

This thick, versatile sauce with a nutty flavor is made of sesame seeds, lemon juice, and garlic. Also known as *tahina*, the

Recipe continues on the following page . . .

sauce is used over fish and vegetables in Turkey, in the dips of Syria, Lebanon, and Egypt, and as an alterative to yogurt sauces by the Jews of the Middle East. You can make your own sesame seed paste by grinding sesame seeds in a food processor, but the purchased pastes available in health food and Middle Eastern stores will probably be smoother than the homemade. Like natural peanut butter, the oil in sesame seed paste separates upon standing, so stir the paste before using it in the recipe.

> **2 cloves garlic, minced**
> **½ cup sesame seed paste (tahini or tahina)**
> **Cold water**
> **¼ cup fresh lemon juice**
> **Salt**

In a medium-size mixing bowl, mash the garlic with the back of a spoon (or squeeze it through a garlic press). Stir in the sesame seed paste, using a fork if the paste is stiff. Blend in about ¼ cup cold water, then stir in the lemon juice. The mixture will turn whitish and should be thick and creamy. Add salt to taste, and more lemon juice if you like. Now add water a tablespoon at a time until you have the consistency desired. As a dip, it should be thick, but as a sauce for Felafel (page 162) it should flow off the spoon. Refrigerate leftovers, but bring to room temperature before serving, and dilute with a little water if necessary.

EGG-AND-LEMON SAUCE
Saltsa Avgolemono

Greece, Turkey, Armenia

Makes 1 cup

This egg-lemon mixture, one of the most famous of all Greek sauces, is used in Turkish and Armenian cooking as well. It is served over vegetables, meats, and fish and stirred into chicken broth to make the creamy, lemony *avgolemono* soup of Greece. Since it is not traditional in kosher homes to mix meat and fish in the same preparation, substitute vegetarian broth when the sauce is to be used over fish.

2 eggs (graded large)
¼ cup fresh lemon juice
1 cup chicken or vegetarian broth

In a small mixing bowl, beat the eggs with a whisk until they are foamy. Whisk in the lemon juice. In a 1-quart pot, bring the broth to the boil. In a thin, constant stream, blend the hot broth into the egg-lemon mixture, stirring rapidly and constantly with a whisk or a fork. Now pour the mixture back into the pot, and set over very low heat, stirring constantly until the sauce is thickened. Do not allow the mixture to boil, or it will curdle. This sauce is best when used immediately.

PRESERVED LEMONS
Msir

Morocco

Makes 1 pint

Lemons preserved in a mixture of their own juice and salt give a unique pickled taste to the Moroccan dishes in which they are used. The lemons are salted and very tightly packed in a canning jar. This packing squeezes the lemons, releasing their juice. Extra lemon juice is added as necessary to cover the lemons. Moroccan Jews use olive oil instead of lemon juice to fill up the jar. Small lemons are recommended because they pack better than large ones.

Although Moroccans store the lemons at room temperature without any heat treatment, standard canning procedure in a boiling water bath is recommended for this recipe. Once the jar of lemons is opened, store the remainder in the refrigerator. Just before using, rinse the lemons well to wash off the salt.

Recipe continues on the following page . . .

6 to 8 small lemons
¼ cup salt
Juice of 1 to 2 additional lemons, or olive oil,
    as necessary

Cut the lemons into quarters from top to bottom, but not quite all the way through. The lemon wedges should remain connected at the bottom. Into a clean 1-pint canning jar that has been sterilized in boiling water, place a tablespoon of the salt. Spread open the lemons and sprinkle the cut surfaces lightly with salt, using about a tablespoon more salt in all.

Hold a lemon over the jar, squeeze out the juice, drop in the lemon, then press out as much additional juice as you can. Do this with the remaining lemons, pushing each one down with a spoon or your fingers and packing them in. As you add the lemons, sprinkle the layers of lemon alternately with the remaining 2 tablespoons of salt.

When you can no longer get any more lemons in, use a narrow spatula to press out any air bubbles. Now add fresh lemon juice or olive oil to within half an inch of the top of the jar, covering the lemons completely. Place a canning lid on the jar, close, and process in a boiling water bath for 15 minutes. Upon cooling, the lid must be concave to ensure that proper sealing has occurred. Store at room temperature as long as the seal is intact. From time to time, turn the jar upside down for several hours at a time to redistribute the salt.

Main Dishes

All Middle Eastern cuisines use lamb as the principal meat. This is partly because, like the Jews, the Moslems (who make up the majority population in the region) follow a biblical prohibition against eating pork. Sheep were the first animals to be domesticated in the world, and this initial step toward civilization took place in the area just north of ancient Mesopotamia, a region that encompasses parts of what are now Turkey, Iran, and Iraq. Over the centuries, lamb soups, meat pies, roasts, and kebobs have been enjoyed all over the Middle East, even among the Christian populations of Lebanon and Greece. While beef is not shunned, its availability is limited and it has therefore not found favor in the Middle Eastern countries.

Chicken is popular throughout the area. It may be grilled, spit-roasted, simmered with vegetables in Moroccan *tagines* (stews), cooked with fruits in Iranian *khoreshes* (stewlike sauces), or served cold in salads. Duck is especially popular in Iran, and pigeon is common in Morocco and Egypt.

Because yogurt is standard fare, cheese is a staple food, and a kind of clarified butter is used extensively in Middle Eastern cooking, it is necessary to make some adaptations when cooking for the kosher home. Of course the Jews of the Middle East have made these adaptations since ancient times, and Israelis have built adjustments into their cuisine. It is not difficult for us to do the same, using nondairy sauces in place of yogurt, substituting oil or *pareve* margerine for butter, and omitting the meat from such dishes as *moussaka* (page 160).

The recipes in this section range from easy-to-prepare everyday dishes to more elaborate preparations, some obviously the foods of wealthy classes who have servants to do the cooking and cleanup. If cooking is your hobby, you'll enjoy fussing over some of these fancier recipes. And if you are lucky, maybe some nice member of your family will volunteer to clean up.

LAMB STEW
Tas Kebab

Armenia, Turkey

Serves 4

A simple stew of lamb, onions, and tomatoes, sprinkled lavishly with parsley, is traditionally served with an eggplant purée by Armenians and Turks. To complete the Middle Eastern effect, serve the lamb and eggplant with a rice or *burghul pilaf.*

> **2½ pounds boneless lamb shoulder, cut into**
> **1- inch cubes**
> **Salt and freshly ground black pepper**
> **¼ cup olive oil or pareve margarine**
> **1 cup chopped onion**
> **1 pound ripe red tomatoes, diced**
> **½ cup water**
> **¼ to ½ cup chopped fresh parsley**
> **Eggplant Purée (page 168)**

Sprinkle the lamb cubes lightly with salt and pepper if desired. In a 4-quart pot, heat the oil or margarine over moderate heat. Add the lamb and chopped onion, and cook, stirring occasionally, until the meat is lightly browned. Mix in the tomatoes and the water. Bring to the boil, cover the pot, reduce the heat to a gentle boil, and cook until the lamb is tender, about 1½ hours. From time to time add a little water to the pot to prevent the meat from sticking.

When the lamb is tender, taste the gravy for seasoning, and add salt and pepper to taste. To serve, place the lamb on a platter, garnish with the chopped parsley, and surround the meat with the puréed eggplant. Serve with the *burghul pilaf* (page 168) or a rice *pilaf*.

LAMB "PIES"
Sfeeha, Lahmejoun

Armenia, Syria, Turkey

Makes twelve 8-inch rounds

These "pies" (*sfeeha* in Arabic, *lahmejoun* in Armenian) will remind you of pizza. Pieces of dough are rolled out and topped with ground lamb, fresh tomatoes, and herbs. They are then broiled to complete the cooking. The crust is thin and crisp, the topping savory. Serve them open-faced or as sandwiches, hot or cold. Very small rounds may be served as appetizers.

> **1 recipe Armenian Thin Bread (page 165)**
> **1½ pounds lean boneless shoulder of lamb, ground**
> **1 cup finely chopped onion**
> **½ cup chopped green pepper**
> **1 large clove garlic, minced**
> **½ pound ripe red tomatoes, peeled, seeded, and chopped**
> **½ cup chopped fresh parsley**
> **1 tablespoon chopped fresh mint leaves**
> **Salt and freshly ground black pepper**
> **⅛ teaspoon ground cayenne pepper**
> **½ teaspoon paprika**

Prepare the bread dough and allow it to rise until it has doubled, 1½ to 2 hours. Meanwhile, mix together all the ingredients for the topping, and use your hands to knead the meat mixture for 5 minutes. Break off a small piece, broil it until it is cooked, taste for seasoning, and adjust the seasoning as necessary. Refrigerate the topping until ready to use.

To shape the dough, follow the directions on page 166. Do not brush the rounds with egg or sprinkle them with sesame seeds.

Recipe continues on the following page . . .

Preheat the oven to 450 degrees F. Divide the topping into 12 equal portions. Using the back of a spoon or your fingers, spread a portion of topping to within ⅛ inch of the sides of a round of dough. Repeat with all the dough and topping. Bake at 450 degrees F. for about 10 minutes, or until the dough is lightly browned. Finish the cooking by broiling the meat 4 to 6 inches from the heat for a few minutes, until brown and bubbly. Serve immediately, or place two rounds together, meat sides facing each other, and wrap in foil to keep warm.

MEAT WITH YELLOW SPLIT PEAS AND HERBS
Khoresh Qai'Meh Sabsi

Iran

Serves 4

An ever-changing combination of meat, fruit, vegetables, herbs, and spices, *khoresh* is served daily in Iran. More a sauce than a stew, it is always served over rice. The *khoresh* of the day varies, depending on what ingredients are available at the market and what the cook chooses to prepare. Lamb is the preferred meat, but poultry or fish are sometimes used in preparing the sauce. Eggplant, tomatoes, dried beans, spinach, apples, quinces, dried fruits, parsley, scallions, leeks, dill, lemons, and limes are among the other ingredients used. No matter what ingredients are selected, *khoresh* is a blend of subtle flavors, tasty but not spicy.

In the recipe below, lamb, beef, or veal and yellow split peas are seasoned lavishly with chopped scallions, parsley, and dill, with more than a touch of fresh lemon juice. The fresh herbs predominate, and the *khoresh* has a refreshing lemony tang enhanced by the tartness of the sliced quince.

In Iranian cuisine, a small amount of *khoresh* accompanies a large portion of rice, so that a pound of meat is enough to serve four.

**1 pound boneless shoulder of lamb or veal, or
    stewing beef**

Salt and freshly ground black pepper
2 tablespoons vegetable oil
1 cup chopped onion
½ teaspoon ground turmeric (optional)
1 cup (8 ounces) tomato sauce
2 cups water
½ cup dried yellow split peas
1 quince (1 pound), optional ·
1 tablespoon vegetable oil
1 cup chopped scallions (white and crisp
   green parts)
1 cup packed chopped fresh parsley
¼ cup packed chopped fresh dill
¼ cup freshly squeezed lemon juice

Cut the meat into ½-inch cubes, removing any fat or gristle. Sprinkle with salt and pepper. Set aside.

In a 4-quart pot, heat the 2 tablespoons of oil over moderate heat. Stir in the onion and the optional turmeric, and cook until the onion is softened and golden but not brown. Add the meat. Cook, stirring occasionally, until the meat is lightly browned all over. Add the tomato sauce and 2 cups water. Bring to the boil over high heat, then reduce the heat so the liquid boils gently. Cover and cook for 1 hour. From time to time check the meat to make sure it is covered by liquid, and add boiling water as necessary.

Now stir in the split peas. Continue cooking, covered, for about an hour, until the meat and peas are tender. Every 20 minutes, stir the meat and peas to make sure they are not sticking, and add boiling water as necessary. Toward the end of the cooking time, peel and core the quince and slice the fruit into 16 wedges. Add the sliced quince to the pot and cook 10 to 15 minutes longer, until tender. (Quinces are starchy and inedible when raw, but they cook quickly.)

In an 8-inch skillet, heat the remaining tablespoon of oil over moderate heat. Stir in the chopped scallions, parsley, and dill. Cook, stirring constantly, for one minute, then sprinkle the lemon juice over the herbs and toss lightly. Add the herbs to the meat mixture, stir to blend, and serve.

VEGETABLE AND LAMB COUSCOUS

Morocco

Serves 6

The national dish of Morocco, *couscous* refers both to a grain made of semolina and to the preparation itself. The *couscous* is steamed on a perforated pan that is set over a stew of vegetables and lamb, chicken, or fish. To serve, the steamed *couscous* is piled high, a well is made in the center (picture a volcano), and the stew is placed in the well. A spicy hot pepper condiment, *harissa*, is served with *couscous*.

Couscous grains, which look like little pellets when raw, are tender but more chewy than rice when cooked. Seasonings of ginger, saffron, cinnamon, and turmeric color the stew an attractive yellow-orange, and the vegetables selected enhance the effect. The stew itself is bland, relying more on many different textures than strong tastes.

In Morocco, *couscous* is served as a luncheon dish or as the last dish at a banquet, where abundance is a sign of hospitality and total satisfaction is a must. The Jews of North Africa serve *couscous* as the Sabbath meal and for other festive occasions.

There is no getting around it, this recipe for *couscous* is a production. The grains require special handling just to prepare them for cooking, including ten minutes of rubbing moistened *couscous* between the fingers. And setting up the steaming equipment may require a little ingenuity. There is a packaged precooked *couscous* available in supermarkets that requires only mixing with boiling broth, but it does not produce the lovely separate grains of the unprocessed *couscous*. If you are looking for shortcuts, you may want to substitute a one-pound can of chickpeas for the dried chickpeas, but the packaged *couscous* that has been prerinsed and presteamed is not recommended.

> **1 cup dried chickpeas, soaked overnight in water to cover by 2 inches**
> **4 cups couscous**
> **Cold water**
> **¼ cup olive oil or vegetable oil**
> **2 pounds lean boneless lamb or veal shoulder, cut into ¾-inch cubes**

1 large Spanish onion, coarsely chopped
Salt and freshly ground black pepper
1 teaspoon ground ginger
Pinch of pulverized saffron (optional)
½ teaspoon ground cinnamon
½ teaspoon ground turmeric
1 pound carrots, peeled, halved lengthwise,
    then cut into 2-inch chunks
1 to 2 pounds fresh pumpkin, turnip, and/or
    sweet potatoes or yams, peeled then cut
    into 1-inch cubes
1 cup golden raisins
¼ cup (½ stick) pareve margarine (optional)

Drain the soaked chickpeas, then place them in a 2-quart pot and cover the chickpeas with water. Bring to the boil, then reduce the heat to a gentle boil, cover the pot, and cook gently for 1½ hours or until nearly tender. Drain and set aside.

Meanwhile, spread the *couscous* in a large flat pan. Pour enough cold water over the grains to cover them completely, stirring with one hand while pouring with the other so the grains don't stick together. Immediately pour off the excess water, spread the *couscous* evenly in the pan, and allow the grains to swell for about 10 minutes. To prevent lumps from forming, use your fingers to sift through the grains as they swell.

Now if you are Moroccan, or if *couscous* is your standard Sabbath dinner, or if you collect fancy kitchen equipment, you will have the specialized two-section tray called a *couscousière* for the next step. Chances are you will need to improvise a *couscousière* as I do. You will need a 4- to 8-quart pot onto which a 2-inch-deep perforated tray or a colander will fit snugly.

In the bottom of the pot place the oil, the lamb or veal, the onion, chickpeas, and spices. Add 8 cups of water, bring the liquid to the boil, reduce to a gentle boil, and cook covered over moderately low heat for 40 minutes, stirring occasionally.

The next step involves the steaming of the *couscous*. If the holes of the colander or steamer tray are large, line the colander or tray with cheesecloth so the *couscous* cannot fall through. Fit the perforated tray or colander into the pot with the stew, stuffing

Recipe continues on the following page . . .

strips of cheesecloth or muslin between the pot and the rim of the tray or colander for a snug fit. The bottom of the tray *must* be above the boiling liquid of the stew. If necessary, steam the *couscous* over a pot of plain boiling water—it is more important for the *couscous* to be steamed without coming into contact with the liquid than it is for it to be steamed over the stew.

Place a heaping cup of the swelled *couscous* on the steamer, and when you can see that the steam is coming through the perforations and not around the rim of the tray, add the remaining *couscous*. If necessary, stuff additional strips of cheesecloth or muslin between the rim of the steamer tray or colander and the pot. For fluffy and tender *couscous,* do *not* cover the pot. Steam the *couscous* for 15 minutes, then remove the steamer tray or colander and add the carrots along with the pumpkin, turnip, and/or sweet potato or yam cubes and the raisins to the bubbling stew. Replace the tray of *couscous,* dot with margarine if desired, and steam for an additional 25 minutes, until the vegetables are tender.

To serve, heap the *couscous* on a large serving platter, make a deep well in the center, and with a slotted spoon transfer the meat and vegetables to the well. Pour in a little gravy, and pass the remaining gravy around separately. Serve with *harissa* (recipe below) for those who like peppery hot touches.

Note: The stew without the *couscous* is a Moroccan *tagine.*

Harissa:

> ¼ **cup dried chili peppers**
> **Boiling water**
> **2 large cloves garlic, minced**
> **1 tablespoon ground cumin**
> **1 to 2 teaspoons olive oil**

In a small heatproof bowl, place the chili peppers with enough boiling water to cover. Drain after 5 minutes. Using a mortar and pestle or a chopping block and a sharp knife or a cleaver, begin to grind or chop the peppers into small pieces. Add the garlic and continue to grind or chop. Work in the cumin, then add a few drops of olive oil at a time, working the mixture into a paste. Store leftovers in a covered jar in the refrigerator, where the *harissa* will keep for several weeks.

GROUND LAMB SANDWICHES
Gyros

Greece, Turkey

Serves 4 to 6

If you've ever looked in the window of a Greek-American restaurant and wondered about the giant loaves of ground meat that are spit-roasted on a vertical grill, you've been looking at the main ingredient of *gyros* (pronounced "heroes"). In Turkey, the meat is known as *döner kebab*. Thin slices of browned lamb are sliced off as the meat cooks and served in large flat breads with onions, tomatoes, and a yogurt sauce. We can use *tahini* (sesame) sauce, *avgolemono* (egg-and-lemon) sauce, or even tomato sauce as a fine alternative to the dairy yogurt because they all go well with lamb.

Herb-seasoned ground lamb mixtures are common in the cuisines of Turkey, Armenia, Greece, and Egypt. The secret to the meat is the texture—it is kneaded to a paste either by hand or in a food processor. Plenty of fresh parsley and dill contribute flavor without dominating.

> **2 pounds lean ground lamb**
> **1 cup minced or grated onion**
> **½ cup packed minced fresh parsley**
> **½ cup packed minced fresh dill**
> **Salt and freshly ground black pepper**
> **6 large pita breads (8-inch diameter)**
> **1 pound ripe red tomatoes, sliced into thin**
>   **rounds**
> **Onion rings, sliced thin**
> **Tahini (page 137), Egg-and-Lemon**
>   **Sauce (page 138), or tomato sauce**

In a large mixing bowl, combine the ground lamb, minced or grated onion, the parsley, dill, and salt and pepper to taste. Knead for 5 minutes by hand, for 3 minutes with an electric mixer, or for 1 minute in a food processor. (If using a food processor, you'll have to do it in several batches.) The mixture will have a soft, pastelike consistency and will be green-flecked throughout. Use immediately or wrap well and refrigerate overnight.

Recipe continues on the following page . . .

For home cooking, it is more practical to grill patties than to spit-broil one large piece of ground lamb. Divide the meat evenly into 12 pieces, and shape each piece into a patty about ½ inch thick. Broil the patties until they are well browned on both sides and cooked through. To serve, slice each patty in half crosswise, place the meat on top of a large *pita,* top with sliced tomatoes and onion rounds, and drizzle with a tablespoon or so of sauce. Wrap the *pita* around the meat and toppings.

EGYPTIAN GRILLED CHICKEN
Farareej Mashwi

Egypt

Serves 4 to 6

Olive oil, lemon juice, and garlic are in the marinade, and olive oil, lemon juice, and garlic are what you'll taste.

**2 broiling chickens (3 pounds each),
  quartered
Salt and freshly ground black pepper
⅓ cup olive oil
Juice of 2 lemons (about ½ cup)
4 large cloves garlic, minced to a paste**

Sprinkle the chicken quarters with salt and pepper, and rub the seasonings into the chickens. If desired, disjoint the legs and wings, and cut the breast halves in half again. In a pan or baking dish just large enough to accommodate the chicken pieces, combine the olive oil, lemon juice, and garlic. Place the chicken pieces skin side down in the marinade, turn the pieces over to coat them well, cover the pan, and allow the chicken to marinate for 1½ hours or longer, turning every 20 minutes to keep the chicken coated.

For outdoor grilling, heat the coals to medium-hot. Place the chicken pieces on the grill, reserving the marinade. Grill the chicken pieces for 30 to 45 minutes, turning as necessary, until they are golden brown all over and thoroughly cooked. During the last 10 minutes of cooking, brush frequently with the marinade.

For indoor broiling, broil the chicken pieces 4 inches from the heat for 15 minutes. Turn the chicken over and broil 15 minutes longer. Turn the chicken again, then broil for an additional 15 minutes, turning often and basting the chicken pieces with the pan juices.

Note: This recipe can be prepared without the skin as long as you baste well. Remove the skin before marinating the chickens.

CHICKEN WITH HONEY AND LEMON
Dajaj

Lebanon

Serves 4 to 6

In *dajaj* the taste of honey predominates, so you may want to serve this chicken dish on Rosh Hashanah. The chicken is usually roasted whole, but if you prefer to serve chicken without the skin, remove the skin and cut up the chickens into serving-size pieces before brushing them with the honey-lemon mixture.

> **2 whole chickens (3 pounds each)**
> **2 lemons**
> **Salt**
> **½ cup honey**
> **¼ cup (½ stick) pareve margarine, melted**

Preheat the oven to 450 degrees F. Rinse the chickens and pat them dry. Using the cut side of half of one lemon, rub the chickens all over. Squeeze the juice from the remaining 1½ lemons; set the juice aside. Sprinkle the chickens lightly with salt.

In a small mixing bowl, stir the honey with a fork, then blend in the margarine and lemon juice, beating lightly with the fork for one minute. Brush the chickens with this mixture.

Recipe continues on the following page . . .

Place the chickens in a greased or oiled baking pan. Roast for 10 minutes at 450 degrees F., then reduce the heat to 350 degrees F. and continue roasting the chickens for 1 to 1½ hours, until golden and tender and cooked through. Brush the chickens occasionally with the pan juices. If they are not yet brown by the time they are tender, raise the heat for a few minutes.

For cut-up skinless chickens, bake for 10 minutes at 450 degrees F., then continue baking for 30 to 45 minutes at 350 degrees F., turning the chicken pieces every 10 to 15 minutes and basting often.

BASTED HERB-AND-SPICE CHICKEN
Djej Mechoui

Morocco

Serves 4 to 6

A combination of herbs and spices subtly flavors this chicken. In Morocco, the base of the sauce is a preserved butter called *smen*, with which the spit-barbecued chickens are basted constantly as they cook. *Pareve* margarine is substituted for the butter in this adaptation, and just in case you don't feel like standing and basting the chickens for an hour or so, the recipe for the sauce is doubled so the diners can moisten the chicken themselves at the table.

> **6 scallions (white and crisp green parts), chopped**
> **2 large cloves garlic**

¼ cup chopped fresh parsley
2 tablespoons chopped fresh coriander leaves
(optional)
1 teaspoon salt (optional)
1 tablespoon paprika
1 tablespoon ground cumin
Dash of ground cayenne or crushed red
pepper
½ cup (1 stick) pareve margarine, softened
2 broiling chickens (3 pounds each), whole
(for spit-barbecuing), quartered, or cut into
smaller pieces

Using a mortar and pestle, pound the scallions and garlic into a paste with the parsley, coriander, and seasonings. Or use a blender or food processor to make a paste. Add the margarine and continue to blend.

Pat the chickens dry. Using about half the blended margarine, rub the paste all over the chickens, including the cavities of the whole chickens. Let stand at room temperature for 1 hour, then cover with plastic wrap or foil and refrigerate the chickens until cooking time.

When ready to cook, heat the remaining herb-spice-margarine mixture over low heat until the margarine is melted and bubbly but not browned. Keep warm over low heat.

For outdoor grilling, spit-barbecue the chickens over hot coals for 1 to 1½ hours, until they are golden brown all over and cooked through. Baste frequently with the extra sauce. Or grill cut-up chickens over medium coals for about 45 minutes, turning as necessary. During the last 20 minutes baste often. Watch out for flare-ups.

For indoor broiling, broil the chicken pieces 4 inches from the heat for 15 minutes, then turn over and broil 15 minutes longer. Turn the chicken again, then broil an additional 15 minutes, turning frequently and basting the chicken pieces with the pan juices or extra sauce.

Serve the chicken with rice, and pass around extra sauce.

CHICKEN WITH PRESERVED LEMONS AND OLIVES
Djej Emshmel

Morocco

Serves 4

Recipes for chicken with lemon and olives are often simplified, calling for fresh lemons and California olives. However, to duplicate the intriguing tartness of the authentic Moroccan preparation, preserved lemons (page 139) and olives from the Mediterranean area are recommended. Unless you keep a supply of preserved lemons on hand routinely, this recipe must be started two weeks in advance to prepare the lemons.

> 1 frying chicken (4 pounds), cut up
> 1 teaspoon ground ginger
> 1 teaspoon paprika
> ½ teaspoon ground turmeric
> ½ teaspoon salt
> ¼ teaspoon freshly ground black pepper
> ¼ teaspoon crushed saffron
> 1 cup minced onion
> 1 cup water
> 1 cup Royal Victoria, Kalamata, or other purple Greek olives
> 1 preserved lemon (page 139)
> 1 to 4 tablespoons fresh lemon juice

Remove and discard the chicken skin. In a small bowl, mix together the ground ginger, paprika, turmeric, salt, pepper, and saffron. Rub this spice mixture into the chicken. In a 4- to 5-quart pot, place the chicken, onion, and water. Bring to the boil over high heat. Reduce the heat to a gentle boil, cover the pot, and cook the chicken until very tender, 45 minutes to an hour. Turn over the chicken pieces every 10 to 15 minutes. The chicken can be refrigerated in its sauce at this point.

To continue cooking, reheat the chicken. Rinse the olives and remove the pits. Taste one. If it is bitter, in a 1-quart pot cover the olives with cold water, bring to the boil, and drain.

Rinse the preserved lemon, cut it into quarters, and stir the lemon and olives into the sauce. Cook for 5 minutes. Using a slotted spoon, remove the chicken, lemon, and olives to a serving bowl. Taste the sauce; if it is thin and watery, raise the heat to boil away some of the liquid. Now blend in 1 tablespoon of fresh lemon juice at a time, tasting after each addition, until the sauce is lemony and tart to your taste. The lemon juice will give the sauce a creamy, slightly glazed look.

Pour the sauce over the chicken and serve.

ROASTED FRUIT-STUFFED CHICKENS
Dejaj Mugalla

Iran

Serves 6

Fruit-and-meat combinations are common in Iranian cuisine, and this naturally sweet breadless fruit stuffing serves both as a delectable side dish and as a chutney-like condiment. A perfect chicken to serve during Passover.

> **2 cups pitted prunes**
> **2 cups dried apricots**
> **Boiling water**
> **2 tablespoons chicken fat or pareve**
>   **margarine**
> **1 cup finely chopped onion**
> **2 cups chopped peeled apples**
> **1 teaspoon cinnamon**
> **2 frying chickens (3 pounds each)**

In a heatproof bowl, place the prunes and apricots and enough boiling water to cover the fruit by an inch. Soak the fruit for 30 to 45 minutes, then drain. Chop the prunes and apricots coarsely.

In a 10-inch skillet, heat the chicken fat or margarine over moderate heat. Sauté the chopped onion until it is soft but not browned. Stir in the apples, cook for a minute, then add the chopped prunes and apricots, mixing well. Sprinkle the cin-

Recipe continues on the following page . . .

namon over the mixture, and cook over low heat for about 5 minutes, stirring occasionally. The stuffing can be refrigerated overnight at this point.

Preheat the oven to 350 degrees F. Stuff the chickens with the fruit mixture. Roast for 1½ to 2 hours. After the first half-hour, baste the chickens with the accumulated pan juices, and continue basting every 15 to 20 minutes. When the chickens are tender and golden brown, they are ready to serve.

DUCK IN POMEGRANATE SAUCE
Fesenjan

Iran

Serves 4

In one of the classic dishes of Iran, duck simmers in a delectable fruit and nut sauce made of pomegranate juice and walnuts. Sugar and lemon juice contribute a sweet-sour taste. Steamed rice is the traditional accompaniment, for there is plenty of the rich, tasty sauce to spoon over the rice. The seeds of fresh pomegranates are squeezed to make the juice, or pomegranate syrup can be purchased in Middle Eastern food shops.

> **1 large duck (5 pounds)**
> **2 tablespoons olive oil or vegetable oil**
> **½ teaspoon ground turmeric (optional)**
> **1 cup sliced onion**
> **1½ cups walnut meats, ground**
> **4 cups chicken broth**
> **1 pomegranate or 3 tablespoons bottled**
>   **pomegranate syrup**
> **¼ cup fresh lemon juice**
> **¼ cup granulated sugar**
> **Salt and freshly ground black pepper**

Remove all visible fat from the duck. Cut the duck into quarters. In a 12- to 14-inch skillet, heat the oil over moderate heat

(350 degrees F.). Add the duck quarters, skin side down. Regulate the heat so the duck browns without burning, and brown the duck pieces all over. Transfer the duck to a platter or a bowl and set aside.

Spoon off all but about 3 tablespoons of fat from the skillet, then add the optional turmeric and stir for a minute. Add the sliced onion. Cook, stirring frequently, until the onion is light brown. Stir in the ground walnuts, reserving one tablespoon for garnish. Transfer the onion-walnut mixture to a 5- to 6-quart pot, add the chicken broth, and bring to the boil over high heat. Reduce the heat so the mixture boils very gently. Cover the pot and cook for 15 to 20 minutes. Add the browned duck pieces. Turn the duck to coat the pieces all over with the sauce. Cover the pot and cook the duck for 1 to 1½ hours or until it is tender when pierced with a fork.

Meanwhile, prepare the pomegranate juice. Cut the pomegranate in half and scoop out the seeds. Use a lemon juicer to squeeze the juice from the seeds; or line a colander or strainer with cheesecloth and use the back of a large spoon to crush the seeds, releasing the juice. There should be about ½ cup of pomegranate juice. Set aside.

When the duck is tender, skim off any fat from the top of the bubbling liquid. Now add the pomegranate juice, the lemon juice, and the sugar. Cover and cook for an additional 30 minutes. The duck should be very tender, the sauce thickened and somewhat syrupy. Taste for seasoning, adding lemon juice or sugar to heighten the sweet-sour taste. Season with salt and pepper and simmer another minute or two.

Transfer the duck pieces to a large casserole or a tureen, and pour some of the sauce over the duck. Sprinkle the duck with the reserved tablespoon of ground walnuts. Serve the duck with rice, passing around the remaining sauce separately.

Variation:

To substitute chicken for the duck, use 4 whole chicken breasts cut in half. Brown the chicken in 4 tablespoons oil, and proceed with the recipe, decreasing the initial cooking time to 45 minutes. If desired, remove the skin and bones from the chicken before serving.

STUFFED MACKEREL
Uskumru Dolma

Turkey, Armenia

Serves 4

The Jews fleeing Spain in the late fifteenth century were welcomed into the Ottoman Empire, and this stuffed mackerel is one of the dishes brought by the Sephardic Jews to Turkey. The mackerel is stuffed with a sweet crunchy mixture and fried crisp.

4 mackerel, heads and tails removed (½
pound dressed weight each)
2 tablespoons olive oil
1 cup chopped onion
¼ cup pine nuts
½ cup chopped walnuts
¼ cup seedless raisins
¼ teaspoon ground allspice
¼ teaspoon ground nutmeg
¼ teaspoon ground cinnamon
Pinch of ground cloves
½ cup chopped fresh parsley
½ cup soft breadcrumbs
1 egg (graded large), beaten
Flour for coating the fish
Oil for frying

To prepare the mackerel, with a sharp boning knife remove and discard all bones. Carefully scrape the meat from the skin, leaving the skin intact. Wash the fish skin under cold water, pat dry, and set aside. Chop the fish coarsely. Set aside.

In a 10-inch skillet, heat the olive oil over moderate heat. Add the onion and sauté until the onion is softened and golden but not brown. Stir in the pine nuts, walnuts, and raisins. Continue cooking for 2 minutes to lightly toast the nuts, then stir in the ground spices. Mix in the chopped parsley, the breadcrumbs, and the chopped fish. Cook 5 minutes longer, stirring often.

Divide the stuffing into 4 equal portions and stuff each fish skin with a portion of the mixture. Secure the edges with toothpicks, or sew the edges together. Roll the fish in the beaten egg and then the flour, coating the fish skin completely with flour.

In a skillet 12 inches or larger and at least 3 inches deep, heat 1 inch of oil to 375 degrees F. The oil should be hot but not yet smoking. Carefully add the fish to the oil, making sure they do not touch each other. Fry the fish for a few minutes on one side until golden, then carefully turn and fry the other side. Drain well on paper towels and serve immediately.

Variation:

For baked stuffed mackerel, omit the coating of egg and flour. Place the fish on a foil-lined baking sheet, and oil the foil. Bake in a preheated 400-degree F. oven for 15 to 20 minutes, until the stuffing is sizzling. Serve hot as a main dish, or chill the fish, slice crosswise into 1-inch pieces, and serve cold as an appetizer.

FISH KEBOBS
Kiliç Şiş

Turkey, Armenia

Serves 4

Grilled fish on skewers is a variation on the more well known *shish kebobs*. A simple marinade of lemon juice and olive oil lightly seasoned with dill and paprika complements the flavor of the fish. For the swordfish used in most Turkish and Armenian recipes, halibut steaks or fillets are used here.

> **2 pounds halibut steaks or fillets**
> **Salt and freshly ground black pepper**
> **⅓ cup freshly squeezed lemon juice**
> **3 tablespoons olive oil**
> **2 teaspoons chopped fresh dill**
> **½ teaspoon paprika**
> **Lemon wedges**

Remove the skin from halibut steaks. (The skin is left on halibut

Recipe continues on the following page . . .

fillets.) Sprinkle the fish with salt and pepper, then cut into 1-inch cubes or squares.

In a bowl large enough to hold the fish, mix together the lemon juice, olive oil, dill, and paprika. Add the fish and stir gently to coat the fish with the marinade. Marinate for about an hour in the refrigerator, turning occasionally. Do not leave the fish in the marinade for more than two hours or it will begin to "cook." (See *poisson cru*, page 194.)

Remove the fish from the marinade and thread onto skewers. Grill the fish over hot coals, turning once after 5 minutes. The fish will be lightly browned on the outside, white on the inside. Serve immediately with lemon wedges.

Variation:

For a more pronounced herb flavor, add 24 bay leaves to the marinade. Thread the bay leaves onto the skewers alternately with the fish.

MOUSSAKA

Greece, Turkey

Serves 6

Broiled eggplant layered with a seasoned mushroom-tomato sauce, a white sauce, and grated cheese makes a hearty main dish. *Moussaka* usually features ground lamb in the tomato sauce, and most kosher recipes include the meat and omit the cheese. I think you will like this dairy version better.

> **2 eggplants (1 pound each)**
> **Olive oil**
> **¼ cup (½ stick) unsalted butter**
> **1 large Spanish onion, chopped**
> **2 large cloves garlic, minced**
> **1 pound mushrooms, sliced**
> **1 cup tomato purée**
> **¼ cup chopped fresh parsley**
> **⅛ teaspoon ground cinnamon (optional)**
> **Salt and freshly ground black pepper**

¼ cup (½ stick) unsalted butter
¼ cup unsifted all-purpose flour
4 egg yolks (from eggs graded large)
2 cups warm milk
1 cup grated Parmesan cheese

Select shiny eggplants—eggplants with dull skins will be seedy and bitter. Peel the eggplants and slice them ½ inch thick. Place on a baking tray, brush with olive oil, and broil 4 inches from the heat until light brown in spots. Turn over the eggplant slices, brush the tops with olive oil, and broil until light brown. Set the eggplant aside.

In a 10-inch skillet, melt ¼ cup butter over moderate heat. Stir in the onion and garlic, and sauté for about 2 minutes, until the onion begins to soften. Now add the sliced mushrooms and continue to cook for about 5 minutes, stirring often. Add the tomato purée, parsley, cinnamon, and salt and pepper to taste. Mix well and cook for another 5 minutes, adding a little water if the mixture sticks. Set aside the mushroom-tomato sauce.

In a 2-quart pot, melt the remaining ¼ cup of butter over moderately low heat. Add the flour, stirring rapidly to make a smooth mixture. Cook the flour and butter mixture for a minute; the mixture should be thick and bubbly but not brown. Using a fork or a whisk, in a medium-size mixing bowl beat the egg yolks well, then beat in the warm milk. Now gradually add this egg yolk-milk mixture into the flour and butter mixture, stirring rapidly with a fork. Cook, stirring constantly, until the mixture comes to the boil. Remove the white sauce from the heat.

Preheat the oven to 350 degrees F. Lightly oil or butter a 9 x 13 x 2-inch baking dish. Arrange half the eggplant in one layer in the baking dish. Cover with half the mushroom-tomato sauce, then add a second layer of eggplant and the remaining mushroom-tomato sauce. Spread the white sauce evenly over the tomato sauce, then sprinkle on the cheese. The moussaka may be covered and refrigerated at this point.

Bake at 350 degrees F. for 35 to 45 minutes. The eggplant should be tender and the cheese light brown and bubbly. Carefully cover the casserole with foil if the cheese browns too rapidly.

FELAFEL

Egypt

Serves 6

We may think of *felafel* as a national dish of Israel, but it has its origins in Egypt, where it is prepared with Egyptian brown beans. In most parts of the United States, chickpeas are much easier to obtain than brown beans, so the chickpea version is given here. Cooked chickpeas are puréed with garlic and spices then deep-fried until crisp on the outside and soft on the inside. *Felafel* is served in *pita,* usually with a *tahini* sauce or a yogurt sauce. Lettuce, tomatoes, cucumbers, and surprises such as pieces of pickle complete the sandwich. Although *felafel* is sold on stands as a snack food, this triple-size recipe can be enjoyed as a complete vegetarian family dinner.

> 3 cups dried chickpeas soaked overnight, or
>   3 cans (1 pound each) chickpeas, drained
> 6 large cloves garlic, minced
> ¼ cup chopped fresh parsley
> ¼ cup minced fresh chives
> 1 to 2 tablespoons ground cumin, to taste
> 2 to 4 teaspoons ground coriander, to taste
> ¾ to 1 teaspoon ground cayenne pepper, to
>   taste
> 3 eggs (graded large)
> ½ cup plus 1 tablespoon unsifted all-purpose
>   flour
> Shredded lettuce
> Chopped tomatoes
> Tahini (page 137)
> 1 cup plain yogurt mixed with the juice of
>   1 lemon
> Pita breads, 2 to 3 per person, depending on
>   size
> Oil for deep-frying

If you are starting with dried chickpeas, begin soaking them a day ahead. In a large bowl, place the chickpeas with enough cold water to cover them by two inches. Allow them to soak overnight or a minimum of 6 hours. Drain the soaked chickpeas, and place them in a 4-quart pot with enough water to cover them by several inches. Bring the water to the boil, reduce the heat to a gentle boil, partially cover the pot, and cook the chickpeas for 2 to 3 hours, until very soft.

Drain the cooked or canned chickpeas, then mash them well with a potato masher until smooth. Mash in the garlic, parsley, chives, cumin, coriander, and cayenne. Beat in the eggs, then the flour. To use a food processor, work with one-third of the ingredients at a time. Use the chopping blade to purée the chickpeas, then mix in the remaining ingredients, processing just until combined. Chill the *felafel* mixture for at least one hour or as long as overnight.

Before you begin frying the *felafel*, place the lettuce, tomatoes, and the sauces in serving bowls on the dining table. If desired, warm the *pita* breads in a 250-degree F. oven while the *felafel* are cooking.

In a 2-quart pot, heat 2 inches of oil over moderately high heat until it is hot but not yet smoking, 375 degrees F. Wet your hands and shape the *felafel* into 1¼- to 1½-inch balls. Carefully drop one ball into the oil; it will immediately start sizzling if the oil is hot enough. Add about 9 more chickpea balls, and cook until they are golden brown all over. Drain well on paper towels, and continue cooking until the mixture is all used up. Keep the cooked *felafel* hot in a bowl covered with a kitchen towel. You may want to keep two pots going to fry the *felafel* more quickly.

To assemble, each person slices off the top of a *pita* and stuffs the pocket with a few chickpea balls, lettuce and tomatoes, and either or both of the sauces.

Note: If the mixture is too moist and the *felafel* do not hold together well during frying, roll the balls in flour immediately before frying.

Side Dishes

The staff of life is also the cutlery of the Middle East, for some form of small, flat round bread is used in most of the area to pick up food to be eaten. Pieces of the bread, known as "Arab bread" (*pita* in Israel, "Mideast bread" in the United States) are torn off and used as edible forks. Certified kosher whole-wheat and white-flour versions are readily available in supermarkets throughout the United States. Variations include a thinner Armenian bread (page 165) that is not so tricky to prepare (it doesn't have to puff to form a pocket) but is very satisfying to eat.

In addition to breads, two wheat products that are not so common in American households are served daily in the Middle East, namely *burghul* and semolina. While the sun-dried brown cracked wheat known as *burghul* is a most important grain in Turkish, Syrian, Lebanese, and Armenian cooking, the yellow-to-white semolina appears in Egyptian and Greek dishes and as *couscous* on Moroccan tables. Steamed rice and wheat preparations known as *pilafs* (pages 167 and 168) are made by sautéing the grain in butter or margarine then cooking it in seasoned broth. Diced fruits and nuts are added to make the *pilafs* fit for festive occasions such as weddings and holidays. Rice is *the* grain of Iran, and nowhere in the world, not even in the other rice-dependent cuisines of Asia (see page 184 and 212) is so much attention given to the daily preparation of basic rice.

To round out a Middle Eastern dinner, you can't go wrong adding a salad of romaine lettuce, tomatoes, green peppers, and olives, dressed with olive oil and fresh lemon juice. For a Moroccan lunch or dinner, a more unusual (to us) salad mixture of grated carrots and raisins or orange sections and dates would be typical. Another out-of-the ordinary salad, from Turkey, uses leeks as the principal ingredient.

Hot and cold vegetables—most often stuffed eggplants, peppers, tomatoes, artichokes, and grape leaves—are served all over the Middle East as appetizers and main dish accompaniments. If you already make stuffed peppers and stuffed cabbage, then stuff them with rice, parsley, pine nuts, onions, garlic, a little cinnamon, some lemon juice, and olive oil, call them *dolmas,* and you're on your way to making a Middle Eastern meal.

ARMENIAN THIN BREAD
Lavash

Armenia

Makes twelve 8-inch rounds

Thin, crisp, crackerlike rounds can be made very small to be served with appetizers or rolled into circles as large as eighteen inches in diameter. The eight-inch rounds suggested here are just the right size for individual dinner breads.

> 3½ cups unsifted all-purpose flour
> 2 teaspoons sugar
> 2 teaspoons salt
> 1 package active dry yeast
> 1 cup hot water (120 degrees F.)
> ¼ cup vegetable oil
> 1 egg (graded large), beaten
> Sesame seeds

In a large mixing bowl, mix 2 cups of the flour with the sugar, salt, and the yeast. Stir in the hot water and the oil. Using an electric mixer with a dough hook or a large kitchen spoon, stir in the remaining flour ½ cup at a time, beating until the dough holds together and is smooth. Turn out onto a clean, smooth, lightly floured work surface and knead for about 5 minutes. Add a little flour as necessary to keep the dough from sticking to your hands or the work surface. Lightly poke your finger into

Recipe continues on the following page . . .

the dough. If the indentation does not remain, the dough is ready for rising.

Place the dough in a clean, dry bowl that will be large enough to accommodate the dough when double in size. Cover the top of the bowl with plastic wrap. Allow the dough to rise in a warm place (85 degrees F. is ideal) for an hour, until it has doubled. To create a warm environment for the dough to rise, place a pan of hot water on the bottom shelf of the oven, and put the bowl of dough on the shelf above the hot water.

When you think the dough has risen enough, poke a finger into the dough. This time the indentation should remain. Punch down the dough, then turn it out onto a clean, smooth, dry work surface. Knead for about half a minute, until the dough is smooth again. Divide the dough into 12 pieces, and shape each piece into a smooth ball. Cover the balls of dough with a clean kitchen towel.

Preheat the oven to 375 degrees F. Working with one ball of dough at a time (and keeping the remainder covered), use a rolling pin to roll the dough into an 8-inch circle that will be about ⅛ inch thick. Turn the dough a quarter-turn to the left or right each time you roll. This helps ensure that the dough is rolled out evenly, and will also help keep the dough from sticking to the work surface. Stretch the dough with your fingers if it is difficult to roll.

Transfer the 8-inch round to one corner of a large ungreased cookie or baking sheet. Roll out another round and place it on the opposite corner of the baking sheet. Repeat with two more balls of dough on a second baking sheet.

Brush the 4 rounds with beaten egg, and sprinkle lavishly with sesame seeds. Bake at 375 degrees F. for about 15 minutes, until crisp and golden. Transfer the baked *lavash* to a wire rack.

Meanwhile, if you have more large baking sheets, prepare more *lavash* as above and bake them when the first batch is done. If not, wait until the first rounds are baked, allow the baking sheets to cool on a wire rack (or wave them in the air to hasten cooling), then roll out the next rounds.

To serve *lavash* warm, wrap the hot breads in foil while the remaining rounds bake. Or line a wicker basket with a linen towel, place the *lavash* in the basket, and cover with another linen towel. To keep for a day or two, cool the *lavash* on wire racks, wrap in foil or heavy plastic bags, and store at room temperature. Freeze for longer storage. Before serving, thawed *lavash* can be warmed in a 250-degree F. oven for a few minutes.

BURGHUL PILAF
for Vegetarian or Dairy Meals

Armenia, Turkey

Serves 4 to 6

Wheat *pilaf* is a wonderful change from rice. This plain *pilaf* is chewy, with a wholesome wheat taste. Chopped apricots and toasted almonds will dress it up.

½ cup (1 stick) unsalted butter or margarine
1 cup chopped onion
2 cups burghul (cracked wheat)
4 cups water or vegetable broth
Salt
Optional additions: ¼ to ½ cup dried apricots, soaked in boiling water for 20 minutes then chopped; ¼ cup blanched slivered almonds, sautéed in 1 tablespoon vegetable oil until golden

In a 4-quart pot, melt the butter or margarine over moderate heat. Add the onion and cook for a minute or two, stirring occasionally. Mix in the *burghul* and cook for another minute, stirring frequently. Add the water or broth and salt to taste, raise the heat to bring the liquid to the boil, and boil for 5 minutes without stirring. Regulate the heat so the liquid doesn't boil over. Reduce the heat to a simmer, cover the pot, and cook the *burghul* for 20 minutes. Turn off the heat and allow the *burghul* to finish cooking on the turned-off burner for another 20 to 30 minutes. Meanwhile, prepare the apricots and almonds if desired. Just before serving, fluff the *burghul* with a fork, stir in the apricots and almonds, and serve.

BURGHUL PILAF

for Meat Meals

Armenia, Turkey

Serves 4 to 6

Once you've served a plain *burghul pilaf,* you'll see how easy it is to prepare and will be making up your own variations. Here's one with chicken broth and diced lamb.

> ½ cup (1 stick) pareve margarine
> ½ cup lamb, cut into ¼-inch cubes
> ½ cup chopped onion
> 2 cups burghul (cracked wheat)
> 4 cups chicken broth
> Salt
> ¼ cup slivered blanched almonds, sautéed in 1 tablespoon vegetable oil until golden (optional)

In a 4-quart pot, melt the margarine over moderate heat. Add the lamb and onion and cook for 2 or 3 minutes, stirring often. Mix in the *burghul* and cook for another minute, stirring frequently. Add the chicken broth and salt to taste, raise the heat to bring the broth to the boil, and boil for 5 minutes without stirring. Regulate the heat so the broth doesn't boil over. Reduce the heat to a simmer, cover the pot, and cook the *burghul* for 20 minutes. Turn off the heat and allow the *burghul* to finish cooking on the turned-off burner for another 20 to 30 minutes. Just before serving, fluff with a fork, adding the optional almonds.

EGGPLANT PURÉE

Hunkar Bejendi

Armenia, Turkey

Serves 4 to 6

Eggplant purée made with a cream sauce and grated cheese is a favorite of Armenians and Turks. Because the purée is usually served with stewed lamb, this adaptation uses a chicken broth base instead of milk. The cheese is omitted. If you like, serve the vegetable as people do in the Middle East: the lamb is placed on a platter and is surrounded by the eggplant. Always select eggplants with a dark, shiny skin. Lackluster eggplants will be bitter.

> **2 eggplants (1 pound each)**
> **2 tablespoons olive oil or pareve margarine**
> **2 tablespoons unsifted all-purpose flour**
> **½ cup chicken broth**
> **2 tablespoons fresh lemon juice**

Prick the eggplants in several places and use a large fork to hold them (one at a time) over a gas flame, or place them on a piece of foil under the broiler. Cook, turning frequently, until the skin is evenly charred and the meat is tender, 10 to 20 minutes over a flame, 20 to 30 minutes under the broiler. Remove from the heat. When the eggplants are cool enough to handle, cut them in half, scoop out and discard the seeds, and mash the eggplants with a fork.

In a 2-quart pot, heat the oil or margarine over moderate heat. Use a fork to blend in the flour, and after it bubbles for a minute, add the chicken broth. Stir rapidly until the sauce is smooth and thickened. Cook 1 minute longer, stirring constantly, then add the mashed eggplant. Add salt to taste. Continue to cook for a few minutes, until hot, and continue to mash the eggplant until it is a smooth purée. Blend in the lemon juice and serve.

Variation:

To serve with a dairy meal, substitute milk for the chicken broth and add ¼ cup grated Parmesan cheese with the eggplant. Cook until the cheese has melted.

Desserts

Fresh fruit, delicate rice puddings flavored with rose water and orange blossom water, sweetened semolina puddings, and rich honey-and-nut laden pastries are enjoyed in the Middle East. While fruit is the most typical dessert, pastries are eaten with coffee or tea as between-meal snacks rather than at the conclusion of a meal. The pastries have a range I love: sweet, sweeter, sweetest.

CUSTARD-FILLED PASTRIES
Galatoboureko

Turkey, Armenia, Greece

Makes about 36 pastries

Surprise your friends with a rich, thick custard sandwiched between layers of phyllo. The bottom layers are drenched in a sugar syrup; the top pastry is crisp and buttery. The secret ingredient in the filling is farina, giving the custard a unique taste and a slightly chewy consistency.

> ½ **cup regular (not quick-cooking or instant) farina**
> ½ **cup granulated sugar**
> **4 eggs (graded large), beaten**
> **1 quart milk**
> **2 tablespoons unsalted butter**

2 teaspoons vanilla extract
10 sheets phyllo dough (about ½ pound)
½ cup (1 stick) unsalted butter, melted

Syrup:

1½ cups water
1½ cups granulated sugar
Quarter of a large lemon

In a 4-quart pot, mix together the farina and sugar. Combine the beaten eggs with the milk, and gradually pour the liquid into the dry ingredients, stirring until the mixture is smooth. Cook over moderate heat, stirring constantly, until the mixture comes to the boil. If the heat is moderate and the mixture is stirred continuously, the custard will not curdle. Allow the mixture to boil for one minute, stirring all the while. The custard will be thick, more granular than a regular custard but not as grainy as cooked cereal. Remove from heat. Stir in the 2 tablespoons butter and the vanilla, stirring until the butter melts.

Open a package of phyllo dough, lay the dough out flat, and carefully remove 10 sheets. Immediately refold and rewrap the remaining phyllo and place in the refrigerator. Cover the 10 sheets of phyllo with a slightly damp but not wet towel. Work with one sheet of phyllo at a time, keeping the remainder covered with the towel so the dough does not dry out.

Using a pastry brush, coat a 9 x 13 x 2-inch baking dish with a thin layer of melted butter. Butter one whole sheet of phyllo with the melted butter. Line the bottom and sides of the baking dish with the buttered sheet, easing the phyllo in so it does not tear. Do not trim the phyllo. Repeat with 4 more sheets of phyllo.

Preheat the oven to 350 degrees F. Pour the warm custard into the baking dish, and level the custard with a spoon. Now cut the remaining 5 sheets of phyllo in half crosswise, making 10 pieces approximately 9 x 13 inches each. Butter one sheet and lay it on top of the custard. Repeat with the remaining sheets of phyllo. It may be easier to first place the unbuttered phyllo on the custard then brush the dough with butter. Do not worry if the

Recipe continues on the following page . . .

pastry tears a bit. Pour any remaining melted butter on the top sheet of dough.

Using a very sharp knife, cut through the top sheets of phyllo in a diamond-shaped pattern, making about three dozen 2-inch pieces. Bake for about 45 minutes, until the pastry is a golden brown.

Meanwhile, prepare the syrup. In a 2-quart pot, mix the water and sugar. Remove the seeds from the lemon, squeeze the juice into the sugar-water mixture, and drop in the squeezed rind. Bring to the boil over high heat. Reduce the heat to a moderate boil and cook, uncovered, for 15 minutes. Remove the lemon rind, and remove the syrup from the heat.

As soon as the pastry is baked, remove it from the oven and pour the sugar syrup evenly over the hot pastry. Allow the *galatoboureko* to cool to room temperature. When cool, use a sharp knife to cut through to the bottom of the pastry. Refrigerate, uncovered, until serving. The pastry will keep for 2 days in the refrigerator, but it will become soggy with age. The syrup that is not absorbed by the pastry is not served.

NUT ROLLS IN HONEY SYRUP
Bourekakia

Turkey, Armenia, Greece

Makes 36 pastries

An obvious antecedent of the strudels of Europe, *bourekakia* is a link between the well-known Turkish pastry *baklava* and the nut-laden flaky European strudels. The pastry begins as a strudel, with paper-thin sheets of dough buttered, laced with jam and nuts, and rolled up. The roll is sliced before it is baked, and immediately after baking, the pastry is bathed in a honey syrup typically used for making *baklava*. The resulting nut rolls are not crisp like strudel; they are softened by the syrup and permeated with the taste of honey.

> 2 cups chopped walnuts
> ½ teaspoon ground cinnamon
> 12 sheets phyllo dough (about ½ pound)
> 1 cup orange marmalade or apricot jam
> 1 cup (2 sticks) clarified unsalted butter (page
>   17) or margarine, melted

Syrup:

> ½ cup granulated sugar
> 1½ cups water
> ½ cup honey
> Half of a large lemon
> 1 cinnamon stick (3 inches)

Combine the walnuts with the ground cinnamon and set aside.

Using a pastry brush, coat a 9 x 13 x 2-inch baking dish with a thin layer of melted butter.

Lay the 12 sheets of phyllo out flat, and cover them completely with a slightly damp but not wet towel. Always keep unused sheets of phyllo covered or they will dry out. Carefully peel off one sheet of phyllo, place it flat on a table or counter, and brush it completely with melted butter. Place a second sheet of phyllo on top of the first, brush with butter, and repeat with a third sheet. Using the back of a spoon or a spatula, spread half the jam on the top sheet of phyllo, then sprinkle with half the walnut-cinnamon mixture. Now place another sheet of phyllo on top of the nut mixture, brush with butter, and repeat with 2 more sheets of dough. There will be 6 layers of dough in all, with one layer of jam and nuts in the middle.

Starting with the long end nearest you, roll the dough into a tight jellyroll. Using a sharp knife, cut the pastry into eighteen 1-inch slices. Place the sliced pastry in the buttered baking dish, nut side up.

Preheat the oven to 350 degrees F. Prepare the remaining phyllo, jam, and nuts. Brush all the remaining melted butter over the pastries. Bake the nut pastries for 45 minutes, or until they are golden brown.

Meanwhile, in a 2-quart pot combine the sugar, water, and

Recipe continues on the following page . . .

honey. Remove the seeds from the lemon and squeeze the lemon, extracting as much juice as possible. Add the lemon juice to the honey mixture, along with the squeezed rind and the cinnamon stick. Bring the mixture to the boil over high heat, stirring constantly to dissolve the sugar and to keep the mixture from boiling over. Reduce the heat to a moderate boil and cook, uncovered, for 20 minutes. Remove the cinnamon stick and the lemon rind, and set the syrup aside.

As soon as the pastry is baked, remove the baking dish from the oven and pour the syrup evenly over the hot pastry. The nut rolls will absorb the syrup. Serve the pastries warm or at room temperature. Store the pastries at room temperature, covered, for 3 or 4 days. Cooled pastries may be frozen. Serve at room temperature or slightly warm.

APRICOT CREAM PARFAIT
Kremli Kuru Kaytst

Armenia, Turkey

Makes 8 servings

This is considered one of the lighter Turkish desserts. Dried apricots are cooked in a sugar syrup, cooled, and topped with ground almonds and whipped cream. (By my standards, this is a rich dessert.) It is especially attractive if served from a glass bowl. In the version below, the apricots, nuts, and whipped cream are layered in individual parfait glasses.

If you enjoy the taste of real whipped cream, save this dessert to follow a dairy or vegetarian meal.

> **1 pound dried apricots**
> **4 cups boiling water**
> **¾ cup granulated sugar**
> **2 tablespoons fresh lemon juice**
> **½ cup finely chopped blanched almonds**
> **1 cup heavy or whipping cream, or 2 cups
> nondairy whipped topping**
> **¼ cup sifted confectioners' sugar**

In a medium-size heatproof bowl, place the apricots and boiling water. The water should cover the apricots by an inch. Add more boiling water if necessary. Allow the apricots to stand for an hour, until they are plump. Very dry apricots will take longer to plump than moist apricots. Drain the apricots, reserving the liquid. There should be about 3 cups of liquid.

In a 2-quart pot, mix together the apricots, reserved liquid, and the ¾ cup sugar. Add water if the apricots are not completely covered. Bring the liquid to the boil over high heat, stirring frequently. Reduce the heat to a gentle boil, and cook the apricots, uncovered, for 45 minutes to 1 hour, stirring occasionally. Most of the liquid will boil away, and the remainder will become very thick. If the liquid boils away too rapidly, reduce the heat, and add a little water from time to time so you don't end up with a pot of burned apricots. When the apricots are tender and the syrup is thick, stir in the lemon juice and continue to cook a minute longer. Cool the apricots to room temperature.

Meanwhile, toast the almonds in a 300 degree F. oven for 15 minutes. Chill a small mixing bowl and beaters for 1 hour in the refrigerator or 15 minutes in the freezer.

When you are ready to assemble the parfaits, place the cream and confectioners' sugar in the chilled bowl. Whip the cream until it is stiff, being careful not to overbeat or the cream will turn into butter. Place a ½- to 1-inch layer of apricots in each of 8 parfait glasses, sprinkle with almonds, then add a layer of whipped cream. Continue layering the parfaits, and top the final layer of whipped cream with a sprinkling of nuts. The parfaits can be put together an hour before serving if refrigerated.

To serve from one large bowl, pack the apricots into a bowl, sprinkle with nuts, reserving a few for garnish, and spread the whipped cream over the apricots. Sprinkle on the remaining nuts. Chill until serving.

3

ASIA
AND THE
PACIFIC
ISLANDS

Introduction

As we enter the Orient, prepare to enjoy some of the most aromatic and spicy cooking in the world. Wafts of coriander, cardamom, and cumin will float through the kitchen as you cook India's Mogul chicken, a reminder that Columbus discovered America in search of the precious spices of India and Indonesia. As you become familiar with the cooking of Thailand, you will learn how to prepare an eye-watering, palate-tingling hot green curry paste flavored with fresh lime peel and lemon grass, using coconut milk to temper the hot curries of this southeast Asian country. A pungent pickled vegetable will be served with your Korean meals, and Philippine dishes will be flavored with vinegar and garlic, giving them a characteristically tangy taste.

Not all Asian cooking is equally intense. Japanese cuisine, for example, is subdued rather than spicy, with delicate soups and *teriyaki* sauces. And Chinese cuisine ranges from light Cantonese marinades to the fiery hot preparations of Szechwan and Hunan provinces.

The island of Tahiti, in the South Pacific, also has a subtle cuisine, one which uses fresh fruits, vegetables, and fish with few embellishments. Thus, many foods are flavored by simply wrapping them in freshly picked native leaves and then cooking them over outdoor fires. Hawaiian cuisine can be characterized as somewhat "native," but it also features dishes that originated in Tahiti, Korea, Japan, and on the United States mainland.

INDIA

Located in southern Asia, India is one-third the size of the United States, with triple its population. From a culinary standpoint, India can be considered two countries, each of whose food patterns is affected by climate and religion. In the cooler North, where wheat is grown, small pieces of the flat whole wheat Indian breads called *chapatis* (page 246) are used in place of forks for getting food from plate to mouth. Throughout India there is a Hindu prohibition against eating beef (cows are considered sacred), and lamb is the meat eaten in the North, where both a tradition of lamb cookery and a prohibition against eating pork were inherited from the Moguls who invaded India in the sixteenth century.

Rice is the grain of the warmer South, where the rice is scooped up with the fingers, absorbing the liquid of deliciously seasoned sauces. There, the Hindu prohibition against beef extends to strict vegetarianism. The southern climate, which makes it possible to grow all kinds of vegetables year 'round, contributes to the success of vegetarianism.

The wonderful variety of tastes in authentic Indian cookery is made possible by the myriad of herbs and spices used. Forget commercial curry powder and learn to create the homemade blends known as *masalas*. Turmeric, cumin, fresh coriander leaves, cloves, peppercorns, cardamom, coriander seeds, fenugreek, cinnamon, cayenne, mustard seeds, and saffron (the world's most expensive spice) are among the items blended in varying combinations to create dishes that range from delicate to fiery. If you expect to do a good deal of Indian cooking, you will want to have on hand a supply of fresh ginger root, garlic, and onions. Plenty of onions. (I once gave an Indian friend a 100-pound bag of onions as a gift. She loved it.)

Spices are used lavishly in the preparation of the dozens upon dozens of different kinds of lentils, beans, and chickpeas— all known in India as *dal*—that are eaten daily in India. Another mainstay of the Indian diet is yogurt. Yogurt is used in Indian cooking to flavor and thicken gravies; it is mixed with vegetables and offered as a condiment; and it is served plain to cool down some of the hotter and more spicy dishes. Yogurt is also consumed as a beverage.

Indian meals can be thought of as one glorious buffet: foods are not served in courses but set out at once. Even sweets—some milk-based, others made of grains—are eaten with meals instead of as desserts. Sweetened fermented black tea, often mixed with milk, is considered the national beverage. Green tea is also consumed, along with spiced milk and buttermilk and yogurt drinks.

With milk products so important in Indian cuisine, the major concern in adapting Indian cookery to the kosher home is the prohibition against mixing milk with meat. In dairy preparations, we can use the yogurt-based marinades and sauces, as well as clarified butter, known as *ghee*, for flavoring. When preparing meat dishes, however, we must omit yogurt from recipes and substitute vegetable oil or margarine for *ghee*. Even with these changes, however, the spices and seasonings so characteristic of Indian dishes will give the kosher adaptations the unmistakable stamp of the Indian kitchen.

CHINA

Leaving India by way of its northeastern border, we find that we have to climb the awesome Himalaya Mountains to enter the vast country of China. This would explain why Indian and Chinese cuisines are not even remotely related. China sees very different vegetables and seasonings, yogurt is absent in Chinese cooking, and meat—particularly pork—plays an important role in its cuisine.

China is actually a country of many cuisines, and just as we identify baked beans with Boston, and fried chicken with the southern United States, each Chinese province or major city has its own characteristic dishes. The technique known as stir-frying comes from the province of Canton, where vegetables and meat combinations are cooked quickly over high heat. The use of chicken stock and light marinades of soy sauce, ginger root, and rice wine is also characteristic of Cantonese cuisine. By contrast, Szechwan and Hunan dishes are hot and peppery, while Peking cookery uses garlic and scallions in very tasty but not overly spicy preparations. From Honan Province come sweet-and-sour dishes that have become standard on Chinese as well as Polynesian menus in the United States. China also has its stews, and Fukien is most famous for red-stewing, or cooking foods in soy sauce over low heat for long periods of time.

Brown and glutinous rices and *tofu* are eaten throughout China. Noodles made from rice, mung beans, and northern-grown wheat are also eaten extensively.

Chinese meals do not follow an appetizer-soup-main dish sequence as they do in Chinese-American restaurants. For family meals, all the foods, including soup, are set out on the table at once, and the soup is available throughout the meal as a beverage. Family members use chopsticks to take food directly from shared dishes to their own rice bowls. A humble family meal might consist of rice mixed with bits of vegetables, egg, *tofu*, or meat and a soup made simply of greens and boiled water. Lunches are often eaten in *dim sum* houses where a selection of small fried and steamed dumplings, filled buns, stuffed bean curd, and noodle dishes are enjoyed.

Banquets are elaborate, served course by course in special sequence. Whether preparing a family meal or a magnificent banquet, Chinese always pay particular attention to balance and contrast in tastes, textures, and colors. Tea, the beverage of China, is consumed throughout the day and before and after meals.

Because pork is virtually synonymous with meat in China and because many Chinese dishes feature shellfish, many Chinese recipes need to be modified for the kosher kitchen. By using cooking methods and seasonings typical of Chinese dishes, it is possible to substitute beef and lamb for pork in wontons and spareribs respectively, and fillets of flounder for the shellfish in many preparations, and end up with kosher dishes having a distinctly Chinese flavor. Dairy products have traditionally been almost nonexistent in China, so it is easy to avoid mixing meat and dairy foods in preparing Chinese meals.

VIETNAM

International cookbooks sometimes class Vietnamese cooking as a subset of Chinese cooking. However, even though northern Vietnam borders southeastern China, the seasonings used in its dishes are fundamentally different from Chinese flavorings. The first thing you'll notice about Vietnamese recipes is the absence of soy sauce. The universal seasoning of Vietnam is *nuoc mam,* a fermented, salty sauce made of anchovies. While we are likely to set a table with salt and pepper, the Vietnamese accompaniment to be sprinkled on almost all dishes is *nuoc cham,* a spicy mixture of *nuoc mam,* hot peppers, garlic, fresh lime juice, and sugar. Another departure from Chinese cuisine is the use of shallots (French influence) and lemon grass. Although, like the Chinese, the Vietnamese favor stir-frying, fresh raw vegetables are served at most meals, and a vegetable plate consisting of fresh coriander leaves, lettuce, and carrots is common. In general, Vietnamese cooking is light and subtle.

THAILAND

Not so Thai dishes. Spicy meat, poultry, and fish curries are the rule. "Come and eat rice" is the standard invitation to dinner, and the table is set with a mountain of rice surrounded by smaller bowls of rich curries.

Artistry is so important in Thai cuisine that there are classes taught in ginger root and vegetable sculpture. Some of the sculptures are so breathtaking that one wonders if the first caterer to use an ice sculpture as a centerpiece was inspired by creations seen in Thailand. Originality and creativity are considered virtues in Thai cookery, so if you taste something marvelous in someone's home, it would not be considered insulting the cook to make your own inventive changes when preparing the dish in your own home. Because of this emphasis on originality, kosher adaptations, such as omitting shrimp paste or fish sauce or using beef in place of pork, can be considered creative changes that would be encouraged by the cooks of Thailand.

INDONESIA

To the southeast of mainland Asia is the string of islands collectively known as Indonesia. These thousands of land masses stretch 3,000 miles between the Indian and Pacific Oceans, and down the centuries, either through invasion or trade, they have been influenced by the Netherlands, Portugal,

China, and India. So, it is not surprising that Indonesia boasts a varied cuisine featuring peanut sauces, barbecues or *satés* (page 231), thick soups, hot curries, sweet soy sauces, sweet-and-sour dishes, and spicy hot *sambals,* all accompaniments to the most important Indonesian food, rice. As in other Asian countries, rice is the heart of the meal, and small portions of many meat, fish, and vegetable dishes and condiments are mixed with the rice. (The famous *rijsttafel,* or rice table, originated as the Dutch colonists' version of the basic Indonesian way of eating. Using Indonesian servants to present the food, the Dutch made a banquet out of the Indonesian approach to everyday eating. With a great number of preparations as a goal and each dish brought in by a different servant, it is easy to see why the Indonesians considered the *rijsttafel* a degrading extension of their approach to food.)

Indonesian food is always well seasoned but not always spicy. Stock the pantry with hot peppers, coconuts, and peanuts; plan on using garlic, shallots, ginger root, scallions, soy sauce, cinnamon, cloves, and other spices; and be prepared for more unusual ingredients such as lemon grass and tamarind. Tea can be served with Indonesian meals, but "java" (from the Indonesian island of the same name), or coffee, is considered more the national beverage.

THE PHILIPPINES

On the map, from the Indonesian Islands to the Philippine Islands looks like a short hop to the north, but from a cook's point of view the two countries might as well be on opposite sides of the globe. Spanish, American, Chinese, and native influences are reflected in the Philippine cuisine, which features sour and salty tastes, lots of garlic and onions, and the cooking of many foods together. A typical main dish will consist of chicken and pork or fish, often cooked with vegetables and noodles, then served with rice. As with many other cuisines, one can duplicate the Filipino taste in the kosher home by using appropriate cooking methods and seasonings while substituting beef for pork and avoiding combinations of meat and fish in the same preparation.

KOREA

Heading north toward mainland China once again, we reach Korea, whose northern frontier borders northeast China. The Chinese influence on Korean cuisine is clear: soy sauce, garlic, and scallions are among the most important seasonings; *wontons* (page 195) and various dumplings are commonly served; and the basic Korean meal is rice (what else?), a soup, and small servings of other dishes (mainly vegetable, sometimes fish). When affordable, beef is the meat served. And Korean meals *always* include a pungent pickled vegetable called *kimchee*, page 209. (You can tell you're in a Korean household by the powerful aroma of the *kimchee*.) Sesame seeds, appearing more and more in Chinese-American restaurant preparations (in sesame-beef dishes, for example), are actually an important ingredient in numerous Korean preparations, including the famous Korean barbecue (page 212).

JAPAN

The Chinese influence is apparent in Japanese cuisine as well. Noodles found their way from China to Japan, and noodles are commonly served as lunch and as a snack. Rice is served at most other meals—in fact, the Japanese word *gohan* means both "cooked rice" and "meal." Each diner must have a rice bowl. Remember, when you have Japanese guests, to serve rice in individual bowls so you won't offend them. Both *tofu* and fish are important protein sources in the Japanese diet.

As in China, balance and harmony are pervasive in the culture of Japan, extending even to the preparation and serving of food. Every Japanese dish is classified according to one of twelve methods of preparation. For example, *yakimono* refers to grilled foods and *sunomono* to vinegared dishes. A balanced meal is created by selecting a number of preparations from the categories, but never more than one dish from each category. Simplicity is a key to Japanese cookery, and the cook is not encouraged to be creative or inventive. Artful presentation, however, is a must.

186 ° ASIA AND THE PACIFIC ISLANDS

HAWAII

Far to the east and slightly south of Japan are the Hawaiian Islands, the population of which is comprised largely of Japanese, Tahitians, Chinese, Portuguese, Koreans, Filipinos, and people from the American mainland. All of these groups are represented in the cuisine of Hawaii, and Hawaiian cookbooks, menus, and everyday meals include delicacies ranging from Korean meatballs to Chinese chicken wings. Sweet-and-sour dishes and soy sauce marinades play an important role in Hawaiian cuisine.

Think Hawaii and you probably think pineapples. Chicken and pineapple, chicken *in* pineapple shells, pineapple appetizers, pineapple desserts—all these are indeed part of Hawaiian cuisine, especially as presented in mainland Hawaiian restaurants. Coconuts grow and are eaten all over the Pacific and throughout much of Asia (they float, hit land, and grow), and Hawaii is no exception. Coconuts are eaten fresh, grated for recipes, combined with water for coconut "milk," and even the shells are used as unique serving bowls. But perhaps the best-known Hawaiian plant is the taro plant, the starchy root that gets mashed into *poi* (page 258), the infamous paste eaten by natives at every festive occasion. The taro root may also be prepared as a potato-like vegetable or used as a thickener. Taro leaves are served as a vegetable, or they may be used for wrapping foods to be baked, steamed, or broiled.

TAHITI

Although some Hawaiian cooking remains "unspoiled" by other cultural influences, it is to Tahiti that we turn for a look at pure, unadulterated Pacific Island cuisine. On parts of the island, hot stones are still used to bake foods or boil water. Tropical leaves of the banana, ti, and taro plants are used to wrap fish and vegetables. Because in most preparations little or no seasonings are used, spicy and pronounced tastes are usually absent from Tahitian preparations. If you're on a low-salt, low-sugar diet, discover Tahitian cooking.

Appetizers and Soups

Even though in most Asian countries appetizers are served along with the rest of the meal rather than as a first course, the wonderful tidbits presented here can be served as appetizers in the traditional sense, either with cocktails or at the dinner table. The festive meals of Hawaii and Tahiti do have courses, and three appetizers from these Pacific islands appear in this section under their native names.

In some Asian cultures—especially China, Japan, and Vietnam—soups are an essential part of meals. The Chinese eat a thick porridge-like soup *(congee)* for breakfast and snacks, the Japanese consume a soybean soup *(miso* soup, page 199) at most meals, and in northern Vietnam a cellophane noodle and beef soup called *pho* is the standard lunch. Quite the opposite is true in India, where soup is not featured at meals or as a snack.

In this section, three of the most important everyday soups of China and Japan are included. While the Japanese *dashi* (page 198) is used as an ingredient in other recipes, the *wonton* (page 197) and *miso* soups are tasty new ways to start off meals with a foreign flavor.

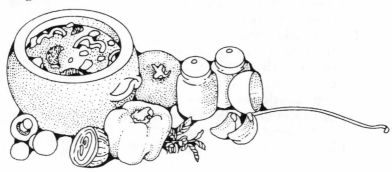

SPICY VEGETABLE FRITTERS
Pakoras

India

Serves 6

Pakoras, known as *bhajia* in some parts of India, are my favorite way of cooking eggplant. The crust has a marvelous blend of spices, and the few minutes of cooking leaves the vegetable as tender as can be. Cauliflower, onions, and green peppers are also particularly good with this batter.

These vegetable fritters of India are related to Japan's *tempura* (page 237), but the *pakora* batter is considerably heavier and much more tasty. While chickpea flour is the more authentic flour to use, it is sometimes difficult to find, and regular white flour is an acceptable alternative. Because it is difficult to distribute small quantities of minced onion and garlic in a large quantity of batter, onion and garlic powders are used here.

> 2 cups unsifted chickpea flour or all-purpose
> flour
> 2 teaspoons double-acting baking powder
> 1 teaspoon salt
> 1 teaspoon sugar
> 1 teaspoon ground coriander
> ½ teaspoon ground turmeric
> ½ teaspoon onion powder
> ¼ teaspoon garlic powder
> ¼ teaspoon crushed dried red pepper
> ¼ teaspoon mustard seeds
> ¼ teaspoon ground ginger
> ¼ teaspoon ground cloves
> 1½ cups cold water
> Oil for deep-frying
> 1 medium-size eggplant (1 pound), peeled and
> cut into strips ⅛ x ⅛ x 2 inches
> 1 cup cauliflower florets
> 1 Spanish onion, sliced into ¼-inch rounds
> and separated into rings
> 1 large green pepper, sliced into ¼-inch rings

In a large mixing bowl, combine the flour with the baking powder, salt, sugar, and all the spices. Mix well with a fork or spoon, then blend in the water. The batter will be smooth and very thick.

In an electric skillet, deep fryer, or a pot at least 4 inches deep, heat a minimum of 1½ inches of oil to 375 degrees F. The oil should be hot but not yet smoking. If it is too hot, the batter will brown before the vegetables cook through.

Cook one kind of vegetable at a time. Drop pieces of the vegetable into the batter, coating completely. Carefully put the coated vegetable pieces into the oil. Cook until brown on one side, then turn to cook the other side. (The eggplant and cauliflower pieces may turn themselves.) Drain well on paper towels, and serve immediately. If you find that the vegetables are not tender, reduce the heat slightly so the fritters cook longer before browning. If the crust is not crisp, raise the heat.

FRIED CHICKEN NUGGETS
Sheng Zha Qu Gu Ji

China

Serves 6 to 10

If you pay attention to television commercials, you know about the competition between two fast-food chains over their boneless chicken nuggets. I was told by a five-year-old expert, that these compare favorably with both. And well they should. Tender, juicy chunks of boneless chicken are encased in a crisp, golden brown crust. The chicken can be served plain or with fresh fruit duck sauce (page 207) and Chinese mustard as dips. To use this chicken for a main dish, mix the hot chicken pieces with any stir-fried vegetables you like.

> **1 pound chicken meat (breasts, thighs, or a**
> **combination)**
> **1 egg (graded large)**
> **¼ cup water**
> **½ cup unsifted all-purpose flour**

Recipe continues on the following page . . .

½ **teaspoon salt**
½ **teaspoon double-acting baking powder**
½ **teaspoon vegetable oil**
  Oil for frying

Trim off all the fat from the chicken, then cut the chicken into 1-inch squares. Set aside. To make the batter, in a medium-size mixing bowl beat the egg. With a fork, beat in the water, then beat in the flour until the mixture is smooth. Stir in the salt, baking powder, and the ½ teaspoon of oil. Add a little water if the batter is too thick or heavy; add flour if the batter is thin and runny. The batter can be prepared a day ahead and refrigerated.

To fry the chicken, in a wok, deep fryer, or 10-inch skillet heat at least ½ inch of oil to 375 degrees F. Mix the chicken pieces with the batter, coating the chicken completely on all sides. Carefully drop the coated chicken pieces one at a time into the oil, making sure they do not touch each other—if the pieces stick together, you will end up with a giant chicken pancake. Fry the chicken pieces until golden brown on one side, then turn them over and fry the other side. Drain well on paper towels and serve immediately while still hot and crisp.

BROILED MARINATED CHICKEN
Tikka Murg

India

Serves 6

A thick spicy marinade clings to chunks of boneless chicken when it is broiled, so you get to really taste the wonderful blend that coats the chicken. Fourteen ingredients go into the marinade, but the blender does all the work.

This recipe requires no kosher adaptation and could have come from India's viable community of about 6,000 Jews, known as Bene Israel, living in Bombay. Another 1,000 Jews live in other parts of India, most notably in Cochin, where about 200 remain out of a once-thriving community of over 2,500.

> 2 whole chicken breasts (1 pound each),
>   skinned and boned
> ¼ cup vegetable oil
> 3 tablespoons red wine vinegar
> ½ cup chopped onion
> 10 cloves garlic, chopped
> 1 tablespoon chopped fresh ginger root
> 2 teaspoons ground cumin
> 1½ teaspoons ground coriander
> ½ teaspoon ground cinnamon
> Seeds from 6 cardamom pods
> 6 whole cloves
> 12 black peppercorns
> ½ teaspoon ground cayenne pepper
> 1 teaspoon salt
> 2 tablespoons tomato sauce

Cut the chicken meat into strips approximately 1 x 2 inches. You will get 5 or 6 strips from each breast half.

In an electric blender or a food processor, in the order listed, place all the ingredients except the chicken. Process on high until the ingredients blend into a paste. Scrape out the marinade into a bowl big enough to hold the chicken and the marinade. Combine the chicken and marinade, mixing well. Allow the chicken to stand at room temperature for no longer than 1 hour (less if it is a hot day), then refrigerate for up to 24 hours. Stir the chicken at least once during this period.

To cook, line a baking pan with aluminum foil. Lay the chicken pieces on the foil in one layer, sides not touching. The marinade should cling to the chicken. Preheat the broiler, and broil the chicken a few inches from the heat for 5 to 10 minutes, until it is lightly browned and a little darker in spots. Turn over each piece of chicken to brown the other side. Watch the chicken carefully so it doesn't burn. Serve hot, speared with toothpicks. No additional dip or sauce is needed.

Variation:

For grilled kebobs, skewer the chicken, leaving a little space between each piece. Cook over hot coals for 10 to 15 minutes, turning as necessary so the chicken browns without burning.

SMOKED "SPARERIBS"
Xun Pai

China

Serves 6

In this version of spareribs from Peking, lamb or veal breast that has first been simmered in a black bean and garlic sauce is steamed over brown sugar and tea leaves. The meat has a deep brown color and a smoky flavor that has the definite taste of tea. If you use lamb, the meat itself will have a strong taste; veal is much more delicate, and the smoky tea taste will be stronger if veal is used.

> **1 recipe "Spareribs" in Black Bean Sauce**
> **(page 225), hot or cold**
> **½ cup firmly packed brown sugar**
> **½ cup tea leaves**
> **1 tablespoon sesame oil**

Cover the bottom of a large, heavy pot completely with aluminum foil. (The foil is absolutely necessary unless you want a big mess to clean up.) Sprinkle the brown sugar and tea leaves over the foil. Place the precooked lamb or veal on a wire rack or a steamer tray with large holes; set the rack over the foil. Cover the pot tightly, and set the pot over moderately high heat. Do not use a red-hot burner. The temperature must be high enough to caramelize the sugar and create smoke, but not so high that the pot burns. When you begin to smell the sugar, quickly lift the lid and check to see if there is smoke. If there is, the heat is high enough. If the sugar is becoming black and crusty, the temperature is too high. Smoke the meat for 15 minutes, then turn off the burner but leave the meat in the covered pot on the turned-off burner for an additional 15 minutes. Brush the ribs all over with the sesame oil and serve.

RUMAKI

Hawaii

Serves 6 to 8

This Polynesian *hors d'oeuvre* is traditionally made of chicken livers marinated in a sweetened ginger-flavored soy sauce then wrapped, along with a slice of water chestnut, in bacon and broiled or grilled. Pastrami is used here in place of the bacon. The *rumaki* are soft, crisp, and chewy, at once sweet and salty. If you like chicken livers, you'll surely enjoy *rumaki*.

> 1 pound chicken livers
> ⅓ cup Japanese soy sauce
> 2 thin slices ginger root
> 1 tablespoon sugar
> 15 water chestnuts, approximately, sliced crosswise
> ½ pound pastrami, *not* too lean

Broil the chicken livers, then cut each into 2 or 3 small pieces, discarding any membranes and fat. In a small bowl combine the soy sauce, ginger root, and sugar. Marinate the broiled livers in this mixture for 15 to 30 minutes.

Cut the pastrami lengthwise into strips. Wrap each pastrami strip around a piece of chicken liver and a water chestnut slice. Refrigerate until serving time. Just before serving, broil the *rumaki* a few inches from the heat for about 5 minutes, until the pastrami is sizzling all over. It is not necessary to turn the *rumaki*. Spear with toothpicks and serve.

LOMI LOMI SALMON

Hawaii

Serves 6

The Hawaiian word *lomi* means "massage," but don't get your hopes up—it's the salmon that gets the massage, not you.

Recipe continues on the following page . . .

Traditional *lomi lomi* is made from salted (but not smoked) salmon, soaked to remove some of the salt then rubbed between the fingers (the first *lomi*). The salmon is then tossed with chopped tomatoes, scallions, and crushed ice (the second *lomi*).

Traditional *lomi lomi* is served as one of the dishes at a *luau*. The recipe here, a variation on the traditional one, uses smoked salmon. Served on a bed of lettuce, it makes a wonderful first course for any special meal. And if you like lox spreads, try this on bagels.

> ½ **pound smoked salmon (salted lox or Nova**
> **Scotia), diced**
> 1 **pound ripe red tomatoes, diced**
> ¼ **cup chopped scallions (white and crisp**
> **green parts)**
> ¼ **cup finely chopped onion**
> **Salt to taste**
> ½ **cup crushed ice**

In a medium-size bowl, combine the chopped salmon, tomatoes, scallions, and onion. Using your fingers, mix well, breaking up the lox into smaller bits. Refrigerate until serving time. Just before serving, mix with the crushed ice. Or, if you prefer, refrigerate the mixture (without the ice) until it is well chilled, and serve it on a bed of lettuce, preferably set on crushed ice.

FISH MARINATED IN LIME
Poisson Cru

Tahiti

Serves 6

It's like magic. Fish marinated in lime juice turns opaque just as though it were cooked by heat—and the fish *tastes* cooked as well. In the Tahitian version, coconut cream is poured over the fish just before it is served. The final preparation looks a bit like herring in cream sauce, and while the consistency is similar to pickled herring, the taste is more delicate.

If you prefer to avoid the cholesterol of coconut oil, omit the coconut cream and garnish the fish with chopped tomatoes and green peppers. (And if you add jalapeño peppers to the tomato and pepper garnish, you will be serving Mexico's *seviche*.)

1 pound very fresh fillets of flounder or sole
1 cup fresh lime juice (about 6 limes)
4 scallions, chopped (white and crisp green
**   parts)**
¾ cup Coconut Cream (page 205)
Optional garnishes: cherry tomatoes and
**   green pepper strips or rounds, or chopped**
**   tomatoes and peppers**

Rinse the fish under cold water, then cut it into 1-inch squares. Place the fish in a bowl, cover it with the fresh lime juice, and allow it to marinate for about 2 hours. Gently stir the fish and juice from time to time. Refrigerate the fish when it turns white and looks cooked. Or, marinate the fish in the refrigerator for about 6 hours.

Just before serving, drain off the juice, mix in the scallions, and pour the coconut cream over the fish. Garnish as desired. Spear with toothpicks to serve.

FRIED WONTONS
Zha Hun Tun

China

Makes 32 wontons

Until recently I used different recipes for soup *wontons* and fried *wontons*. Then, after our sisterhood's annual Chinese banquet a few years back, we found ourselves with a whole bag of thawed, uncooked soup *wontons* but no chicken broth handy to

Recipe continues on the following page . . .

cook them in. We decided to fry them and found that the filling not only cooked through perfectly but was juicier than a pre-cooked ground beef filling. So make the filling, shape the *wontons*, and take your pick—appetizer or soup.

½ **pound minced beef**
2 **tablespoons chicken broth or water**
1 **teaspoon vegetable oil**
1 **tablespoon soy sauce**
1 **tablespoon rice wine or dry sherry**
2 **tablespoons chopped scallions (white and**
  crisp green parts)
1 **tablespoon cornstarch**
½ **teaspoon salt (optional)**
½ **teaspoon sugar**
32 **wonton wrappers**
  Oil for frying

Mix together the ingredients for the filling. Use a fork or your fingers to distribute all the ingredients evenly.

Working with only 6 to 8 wrappers at a time (keep the remainder covered with a clean kitchen towel so they do not dry out), place a rounded teaspoonful of filling just off-center on each square. Brush the edges of the wrapper lightly with water or beaten egg, then fold the dough over the filling to form a triangle. Press together the edges of the dough to firmly enclose the filling. Now bring the tips of the long edge of the triangle back to meet behind the folded edge, gently stretching the dough. Pinch together the tips of the dough. Repeat with the remaining squares of dough and filling. If desired, freeze the *wontons* on a tray lined with wax paper, then transfer them to a freezer bag or container.

A 12-inch electric skillet is ideal for frying *wontons* because as many as 20 can be fried at once, but any deep fryer, wok, or pot with sides at least 3 inches high can be used. The *wontons* will cook well in as little as ½ inch of oil, or you may use more. Heat the oil to 375 to 400 degrees F. Carefully add the *wontons* one at a time so they do not touch each other. Fry them until golden all over, turning as necessary. Drain well on paper towels. Serve the fried *wontons* with fresh fruit duck sauce (page 207), Chinese mustard, or any condiment of your choice.

WONTON SOUP
Hun Tun Tang

China

Serves 6

In China, *wontons* are invariably filled with pork. *Wonton* soup may appear on the table with other dishes, or it may be a complete luncheon meal in which as many as a dozen *wontons* are served in a small amount of broth. Garnishes of cooked greens, chopped scallions, and ham are used in China. In the kosher home, beef is used in place of the pork and ham. *Kreplach* dough can be used for the *wonton* wrappers, and certified kosher *wonton* wrappers may be purchased in some large cities.

> **32 uncooked wontons from Fried Wontons (page 195)**
> **3 quarts chicken broth**
> **Soy sauce or salt**
> **Garnishes: chopped scallions; diagonally-cut strips of Chinese cabbage; bite-size pieces of fresh spinach, washed thoroughly; diced cooked chicken or beef; thinly sliced fresh mushrooms; sliced water chestnuts; dried Chinese mushrooms, soaked in hot water then sliced**

If you are using a homemade dough, roll out the dough as usual and cut it into 3-inch squares. Wrap the *wontons* as directed on page 196.

To cook the wontons, in a 5- or 6-quart pot bring the 3 quarts of chicken broth to the boil. Carefully drop in the *wontons* and cook them for 4 to 7 minutes, until the dough is tender. (Frozen *wontons* may take a little longer.) Season the soup to taste with soy sauce or salt. Pour the *wonton* soup into a tureen, garnish as desired, and serve.

JAPANESE SOUP STOCK
Dashi

Japan

Makes 1 quart

If you intend to get serious about Japanese cooking, let me introduce you to *dashi*, the base used for most Japanese soups and some seasonings. (Chicken broth flavored with ginger root is also used in Japan, but it does not have the smoky taste associated with *dashi*.)

Made from dried seaweed and dried bonito flakes, *dashi* is sweet and smoky but bland. Bonito, related to the tuna, is a fish that can be used in the kosher kitchen, but the packaged dried flakes are not certified kosher, so for the one-half to three-quarter cup of bonito flakes usually used in making *dashi*, the skin of smoked whitefish is used in this recipe. For meat dishes, use a vegetarian broth with the seaweed, and omit the white-fish skin. The seaweed sees a double use in Japanese kitchens, for after it flavors the *dashi* it is cut into pieces and used as a vegetable in other dishes.

1 piece dried seaweed, 4 x 8 inches
4 cups cold water
Skin of ½ pound smoked whitefish, rinsed
    under cold water

In a 2-quart pot, combine the seaweed and water. Cover the pot, bring the water to the boil over high heat, remove the pot from the heat, and immediately remove the softened seaweed. The water will now have a slightly sweet, salty, smoky, and faint vegetable taste. Add the smoked whitefish skin, and allow the skin to remain in the soup for 2 minutes. Remove the whitefish skin. Line a colander or strainer with paper towels, set the colander or strainer over a bowl, and strain the broth through the paper towels. Refrigerate for up to 3 days. Freezing is not recommended because the delicate taste of the stock may be lost.

BEAN PASTE SOUP
Misoshiru

Japan

Makes 1 quart

Miso, a red paste made from fermented soybeans, is added to *dashi* to a make a flavorful soup served by Japanese at breakfast and at other meals. The bean paste both thickens the broth and gives it a lovely reddish-brown hue. *Miso* is very salty, so add a tablespoon at a time, and taste after each addition.

> **4 cups Dashi (see previous recipe)**
> **2 to 4 tablespoons miso, to taste**
> **Optional: ½ cup tofu cubes (¼-inch cubes)**

In a 2-quart pot, heat the *dashi* to boiling, then reduce to a simmer. In a small bowl, stir the *miso* with a fork until smooth. Blend the *miso* into the soup a tablespoon at a time, tasting after each addition. Add the *tofu* cubes and serve. The *miso* has a tendency to separate and give the soup a curdled appearance, so stir the soup just before serving.

Condiments
and Sauces

With spices and seasonings so important in cuisines of the Orient, it is no wonder that seeing a certain condiment on the dinner table or slowly scenting the delectable aroma of a sauce will tell you which country's food is on the menu tonight. When you get good at it, you will even be able to tell the difference between a Japanese and a Chinese soy sauce, or identify one of the sweet soys of Indonesia.

Four homemade condiments you'll want to serve with your ethnic meals are in this section, along with the curry pastes that are the backbone of many Thai preparations and the coconut milk and cream used throughout Asia and the Pacific. We begin with a famous spice mixture of India.

INDIAN SPICE BLEND
Garam Masala

India

Makes ¼ cup

Garam masala, a blend of ground "hot" spices, is called for in many Indian recipes. Turmeric, which gives a yellow color to many Indian preparations, is *not* included here, so the mixture will not look like any of the prepared curry powders you may have seen. *Garam masala*, made simply by combining ground spices or by grinding whole spices, can be purchased in Indian food stores. In this recipe, whole spices are roasted in a very slow oven before they are ground. This has two advantages: your kitchen will have a wonderful smell and the spices will dry out a bit, increasing the shelf life of the blend.

> **1 cinnamon stick (3 inches)**
> **1 tablespoon whole cardamom pods (about 30)**
> **10 whole cloves**
> **1 tablespoon whole coriander seeds**
> **1 tablespoon whole cumin seeds**
> **1 tablespoon black peppercorns**

Preheat the oven to 200 degrees F. Place all the spices in a baking pan in one layer. Roast for 30 minutes, stirring the spices around every 10 minutes. If they begin to darken, remove them from the oven.

Place the cinnamon stick between 2 sheets of wax paper, and crush it with a rolling pin. Remove the cardamom seeds from the pods, discarding the pods. (Slit open the pods with your fingernail or a small sharp knife, and dislodge the seeds with your nail or the knife.) Using a mortar and pestle, a spice grinder, or a blender, grind all the spices together to make a powder. Store the *garam masala* in an airtight jar at room temperature. It will retain its power for several months.

HOT GREEN CURRY PASTE
Krung Gaeng Keo Wan

Thailand

Makes about ½ cup

The aroma of this mixture is heavenly even before it is cooked—sometimes I actually take it out of the refrigerator just for a whiff. Nearly a dozen ingredients go into the recipe, but once prepared it will keep in the refrigerator for weeks. The lemon grass, *laos*, hot peppers, and shallots are among the ingredients in this curry paste that make it characteristic of Thai cookery. Lemon grass gives off an aromatic lemony flavor

Recipe continues on the following page . . .

and is enhanced by the fresh, fruity presence of lime peel. *Laos* will remind you of ginger root, but it is not nearly so strong. Coriander leaves are listed as an optional ingredient because their peculiar pungency is not appreciated by everyone.

Thai curries are identified by color, and the pastes that are used to season meat, poultry, and fish dishes may be very similar, with variations in one or two ingredients changing the color of the whole paste. This green paste, for example, can be made into a red paste by substituting hot red chili peppers for the green, omitting the coriander leaves, and using lemon peel instead of the lime.

1 or 2 stalks lemon grass, fresh or dried
3 pieces dried laos or 1 teaspoon
powdered laos
Boiling water
6 fresh hot green chili peppers (serrano
or jalapeño)
3 tablespoons minced shallots
1 tablespoon minced garlic
¼ cup minced fresh coriander leaves (optional)
¼ teaspoon freshly ground black pepper
1 teaspoon caraway seeds
1 teaspoon coriander seeds
1 teaspoon grated lime peel
¼ cup vegetable oil

If using dried lemon grass, soak it in boiling water for 30 minutes, until softened. For both fresh and dried lemon grass, cut off the root end and the top where the "leaves" begin to separate, and peel off any tough outer layers. Now chop the remaining stalk coarsely.

Soak the dried *laos* in boiling water for 15 to 20 minutes, then drain well and chop fine. (Powdered *laos* is used as is.)

Slice the hot peppers in half, discarding the stems, membranes, and most of the seeds. The more seeds you use, the hotter the curry paste. Chop the peppers coarsely. Now wash your hands thoroughly to rid them of the caustic pepper oils.

Place all the ingredients in a blender and process them to a paste, turning off the motor and scraping down the sides as necessary. Transfer the curry paste to a small jar and place in the refrigerator, where it will keep for 3 or 4 weeks. Use it in recipes from Thailand that call for a hot green curry paste.

The more authenic method for making the paste is to use a mortar and pestle to mash the ingredients. First grind the caraway and coriander seeds in a spice grinder, or pulverize them with the mortar and pestle and set them aside. Place the chopped green peppers in the mortar, grind them to a paste, then grind in the shallots and garlic, then the *laos*, lemon grass, and the fresh coriander. Work in the black pepper, caraway and coriander seeds, and the lime peel. Now add one tablespoon of oil at a time, grinding until the paste is blended well.

COCONUT MILK

Hawaii, India, Indonesia, Philippines, Tahiti, Thailand, Vietnam

Makes about 3 cups

Coconut "milk" is made by steeping freshly grated coconut in boiling water then straining out the coconut shreds. Although milk can be used instead of water, it is certainly not mandatory, and coconut milk made with water may of course be used in meat dishes and with meat meals. The proportions here of one cup of water to one cup of chopped coconut produce a good coconut flavor, and the recipes in this book were tested with this one-to-one ratio.

Select a heavy uncracked coconut and shake it. If you don't hear liquid sloshing around, that signifies that the coconut is old and dry—don't buy it. The liquid, which is thin and sweet with a mild coconut flavor, is known as coconut water. Some people like to drink it as a beverage. I use the coconut water as part of the water called for in making coconut milk.

Recipe continues on the following page . . .

1 medium-large coconut (about 8 inches long)
Coconut water reserved from the fresh coco-
nut, plus water
Cheesecloth for straining (available in
supermarkets and housewares stores)

Opening the Coconut:

The most difficult part of making coconut milk is cracking open the coconut and getting out the meat. Unless you have a monkey who likes to climb palm trees, you'll need a sharp tool such as a screwdriver or an ice pick (my husband uses a drill) to puncture two of the three "eyes" at one end of the coconut. Drain *all* of the coconut water into a cup or bowl, and reserve this liquid for later use.

Preheat the oven to 400 degrees F. Place the drained coconut in the oven for about 15 minutes. (The coconut *must* be drained or it can explode.) This will make it easier to remove the meat from the shell once the coconut is opened. Cool to room temperature.

Using the broad side of a large heavy knife or a cleaver, rap the drained baked coconut sharply all around the circumference. Eventually a crack will develop around a "fault line" on the circumference, and the coconut will be easy to split open. If necessary, use a hammer and chisel to pry open the cracked coconut. An alternative method of cracking open a coconut is to place the drained coconut in a vise, then squeeze it until it breaks open.

Pry the coconut out of the shell with a knife or a chisel. Use a vegetable peeler to peel off the thin brown layer that is edible but not attractive in coconut milk. Rinse off the coconut pieces. If you will not be using the coconut immediately, place in a bowl or container, cover the coconut pieces completely with water, and refrigerate.

Making the Coconut Milk:

Chop the coconut coarsely. Measure the chopped coconut. This will be the amount of liquid you use in making the coconut milk, and will probably be at least 2 cups. Measure the coconut water reserved from the coconut, then add enough water to equal the amount of liquid you need. Or use plain water only for the liquid.

In a 1-quart pot, bring the liquid just to the boil. In a blender or a food processor, place half the chopped coconut. Pour half the liquid into the blender or processor. Process the coconut and water on a high speed until the coconut is in the smallest pieces possible. Pour the mixture into a large bowl, then repeat the process with the remaining coconut and water. Combine the two batches in the large bowl, and set aside the mixture for about 45 minutes. (If you do not have a blender or food processor, grate the coconut by hand, then pour the boiling water over the coconut and let stand.)

Line a colander or strainer with a double layer of cheesecloth, and set the colander or strainer over a large pot or bowl. Carefully pour the coconut mixture into the cheesecloth-lined colander or strainer, pressing out the liquid with the back of a spoon. Now draw together the 4 ends of the cheesecloth, making a ball around the coconut. Use your hands to squeeze out *all* the excess liquid. You should end up with 3 cups of coconut milk.

If you do not have quite enough for a recipe, mix a little more boiling water with the coconut shreds, steep for 30 minutes, and strain.

Coconut milk will keep a few days in the refrigerator, and it can be frozen.

Note: Unsweetened shredded coconut, available in health food stores, can be used. However, a slightly thinner coconut milk will result, so use 2 cups of coconut to 1 cup of water.

COCONUT CREAM

Hawaii, India, Indonesia, Philippines,
Tahiti, Thailand, Vietnam

Makes about 1 cup

Coconut cream is the thick white "cream" that rises to the top when coconut milk is allowed to stand. It contains the

Recipe continues on the following page . . .

coconut oil that is used as a cooking oil in some countries. It is also used to enrich gravies, and it is an all-natural nondairy substitute for heavy cream on desserts.

1 recipe Coconut Milk (from above)

Pour the coconut milk into one or two jars. Cover and refrigerate for at least an hour. A thick white "cream" will rise to the top, leaving a more watery layer on the bottom. (For some, this will bring back memories of nonhomogenized milk.) Spoon off the amount of cream you need for a recipe. The remaining coconut milk will be thin, but it can still be used to flavor gravies.

FRESH FRUIT CHUTNEY
Chatni

India

Makes about 3 cups

Indian meals always contain a condiment—from something as simple as a hot pepper or an onion sprinkled with lemon juice to a preparation as elaborate as a fruit chutney prepared with a dozen or more ingredients. Chutneys, of which there are many kinds, generally are made from a combination of fruits and aromatic herbs and spices. Here is a recipe for a thick fruit chutney, sweet and spicy, made from apples, nectarines or peaches, plums, and raisins. The ginger root and vinegar contribute a pungency.

½ **pound green cooking apples**
½ **pound nectarines or peaches**
½ **pound plums, variety of your choice**
½ **cup light or dark raisins**
1 **to 3 slices (⅛ inch thick) ginger root**
2 **cloves garlic, minced**
¼ **cup firmly packed light or dark brown sugar**
½ **teaspoon each ground cumin and coriander**

¼ teaspoon each ground cloves, cinnamon,
   and cardamom
Dash to 1 teaspoon ground cayenne pepper
½ cup distilled white vinegar

Core the apples and remove the pits from the nectarines and
plums, but do not peel the fruit. Cut the fruit into 1-inch
chunks. In a 2- or 3-quart pot, combine all the ingredients. Bring
to the boil, reduce the heat to a gentle boil, and cook, covered,
for 1 hour, stirring occasionally. When the fruit is tender and
the mixture is thickened, the chutney is ready. If there is too
much liquid, remove the cover and boil away some of the liquid,
taking care not to burn the fruit. Remove the ginger root before
serving. Serve hot, warm, or chilled. Leftovers will keep in the
refrigerator for at least a week. Although the chutney can be
frozen, there may be changes in the consistency.

FRESH FRUIT DUCK SAUCE
Tao Xing Li Jiang

China

Makes 1½ cups

Duck sauce has been popularized so much by Cantonese
Chinese-American restaurants that it is available in most
supermarkets. At least one national brand is kosher, but you
still may want to make your own duck sauce with fresh fruit,
because it will be tastier than anything you can buy. Incidentally, there's no duck in duck sauce—it was originally used as a
sauce for duck, hence the name.

1 pound mixture of fresh peaches and
   apricots
1 cup water
1 tablespoon sugar
1 tablespoon light corn syrup
1 tablespoon distilled white vinegar
1 slice (⅛ inch thick) ginger root

Recipe continues on the following page . . .

Cut the unpeeled fruit into chunks, discarding the pits. In a 2-quart pot, combine the peaches and apricots with the water. Bring to the boil, mix in the remaining ingredients, and boil for 1 minute, stirring constantly. Reduce the heat to low, cover the pot, and simmer the fruit for 15 to 20 minutes, until tender. Stir the mixture occasionally, making sure it doesn't stick to the bottom of the pot. Add a little water as necessary to prevent sticking. When the fruit is nice and soft, remove the cover and cook until the mixture is thick, stirring to prevent sticking. Remove the piece of ginger root, and chill the duck sauce before serving. Refrigerate leftovers.

ONION AND TOMATO RELISH
Cachumbar

India

Makes about 3 cups

This hot relish will perk up your appetite, bring tears to your eyes, and maybe even clear out your sinuses. For an even sharper relish, omit the tomatoes. Serve the condiment with any Indian meal.

> **1 teaspoon cumin seeds**
> **1 pound ripe red tomatoes, chopped**
> **2 cups chopped onion**
> **2 tablespoons fresh lemon juice**
> **Dash of ground cayenne pepper**
> **Salt and freshly ground black pepper**

In a small cast-iron skillet, heat the cumin seeds over moderate heat for 2 to 3 minutes, until they begin to darken. Shake the pan to prevent sticking or burning. Remove the pan from the heat. Grind the seeds in a mortar and pestle, or place them between 2 sheets of wax paper and crush them with a rolling pin.

In a medium-size bowl, combine the tomatoes, onion, cumin seeds, lemon juice, and cayenne. Add salt and pepper to taste. Refrigerate until serving.

KOREAN PICKLED VEGETABLES
Kimchee

Korea

Makes 2 cups

No Korean dinner is complete without one or two pickled vegetables known as *kimchee. Kimchee* serves as both a relish and a vegetable and is used as a way of preserving vegetables following a short growing season. The turnip *kimchee* is strong, pungent, and salty. Not everyone finds it palatable at first, but it is a good representative of *kimchee*. The cucumber *kimchee* is closer to the kinds of pickles found on Western tables.

TURNIP PICKLES
Moo Kimchee

> 2½ cups grated turnip
> 1 tablespoon salt
> 1 teaspoon minced ginger root
> ½ teaspoon sugar
> 2 dried red chili peppers, minced
> ½ cup water mixed with ¼ teaspoon salt

In a medium-size bowl, combine the grated turnip and 1 tablespoon salt. Cover with plastic wrap and allow to stand overnight. The next day, mix in the ginger root, sugar, and chili peppers. Pack the turnip mixture into a 1-pint jar, and pour in enough salted water to cover the turnips. Leave an inch headspace in the jar. Close the jar, but not too tightly. Set the jar in a bowl or in the kitchen sink. As the turnips ferment, the liquid expands and may seep out over the top. From time to time, stir the turnips to allow gas bubbles to rise to the top. Allow the turnips to stand at room temperature for 3 to 4 days in hot weather, twice as long when it is cold. Close the jar securely and refrigerate. The turnip *kimchee* can be served at any time and will keep in the refrigerator for many weeks.

CUCUMBER PICKLES

Oye Kimchee

2 cucumbers (7 inches long)
1 tablespoon salt
3 scallions (white and crisp green parts),
   chopped
1 teaspoon minced ginger root
2 cloves garlic, minced
1 dried red chili pepper, minced
Salt water

Wash the cucumbers, slice in half lengthwise, and scoop out the seeds. Slice in half lengthwise again, then cut the cucumbers into 1-inch pieces. In a medium-size bowl, combine the cucumbers and salt. Allow them to stand for an hour, then rinse and drain. Return the cucumbers to the bowl, and mix them well with the scallions, ginger root, garlic, and chili pepper. Cover the bowl with foil, and allow the cucumbers to ferment at room temperature for 2 days, stirring once or twice a day. In very hot weather, they will take only a day to soften and acquire a pungent odor. Pack into a 1-pint canning jar. Include any accumulated liquid. As you press down to fit in all the cucumbers, you'll squeeze out liquid which will probably cover the cucumbers completely. If the liquid does not cover the top cucumbers, add a little salted water, leaving half an inch headspace in the jar. Close the jar securely and refrigerate. The cucumber *kimchee* can be served at any time and will keep in the refrigerator for several weeks.

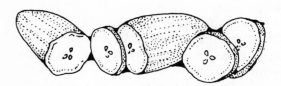

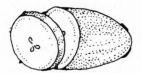

Main Dishes

"Meat" may mean brisket, steak, or veal chops to you, but the term means different things in different cultures. In China, meat most often refers to pork, and the *luaus* of Hawaii and major feasts of Tahiti center around whole roast pig. Not every Asian cuisine depends on pork, of course: in both India and Indonesia there are areas where goat is the common meat. India's Moslems are forbidden to eat pork, and the preferred meat of Korea is beef. Although Japanese eat beef, they'd rather have fish, and the most important seasoning in Vietnamese cuisine is a fish-based preparation. Shrimp paste is used in Indonesian and Thai cookery, but all kinds of fish (those with fins and scales as well as shellfish) are caught in the waters surrounding Vietnam, Indonesia, the Philippines, Tahiti, Hawaii, Korea, and Japan, and along coastal China, India, and Thailand. Home-raised chickens are eaten all over Asia and the Pacific Islands.

It is obviously necessary to adapt pork and shellfish preparations to the kosher kitchen. Veal is outstanding in the black bean sauce of China (see page 225), and anchovy paste is a practical substitution for shrimp paste. Lamb shoulder rubbed with a little garlic, soy sauce, and brown sugar, then wrapped completely in banana or ti leaves or even corn husks and roasted along with foliage-wrapped yams and plantains makes a wonderful *luau* dish. To cook lamb for a *luau*, roast the wrapped lamb, yams, and plantains in a 425-degree F. oven for 45 minutes, then reduce the heat to 350 degrees F. and continue roasting for another 2¼ hours.

But whether or not they require any kind of kosher adaptation, many dishes from Asian countries need modification to make them *main* dishes in Western homes. This is because rice is, in effect, the main dish in most Asian diets, and small portions of other dishes are served to accompany the rice. In China, for example, while many different bowls of food might be set out, no one dish stands out as the main course (except at banquets, where one elaborate, expensive dish is highlighted). Indonesian meals consist of small amounts of numerous foods, none of which can be said to be the main dish because all are important to the complete meal. And Japanese meals are known for small portions that don't always satisfy American stomachs.

A typical Asian meat preparation usually contains a lot less meat than a Westerner would expect. Authentic curries of Thailand, for example, have relatively little meat, but gravy abounds. So, in planning a meal featuring a preparation of this type, one thing to do is to increase the amount of meat in the dish. Or, some preparations can simply be doubled or tripled for use as a main dish. On the other hand, the quantities of food needed for a native Tahitian shindig may have to be cut down a bit for a backyard party in the United States. But you don't have to worry about making changes, because the recipes in this section have all been adjusted to American tastes, and usually serve 4 to 6 as the main dish.

KOREAN BARBECUE
Bul-Kogi

Korea

Serves 4 to 6

Thin beef slices coated with ground, roasted sesame seeds, scallions, and soy sauce are cooked rapidly over hot coals and are then traditionally served with rice and *kimchee* (page 209). For one of our banquets at Temple Emanuel, we made up hundreds of skewers of the beef, broiled them, and served them over fried rice noodles. They also make a wonderful appetizer as kebobs.

The *bul-kogi* marinade has become one of my favorites—it is outstanding with lamb cubes, grilled chicken, and broiled fish, and it adds a new dimension to hamburgers when it is mixed with the uncooked chopped meat.

> ½ cup sesame seeds
> 2 pounds London broil, partially frozen
> ¼ cup granulated sugar
> 1 to 2 tablespoons sesame oil
> ¼ cup soy sauce
> 4 scallions (white and crisp green parts),
> chopped
> 2 cloves garlic, minced

In a heavy 7- or 8-inch skillet, heat the sesame seeds over moderate heat until they are light brown. Shake the pan often to keep them from burning. Remove from the heat and pulverize the seeds with a mortar and pestle, or use a blender to grind them almost to a paste.

Slice the partially frozen beef on the diagonal into pieces ⅛ inch thick, then cut into 3-inch pieces. Combine the beef slices with the sesame seeds, sugar, sesame oil, soy sauce, scallions, and garlic. Mix lightly with your hands, then transfer to a bowl and allow the meat to marinate for an hour at room temperature, or as long as overnight in the refrigerator.

Preheat a charcoal grill or a broiler. Cook the beef over hot coals or under a broiler, tossing with chopsticks to cook completely. If your grill is widely spaced and the beef will fall through, place some kind of nontoxic heatproof screening on top so you can cook the meat in the authentic manner. To cook on aluminum foil, allow a few minutes extra time for the beef to cook. Use tongs, a fork, or chopsticks to turn the beef once during cooking.

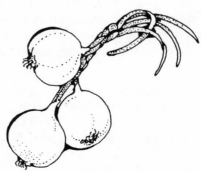

OXTAIL STEW
Kari Kari

Philippines

Serves 4 to 6

While beef neck bones are a logical substitute for the oxtail of *kari kari*, most of us non-Filipinos probably don't enjoy picking meat off bones for our protein, so boneless stewing beef is suggested here. This is considered an ordinary stew for the home table in the Philippines, but to me, when I use annatto for color, ground peanuts as a gravy enhancer, and homemade rice powder as a thickener, I'm cooking something unusual. If your preference is for bland rather than spicy foods, you'll enjoy this stew.

> 2 tablespoons vegetable oil
> 1 tablespoon annatto seeds
> 2 pounds well-trimmed stewing beef, cut into
>   1-inch cubes
> Salt
> 2 tablespoons vegetable oil
> 1 large onion, cut into paper-thin rounds
> 2 cloves garlic, minced
> 2 cups water
> ¼ cup distilled white vinegar or lemon juice
> ¼ cup salted peanuts
> ½ cup raw white rice
> 1 pound fresh green beans, tips removed, cut
>   into 1-inch pieces

In a small heavy skillet, heat the oil until it is hot but not yet smoking. Add the annatto seeds, mix to coat the seeds with oil, and cook for a minute. Remove the skillet from the heat, allow the oil to cool to room temperature, and strain out the seeds. Set the oil aside.

Sprinkle the stewing beef with salt. In a 4-quart pot, heat the remaining 2 tablespoons of oil over moderate heat. Using about a quarter of the beef at a time, brown the stewing beef in the oil. Use a slotted spoon to transfer the meat to a bowl as it browns. When all the meat is browned and removed from the pot, pour the annatto oil into the pot, then stir in the onion rounds and the garlic. They will immediately turn orange. Cook, stirring frequently, until the onion is softened but not browned. Return the browned meat to the pot, mix the onions and meat, and add the 2 cups of water and the vinegar or lemon juice. It will now look as though you poured a whole can of paprika into the pot. Bring the liquid to the boil, reduce the heat to a gentle boil, cover the pot, and cook for about 2 hours, until the meat is tender.

Meanwhile, in a blender or food processor pulverize the peanuts until the pieces are almost powdery, but don't make peanut butter. Set aside.

While the beef is cooking, in a heavy 8-inch skillet heat the rice without adding any water. Using moderately low heat, cook the rice for about 20 minutes, until it is golden brown. Shake the pan often to keep the rice from sticking and to help the rice brown evenly. Reduce the heat if the rice browns too quickly. Using a blender at high speed, pulverize the toasted rice until it is a powder. Set aside.

When the meat is tender, stir in the peanuts, then the green beans. Add water if necessary to cover the meat and beans, then bring the liquid to the boil. Regulate the heat to a gentle boil and continue cooking for 20 to 30 minutes, until the green beans are tender. Now stir in the powdered rice and cook, covered, for an additional 15 minutes. The rice will thicken the gravy, and you may need to add water to keep the thick gravy from sticking. Check the pot from time to time, stir things up, and add water as necessary. This stew can be prepared in advance and reheated.

SUKIYAKI

Japan

Serves 4 to 6

Sukiyaki is the most famous of the Japanese dishes falling under the category of *nabemono*, one-pot dinners that are braised or simmered. Although its historical antecedents may have

Recipe continues on the following page . . .

been simply chunks of boar or buffalo meat roasted over an open fire, present-day *sukiyaki* consists of an array of meat or fish and vegetables cooked at the table in a thin brown sweet-and-salty sauce.

As a Japanese preparation the ingredients are cooked in the same pot without being tossed together. Only a quarter of the ingredients are cooked at a time, ensuring quick cooking and hot food for all. A large electric skillet makes the perfect cooking pan. The table is set with chopsticks for everyone, and each person gets a bowl of rice and a bowl with a raw egg in it. Diners pick out one kind of food at a time, dip it into a beaten raw egg, mix it with a little rice, and eat.

To serve *sukiyaki* as an American dish, omit the raw eggs and toss the contents of the pan together before spooning out servings over rice. The *sukiyaki* will be a tasty combination of meat and vegetables.

> **2 pounds London broil, partially frozen then thinly sliced on a 45-degree angle and cut into 2-inch pieces**
> **1 pound tofu, cut into 1-inch cubes**
> **10 scallions (white and crisp green parts), sliced on the diagonal into 1-inch pieces**
> **1 large red onion or 1 medium-size Spanish onion, cut into thin rounds**
> **½ pound Chinese cabbage (any kind), cut into pieces 1 x 2 inches**
> **½ pound very small fresh mushrooms, whole; or larger mushrooms, thickly sliced**
> **8 large dried Chinese mushrooms, soaked in boiling water until softened then sliced into ¼-inch strips (optional)**
> **½ pound cellophane noodles, soaked in warm water until softened then cut into 2-inch pieces**
> **4 cups beef broth, chicken broth, or water**
> **1 cup Japanese soy sauce**
> **1 cup rice wine or mirin**
> **Granulated sugar**
> **1 teaspoon sesame oil or a fresh piece of beef fat**
> **6 eggs (graded large)**

Arrange the beef in 4 separate piles on one large plate. Arrange the *tofu,* scallions, onion, Chinese cabbage, fresh and dried mushrooms, and cellophane noodles attractively on four platters, keeping each vegetable in its own place. Each platter should consist of one-quarter of each ingredient. Cover and refrigerate until cooking time.

In a large bowl, combine the broth or water with the soy sauce and the rice wine or *mirin.* Have this mixture and a ladle, along with a bowl of sugar, available at the cooking table.

Just before the diners are seated, break each egg into a separate small bowl or cup. Place each bowl or cup next to each dinner plate along with a bowl of rice.

To cook, heat a large electric skillet to 350 degrees F. Dampen a piece of paper towel with the sesame oil and wipe the skillet all around with the paper towel, or wipe the skillet all around with the beef fat. Place one-quarter of the beef in the pan, sprinkle it lightly with sugar, and ladle on enough of the broth mixture to cover the beef. Now place one-quarter of each of the other ingredients on top of the beef. Cook, uncovered, for about 5 minutes, until the vegetables look partially cooked. Add a little liquid to the pan if necessary. The *sukiyaki* is eaten when the vegetables are still crisp.

While the mixture is cooking, each diner beats an egg with chopsticks. To eat, each person selects a piece of beef or vegetable or some noodles from the pan (with chopsticks), dips it into the beaten raw egg, and mixes the food with rice before eating. When the pan is emptied, the cooking procedure is repeated, although it will not be necessary to grease the pan after the first time.

Variation:

For fish *sukiyaki,* use very fresh fillets of sole or flounder, and substitute *dashi* for the beef or chicken broth.

MU SHU PANCAKES
Bao Bing

China

Makes 24 pancakes

Flexible, thin flour-and-water pancakes are flavored by a hint of sesame oil. These are the pancakes used for *mu shu* dishes and for Peking duck. They are rolled out in pairs, cooked on a griddle, then separated and steamed. They do take a while to prepare, but fortunately they can be made ahead of time and frozen.

> **2 cups unsifted all-purpose flour**
> **¾ cup boiling water**
> **1 tablespoon sesame oil, approximately**

Place the flour in a medium-size mixing bowl. Make a well in the center and pour in the boiling water. Using a wooden spoon, gradually mix together the flour and water until a soft dough is formed. The dough will seem crumbly and won't hold together at first, but soon it will become workable. As the dough cools down, use your hands for easier mixing.

Round the dough into a ball, then knead it on a smooth, lightly floured work surface for 10 minutes, until very smooth. Cover the ball of dough with a bowl or a kitchen towel and let it rest for 15 minutes, which will make rolling easier.

Divide the dough into 24 equal pieces, shape each piece into a smooth ball, then flatten each piece with the palm of your hand. Now, with a rolling pin, roll each of the 24 pieces into a 3-inch circle. Place the circles side by side in pairs and brush each one lightly with sesame oil, covering the surface completely with a thin layer of oil. Now put each pair of circles together, oiled sides together. You should now have 12 pairs of circles. Use a rolling pin to roll out each pair into a 5- or 6-inch circle. The oiled surfaces may make the pancakes slippery at first, but they will become more manageable as you continue rolling. Rotate as you roll so the circles keep their shape relatively well and so they do not stick to the work surface. If you work slowly, cover the pancakes with a towel after rolling.

Cook the pairs of pancakes on a moderately hot ungreased griddle. The cooking time is about 1 minute on each side. The pancakes will bubble slightly and get a wet look. It's okay if they brown slightly in spots, but be careful not to burn them. As each set is finished, gently separate the halves and fold each pancake in half, oiled side inside. If it's difficult to separate the pancakes, let them cool a bit, then look for a small opening anywhere on the edge and stick in a knife to get them started.

Place the separated and folded pancakes on an ungreased steamer tray, overlapping them to fit. Steam for 10 minutes. These pancakes can be left in the steamer on a turned-off burner for as long as half an hour. They can be completely prepared in advance and refrigerated or frozen before or after steaming. Resteam immediately before serving.

MU SHU BEEF
Mu Xu Niu Rou

China

Serves 4

In this adaptation of a popular restaurant dish, paper-thin pancakes are rolled around an unusual filling of chewy golden needles (tiger lily buds), tree ears, and dried Chinese mushrooms cooked with strips of beef, scrambled eggs, and chopped scallions. The distinctively flavored *hoisin* sauce is spread on the pancakes just before they are filled.

> 1 recipe Mu Shu Pancakes (preceding recipe)
> 24 tiger lily buds
> ¼ cup tree ears (wood ears)
> 4 medium-size dried Chinese mushrooms
> Boiling water
> 2 tablespoons vegetable oil
> 1½ cups shredded beef (1-inch-long matchstick
>   pieces)
> ¼ cup chopped scallions (white and crisp
>   green parts)

Recipe continues on the following page . . .

2 tablespoons vegetable oil
4 eggs (graded large), beaten
Hoisin sauce, about ½ cup

Prepare the pancakes and keep them warm in the steamer.

In a medium-size heatproof bowl, place the tiger lily buds, tree ears, and dried Chinese mushrooms. Cover with boiling water by 2 inches and allow the dried ingredients to soak until they are soft, about 20 minutes. Drain off all the water. Cut the tiger lily buds into 3 pieces each, chop the tree ears coarsely, and slice the mushrooms thin, discarding the stems.

In an 8-inch skillet, heat 2 tablespoons of oil until it is hot but not yet smoking, about 375 degrees F. Add the beef and stir continuously until the beef is cooked. This will take only a minute or two. Now mix in the tiger lily buds, tree ears, and Chinese mushrooms, then the chopped scallions. Remove the skillet from the heat.

In a 10-inch skillet, heat 2 tablespoons of oil until it is just beginning to smoke, about 400 degrees F. Add the beaten eggs, and scramble them quickly until they are set. Mix in the cooked meat mixture.

Arrange the warm pancakes attractively on a plate, and put the filling and *hoisin* sauce in separate bowls. Each person opens up a pancake, spreads a thin layer of *hoisin* sauce on the pancake with a chopstick or a spoon, places some filling down the center, rolls the pancake around the filling, and folds over the bottom an inch or two so no filling falls out. The pancakes are held and eaten as a sandwich.

LION'S HEAD
Shih Tzu Tou

China

Serves 4

Lion's Head is the stuffed cabbage of eastern China. In the classic preparation, one pound of meat is divided into four meatballs to represent the four blessings of happiness, prosperity, longevity, and health. As you might guess, it is a traditional New Year's dish. The large, delicately seasoned meatballs are cooked on a bed of Chinese cabbage leaves and are covered by the leaves as well. With some stretch of the imagination, we can describe the dish as looking like the head and mane of a lion.

> **2 pounds lean ground beef**
> **⅓ cup Japanese soy sauce**
> **2 tablespoons rice wine or sherry (optional)**
> **3 scallions, chopped (white and crisp green parts)**
> **8 water chestnuts, coarsely chopped**
> **2 teaspoons granulated sugar**
> **2 tablespoons cornstarch**
> **½ cup water or chicken broth**
> **Oil for shallow-frying**
> **2 pounds celery cabbage or nappa, cut into 2- inch pieces**
> **1 cup chicken broth**

For the meatballs, use your hands to mix together the ground beef, soy sauce, wine, scallions, water chestnuts, sugar, and the cornstarch. Gradually add the ½ cup of water or chicken broth. Divide the meat evenly into 8 pieces, and shape each piece into a compact ball.

Into a large skillet, pour ¼ inch of vegetable oil, and heat the oil over moderate heat. Brown the meatballs, gently shaking the skillet so the meat browns all over without sticking. Using a slotted spoon, remove the meatballs to a bowl or plate.

In a 5-quart pot, place half the cabbage pieces. Arrange the meatballs on top of the cabbage, then scatter the remaining cabbage on top of the meat. Pour the cup of chicken broth into the pot, distributing it evenly. Bring to the boil over high heat, then reduce the heat to a gentle boil, cover the pot, and cook for 45 minutes to an hour. Check the pot from time to time, regulating the heat so the meat simmers but the liquid doesn't boil away. Add a little chicken broth if necessary. When the cabbage is tender and the meatballs are cooked through, the Lion's Head is ready to be served.

GROUND MEAT WITH PEAS
Matar Keema

India

Serves 4 to 6

By mixing together the spices in this recipe, you are actually creating your own *masala* (see page 23). Don't be deterred by the long list of ingredients; this colorful meat-and-vegetable combination is easy to prepare. Serve it with plain rice or *chapatis* (page 246).

- ¼ cup vegetable oil
- 1 large onion, finely chopped
- 2 cloves garlic, minced
- 1 tablespoon ground coriander
- 2 teaspoons ground cumin
- ½ teaspoon ground turmeric
- ¼ teaspoon ground fenugreek
- ¼ teaspoon crushed dried red pepper
- 2 pounds extra-lean ground beef, lamb, or veal
- 1 pound ripe red tomatoes, peeled and chopped
- 1 package (10 ounces) frozen peas, thawed
- Optional: 1 tablespoon fresh lemon juice

In a 12-inch skillet, heat the oil until moderately hot. Add the onion and garlic and cook until softened and just beginning to brown, strirring frequently. Add the spices and continue cooking for about 3 minutes, stirring all the while. Raise the heat to high, add the ground meat, and cook, stirring to break up the meat into very small pieces. When the meat is completely browned, mix in the tomatoes and peas. Reduce the heat to moderately low, cover the skillet, and cook 10 minutes longer. Sprinkle on the lemon juice if you like. Uncover and cook for another minute, stirring all the while, and serve.

LAMB STEW
Korma

India

Serves 4

This richly seasoned but not spicy-hot lamb stew is well worth the effort to prepare. The lamb is first browned in oil flavored by a combination of whole spices. (The cook does not usually remove the whole spices from Indian preparations—the diner is expected to do that discreetly.) Then a selection of ground spices is fried in an onion-garlic-ginger paste and the browned lamb is cooked in this delicious mixture. After you enjoy the basic recipe, you'll want to try the beef and chicken variations. Serve lamb *korma* with plain rice or yellow rice (page 256). The *korma* may be made a day ahead and reheated.

> 2 pounds boneless lamb shoulder
> ½ cup vegetable oil
> 1 cinnamon stick (3 inches long)
> 2 dried hot chili peppers
> 6 whole black peppercorns
> 4 whole cardamom pods, crushed with the back of a spoon
> 4 whole cloves
> 1½ cups chopped onion
> 4 large cloves garlic, chopped
> 1 piece ginger root (1 inch square), chopped
> Additional vegetable oil if necessary
> 2 tablespoons ground coriander
> 1 tablespoon ground cumin
> 1 teaspoon ground turmeric
> 1 pound ripe red tomatoes, peeled and chopped
> 1½ cups water
> 1 tablespoon paprika or ½ teaspoon saffron soaked in 1 tablespoon warm water
> Salt (optional)

Remove all fat and gristle from the lamb, then cut the meat into 1-inch cubes.

Recipe continues on the following page . . .

In a 12-inch skillet, heat the oil over moderate heat. Add the cinnamon stick, chili peppers, peppercorns, cardamom pods, and cloves. Stir to coat the spices with the oil. As soon as they darken (a matter of seconds), add enough lamb cubes to fit comfortably in the skillet. Brown the lamb lightly on all sides, then use a slotted spoon to remove the lamb to a 4-quart pot. Repeat with the remaining lamb. Use the slotted spoon to transfer the whole spices to the pot of browned lamb.

In a blender or a food processor, place the chopped onion, garlic, and ginger root. Blend at high speed to form a smooth paste, adding a tablespoon of water at a time if necessary. To the skillet used to brown the lamb, add enough oil to make about ¼ cup. The oil should coat the pan liberally. Heat the oil to 375 degrees F.—a drop of water will spatter instantly. Pour in the onion paste, taking care not to get burned by any spattering onions. Fry the paste for a few minutes, stirring constantly, until all the liquid is evaporated and the paste thickens. Remove the skillet from the heat if the paste begins to burn.

Now add the ground coriander, cumin, and turmeric, stirring constantly for 3 minutes. Again, take care not to burn the onions and spices. Stir in the chopped tomatoes, then scrape the entire contents of the skillet into the 4-quart pot containing the lamb.

Mix together the lamb and onion-spice mixture. Add the paprika if desired (if using the saffron, do *not* stir it in at this point). Stir in 1½ cups water, and bring the liquid to the boil. Reduce the heat to a gentle boil, cover the pot, and cook for 1½ hours, until the lamb is tender. From time to time stir the lamb, and add a little water if the liquid is evaporating. Taste the gravy after an hour, and add salt if desired.

If you are using the saffron, stir it into the pot during the last 5 minutes of cooking.

If the gravy is too thin when the meat is tender, remove the cover and cook for a few minutes to evaporate some of the liquid.

Variations:

To substitute beef for the lamb, increase the cooking time to 2 hours or until the beef is tender.

To substitute chicken, remove the skin from a 4-pound chicken (or 4 pounds of chicken parts) and cut the chicken into small pieces: disjoint the wings and legs, cut the breasts into 3 pieces each, cut the thighs into 2 pieces each. Cook the browned chicken in the sauce for 30 to 40 minutes, turning occasionally.

"SPARERIBS" IN BLACK BEAN SAUCE
Dou Shi Pai Gu

China

Serves 4

Succulent ribs of lamb or veal simmer in a rich, dark sauce seasoned with salted fermented black beans and garlic. This recipe is the way spareribs are prepared in Cantonese tea-houses. The ribs are quite different from the barbecued spare-ribs you may have seen hanging in the windows of Chinese groceries.

This is actually two recipes, because if you use lamb, the taste of the meat will be strong and will be noticeable in the gravy, whereas veal is delicate and won't impart a taste of its own to the gravy. Therefore, when veal is used, the taste of the black bean sauce will be more obvious.

> **4 pounds breast of veal riblets or breast of lamb**
> **1 tablespoon salted fermented black beans**
> **2 tablespoons vegetable oil**
> **2 cloves garlic, minced**
> **¼ cup soy sauce**
> **1 tablespoon granulated sugar**
> **½ cup chicken broth**

Slice the veal or lamb between the ribs. Remove and discard as much fat as possible.

To remove some of the salt, soak the salted fermented black

Recipe continues on the following page . . .

beans in warm water for 20 minutes. Drain well, then mash the beans with a fork.

In a wok, a large skillet, or a 4-quart pot, heat the oil to 350 degrees F. Add the veal or lamb and cook until the ribs are brown all over, turning occasionally. Do this in more than one batch if necessary. You may need to add a little more oil to brown the veal, but the lamb has its own fat which will be rendered out. Spoon off accumulated fat. When all the ribs are browned, sprinkle them with the black beans, the garlic, soy sauce, and sugar. Stir to coat the ribs, then add the chicken broth. Bring to the boil, reduce the heat to a gentle boil, cover the wok, skillet, or pot, and cook the meat gently for 30 to 40 minutes, until tender. Serve hot, with plenty of rice for the sauce.

MOGUL CHICKEN
Murg Moghlai

India

Serves 6

Looking for a new way to serve chicken? Here's a special-occasion chicken replete with the spices for which the Orient is known, including saffron, which colors the chicken a beautiful reddish-brown. The dish is enriched with fried onions, but we omit the yogurt thickener used in India. The list of ingredients may be formidable but, happily, Mogul chicken can be prepared completely in advance and reheated.

> 2 whole chicken breasts (2 pounds)
> 4 chicken thighs with legs (2 pounds)
> 2 cinnamon sticks (3 inches each)
> Seeds from 10 whole cardamom pods
> 8 whole cloves
> 1 teaspoon whole cumin seeds
> ½ teaspoon turmeric
> ½ teaspoon ground cayenne pepper
> 1 tablespoon ground coriander
> 2 teaspoons ground cumin

1 teaspoon tightly packed saffron
1 cup chopped onion
1 tablespoon chopped ginger root
8 large cloves garlic, chopped
½ cup vegetable oil
¼ cup tomato sauce or 1½ tablespoons tomato
  paste
½ cup chicken broth or water
1 teaspoon salt (optional)
2 tablespoons vegetable oil
1 cup sliced onion

Remove the skin from the chicken pieces. Cut each breast in half, then in half again. Disjoint the legs. You now have 8 pieces of breast meat, 4 thighs, and 4 drumsticks. Set aside the chicken.

Combine the cinnamon sticks, cardamom seeds, cloves, and cumin seeds; set aside. Set aside the turmeric and cayenne.

In a small heavy skillet (cast-iron is ideal), place the ground coriander and cumin. Turn the heat to moderate and toast the spices for 2 or 3 minutes, shaking the pan often so the spices do not burn. When they turn light brown and begin to give off a pleasant odor, transfer the spices to a bowl and set aside. Wipe the pan clean. Now roast the saffron. Place the saffron in the pan, turn the heat to moderate, and cook the saffron for a minute or two, shaking the pan constantly. Saffron is too expensive to burn, even slightly. Turn out the saffron onto a piece of wax paper, and crush the saffron by folding the wax paper in half and pressing with the palm of your hand. Set aside the saffron. Later on, it will be soaked in warm water before it is added to the chicken.

In a blender or a food processor, combine the chopped onion, ginger root, and garlic. Process until you have a smooth paste, adding a little water only if necessary.

And now, the cooking begins. In an 8-quart pot, heat the ½ cup of oil until moderately hot. Brown the chicken pieces all over, removing them with a fork or a slotted spoon as they brown. When all the chicken is browned and removed, stir in the cinnamon sticks, cardamom seeds, cloves, and cumin seeds, coating them with the oil. Carefully add the paste from the

Recipe continues on the following page . . .

blender, and fry the paste, stirring all the while, until it is thick and light brown. This will take at least 5 minutes, so regulate the heat to prevent burning. Now add the toasted ground coriander and cumin, the turmeric, and the cayenne. Stir for about a minute, then blend in the tomato sauce or paste. Add the chicken pieces, turning them to coat all over. Mix in the ½ cup water or chicken broth, add the salt if you like, and bring to the boil. Reduce the heat to a gentle boil, cover the pot, and cook the chicken for 30 to 45 minutes, turning occasionally, until tender.

Meanwhile, soak the saffron in a tablespoon of warm water for at least 20 minutes.

A few minutes before the chicken is done, in an 8-inch skillet heat 2 tablespoons of oil until it is moderately hot, about 350 degrees F. Add the sliced onion and fry, stirring often, until beautifully browned but not burned. Set aside.

When the chicken is tender, stir in the soaked saffron and saffron water and the fried onion. Cook for a minute to blend the flavors. Enjoy this wonderful dish at once, or if you can wait, refrigerate and reheat to serve.

CHICKEN AND BEEF STEW
Adobo

Philippines

Serves 4 to 6

The national dish of the Philippines, *adobo* combines the three things most characteristic of the Philippine cuisine— vinegar, garlic, and the use of more than one meat. Small pieces of unboned chicken are combined with beef (pork in the Philippines) and simmered in a tasty, slightly tangy garlic-and-vinegar sauce. The optional coconut milk will add a sweet touch and distinct coconut flavor to the gravy.

> **2 pounds well-trimmed stewing beef, cut into
> 1-inch cubes
> Salt and freshly ground black pepper**

3 tablespoons vegetable oil
1 tablespoon minced garlic
½ cup distilled white vinegar
1½ cups chicken broth, approximately
1 chicken (3 pounds), skinned if desired and
    cut into at least 12 pieces
2 tablespoons vegetable oil
1 cup Coconut Milk (page 203), optional

Sprinkle the stewing beef with salt and pepper. In a 5-quart pot, heat the 3 tablespoons of oil over moderate heat. Brown the beef cubes in 2 or 3 batches, then return all the beef to the pot. Mash the minced garlic to a paste. Add the garlic, vinegar, and 1½ cups of chicken broth to the beef. Bring to the boil over high heat, and boil for about 15 seconds. Reduce the heat to a gentle boil, cover the pot, and cook the meat for one hour.

Toward the end of the cooking time sprinkle the chicken pieces with salt and pepper, rubbing the seasonings into the chicken. In a large heavy skillet, heat the 2 tablespoons of oil over moderate heat. Brown the chicken pieces all over. Using a slotted spoon or a fork, transfer the browned chicken to the pot of beef. Gently stir the chicken into the contents of the pot, coating the pieces all over with sauce. Cook, covered, for an additional 45 minutes or until the beef and chicken are tender. The meats will not be completely covered by gravy, so stir them around from time to time to coat them. Add a little chicken broth as necessary if too much liquid cooks away—there should be a minimum of an inch of gravy in the pot at all times.

When the beef and chicken are tender, taste and correct the seasoning. Add the optional coconut milk and simmer a few minutes longer. *Adobo* is traditionally served with plain white rice.

ROAST STUFFED CHICKEN
Rellenong Manok

Philippines

Serves 4 to 6

Filipinos enjoy poultry and meat combinations to the point where meat is a likely stuffing for roast chicken or duck. This *chorizo*-stuffed chicken reflects the Spanish influence on Philippine cuisine. Chopped raisins added to the spicy *chorizo* make the stuffing sweet. Capers, pickles, pimientos, and hard-cooked eggs are ingredients sometimes added to the stuffing to make it more festive.

> **1 roasting chicken (6 pounds)**
> **1 clove garlic, cut in half**
> **1 lemon, cut in half**
> **Salt and freshly ground black pepper**
> **2 pounds Chorizo (page 79)**
> **2 eggs (graded large), beaten**
> **¼ cup light or dark raisins, chopped**

Preheat the oven to 350 degrees F.

Rub the chicken all over, inside and out, with the halved garlic cloves, then rub the chicken with the halved lemon, squeezing the juice onto the chicken as you rub. Use the entire lemon. Season the chicken lightly with salt and pepper.

Combine the *chorizo,* eggs, and raisins, mixing well. Stuff the chicken with this mixture. Leftovers can be baked separately at 350 degrees F. for 45 minutes.

Set the chicken on a rack in a pan and roast at 350 degrees F. for approximately 2 hours. Now baste the chicken with the pan drippings, margarine, or chicken fat, and raise the heat to 425 degrees F. Continue roasting for about 15 minutes, until the chicken is beautifully browned.

CHICKEN KEBOBS
Saté Ajam

Indonesia

Serves 4

Satés are Indonesian kebobs. Pieces of meat are marinated in a sauce that can be simple or very elaborate. The meat is broiled on special *saté* skewers, then dipped into a spicy peanut sauce at the table. The marinade below uses a sweetened soy sauce lightly seasoned with garlic, coriander, and lime juice. Although the marinated kebobs are very good alone, the peanut-based dip brings in a new flavor, and the contrast is enticing. Crushed red pepper makes the dip moderately hot. Use chunky peanut butter if you want a more fluid dip and ground peanuts for a dip that is a bit more coarse.

> **2 pounds chicken cutlets**
> **2 tablespoons soy sauce**
> **1 tablespoon firmly packed dark brown sugar**
> **1 tablespoon molasses**
> **1 teaspoon minced garlic**
> **½ teaspoon ground coriander**
> **1 tablespoon fresh lime juice**
> **Spicy Peanut Sauce (below)**

Cut the chicken into 1-inch cubes. In a medium-size bowl, combine the soy sauce, brown sugar, molasses, garlic, coriander, and lime juice. Marinate the chicken for 30 minutes or longer. Refrigerate after the first 30 minutes. Meanwhile, prepare the peanut sauce.

When ready to serve, preheat a charcoal grill or a broiler. Thread the chicken onto small skewers, and broil 3 inches from the heat for about 5 minutes, turning as necessary until golden and cooked through.

Spicy Peanut Sauce:

> **1 tablespoon peanut oil or vegetable oil**
> **2 tablespoons chopped shallots (substitute scallions)**

Recipe continues on the following page . . .

1 large clove garlic, minced
1 cup water or chicken broth
½ cup all-natural chunky peanut butter (no
   additives) or ½ cup ground peanuts
1 teaspoon fresh lemon or lime juice
1 tablespoon firmly packed dark brown sugar
½ teaspoon crushed dried red pepper
Salt to taste

In a 1-quart pot, over moderately low heat, heat the oil. Add the shallots and garlic, and stir for one minute. Regulate the heat to prevent burning. Add the water or chicken broth, and raise the heat to bring to the boil. Now stir in the remaining ingredients, reduce the heat to a simmer, and allow the sauce to cook for 5 to 10 minutes, stirring often until thickened. If necessary, thin with a little water. Serve hot in individual small bowls as a dipping sauce.

CHICKEN IN GREEN SAUCE
Gai Krung Gaeng Keo Wan

Thailand

Serves 4

This is a classic method of Thai curry cookery. A very hot curry paste, usually identified by color (red, green, yellow, or orange), is cooked in a highly concentrated coconut cream that is largely coconut oil. Meat, poultry, or fish is mixed in, coconut milk is added, and the meat cooks in this mixture until it is tender.

The sauce is the highlight of the preparation. The aromatic lemon grass, lime peel, gingery *laos,* caraway and coriander seeds, and other ingredients in the paste add texture as well as an interesting combination of tastes (sour, pungent, and spicy) to the natural sweetness of the coconut milk. The coconut milk very effectively tempers the hot curry paste, and the resulting dish is full of the spice, but not the original fire, of the mixture.

There's lots of gravy in the curries of Thailand, so plan to serve with plenty of rice.

> **1 cup Coconut Cream (page 205)**
> **2 to 4 tablespoons Hot Green Curry Paste (page 201)**
> **2 pounds boneless chicken, cut into 1-inch cubes**
> **3 cups Coconut Milk (page 203)**

In a 10-inch skillet, heat the coconut cream over high heat until about three-quarters of it has evaporated, leaving a thick, glossy, oily "cream." Reduce the heat to moderate, add the curry paste, and stir constantly for 2 minutes. Almost all the liquid will evaporate, so take care not to burn the curry paste. Add the chicken cubes and mix them around to coat with the paste. Now add the coconut milk, reduce the heat to low, cover the skillet, and simmer for about 20 minutes, until the chicken is done. Serve hot with rice.

TERIYAKI

Japan

Serves 4

In Japan, when fish or meats are marinated in soy sauce and rice wine and then grilled, they are called *teriyaki*, or glaze-grilled. Fish steaks or fillets, chicken, and steak all lend themselves to this method of preparation. The marinade makes an attractive glaze, and the delicate flavor is typically Japanese—a bit salty, slightly sweet, a tad pungent.

> **¼ cup Japanese soy sauce**
> **2 tablespoons mirin (sweetened rice wine)**
> **2 teaspoons coarsely chopped ginger root**
> **2 pounds fresh fillets of flounder or sole or 2 pounds chicken cutlets**

In a small bowl, combine the soy sauce, *mirin*, and ginger root.

Recipe continues on the following page . . .

Arrange the fish or chicken in a flat pan, then pour the marinade over the fish or chicken. Turn the fillets or cutlets over to coat them on both sides. Allow them to marinate for 30 minutes, then cook immediately or leave the fish or chicken in the marinade and refrigerate.

Transfer the fish or chicken to a baking dish or broiling pan, and broil a few inches from the heat until delicately browned. Or grill over hot coals, being careful not to burn. The chicken needs to be turned once during the cooking, but the fish does not. If desired, brush any leftover marinade over the fish or chicken during cooking.

Variation:

Japanese also prepare fish *teriyaki* by pan-frying. In a 10- or 12-inch skillet, heat 2 tablespoons of oil over moderate heat. Add the fish, pouring the marinade over the fish. As soon as the fish flakes easily, it is ready to serve.

CHARCOAL-GRILLED FISH IN TI LEAVES

Tahiti

Allow 1 fish or fish steak
or fillet per person

Ti leaves are used in the Pacific Islands to enclose fish, chicken, and vegetables that are grilled or baked in outdoor "ovens" heated by stones. The foods emerge moist and tender. (Banana leaves, available in Asian groceries, may be used as a substitute.) Ti leaves are sometimes available from florists, but if you are ambitious, you can grow your own from ti logs advertised in some garden catalogs. They take longer to grow than advertised, but eventually they sprout and produce long, tapered leaves. If you are going to grow your own ti leaves, start this recipe 4 to 6 months in advance.

Select a fish you like for its own taste, because there are no heavy spices or sauces to mask the flavor of the fish, and the ti leaves do not add a significant taste. Salmon steaks or the

Hawaiian fish called *mahi mahi* are used in the Islands, but any kosher fish steaks, fillets, or small whole fish will work well.

**1 fresh salmon steak or fillet (½ pound) or 1
whole whiting (1 to 1¼ pounds), cleaned
and boned, per serving
Salt (optional)
1 fresh lime per serving
Ti leaves or banana leaves**

Ignite the charcoal in advance so the heat is medium-low when the fish is to be cooked.

Sprinkle the fish lightly inside and out with the optional salt, then rub in the salt. Cut the lime into quarters and rub the fish inside and out with the cut side of a lime wedge, squeezing the juice onto the fish as you rub. Use one or two wedges for rubbing, reserving the remainder of the lime for garnishing.

For large ti leaves, cut out the tough part of the rib so the leaf is flexible. (Cut banana leaves into pieces large enough to enclose the fish.) Wrap each fish or fish steak or fillet individually, enclosing it securely in the leaf. Fold the end flaps down underneath the fish to make a tight package.

Grill the fish for 5 to 10 minutes on each side, depending on thickness. The leaves will be scorched in spots but not burned through. Turn once during cooking. Serve the fish in the unopened packages with lime wedges on the side. (If the leaves are very charred, you may want to open and discard them before serving the fish.) Buttered rice and a spinach salad or fresh pineapple wedges will complete the simplicity of the meal.

STUFFED WHOLE FISH
Ca Rut Xuong Dut Lo

Vietnam

Serves 4

You'll find cellophane noodles in Vietnamese soups, vegetable combinations, and even in stuffings. Like other prepara-

Recipe continues on the following page . . .

tions from Vietnam, subtlety is a key to this stuffed fish, for while there are some very interesting ingredients (tree ears, golden needles, and the cellophane noodles), the flavors are not strong. Fresh mushrooms are used in place of the ground meat of the original Vietnamese recipe.

> **1 ounce cellophane noodles**
> **1 tablespoon tree ears**
> **6 tiger lily buds (golden needles)**
> **Boiling water**
> **1 cup chopped fresh mushrooms**
> **3 shallots, chopped fine (substitute scallions)**
> **2 teaspoons minced garlic**
> **⅓ cup finely chopped onion**
> **1 egg (graded large), beaten**
> **¼ teaspoon salt (optional)**
> **1 whole boneless bluefish, sea bass, carp, or**
> **   any fish suitable for baking, head and tail**
> **   intact (2 to 2½ pounds before boning)**
> **Salt and freshly ground black pepper**
> **1 tablespoon vegetable oil**
> **Garnishes: Lime and lemon wedges, shredded**
> **   carrots, sprigs of fresh coriander or parsley**

In a medium-size bowl, soak the cellophane noodles in hot water to cover by an inch for about 15 minutes, until softened. Drain, then cut the noodles into 1-inch pieces.

In a small heatproof bowl, place the tree ears and tiger lily buds, and cover them with boiling water. Soak for 10 minutes or until soft, then chop the tree ears into small pieces and cut the tiger lily buds into 4 or 5 pieces each.

In a medium-size bowl, mix together the cellophane noodles, tree ears, tiger lily buds, mushrooms, shallots, garlic, onion, the beaten egg, and the optional salt.

Preheat the oven to 350 degrees F. Sprinkle the inside of the fish with salt and pepper. Stuff the fish, and transfer the stuffed fish to a baking dish lined with oiled foil. Rub oil over the fish. Bake for 30 to 40 minutes, until the fish flakes easily when poked with a fork. Carefully transfer the whole fish to a serving platter, arrange the lemon and lime wedges around the fish, strew the shredded carrots over the top, and garnish with the coriander or parsley.

TEMPURA

Japan

Serves 4 as a main dish,
8 to 10 as an appetizer

The Japanese have perfected a nongreasy method of deep-frying that leaves a delicate, crisp coating on foods. An assortment of vegetables and very fresh fillets of sole or flounder make a wonderful *tempura* dinner. In addition to the vegetables in this recipe, almost any thinly sliced vegetables can be used, including eggplant, broccoli, turnip, and white and sweet potatoes. The batter is unseasoned, and diners dip the cooked foods into a sauce.

The oil used to deep-fry the *tempura* affects the taste of the fried coating. A mildly-flavored vegetable oil such as soy, corn, peanut, or sunflower oil can be used alone or in combination with the strong-tasting sesame oil in the proportion of three parts mild oil to one part sesame oil.

Small quantities of *tempura* are cooked at one time so that an oil temperature between 360 and 380 degrees F. can be maintained. An electric skillet set up near the dining table is ideal because the *tempura* should be eaten as soon as it is cooked. Have the vegetables and fish all ready for coating, start heating the oil, then prepare the batter so it will be both fresh and cold. It is the combination of the cold batter and the moderately hot oil that ensures the nongreasy crust.

> **1 pound fresh fillets of flounder or sole, cut into 1 x 2-inch pieces**
> **1 cup cauliflower florets**
> **1 cup fresh small whole mushrooms**
> **2 large green peppers, sliced into rounds (discard membranes and seeds)**
> **1 Spanish onion, sliced into rings**

Recipe continues on the following page . . .

> 1 cup whole green beans, tips and ends
> removed
> ½ cup Dashi (page 198), optional
> ½ cup Japanese soy sauce
> ¼ cup shredded daikon (Japanese radish),
> optional
> Oil for deep-frying, 2 to 3 inches deep
> 1 egg (graded large)
> ¾ cup ice water, approximately
> 1 cup unsifted all-purpose flour

Have the fish and cauliflower, mushrooms, green peppers, onion, and green beans all ready. To prepare the dipping sauce, in a small bowl, combine the *dashi*, Japanese soy sauce, and *daikon*. Spoon into small, individual serving dishes and set aside.

In an electric skillet or a 4-quart pot, start heating the oil to 360 to 380 degrees F. A drop of water will spatter instantly but the oil will not be smoking. Break the egg into a 1- or 2-cup liquid measure and beat it lightly, just to mix. Add enough ice water to make 1 cup. Pour this mixture into a medium-size mixing bowl. Using a spoon, stir in the flour. Stir gently until the flour and liquid are combined into a fairly thin batter that will have small lumps in it. Use the back of the spoon to press out any very large lumps of flour, but do not beat the batter or attempt to make it smooth.

Test the oil temperature with a little batter. The batter should sink a little, rise a little, and turn golden. If it browns immediately, the oil is too hot. If it doesn't sizzle at all, the oil is too cool.

Using 4 to 6 pieces of the same kind of food at a time, dip the food into the batter to coat completely, then use tongs, chopsticks, a fork, or your fingers to drop the pieces of food into the oil one at a time. Within 2 minutes the food will be cooked and a light, lacy coating will enclose it. (Mushrooms take less than a minute.) Remove the food with tongs, chopsticks, or a slotted spoon. Drain on paper towels and serve immediately with the dipping sauce. Use a slotted spoon to skim off any pieces of batter that remain in the oil.

To make a lot of *tempura* at once, use several pots of oil. To

increase the quantity of batter, make a second batch after you
run out of the first, so the batter will remain cold longer.

FRIED RICE

Nasi Goreng

Indonesia

Serves 6

Indonesian fried rice is typically laden with shrimp and
chicken, beef, or other meat; seasoned with spices and shrimp
paste; and garnished with strips of cooked egg and fried onions.
The hot pepper paste added at the beginning and the fried onion
garnish at the end make this different from a typical Chinese
fried rice, which is considerably more bland. Because there are
countless recipes for *nasi goreng*—and it is considered desirable
for the Indonesian cook to improvise—this preparation is easy
to adapt to the kosher kitchen.

> 1 tablespoon chopped garlic
> 1 tablespoon chopped fresh cayenne or other
>   hot red chili pepper, or 1 teaspoon dried
>   crushed red pepper, or ½ teaspoon ground
>   cayenne pepper
> 1 cup chopped onion
> ½ teaspoon ground turmeric (optional)
> ¼ cup vegetable oil
> 2 cups diced beef
> ¼ cup soy sauce
> 2 teaspoons dark brown sugar
> 6 cups cold cooked long-grain white rice (2
>   cups raw rice)
> Salt and freshly ground black pepper
> 2 tablespoons vegetable oil
> 1 medium-size onion, cut in half lengthwise
>   then sliced thinly crosswise into
>   half-rounds
> 1 tablespoon vegetable oil
> 2 eggs (graded large), beaten

Recipe continues on the following page . . .

Using a mortar and pestle or a blender, pound or blend together the garlic, hot pepper, onion, and turmeric to make a paste. In a wok, a 12-inch skillet, or an 8-quart pot, heat the ¼ cup oil until it is hot but not yet smoking. Add the paste and cook, stirring constantly, for 1 to 2 minutes, taking care not to burn the spices. Now add the meat and continue to cook and stir until it is done. Mix in the soy sauce and brown sugar, then add the rice, stirring with a large spoon, fork, or chopsticks until everything is mixed well. Add salt and pepper to taste. Reduce the heat to low and keep the rice warm, stirring occasionally.

In an 8-inch skillet, heat 2 tablespoons of oil until the oil just begins to smoke. Add the thinly sliced onion and fry until the onion slices are well browned but not burned, stirring as necessary. Keep the onions warm while cooking the eggs.

In an 8-inch skillet, heat the remaining tablespoon of oil to 350 degrees F. A drop of water will spatter instantly. Pour in the eggs and let them set into a flat pancake. Push cooked egg toward the center and allow uncooked egg to flow toward the sides. Flip the pancake over to cook both sides, then remove the egg pancake from the pan and cut it into strips.

To assemble the *nasi goreng,* heap the rice on a platter, garnish with the fried onions and egg strips, and serve.

CRISPY THAI NOODLES
Mee Krob

Thailand

Serves 6

Here is where Thai artistry comes into play. A mountain of noodles and meat is garnished with unique "nets" made of egg. Scallion "flowers," parsley, hot red peppers, and citrus peel are arranged beautifully around the noodle mixture. Crisp fried rice noodles, tender strips of beef, and soft *tofu* are seasoned with scallions and garlic then blended into a sweet-and-sour lemon-lime sauce. (In Thailand, *mee krob* is made with shrimp and pork, but as we have seen, Thai etiquette encourages the cook to make changes.)

I admit to you that this recipe will take time and your kitchen may be a mess for a while. Start early, eat in the dining room, and revel in your achievement.

> Oil for deep-frying
> ½ pound dried thin rice noodles
> 2 eggs (graded large or extra-large), beaten,
>   for the egg nets
> ¼ cup chopped scallions (white and crisp
>   green parts)
> 1 tablespoon minced garlic
> ½ pound beef, cut into ¼ x ¼ x 1-inch strips
> ¼ pound tofu, cut into ½-inch cubes
> 2 tablespoons soy sauce
> 2 tablespoons fresh lime juice
> ¼ cup fresh lemon juice
> ¼ cup granulated sugar
> 2 eggs (graded large or extra-large)
> Garnishes: 4 scallions, cut into 2-inch pieces,
>   ends slit into a 1-inch deep "x" then placed
>   in cold water to open up into "flowers"; 2
>   tablespoons grated orange or kumquat peel;
>   1 or 2 fresh hot red chili peppers, cut into
>   thin strips; 2 tablespoons chopped fresh
>   coriander or parsley leaves; ½ cup fresh
>   bean sprouts; egg nets from above

Have all the ingredients, including the garnishes, ready and at hand before you begin.

In a deep 4- or 5-quart pot or a wok, heat at least 2 inches of oil until it just begins to smoke, 375 to 400 degrees F. While the oil is heating, break the rice noodles into 2-inch pieces. You will do well to do this in a large, heavy paper bag so the pieces don't fly all over. Drop one test noodle into the oil—it should puff up immediately. Carefully drop a big handful of rice noodles into the oil. Within seconds the noodles will puff up. If some puff but not others, you're adding too many at once. Using a slotted

Recipe continues on the following page . . .

spoon, remove the noodles as soon as they puff, and drain them well on paper towels. Test one noodle again to make sure the oil is still hot enough, then cook another batch. Repeat until all the noodles are fried. Cover the noodles with paper towels until ready to use.

Reduce the oil temperature to 350 degrees F. A drop of water will spatter instantly, but the oil will not be smoking. Using a slotted spoon, remove any bits of rice noodles that remain in the oil.

To make the egg nets, dip your fingers into the 2 beaten eggs, cupping your hand so about a tablespoon of egg remains in your fingers. Holding your hand over the oil, allow the eggs to drizzle from your fingertips into the oil, going back and forth and side to side to form a net. The eggs should congeal immediately upon hitting the oil, but the oil should not be so hot that the eggs burn. Quickly dip your fingers into the beaten eggs again, and drizzle more egg into the pot. When a lacy pancake has formed, allow it to brown lightly on one side, then turn it over with a slotted spoon to brown the other side. Transfer the egg net to paper towels and allow it to drain. Repeat with the remaining eggs, making about 4 egg nets in all. Cover the egg nets with paper towels or a clean kitchen towel to keep them warm.

Now pour off all but a ⅛-inch layer of oil. In the same 4-or 5-quart pot, heat the oil to 350 degrees F. Stir in the chopped scallions and minced garlic until they are coated with oil but not brown. Add the beef strips, stirring constantly until browned, then stir in the *tofu.* Now add the soy sauce, lime and lemon juices, and the sugar, mixing well. Taste for seasoning. The mixture should be salty, sweet, and sour. Add more soy sauce, lemon juice, or sugar as necessary. Now add the remaining 2 unbeaten eggs to the mixture, and scramble until set.

To assemble the *mee krob,* put half the noodles into a clean large pot. Mix with half of the meat mixture. Transfer to a serving platter or bowl, heaping the mixture to create a mountainlike mound. Repeat with the remaining noodles and meat, using a second serving platter or bowl if necessary. Place the egg nets on top of the mound, decorate attractively with the garnishes, and serve immediately.

VEGETABLE SUSHI
Gomoku-zushi

Japan

Serves 4

Sushi is vinegared white rice that is garnished attractively with sliced raw fish (the fish is called *sashimi*) and vegetable and/or egg slices. In Japan *sushi* is a main dish, while in the United States it is served as either an appetizer or a main course. Although *sushi* is most often shaped into individual balls and oblongs, dabbed with *wasabi* paste (see page 31), then topped with one or more garnishes as described above *(nigiri-zushi)*, it can be tossed with other ingredients, mounded on the serving platter, and garnished, as it is in this recipe. The rice has a pronounced sweet-and-sour taste, and the liberal addition of sesame seeds punctuates the soft rice with a crunchy texture. *Miso* soup (page 199) and a salad complete a luncheon or light supper.

Sushi is prepared with fresh-cooked rice and served at room temperature. (Leftover rice is never used.) All the ingredients may be prepared ahead of time, but final assembly does not take place until serving time.

    1 cup short-grain white rice
1¼ cups cold water
    ½ cup Japanese rice vinegar
    ⅓ cup granulated sugar
    ½ teaspoon salt
    ⅓ cup sesame seeds
    2 tablespoons vegetable oil
    4 eggs (graded large), beaten
    ¼ cup sliced bamboo shoots (¼ x 1-inch strips)
    ½ cup fresh or thawed frozen peas
    ½ cup diced tofu (optional)

For the *sushi* rice, using cold water rinse and drain the rice 2 or 3 times. In a 2-quart pot, place the rice and the 1¼ cups of cold water. Allow the rice and water to stand for 15 minutes. Bring to the boil over high heat, then reduce the heat to low, cover the pot, and continue cooking for 15 minutes. Try not to lift the

Recipe continues on the following page . . .

cover off the rice to check it. Now turn off the heat and allow the rice to remain in the pot for 15 to 20 minutes.

Meanwhile, in a 1-quart pot combine the vinegar, sugar, and salt. Bring to the boil over high heat, stirring to dissolve the sugar and salt. Remove from the heat.

While the rice is cooking, in an 8-inch skillet over moderate heat toast the sesame seeds for 3 or 4 minutes, until they are a golden brown. From time to time shake the pan gently so the seeds toast evenly without burning. Transfer to a bowl and set aside.

In a 10-inch skillet, heat the oil over moderate heat, pour the beaten eggs into the skillet, tilt the skillet quickly so the eggs cover the bottom evenly, and allow the eggs to set into a large pancake. Gently push cooked egg toward the center, allowing uncooked egg to flow around the edges. When the egg pancake is set, cover the skillet and remove it from the heat. The eggs will continue to cook without browning or becoming tough. When the egg pancake is cool enough to handle, cut it into ¼ x 2-inch strips. Set aside.

Have the bamboo shoots, the peas, and the optional *tofu* ready and at hand.

As soon as the rice is done, fluff the hot rice with a fork or chopsticks, and sprinkle in the sweetened vinegar. Stir with the fork or chopsticks to distribute the vinegar evenly.

Toss the vinegared rice with the toasted sesame seeds, the bamboo shoots, peas, optional *tofu*, and half of the egg strips. Shape the rice into a compact mound on a serving platter or bowl. Arrange the remaining egg strips attractively over the rice and serve immediately.

Side Dishes

Because meat is not often the focal point of the meal in most Asian and Pacific Island countries, side dishes assume more importance than they do in the United States. As we have seen, rice is treated as the main dish in many Asian cuisines, and no northern Indian meal is complete without individual round breads. Noodles are enjoyed as snacks or lunches in Japan and parts of China and Korea.

Intriguing combinations of deliciously spiced vegetables are well known throughout India. Vegetable cakes from the Philippines use winter squash in an unusual way (see page 251), and the Chinese cooking method known as stir-frying, where small pieces of foods are cooked briefly over high heat while being stirred constantly, has found its way into American kitchens as a timesaving, nutritious, and tasty way to serve vegetables (page 250).

Breads, vegetables, rice, and noodles—here is a selection of the most well-known, colorful, or indispensable side dishes in the cuisines of Asia and the Pacific. From the flaky whole wheat breads of northern India to the famous noodles of Japan, these are recipes you'll enjoy when you want to add an unusual touch to an everyday meal, or when you want to round out a special international dinner.

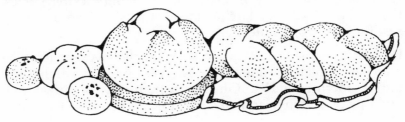

FLAT WHOLE-WHEAT BREADS
Chapatis

India

Makes 12

In India, pieces of the flat, unleavened breads known as *chapatis* are broken off and used to pick up small portions of food. If *chapatis* are not served, food is scooped up with the fingers, and rice absorbs the sauces in the meal. Either rice or *chapatis* is always served in an authentic Indian meal.

Made of whole wheat flour, *chapatis* are chewy with a strong, wheaty taste. For lighter *chapatis*, use half white flour. Indians spread *ghee*—their version of clarified butter (see pages 20 and 17)—on each *chapati* for flavor, a step you may want to omit if you are counting calories.

>**2 cups unsifted finely-ground whole-wheat flour or 1 cup each unsifted whole-wheat and all-purpose flours**
>**1 tablespoon vegetable oil**
>**⅔ cup water, approximately**
>**Melted unsalted butter (clarified if desired) or margarine (optional)**

Place the flour in a medium-size mixing bowl. Sprinkle the oil over the flour, and work the oil into the flour with your fingers. Slowly add ½ cup of water, using a fork or your fingers to mix the water into the flour. Gradually add enough water to make the dough come together to form a ball that is smooth but not sticky.

On a clean work surface, knead the dough for 10 minutes, until it is very smooth. Lightly dust the dough or the work surface with flour as necessary to keep the dough from sticking. Cover the dough with a clean kitchen towel or plastic wrap, and let it rest for 30 to 60 minutes.

Preheat a griddle or an 8-inch cast-iron skillet over moderately high heat. Divide the dough into 12 pieces, and form each piece into a smooth, round ball. On a lightly floured work surface, roll out a piece of dough to make a 5- to 6-inch circle. (Keep the remaining balls of dough covered with a towel so they do not dry out.) Turn the dough a quarter-turn each time you roll to help keep the shape round and even.

Bake the *chapati* on the hot griddle for ½ to 1 minute on a side, turning to cook both sides. The *chapati* may brown lightly in spots, but take care not to burn. If you are lucky, some *chapatis* will puff up, making them lighter and flakier. If desired, brush each cooked *chapati* with melted butter or margarine as it comes off the griddle. Repeat the baking process with the remaining balls of dough, stacking the *chapatis* as they cook. Wrap well in foil until ready to serve; they will keep warm for about 30 minutes. Although they are best when served immediately, *chapatis* can be reheated on the griddle or briefly in a microwave oven. They should be served warm.

PUFFED WHOLE-WHEAT BREADS
Puris

India

Makes 12

When *chapatis* are deep-fried in very hot oil, they puff up and become the special-occasion breads known as *puris*. They are light and flaky, with a hearty wheat taste.

1 recipe Chapatis (previous recipe)
Oil for frying

Prepare the dough as directed on page 246. In a 4-quart pot, heat 2 inches of oil until it just begins to smoke, about 400 degrees F. Divide the dough into 12 pieces, and roll out as directed on page 246. Carefully drop a circle of dough into the hot oil. It should sink to the bottom, puff up within a few seconds, and rise to the top. Turn the *puri* once, continue cooking a few more seconds, then drain well on paper towels. If the *puri* does not sink, push it down with a large spoon or a metal pancake turner. If it does not puff, the oil is not hot enough; if it burns, the oil is too hot.

Recipe continues on the following page . . .

Puris should be eaten as soon as they are all cooked, but leftovers can be reheated for a few minutes in a 300-degree F. oven, under a broiler if watched very carefully, or briefly in a microwave oven.

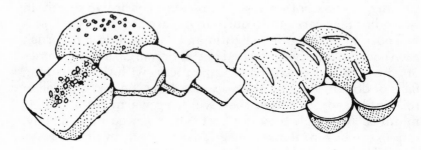

POTATO-STUFFED WHOLE-WHEAT BREADS
Alu Parathas

India

Makes 8

When a spicy potato filling is stuffed between two uncooked *chapatis* that are then rolled together and cooked, you get a filled *paratha*—something like a very thin potato *knish* with a delicious Indian flavor. *Alu parathas* may seem complicated when you read the recipe, but you'll develop a rhythm of filling, rolling, and cooking, and by the last one you may be sorry you didn't double the recipe.

> 1 recipe Chapatis (page 246)
> 1 pound potatoes
> 2 tablespoons vegetable oil
> ¼ cup finely chopped onion
> ¼ teaspoon ground cumin
> ¼ teaspoon ground turmeric
> ⅛ teaspoon crushed dried red pepper
> Salt to taste
> Clarified butter (page 17) or softened butter
>   or margarine for spreading (about 2
>   tablespoons)

Prepare the *chapati* dough, cover, and let it rest while you make the filling.

Peel the potatoes, cut them into quarters, and boil until tender. Drain, then mash the potatoes with a fork or a potato masher.

In an 8-inch skillet, heat the oil over moderate heat. Add the onion and cook until softened and beginning to brown, stirring constantly. Add the spices and continue to cook and stir for 2 minutes, then add the mashed potatoes. Mix well. Divide the potato mixture into 8 equal parts.

Divide the *chapati* dough into 16 equal pieces. Roll each piece into a smooth ball, then flatten each ball with the palm of your hand. Sprinkle a little whole wheat or white flour onto a clean work surface, then roll one of the balls of dough into a 4-inch circle. Repeat with a second ball of dough, keeping the remaining balls of dough covered with a towel so they don't dry out.

Place ⅛ of the potato mixture on one circle of dough, and spread it evenly to within ½ inch of the edge of the circle. Place the second circle of dough over the potato mixture, and use your fingers to press down the edges of the two circles to seal them together. Gently roll out the stuffed *paratha* to a circle of 6 to 7 inches, being careful not to allow any filling to leak out. Turn the *paratha* a quarter-turn each time you roll. This will keep the dough from sticking and will help ensure a round *paratha*.

To cook, heat a griddle or an 8-inch cast-iron skillet until it is moderately hot. Place the filled *paratha* on the griddle, let it cook for 30 seconds to 1 minute, then turn it over to cook for another 30 to 60 seconds. Spread a little butter or margarine on the top side, flip it over again after half a minute, spread butter or margarine on what is now the top side, and continue to cook until the *paratha* is golden on both sides, perhaps darkened in a few spots but not burned. Repeat with the remaining dough and filling. When you get the technique down, you may be able to bake one while you roll the next.

Stack the cooked *parathas* on top of each other, wrap in foil, and serve hot when all are cooked. If you prepare them in advance, reheat on a griddle or very briefly in a microwave oven. *Alu parathas* can be tray-frozen and reheated (unstacked) in a 350-degree F. oven.

STIR-FRIED VEGETABLES
Su Hui

China

Serves 4 to 6

When vegetables are stir-fried quickly over high heat, they retain their bright colors and fresh taste. The vegetables are added according to the length of cooking time each requires, so they all remain crisp. The optional chicken broth-and-cornstarch mixture added at the end makes an attractive glaze. Be sure to have all the ingredients ready and at hand before you begin, for stir-frying takes only a few minutes from the time the oil is heated until the vegetables are ready to serve.

> **2 tablespoons vegetable oil**
> **1 large onion, sliced**
> **1 large clove garlic, minced**
> **1 teaspoon minced ginger root**
> **1 cup fresh small snow peas, tips and strings removed**
> **2 cups sliced fresh mushrooms**
> **Salt or soy sauce (optional)**
> **Optional glaze: 1 tablespoon cornstarch dissolved in ¼ cup cold chicken broth or water**

In a 10-inch skillet, heat the oil over moderately high heat until it just begins to smoke. Add the onion, garlic, and ginger root and stir continuously for a minute. Add the snow peas and cook for an additional 30 seconds, stirring constantly. Now add the mushrooms, stirring all the while. Cook only until the mushrooms wilt slightly. Season with salt or soy sauce as desired. For the glaze, again mix together the cornstarch and broth or water, then stir the mixture into the vegetables. Mix well. As soon as the liquid boils and thickens, turn off the heat. Serve at once while the vegetables are still crisp.

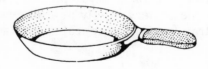

DEEP-FRIED VEGETABLE CAKES
Ukoy

Philippines

Makes 12

Bright orange shredded vegetables flecked with chopped green onion (scallion) are mixed with a thick batter and deep-fried until they are crisp on the outside and chewy inside. For the garlic-and-vinegar dip alone, this recipe is worth trying. Although *ukoy* is made as a shrimp and vegetable cake in the Philippines, and pieces of flounder fillets can be substituted for the shrimp successfully, I think this is superb as a vegetarian preparation, as presented here.

> **2 teaspoons minced garlic**
> **¼ teaspoon salt**
> **½ cup distilled white vinegar**
> **1 cup water**
> **1 teaspoon annatto seeds (optional)**
> **1 cup unsifted all-purpose flour**
> **1 cup unsifted cornstarch**
> **2 cups coarsely grated peeled yams**
> **2 cups coarsely grated peeled butternut or**
>   **acorn squash**
> **⅓ cup chopped scallion tops**
> **Oil for deep-frying**

First prepare the garlic sauce. In a small bowl, using the back of a spoon, mash the garlic and salt to a paste. (Or use a garlic press.) Stir in the vinegar until the mixture is thoroughly combined. Set aside.

In a small pot, bring the water to the boil. Drop in the annatto seeds, remove the pot from the heat, and set aside for 5 minutes. The annatto seeds act as a dye, turning the water orange. If you do not use the seeds, use plain water in the next step.

In a large mixing bowl, combine the flour and cornstarch. Strain the annatto water to remove the seeds, then pour the annatto water into the flour-cornstarch mixture, stirring constantly with a fork. Beat until a thick batter is formed, then stir in a cup

Recipe continues on the following page . . .

252 ° ASIA AND THE PACIFIC ISLANDS

at a time of the grated vegetables. The batter will be very thick and may be difficult to stir. Add a little water if necessary.

Pack a ⅓-cup measure with the mixture, then turn out onto a large sheet of wax paper. Repeat until you have used up all of the mixture. There should be 12 patties. Shape the patties into 3½-inch rounds that are ½ inch thick. Sprinkle each with some of the chopped scallion tops, and press the scallions in lightly. The vegetable cakes can be refrigerated overnight at this point.

Pour an inch of oil into an electric skillet or a heavy pot with sides at least 3 inches deep. Heat the oil until it is hot but not yet smoking, about 375 degrees F. Using a pancake turner, carefully lift up one vegetable cake and place it in the oil. It will come right off the pancake turner. Cook several cakes at a time for a total of 3 minutes, turning once after 2 minutes. Drain well on paper towels.

To serve, spoon a little garlic sauce over each vegetable cake. Serve the remaining sauce as a dip.

DAL AND CABBAGE

India

Serves 4

If Neil Simon's mother had prepared lima beans with Indian spices and crisp onions, they might never have found their way into *Brighton Beach Memoirs* and *Biloxi Blues*. Any dried bean, pea, or lentil—that is, *dal*—can be made special by topping it off with a variety of spices cooked with fried onions. This recipe combines lentils and cabbage with garlic and onions—so far it could be an eastern European dish. The Indian contribution is the cumin and turmeric, cooked with additional onions until the onions become brown, crisp, and so very tasty.

Indians serve *dal* as a vegetable with rice or *chapatis*, but you may want to thin it with a little water and serve it as a thick soup.

1 cup brown lentils, picked through and rinsed
½ cup chopped onion

2 cups water
2 cups shredded cabbage
¼ cup vegetable oil
1 teaspoon ground cumin
1 teaspoon ground turmeric
1 clove garlic, minced
1 cup sliced onion
1 tablespoon tomato paste
Salt
2 tablespoons fresh lemon juice

In a 2- or 3-quart pot, combine the lentils, chopped onion, and water. Bring to the boil over high heat, reduce the heat so the water boils gently, cover the pot, and cook for 15 to 20 minutes. Add the shredded cabbage, and continue cooking (covered) for 45 to 60 minutes, stirring occasionally, until the lentils are soft. From time to time, add a little liquid to the pot to keep the lentils from sticking.

When the lentils are tender, in an 8-inch skillet heat the oil over moderately low heat (300 to 350 degrees F.). Stir in the ground cumin and turmeric; cook, stirring constantly for 3 or 4 minutes, being careful not to burn the spices. This initial cooking will eliminate the raw taste of the turmeric. Now add the garlic and sliced onion, and cook, stirring frequently, until the onion slices are brown but not burned. Stir in the tomato paste, then add the onion mixture to the lentils and cabbage, mixing well. Add salt to taste, then blend in the lemon juice. Keep warm over low heat until ready to serve.

CURD CHEESE WITH TOMATOES AND PEAS
Tamatar Matar Panir

India

Serves 4

Little Miss Muffet must have been preparing *panir* when she was eating her curds and whey. Nowhere will you find a more graphic explanation of just what curds and whey are than when

Recipe continues on the following page . . .

you curdle boiling milk to produce this Indian cheese. If you've never made cheese and are wondering how it's done, here is your chance. The milk immediately separates into a thin, cloudy liquid and a surface of curds that will resemble cottage cheese when strained. The curds, known as *panir,* are kneaded and pressed together. *Panir* is not eaten by itself but is combined with spices and vegetables, adding protein to vegetable dishes. For a meat meal, the *panir* is omitted, water or broth is used in place of the whey, and oil is used instead of butter. The resulting dish can then be appropriately named Tomatoes and Peas With Spices.

The Panir:

> **½ cup plain yogurt**
> **2 tablespoons fresh lemon juice**
> **Cheesecloth for straining (available in**
> **supermarkets and housewares stores)**
> **4 cups milk**

In a small bowl, combine the yogurt and lemon juice. Line a colander or strainer with a double layer of cheesecloth and set over a large heatproof mixing bowl.

In a 3- or 4-quart pot, bring the milk to a rolling, foaming boil, stirring constantly so the milk does not scorch. Turn off the heat, and stir in the yogurt-lemon juice mixture. The milk will curdle immediately, and the curds will rise to the top. Pour the mixture into the cheesecloth-lined strainer and allow the liquid to drip through. Pull the corners of the cheesecloth toward the center to enclose the curds, and squeeze out all the liquid. Now use a piece of string to tie the cheesecloth tightly around the *panir,* and hang the cheesecloth ball over a bowl to catch the drippings. Refrigerate the whey (the cloudy liquid).

After an hour, transfer the *panir* to a sheet of wax paper. Using the palms of your hands, knead the *panir* for a minute or two. To keep the *panir* from sticking to your hands, lift one side of the wax paper to fold the cheese in half, press the paper-covered cheese with your palms, then pull back the paper and repeat the process. Form the kneaded *panir* into a 4-inch square, then wrap it in cheesecloth. Place a very heavy book on top of the cheese-cloth, and press the *panir* for 2 or 3 hours. The *panir* can be used now, or refrigerated for up to 3 days.

The Vegetables:

> ⅓ cup clarified butter (page 17) or vegetable
> oil
> 1 cup Panir, from above, cut into ½-inch
> squares
> ½ cup finely chopped onion
> 1 large clove garlic, minced
> ½ teaspoon Garam Masala (page 200)
> ½ teaspoon ground coriander
> ½ teaspoon ground turmeric
> Pinch of ground cayenne pepper
> 1 teaspoon salt (optional)
> 1 pound ripe red tomatoes, diced
> 1 to 1½ cups whey from Panir
> 1½ cups shelled fresh peas or 1 package
> (10 ounces) frozen peas, thawed
> 1 teaspoon sugar (optional)

In an 8-inch skillet, heat the butter or oil over moderate heat. Add the *panir* and cook it for a few minutes, turning gently as necessary until the cheese is golden all over. With a slotted spoon remove the *panir* and drain on paper towels.

In the same butter or oil, cook the onion until lightly browned, then add the garlic and seasonings. Cook for 2 to 3 minutes, stirring frequently. Now add the tomatoes, cook 5 minutes longer, then stir in ½ cup of the whey. Partially cover the skillet and cook for an additional 5 minutes. Add another ½ cup of whey, stir in the peas, and cook uncovered 5 minutes longer. If there is no liquid left, add more whey. Before serving, taste the sauce and add a little more cayenne or salt as desired. If it is too sour, add the optional sugar.

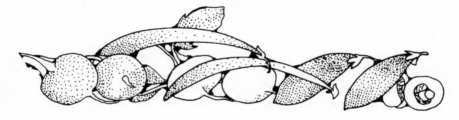

YELLOW RICE
Chaval

India

Serves 6

Lightly spiced and buttery, this lovely yellow rice can be served with any Indian meal. Prepare the rice with *pareve* margarine for meat meals.

> ½ **cup (1 stick) unsalted butter or margarine**
> 2 **tablespoons vegetable oil**
> 1 **teaspoon ground turmeric**
> ¼ **teaspoon ground cumin**
> ⅛ **teaspoon ground fenugreek**
> 1 **tablespoon tomato paste**
> 2 **cups long-grain white rice**
> 4 **cups water**

In a 4-quart pot, over moderately low heat, melt the butter or margarine with the oil. Stir in the spices and tomato paste, and cook for 5 minutes, stirring frequently. Add the rice, mix well, and cook for 5 to 10 minutes, stirring often and taking care not to burn the rice. Now add the water, cover the pot, and cook the rice until all the water is absorbed, about 20 minutes. If the water boils over the top or the rice appears to be burning, reduce the heat. Turn off the burner and allow the rice to remain in the pot on the turned-off burner until serving. Fluff with a fork just before serving.

WHITE NOODLES
Somen

Japan

Serves 6

Japanese eat noodles as snacks and lunches and in soups. The noodles may be mixed with small amounts of vegetables, meat, or fish, or served plain with a dipping sauce. Among the unusual noodles featured in Japanese cuisine are the brown *soba* noodles, made from a flour similar to buckwheat, and the very white, very thin *somen*, made of wheat. During the summer both noodles are often served cold with a sweetened *dashi*-and-soy-based dipping sauce to which each diner adds chopped ginger root, scallions, and the green paste known as *wasabi*, which is made of a horseradish-like root. The combination is sweet, salty, and as tangy as desired.

> **1 pound somen**
> **1 cup Dashi (page 198)**
> **¼ cup Japanese soy sauce**
> **¼ cup granulated sugar**
> **¼ cup chopped scallions (white and crisp**
> **green parts)**
> **2 tablespoons grated ginger root**
> **1 tablespoon wasabi paste**

In a 4-quart pot, bring 3 quarts of water to the boil. Drop in the noodles in bunches, stir with a fork, and cook for one minute or until tender. Drain into a strainer or colander, and run cold water over the noodles to cool them and to keep them from sticking together. Refrigerate the noodles if they will not be served within an hour.

In a 1-quart pot combine the *dashi*, soy sauce, and sugar. Bring to the boil over high heat, stir until the sugar is dissolved, and remove the pot from the heat. Allow the *dashi* mixture to cool to room temperature.

To serve, each person gets a bowl of noodles and a small bowl of the cooled *dashi* mixture. The scallions, ginger root, and *wasabi* paste are placed in bowls within easy reach of all the diners, who make up their own dipping sauce. Noodles are taken with chopsticks and dipped before being eaten.

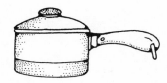

BREADFRUIT PURÉE
Poi

Hawaii

Makes about 1½ cups

Ever since I read *Mutiny On the Bounty* years ago, I've been curious about breadfruit, so when I saw one of these expensive knobby, not the least bit attractive, round fruits in the supermarket, I had to buy one. Baked, boiled, or steamed, breadfruit earns its name, tasting like both a sweet but starchy fermented unripe fruit (similar to a peach picked too soon) and a sweet whole-wheat bread. Its intriguing spongy consistency contributes to the uniqueness of the fruit.

For an authentic *poi* supper or a *luau* some form of *poi* is traditional, and *poi* made from breadfruit is tastier than reconstituted canned *poi* made from taro root. Like potatoes, breadfruit can be boiled, baked, or steamed. Breadfruit cooks more quickly when boiled or steamed, but baking is somewhat easier because the tough skin is not removed prior to baking.

1 breadfruit, slightly soft and turning yellow

To bake the breadfruit: Wrap the breadfruit in foil and bake for an hour in a preheated 400-degree F. oven. Cut the baked fruit in half and scoop out the fruit, discarding the blackened core.

To steam or boil: Using a sharp knife, remove the heavy skin. Cut the breadfruit in half, scoop out the core and cut the fruit into 1-inch cubes. Steam or boil for about 20 minutes, until a fork pierces the breadfruit easily.

Mash the cooked breadfruit with a fork, or use a food processor. Add just enough water so you can scoop up the *poi* with one or two fingers, which is the way it is eaten. Refrigerate unless the *poi* will be served within a few hours. Leftovers will keep for several days in the refrigerator.

Desserts

Most Asian and Pacific Island meals end with fresh fruit. When more elaborate desserts are served in the warmer regions, tropical fruits are usually part of the preparation, as in Tahitian *poe* (page 260), a baked dessert. Custards and puddings made with coconut milk are common, and two recipes that use coconut milk—a rice, fruit, and nut pudding from Thailand and a traditional Hawaiian *luau* pudding—are presented here.

Steamed cakes, bean paste desserts, and sweetened fritters are enjoyed throughout the area, but the kinds of pies, cakes, and cookies Westerners find palatable are not typically a part of Asian and Pacific Island meals. However, one can create delicious desserts based on local ingredients, such as the Macadamia Nut Pie concluding this chapter.

WHIPPED COCONUT CREAM

Hawaii, Tahiti

Makes about 1 cup

Can coconut cream be whipped? Partially freeze the cream, use a chilled bowl and beaters, and make an all-natural nondairy whipped cream that has the consistency of real whipped cream with a coconut taste. Because coconut cream is already sweet, it is not even necessary to add sugar.

½ cup Coconut Cream (page 205)

 Recipe continues on the following page . . .

Chill a small metal mixing bowl and the beaters from an electric mixer in the freezer for 15 minutes. Now add the coconut cream to the chilled bowl and replace the bowl in the freezer for about 30 minutes, until the coconut cream just begins to freeze.

With the electric mixer at high speed, immediately whip the cream. Watch the cream carefully as it begins to thicken or it may curdle. Turn off the mixer when the coconut cream is stiff enough to hold peaks when the beaters are lifted. The whipped coconut cream is ready to serve. Or refrigerate, covered, for up to four days; the cream does not separate the way regular whipped cream does, nor does it spoil as rapidly.

POE

Tahiti

Serves 8 to 10

Both *poe* and *poi* refer to the pounding of fruits or roots into a pulp. But unlike Hawaiian *poi,* this Tahitian *poe* is a sweet, tasty baked tropical fruit dessert, served chilled and topped with coconut cream. Don't taste too much of it before you bake it, for like some cake batters it is delicious uncooked and may not make it into the oven.

> 2 tablespoons unsalted butter or margarine, softened
> 1 ripe pineapple (4 pounds)
> 1 or 2 ripe papayas (2 pounds total)
> 1 or 2 ripe mangos (2 pounds total)
> 1½ pounds ripe bananas
> ½ cup unsifted cornstarch or arrowroot
> ½ cup pineapple juice (optional)
> ½ cup firmly packed light or dark brown sugar
> 2 teaspoons vanilla extract
> 1 cup Coconut Cream, page 205, or Whipped Coconut Cream, page 259 (optional)

Generously butter a 9 x 13-inch baking dish. Preheat the oven to 375 degrees F.

Quarter the pineapple, slice off and discard the core, remove the fruit from the shell, and chop the pineapple fine. Peel the papayas, cut in half, remove and discard the seeds, and chop the fruit fine. Peel the mangos, cut the fruit away from the pit, and chop the mangos fine. Peel and mash the bananas. Purée the fruit in a food mill, blender, or a food processor, or use the coarse blade of a grinder. Because the fruit is usually pounded by hand, not processed in a machine, the texture need not be too smooth.

Mix the fruit together and place in a strainer over a bowl. Mix the liquid that drains into the bowl with the cornstarch or arrowroot, making sure the mixture is very smooth. Or, if you're short on time, mix the ½ cup pineapple juice with the cornstarch or arrowroot and do not drain the fruit.

In a large mixing bowl, using a large kitchen spoon, combine the fruit purée, cornstarch or arrowroot mixture, sugar, and vanilla extract. Spread evenly in the prepared baking dish, and bake for 1 hour, until golden brown. Cool, then cover and refrigerate until well chilled. Serve with coconut cream, plain or whipped, passed around separately.

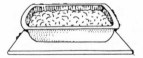

COCONUT PUDDING
Haupia

Hawaii

Serves 4

This light, refreshing pudding looks just like a milk dish and is indeed made from coconut "milk," but the coconut milk is nondairy. *Haupia* is traditionally cut into squares and served as dessert at a *luau*. Coconut milk is naturally sweet, so very little additional sugar is required.

Recipe continues on the following page . . .

2 tablespoons granulated sugar
2 tablespoons unsifted cornstarch or
arrowroot
2 cups Coconut Milk (page 203)

In a 2-quart pot, combine the sugar and cornstarch or arrowroot. Gradually blend in the coconut milk. Bring to the boil over moderate heat, stirring constantly. Cook for 1 minute after the mixture boils, stirring all the while. Pour into a 1-quart square serving dish (6- to 8-inch square). Chill until firm, at least 2 hours. Serve in squares.

To double this recipe, use ¼ cup sugar, ⅓ cup cornstarch or arrowroot, and 4 cups coconut milk. Cook in a 3- to 4-quart pot, and pour into a 2-quart oblong dish, 7 x 12 inches.

COCONUT RICE PUDDING WITH MANGOS
Mamuang Kao Nieo

Thailand

Serves 6

A sweet coconut-flavored rice pudding is made special with the addition of nuts and chunks of fresh tropical fruit. Vietnamese cuisine has a similar dessert that uses sweetened turnip and tiny peas in place of the fruit and nuts.

1 cup glutinous rice
2 cups water
1 cup Coconut Milk (page 203)
½ cup granulated sugar
¼ cup unsalted peanuts
1 ripe mango, peeled and cut into ½-inch
cubes (substitute 1 pound fresh peaches)
Optional garnish: Whipped Coconut Cream
(page 259), chopped unsalted peanuts

Rinse the rice, place it in a medium-size bowl, and cover with cold water. Allow the rice to soak for a minimum of 2 hours or as long as overnight. Drain, then place the rice in a 2-quart pot with 2 cups of cold water. Bring to the boil over high heat, reduce the heat to low, cover the pot, and cook the rice for 20 minutes. The water should be absorbed and the rice tender. Leave the rice on the turned-off burner while preparing the sweetened coconut milk.

In a 1-quart pot, mix together the coconut milk and sugar. Bring to the boil over high heat and boil rapidly for 2 minutes. Fluff the cooked rice with a fork or chopsticks, and mix in the coconut syrup. Transfer to a bowl, cool to room temperature, then mix in the peanuts and the mango cubes. Serve immediately, or spoon into dessert dishes and chill until serving. The pudding becomes more firm and chewy as it chills. If desired top with a dollop of whipped coconut cream garnished with chopped peanuts.

MACADAMIA NUT PIE

Hawaiian influence

Makes one 9-inch pie

Hawaiian supermarkets attest to the popularity and availability of macadamia nuts on the Islands—whole sections of supermarkets are devoted to the display and sale of the nuts. Macadamia nuts are small and round (about ½ inch in diameter), softer than many other nuts, with a cashewlike flavor. When baked in a pie, however, the macadamias become very crisp and their taste becomes more delicate than cashews. This recipe is based on southern pecan pie, but the macadamia nuts make the dessert distinctive.

The Pie Shell:

1 cup unsifted all-purpose flour
Dash of salt (optional)
⅓ cup vegetable shortening
2 tablespoons water, approximately

In a small mixing bowl, mix together the flour and salt. Cut in the shortening with a fork or a pastry blender, until the parti-

Recipe continues on the following page . . .

cles are about the size of coarse meal. Sprinkle the water over the mixture 1 tablespoon at a time, stirring after each addition. The moistened flour should cling together. Sprinkle in a little more water if the dough is crumbly.

With your fingers, gather the dough into a ball. Flatten the ball of dough and place it between 2 sheets of wax paper, 12 inches square. Roll out the dough between the 2 sheets of wax paper to an 11-inch round. Peel off the top sheet of paper, replace it, flip over the dough, and peel off what is now the top sheet of paper. Ease the dough into a 9-inch pie pan. Fold in any overhanging edges, and shape the dough between your fingers to make a stand-up rim. Flute the edges. Do not bake the pie shell.

The Filling:

> 1¼ cups macadamia nuts
> 3 eggs (graded large or extra-large)
> ⅔ cup granulated sugar
> ⅓ cup unsalted butter or margarine, melted
> 1 cup dark corn syrup

Preheat the oven to 375 degrees F. Place the macadamia nuts in the unbaked pie shell, then place the pie shell and nuts in the freezer while you mix the remaining ingredients. (Do not freeze the pie shell and nuts too far in advance; they should only be in the freezer for the time it takes to prepare the filling.)

In a medium-size mixing bowl, beat the eggs with a rotary beater or an electric mixer until the yolks and whites are combined, then beat in the sugar, melted butter or margarine, and the corn syrup. The mixture should be blended well, but do not overbeat. Pour the mixture over the nuts (the macadamia nuts will rise to the top) and place the pie on the middle shelf of the oven. Bake for 50 minutes. Midway during baking check the pie, and if it is browning too quickly, cover lightly with aluminum foil. The filling should be slightly puffed and firm at the end of the baking period. Press a finger lightly on the surface—the filling will spring back when touched. Cool the pie on a wire rack. Use a sharp knife to cut through the nuts when serving the pie. Store leftovers at room temperature, covered with plastic wrap.

4

THE

AMERICAS

Introduction

The range of foods eaten in the Americas is as varied as the cuisines of the world, for Spanish, Portuguese, British, French, and Dutch colonizations and European, Asian, and African emigrations all influenced the indigenous cooking of the Americas. While some preparations were transported intact, many of the most exciting culinary treats resulted from the blend of native cuisines with new ingredients and know-how brought from distant lands.

In most parts of the Americas native Indians helped shape today's cuisines. The Indians in the North gave us wild rice; potatoes were developed by Peruvian Indians; and corn came from several different tribes. But most Indian cooking was unsophisticated, and the New World settlers brought cooking methods and seasonings that transformed the most basic ingredients into enticing fare.

In the United States numerous regional cuisines evolved. Today, while New Englanders enjoy one-pot meals that may even cook over the same stove that heats the house, Texans are smoking meat and poultry outdoors over mesquite wood. There are smaller areas in the United States where unique cooking styles are part of the character of the locale, such as Lancaster County, Pennsylvania, and New Orleans, Louisiana.

Latin American countries developed distinctive cuisines. The four cuisines featured in this section as representative of the cooking of Latin America cover a broad variety of foods. Flavorful Mexican preparations, Brazilian specialties based on dried black beans and a starchy white tropical root (cassava), the unique treatment of potatoes that can be traced back to the Incas of Peru, and subtle meat-and-vegetable combinations from Argentina are presented. While Mexican cooking shows a strong Spanish influence, many Brazilian dishes resemble Portuguese more than South American preparations. Peruvian cuisine, another blend of native Indian and Spanish, offers among the most elaborate and imaginative dishes in South America. Argentina alone had no Indian culture when the Spanish colonized South America, making the Argentinian cuisine closest to the cooking of Spain.

UNITED STATES OF AMERICA

It took Dorothy nearly 101 minutes in *The Wizard of Oz* to discover what you are about to learn in the final chapter of this book: there's no place like home. You don't need to look beyond your own backyard to find exotic and intriguing preparations, for the United States of America is the home of the cuisines of all nations.

If you have ever moved to a new locale, you know it is comforting to bring with you something familiar from your former home. So it was—and still is—that every group of immigrants to the United States has held on to the old, familiar ways of cooking while adjusting to life in America. And even after they have assimilated, they have continued to use the kitchen as one way of preserving their cultural heritage. American Jews may prepare pizza, burgers, and even "chow mein," but they also prepare *gefilte* fish, *knaidlach, chremslach, cholent,* and *kugels* of all kinds. Scandinavians in the Midwest, Armenians in California, the Chinese of New York City and San Francisco— all ethnic groups hold fast to culinary traditions, many on major holidays and annual festivals only, others at one weekly dinner, and some at every meal.

THE PENNSYLVANIA DUTCH

One particular group, the Pennsylvania Dutch of Lancaster County in southeastern Pennsylvania, has set itself apart from the American mainstream by maintaining traditions of a bygone era in all aspects of life. It shuns electricity and modern machinery, clings to old speech patterns, and continues to dress as its ancestors did. The distinctive foods of the Pennsylvania Dutch reflect their Germanic origins. (They are not Dutch, but *Deutsch.*) Sauerkraut, *sauerbraten,* doughnuts, crullers, *hassenpfeffer*—many of the recipes in German cookbooks appear in those of the Pennsylvania Dutch as well.

But even when a cultural or religious group is insulated from the rest of society, where they live affects what they eat. As a resourceful farming community on fertile land with good spring rains, a respectable growing season, and long sunny days during the summer, the Pennsylvania Dutch are naturally known for imaginative fruit and vegetable cookery. If you travel through Lancaster County, you will see restaurant signs advertising "seven sweets and seven sours," letting you know that your meal will include numerous sweet fruit sauces and varied pickled vegetables. Stop in a country general store and you will find hundreds of jars of homemade preserves and relishes along with home baked breads, fruit pies, and the famous molasses pie known as shoofly pie.

To enjoy a Pennsylvania Dutch meal in your home serve a thrifty soup, such as a vegetarian split pea soup, followed by a substantial main course of chicken and dumplings, along with sweet-and-sour red cabbage, a corn relish, a pickled vegetable, perhaps a fresh cranberry-orange relish, mixed sweet pickles, hot bread, and for dessert an apple pie along with a lemony-brown sugar tart if you wish.

NEW ENGLAND

Preserves, relishes, home-baked breads, and fruit pies. This part of Pennsylvania Dutch cookery sounds a lot like New England. Like the Amish, the Puritans who first came to the shores of Massachusetts were a practical, no-nonsense group. Aided by native Indians, not only did they learn to survive on the three Indian staples of beans, corn, and squash (supplemented by seafood and game), but they also built up a cuisine that stands on its own. Beans became the famous baked beans sweetened by molasses in Boston (page 323) and maple syrup in Vermont; corn was made into chowder or eaten right off the cob at picnics; and winter squash became pumpkin pie (pumpkin is actually a kind of squash). New Englanders still have a practical attitude toward food. A good meal should be plentiful but not wasteful, memorable but not flamboyant.

It is not difficult for observant Jews to cook traditional New England foods. The New England boiled dinner of corned beef, cabbage, and potatoes needs no adaptation. Fresh fish such as cod and haddock that are caught in the waters off the coast of Massachusetts make tasty chowders, and barbecued chicken is featured in place of shellfish at the gatherings known as clambakes.

NEW ORLEANS

The most remarkable cuisine in the United States—a cuisine shaped like New England's from the mix of native Indian know-how and the background of the colonists, but worlds apart in tastes, ingredients, and presentation—lies in the southern state of Louisiana, centering around New Orleans. Fashioned from the food tastes of French and Spanish settlers, the culinary skills and food preferences of African slaves, and what was learned from the natives about local ingredients and cooking methods, the cooking of New Orleans blossomed into a cuisine unlike any other. Where else does one spend nearly an hour stirring a mixture of flour and butter or oil until it is exactly the right color to first begin cooking the gumbo?

New Orleans boasts world-famous restaurants and restaurant creations, including oysters Rockefeller and rémoulade sauce for salad. Those of us who are old enough to remember heard all about Louisiana's jambalaya, crawfish pie, and filé gumbo on *Your Hit Parade*. Everyone has a favorite jambalaya, including the Jews of Louisiana who prepare seafood jambalaya by substituting a white fish such as sole for shellfish.

The cooks of New Orleans added a new meaning to the word *creole*. While Creole originally referred to a person descended from the French and Spanish settlers of Louisiana, it has also come to mean a spicy food preparation that starts with a base of sweet green peppers, onions, and tomatoes. Actually, Louisiana's Creole cookery covers all the rich and varied cooking of New Orleans, the rice and red beans, fried catfish (which is nonkosher), broiled pompano, saucy duck dishes, and spicy sausages that can be made with ground beef instead of the pork product eaten by the non-Jewish population. A close cousin of Creole cooking is Cajun cuisine, more the cooking of the people—a bit spicier (more Tabasco peppers and sauce), somewhat less sophisticated.

SOUTHEASTERN UNITED STATES

New Orleans has a unique cuisine, but as a pocket of unusual eating it is not representative of southern cooking in general. While New Englanders and midwesterners are eating corn on the cob, most southerners are turning their corn into hominy. Grits (made of hominy) are enjoyed by all as a side dish for any meal. Southern Jews adapting the cooking of the area to the dietary laws enjoy split pea soup made with smoked turkey carcasses to replace the smoked hams for which the South is noted. Fried chicken and small fried steaks are eaten throughout the South. The "cream" gravy served with some of the meat dishes is made in Jewish homes by thickening pan drippings with flour and then mixing in broth in place of a dairy product.

TEXAS

Southerners enjoy a reputation for graciousness and hospitality, and perhaps no group vies for the title of hospitality king as much as Texans. Colossal Texas barbecues featuring chicken and ribs, gallons of Texas chili, and heaping bowls of side dishes to feed hundreds of people may not be your everyday meal in this southwestern state, but Texans do like to do things bigger and better, barbecues included.

Another acclaimed element of Texas cuisine is known as Tex-Mex cooking. With Texas once a part of Mexico, now separated by the Rio Grande on its entire southwestern border, the Mexican influence in Texas kitchens is profound. *Tacos, enchiladas, tamales,* and chili (see page 298) prepared by Texans are related to their purely Mexican antecedents, but Tex-Mex foods tend to be sauced more heavily than their Mexican counterparts.

NEW MEXICO

Some of the best New Mexican preparations are also a blend of cuisines. Native Indian and Spanish influences are apparent in preparations such as *sopaipillas* (page 331), which may appear in Mexican cookbooks but are in fact New Mexican. Green chilis prepared by Zuñi Indians and the fried breads of the Navajos have become part of the cuisine of New Mexico.

MEXICO

Present-day Mexican cuisine is the result of the influence of Spanish ingredients and cooking methods of two established Indian civilizations: the Mayas and the Aztecs. Spanish settlers introduced the technique of frying to the Indians, making the simple corn-based cuisine more interesting even without the addition of new foods. But when the beef, pork, chickens, rice, wheat, and almonds brought by the Spanish were combined with native corn and hot chilies, unusually tasty preparations were created. (Not that the culinary gains were one-sided: without the food treasures brought back from Mexico and other parts of the New World, the Spanish would have to face the morning without hot chocolate, and *gazpacho* would be tomatoless.)

Beans are another mainstay of the Mexican diet, and the Spanish introduction of lard to Mexico is responsible for the famous refried beans (we can substitute chicken fat or oil for the lard, see page 321) as well as for all the fried variations of the basic Mexican breads, *tortillas* (page 319). Plain baked *tortillas* made of *masa harina* (a corn product) are still eaten with every meal, and boiled or refried beans also appear on the table with most meals, even breakfast. A traditional Mexican breakfast consists of eggs, *tortillas*, a sauce, beans, perhaps avocado slices and fruit, and a cup of Mexican chocolate.

Sweet or hot pepper-based sauces called *moles* are characteristic of Mexican cuisine. The most famous is *mole poblano*, an elaborate concoction using dozens of ingredients including several different kinds of chilies along with pumpkin seeds, nuts, and chocolate. While breakfasts and dinners are substantial and unhurried, small *tamales* (page 301), tortilla chips, sweets, and fruit juices are enjoyed as quick snacks all day long.

BRAZIL

Because of the influence of Portuguese explorations on the New World and Portuguese settlements in Brazil, Brazilian cuisine is unlike that of any other country on the South American continent. To Brazilian cuisine, the Portuguese introduced onions, garlic, and parsley, along with cattle, pigs, goats, and sheep. Perhaps most significant, however, was the importation of African slaves by the Portuguese into Brazil in the 1600s. Already accustomed to torrid weather, the black West Africans were at home cooking in Brazil. They brought their palm oil, coconuts, okra, bananas, and a hot pepper that was actually native to the New World but used in African cooking before it was reintroduced to Brazil. Using these and other African ingredients, Portuguese additions, and the primitive foods of the Brazilian Indians, including crops of corn, sweet potatoes, and cassava, the African slaves became the prime molders of the Brazilian cuisine in the North.

With a 4,000-mile coastline on the Atlantic Ocean and the world's longest river (the 4,000-mile Amazon) running across, it is not surprising that all kinds of fish supplement Brazil's basically starchy diet of rice, beans, and cassava. Although shrimp are the most popular seafood in Brazil, and pork and pork sausages are part of the Brazilian national dish called *fejoada completa* (page 322), we can enjoy Brazilian food in the kosher home by including the staples—black beans and cassava—and using the spices and garnishes always served with Brazilian meals (see page 322). Whatever is eaten, the universal beverage is coffee—consumed throughout the day.

PERU

Ice-covered 14,000-foot peaks of the Andes Mountains with temperate valleys below, a narrow desert coast dotted with

small oases created by water trickling down from the mountains—these were the formidable geographic conditions faced
and mastered in the days of the Inca civilization. Making the
most of available agricultural land, the Incas terraced steep
mountainsides to increase the land available for growing crops,
built irrigation systems, and constructed roads and bridges
linking the farmers and their produce to town markets.

It was in the Andes Mountains that potatoes and other root
crops were first cultivated as long ago as 2500 B.C.E., probably
before the time of the Incas. The heritage of the Incas combined
with the influences of the Spanish conquerors in the 1500s led
to the development of a sophisticated albeit sometimes strange
cuisine. Among the more unusual foods enjoyed by Peruvians
are a kind of guinea pig (*cuy*) and a snack called *antichucos* consisting of pieces of grilled skewered beef heart dipped in a hot sauce.
Seviche, raw fish that is "cooked" in a marinade of lemon or lime
juice, is a favorite appetizer in Peru (see the Tahitian version on
page 194). Potatoes are seasoned and decorated imaginatively,
and an elaborate potato creation that will bring a touch of Peru
to your table is presented on page 314.

ARGENTINA

Temperate, flat, and fertile, central Argentina provided the
perfect land for the cattle brought by the Spaniards from
Europe in the 1600s. And it is beef that dominates Argentinian
cuisine. Broiled beef and roasted beef are most popular, a legacy
of the gauchos who herded cattle and grilled the meat without
fanfare. Nowadays Argentinians enjoy beef sprinkled with a
fiery hot sauce (page 294). Beef stews that are savory but not
spicy are another part of Argentina's varied cuisine, and there is
a festive stew that is cooked and served in a most unusual
container (see page 296).

There was no established Indian civilization when the
Spanish came to Argentina, so the cuisine is not a mix of Indian
and Spanish preparations but the creation of Spanish cooks
using indigenous ingredients. Some of the dishes cooked in
Argentina, such as *paella* and potato omelettes, could as easily
have come from Spanish kitchens. Although some Argentinian

specialties, including *empanadas* and *flan,* are part of Mexican cuisine as well, the meat-and-dairy combinations that are popular in Mexico are not featured in Argentinian dishes. With beef the preferred meat and dairy products not characteristically eaten with meat, most Argentinian recipes do not require kosher adaptations.

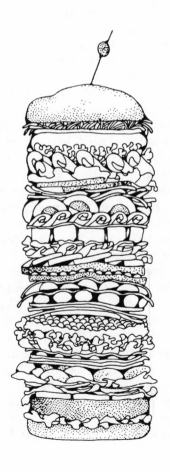

Appetizers and Soups

In the United States, where appetizers are usually meant to tease or whet the appetite, an appetizer may be as modest as a bowl of nuts or vegetables served with a dip. We are most likely to have more elaborate appetizers when we are dining out or when we are entertaining at home. In Latin American countries the appetizers are often more than just a "teaser."

For one cuisine in Latin America, the appetizers are even more important than the rest of the meal. In Peru, there is a tradition of filling up on appetizers and leaving the main course for the servants. Brazilians serve *tamales*, small meat pies, and shrimp preparations to ward off hunger pangs before the late evening meal, and Argentinians enjoy *empanadas* (page 281) and other treats while waiting for their barbecued meats to cook. Mexican finger foods prepared on a base of small *tortillas* are known as *antojitos*, "little whims." Corn chips topped with *guacamole* (page 290) and *salsa cruda* (page 292) is an example of an *antojito*. While *antojitos* are eaten as snacks in Mexico, they make good appetizers. Latin American appetizers are usually well seasoned and tasty combinations of ingredients, and they can be used as an exciting introduction to brighten up routine meals.

"Soup's on!" was the signal that our Friday night dinner at my Grandma's was about to begin. Soup still begins the meal for many people in the United States, especially on formal occasions and holidays. Soup is even more important in Latin American cuisines, where the main meal is not considered complete unless it is preceded by soup. On festive occasions Mexicans sometimes follow the usual noodle, dumpling, avocado, or bean soup with what is referred to as a "dry soup," but turns out to be rice, noodles, or *tortillas* cooked in broth until the liquid is absorbed. Brazilian soups are also rich and satisfying, and throughout South America stewlike *chupes* full of vegetables and fish, cheese, or eggs are popular. Light broths and delicate squash blossom soups (page 287) are also enjoyed, and peanut soups popular in colonial North America are eaten throughout Latin America.

FRIED PLANTAIN CHIPS
Plátanos Fritos

General Latin America

Serves 4 to 6

Plantains look like large green bananas, but they are much starchier, and even when ripe they need to be cooked. The fruit appears in stews and on the dessert table, and when sliced and fried it may be served as an appetizer.

Plátanos fritos are crisp on the outside with a softened center. Somewhat starchy yet a little sweet, fried plantains taste like they are in the banana family, which indeed they are.

1 large plantain (about ½ pound)
Oil for frying

In an electric skillet or a 4-quart pot, heat a minimum of ½ inch of oil to moderate, 350 degrees F.

To peel the plantain, use a sharp knife to slice off the ends. Cut through the skin lengthwise in 3 or 4 places, then peel off the skin. Slice the plantain on the diagonal into thin (⅛ inch) rounds.

Fry the plantain chips for a minute or two until golden brown on both sides, turning as necessary. Remove from the oil with a slotted spoon. Place on paper towels and cover with additional paper towels. Press on the plantain rounds with the palms of your hands. This will squeeze out excess oil and make the rounds thinner. Serve hot or at room temperature, plain or with a dip. Plantains can be refried briefly to reheat.

BATTER-FRIED SQUASH BLOSSOMS

New Mexico

Serves 4 to 6

The Zuñi Indians have a delicious use for the abundance of male blossoms produced by their zucchini, pumpkins, and other fruits in the cucurbit family: they dip freshly picked blossoms in batter then deep-fry them, making a light crisp crust around the fragile blossoms. A *masa harina* batter makes a crust with a definite corn taste, while the use of all-purpose flour allows the delicate flavor of the blossom to predominate. You may notice differences in taste among the blossoms of different plants.

Squash blossoms are available in Spanish, Mexican, and sometimes Italian groceries, but if you grow pumpkins, gourds, and other squashes, you will enjoy picking the blossoms yourself. Pick the male blossoms either before or just after they open (the female blossoms have a swelling behind them that will become the fruit). *Caution:* Make sure there are no bees inside the blossoms you pick.

> 1 cup unsifted masa harina or all-purpose
> flour
> ½ teaspoon salt (optional)
> 1 cup water, approximately
> Oil for deep-frying
> 12 to 24 squash blossoms, depending on size

In a small bowl, place the *masa harina* or all-purpose flour and salt. Stir in the water. Mix well with a fork to make a thin, smooth batter. The *masa harina* will take an additional tablespoon or two of water to reach the proper consistency.

In an electric skillet or a 2- to 4-quart pot, heat 1½ inches of oil to 375 degrees F. The oil will be hot but not yet smoking; a drop of water will spatter instantly. Gently dip one blossom at a time into the batter, covering the petals inside and out. Allow excess batter to drip off, then carefully place the coated blossom in the hot oil. Cook until a golden brown, then turn and fry the other side. Several blossoms can be fried at once as long as they do not touch each other. If the blossoms are absorbing too much oil, raise the heat. Drain the cooked blossoms very well on paper towels and serve immediately.

NACHOS

Southwestern United States,
Mexican influence

Serves 6 to 8

 Nachos are, in a sense, Mexican open-faced grilled-cheese sandwiches. The basic Mexican bread, the *tortilla*, is cut into wedges or strips, fried, sprinkled with cheese, and broiled. Monterey Jack is an excellent cheese to use in Mexican cooking, but Cheddar, Muenster, Swiss, or any other cheese that melts easily is suitable. The simplest way to make *nachos* is to buy *tortilla* or corn chips, cover them with shredded cheese, and broil or bake until the cheese has melted. Or buy soft corn or flour *tortillas* (canned or fresh), cut them into wedges, fry them, and proceed as above. If you like to start from scratch, make your own *tortillas* and proceed as directed below.

> **8 tortillas, purchased or homemade (page 319)**
> **Oil for deep-frying**
> **1 pound shredded cheese (see introduction above)**
> **Green Tomato Sauce (page 291), Uncooked Red Sauce (page 292) or a purchased taco sauce**

Cut the *tortillas* into 8 wedges each. In a large electric skillet or a pot at least 2 inches deep, heat an inch of oil until it just begins to smoke, 400 degrees F. Fry as many *tortilla* wedges at once as will fit comfortably, turning to brown them on both sides. When they are golden brown, remove the chips with a slotted spoon. Drain well on paper towels. When cool, the chips can be stored in plastic bags. They will keep at room temperature for 2 or 3 days, or they may be frozen.

When you are ready to cook, spread the *tortilla* chips out on one or more large ungreased baking sheets. Sprinkle lavishly with the shredded cheese. If desired, drizzle some sauce over the cheese. Broil 4 inches from the heat until the cheese is melted but not browned. Serve with green or red sauce or a purchased *taco* sauce.

BEAN DIP

Frijoles Para Sopear

Mexico

Makes 2 cups

Can you boil water? Then you can make this bean dip from scratch, because all you need to do is boil water with dried beans, mash the beans (or purée them in a food processor), stir in grated cheese to make it creamy if you like, and add a spicy sauce. Although kidney beans are widely used in Mexico, many other beans are tasty and make a smooth, colorful purée also.

> ½ pound (1¼ cups) dried pinto, kidney, or
>   other red or pink beans, picked through and
>   rinsed
> 1 quart water
> ½ cup shredded Monterey Jack, Muenster, or
>   Cheddar cheese (optional)
> ¼ cup Green Tomato Sauce (page 291),
>   Uncooked Red Sauce (page 292), or
>   purchased taco sauce or 1 tablespoon chili
>   powder

In a 2-quart pot, bring the beans and water to the boil. Reduce the heat so the water boils gently, cover the pot, and cook for 1½ to 2½ hours, until the beans are very tender. Check the pot from time to time—the beans must always be covered by water, and the liquid must be boiling or they will not cook. When the beans are tender, drain them, reserving the liquid.

Using a potato masher, a food processor, a food mill, or a fork, mash the hot beans, adding enough liquid to make a thick, smooth purée. If you are using cheese, blend it in while the beans are still very hot so the cheese melts. Stir in one of the sauces or the chili powder. If the dip is too stiff, add a little liquid saved from the beans. Serve hot, warm, or at room temperature as a party dip with *tortilla* chips. Or serve small portions as a first course with a few chips stuck into the beans. Refrigerated leftovers will keep for a day or two, and the dip may be frozen.

LITTLE MEAT-FILLED TURNOVERS
Empanaditas de Carne

Argentina, Brazil

Makes 48

Little turnovers filled with a pleasantly spiced ground beef mixture are finger food for an appetizer party and make an appealing *hors d'oeuvre* for a theme dinner. Optional additions of raisins, nuts, and olives make them even tastier. This recipe uses a homemade pastry dough, although in Argentina and parts of the United States precut dough for *empanadas* (large *empanaditas*) can be purchased. My Argentinian neighbor confessed to me that even though puff pastry is much flakier and not traditional, she buys a frozen puff pastry for her baked *empanadas,* and you may wish to to do the same as a shortcut.

The Filling:

½ **pound extra-lean ground beef**
2 **tablespoons tomato paste**
1 **teaspoon chili powder**
Salt and freshly ground black pepper
3 **tablespoons finely chopped onion**
Optional: 1 to 2 tablespoons chopped raisins,
  1 to 2 tablespoons chopped toasted
  almonds, 1 to 2 tablespoons finely chopped
  green olives or pimiento-stuffed olives

The Dough:

2 **cups unsifted all-purpose flour**
1 **teaspoon double-acting baking powder**
⅓ **cup solid vegetable shortening**
1 **egg (graded large), unbeaten**
¼ **cup water, approximately**
 Oil for deep-frying *or* 1 **egg (graded large) for**
  baking
 Green Tomato Sauce (page 291), Uncooked
  Red Sauce (page 292), or a purchased taco
  sauce

Recipe continues on the following page . . .

For the filling, in an 8-inch skillet cook the ground beef over moderate heat, strring frequently, until it is brown all over. Use the edge of a large spoon to break up all clumps of meat while the meat is browning. Spoon off accumulated fat. Add the tomato paste, chili powder, and salt and pepper to taste, mixing well. Cook over low heat for 5 minutes, stirring to prevent sticking, then transfer the meat to a bowl. Mix in the chopped onion and any of the optional additions. Refrigerate until ready to use, up to 24 hours.

For the dough, in a medium-size bowl, mix the flour and baking powder. Using a fork, cut in the shortening until the particles are small and evenly distributed. Add the unbeaten egg, stirring to moisten the dough. Now sprinkle in the water a tablespoon at a time, stirring after each addition. Add enough water so the dough clings together, but do not make it too moist. Use your hands to gather the dough into a ball, then divide the dough evenly into 3 balls.

Flatten a ball of dough between 2 sheets of wax paper, then roll the dough into a thin 10-inch round. After every few rolls, peel off the top sheet of wax paper, replace it, then flip over the dough and peel off the bottom sheet, replacing it also. This will make the dough easier to roll and will keep the dough from sticking to the wax paper.

Work with one ball of dough at a time, keeping the remaining dough covered.

Using a 3-inch cookie cutter, cut as many rounds as you can from the dough. Reroll scraps, and cut more rounds. You should get about 16 rounds from each third of the dough. You may, of course, cut larger rounds. Obviously, if you cut 4- or 5-inch rounds (most coffee containers are 4 inches, and shortening cans are 5 inches) you will have fewer rounds.

Place about a teaspoon of filling off-center on each 3-inch round. (Four-inch rounds take about 2 teaspoons, and 5-inch rounds use about a tablespoon.) Moisten the edges of the dough with water, then fold the dough over the filling. Press the edges together, and crimp as desired. Place on wax paper, and cover with a clean towel or another sheet of wax paper so the *empanaditas* don't dry out. Repeat with the remaining dough and filling. The filled turnovers may be tray-frozen at this time.

To fry the *empanaditas*, in a large electric skillet, a deep-fryer, or a pot with sides at least 2 inches deep heat ½ to 1 inch of oil to 375 degrees F. Add as many *empanaditas* as you can without crowding them (they should not touch each other), fry until they are golden on one side, and turn to fry the other side. This will take only a minute or two, a little longer for frozen *empanaditas*. Drain well on paper towels.

To bake, preheat the oven to 400 degrees F. Place the *empanaditas* on a cookie sheet or baking tray. Brush the tops with the beaten egg. (It is not necessary to grease the tray, but the turnovers will brown better on the bottom if you do use grease.) Bake for 10 minutes or until golden. Frozen *empanaditas* will take longer.

Serve with green or red sauce or a purchased *taco* sauce.

DEVILED TUNA

Southeastern United States

Serves 4 as an appetizer,
2 or 3 as a luncheon dish

Deviled crab is a popular preparation in Maryland, Virginia, and other southern states. The seafood is combined with just enough mustard powder and lemon juice for a piquant touch. Sometimes a combination of ingredients created for a particular kind of shellfish turns out to be especially well suited for a fish that is a staple in many kosher homes. So it is with deviled crab and tuna fish. Plain, ordinary canned tuna becomes a delicious appetizer or luncheon treat when it is mixed with lots of crunchies and a hint of the spicy, then baked with a breadcrumb topping. Fresh tuna and codfish steaks are tasty as "deviled" fish also.

> **2 cans (6½ ounces each) tuna fish or 1 pound**
>   **fresh tuna or cod steaks**
> **¼ cup mayonnaise**
> **¼ cup minced onion**
> **¼ cup minced celery**
> **¼ cup minced green pepper**

Recipe continues on the following page . . .

2 tablespoons chopped fresh parsley or 2
teaspoons dried parsley flakes
1 teaspoon dry mustard powder,
approximately
4 teaspoons fresh lemon juice, approximately
Salt and freshly ground black pepper
½ cup soft breadcrumbs
2 teaspoons unsalted butter or margarine

For canned tuna, place the tuna in a medium-size bowl and mash it well with a fork. For fresh fish steaks, place the fish in an 8- to 10- inch skillet with enough water to cover by ¼ inch. Bring to the boil over moderate heat, immediately reduce the heat to a very gentle boil, partially cover the skillet, and cook the fish for about 5 minutes, until it flakes easily with a fork. Remove from the skillet with a slotted spoon. Remove and discard the skin and any bones, then place the fish in a medium-size bowl and flake it with a fork.

Preheat the oven to 350 degrees F. To the canned or fresh fish add the mayonnaise, onion, celery, green pepper, parsley, mustard powder, lemon juice, and salt and pepper to taste, mixing very well. To increase the "deviled" taste, add a little more mustard powder or lemon juice. Turn the mixture into 4 small ramekins or ceramic baking shells. Top with the breadcrumbs (2 tablespoons per ramekin) and dot with tiny bits of butter or margarine.

Bake for 12 to 15 minutes, until the crumbs begin to brown but before the fish dries out.

Note: To serve as a luncheon dish, place the mixture in a 1-quart casserole (7 inches square, approximately), top with breadcrumbs, dot with butter, and bake at 350 degrees F. for about 15 minutes.

SALMON WITH CREAM DRESSING

Washington State

Serves 6 as an appetizer,
4 as a luncheon dish

The waters of the Pacific Northwest abound with Dungeness crab and salmon, and the famous crab meat preparation known as Crab Louis originated in Seattle, Washington. The mayonnaise-and-whipped cream dressing that tops Crab Louis is excellent when canned or fresh salmon is substituted for the crab.

> 1½ pounds fresh salmon fillets or 1 can (1
>   pound) red or pink salmon
> 1 cup mayonnaise
> 2 tablespoons prepared chili sauce (not hot
>   Mexican chili sauce)
> 1 tablespoon grated onion or 1 tablespoon
>   finely chopped fresh chives
> 1 tablespoon fresh lemon juice
> 2 tablespoons chopped fresh parsley
> Dash of ground cayenne pepper
> ½ cup heavy or whipping cream
> Lettuce leaves
> Optional garnishes: quartered hard-cooked
>   eggs, black olives, avocado slices, whole
>   cooked green beans

For the fresh salmon, place the fish in a skillet with enough water to cover by ¼ inch. Bring to the boil over moderate heat, immediately reduce the heat to a very gentle boil, partially cover the skillet, and cook the salmon for 4 to 5 minutes, until it flakes easily with a fork. With a pancake turner or a slotted spoon carefully transfer the fish to a flat plate. Refrigerate, covered, until chilled.

For canned salmon, drain the salmon, remove any skin and bones, and flake the salmon. Place in the refrigerator.

The dressing should be prepared at least an hour in advance so it can chill. It can be prepared as long as 24 hours ahead of time and refrigerated, but it does not freeze well.

Recipe continues on the following page . . .

Chill a small mixing bowl and beaters or a whisk in the freezer for 15 minutes, or place in the refrigerator for an hour or longer. Cream will whip better in a chilled bowl.

In a medium-size bowl, combine the mayonnaise with the chili sauce, onion or chives, lemon juice, parsley, and cayenne pepper. Pour the cream into the chilled bowl and whip until the cream holds stiff peaks. Blend the whipped cream into the mayonnaise mixture. Chill until serving.

To assemble, arrange a large lettuce leaf on each serving plate. Cut the fresh salmon into serving-size pieces, or flake the salmon with a fork. Divide the salmon among the plates and top with a generous portion of dressing. Garnish as desired.

NEW ENGLAND FISH CHOWDER

New England

Serves 4 to 6

New England clam chowder is white, creamy, and tomato-less, whereas Manhattan chowder is tomato-y red. By using pollock or haddock in place of clams and omitting the salt pork that is a part of the New England version, a fine fish chowder can be produced. Full of diced fish and cubed white potatoes, the chowder can almost be eaten with a fork. Although it is not typical to top the chowder with spices, a touch of nutmeg adds a nice flavor.

> **1 pound fresh pollock or haddock fillets**
> **2 cups potato cubes (½-inch cubes)**
> **2 cups water**
> **2 tablespoons unsalted butter or vegetable oil**
> **1 cup chopped onion**
> **2 cups milk**
> **1 cup light cream**
> **Salt and freshly ground black pepper**
> **Ground nutmeg (optional)**

Cut the pollock or haddock into ½-inch squares. Refrigerate until ready to use.

In a 2-quart pot, place the potato cubes and the 2 cups of water. Bring to the boil over high heat, reduce the heat to a moderate boil, and cook, partially covered, until the potatoes are tender, 10 to 12 minutes.

Meanwhile, in a 4-quart pot over moderate heat, melt the butter or heat the oil. Add the chopped onion and cook, stirring often, until the onion is tender but not brown. When the potatoes are done, use a slotted spoon to transfer them to the 4-quart pot. Stir gently to mix the potatoes in with the cooked onions. Remove the pot from the heat.

Now add the pieces of fish to the potato water, and bring to the boil over high heat, stirring frequently. As soon as the water boils, turn the heat down to the lowest setting and cook, stirring often, until the fish turns white. Add the cooked fish with the cooking liquid to the potatoes and onions. Stir in the milk and cream, add salt and pepper to taste, then bring just to the boil over moderate heat, stirring often. Reduce the heat to low, simmer a minute or two, then turn off the heat. Allow the chowder to rest, covered, for a few minutes before serving. Serve from a tureen or in individual bowls. If desired, sprinkle the chowder with a little nutmeg just before serving.

CHAYOTE AND SQUASH BLOSSOM SOUP
Sopa de Chayotl y Flor de Calabaza

Mexico

Serves 4

Crisp and delicate, the pale green pear-shaped squash known as chayote originated in Mexico. With a flavor even milder than zucchini, chayote is used in soups, soufflés, and vegetables dishes, and it is stuffed for main dishes and desserts.

Recipe continues on the following page . . .

This refreshing soup uses squash blossoms as well as chayote, adding flecks of orange and the subtle flavor of the blossoms to the purée. Firm, unblemished chayotes will keep in the refrigerator for a week or two.

> **2 large chayotes (¾ pound each)**
> **24 pumpkin, zucchini, or other large squash**
> **blossoms**
> **2 tablespoons vegetable oil**
> **¼ cup chopped onion**
> **1 large clove garlic, minced**
> **1 quart chicken or vegetable broth**
> **Salt**
> **Cucumber, cantaloupe, or other small yellow**
> **blossoms, for garnish**

Peel the chayotes and cut 4 thin slices from each small end. Reserve the slices for garnish. Cut the remaining chayotes into ½ inch cubes. In a 4-quart pot, bring 2 quarts of water to the boil. Add the cubed chayote and cook until tender, about 20 minutes. Drain and set aside.

Fill a large bowl with cold water. Gently swish the large blossoms in the water to remove any dirt or small insects. Drain. Chop the blossoms into small pieces.

In an 8-inch skillet, heat the oil over moderate heat. Sauté the onion and garlic until they are softened and just beginning to brown. Add the squash blossoms and sauté a minute or two longer, stirring often. The blossoms should be soft but not brown, and they will have a lovely aroma when cooked.

In a blender or a food processor, purée the cooked chayote along with the sautéed blossom mixture. Set aside.

In a 4-quart pot, bring the chicken or vegetable broth to the boil over high heat. Reduce the heat to moderate and add the purée. Bring back to the boil, add salt to taste, then reduce the heat and simmer for a minute or two. The soup can be cooled and refrigerated or frozen at this point. To serve, reheat the soup and transfer to a tureen or individual bowls. Just before serving, rinse the small blossoms in cold water. Garnish the soup with the reserved chayote slices and the small whole blossoms.

Condiments
and Sauces

If you have a favorite kosher deli or restaurant, you probably have come to anticipate a certain array of pickles and other condiments that may be on the table even before you place your order. Sour pickles and tomatoes smelling heavily of garlic and dill, black and green olives, and sauerkraut or cole slaw are some of the extras that complete the meal. As we have seen, the Pennsylvania Dutch serve an imposing assortment of condiments, including mouthwatering relishes and pickled vegetables, sweet jams, conserves, and fruit sauces. Tomato, corn, and cucumber relishes are prepared throughout the United States. Apple butter is a breakfast accompaniment in the Northeast and Northwest, maple syrup is one of Vermont's most famous products, while in the South pancakes are drenched with a dark corn syrup.

Salt and pepper are the universal seasonings in American homes. The Latin American counterpart is a kind of hot sauce that is present on the table for all meals. A superb Brazilian hot sauce flavored with fresh lemon and lime juices is presented in this section, along with a liquid pepper sauce used by Argentinians to season grilled meats at the diner's discretion.

Mexican sauces range from a simple condiment of uncooked chopped hot peppers with onions, tomatoes, and sometimes vinegar to more complicated *moles*. As in Peruvian dishes, many Mexican sauces are an integral part of the preparations themselves (for example, *mancha manteles*, page 311). Whether incorporated into the preparation or passed around separately, Mexican sauces tend to be spicy. However, the famous avocado sauce (*guacamole*, page 290) that is served as a dip, sauce, and side dish ranges from temperate to spicy.

GUACAMOLE

Mexico

Makes 1 cup

A Texan friend of ours used *guacamole* as a character builder for his daughter, who considered this avocado preparation to be one of her worst enemies. He told her that if she just learned to eat *guacamole*, she would find that she could do all sorts of things she had thought impossible. Encouraging rather than forcing his daughter to take little tastes from time to time, our friend reported that after a year or two the young lady not only ate *guacamole*, she began to enjoy it. "Remember the *guacamole!*" became the answer to "I can't do it."

As an avocado-lover I have an affinity for *guacamole*, so I cannot use it as a character builder for myself. But I can vouch that as a food *guacamole* is superb. Mexicans use it as a sauce for *tacos* and plain *tortillas*, and *guacamole* accompanies most Mexican meals. The addition of a hot pepper makes this *guacamole* spicy and the lime juice gives it a unique flavor. Use it as a dip, a salad, *tostada* topping (see page 304), *taco* sauce, and, if appropriate, a character builder.

> **1 large ripe avocado (about 1 pound)**
> **1 small hot jalapeño pepper (about 2 inches long)**
> **1 tablespoon chopped scallion or onion**
> **1 to 2 tablespoons fresh lime juice**
> **1 medium-size ripe red tomato, peeled, seeded, and chopped**
> **1 teaspoon chopped fresh coriander (optional)**

The avocado must be soft to the touch (but not mushy) or it will have no flavor. Avocados will usually ripen at room temperature, but they should be refrigerated when soft.

Cut the avocado in half, remove the large seed (plant the seed if you like), and use a spoon to scoop out the fruit. If you find it easier, use a vegetable peeler to peel the skin from the fruit. In a medium-size bowl, mash the avocado with a fork. Cover tightly with plastic wrap and set aside.

Cut the hot pepper in half and remove and discard the seeds and ribs. Slice the pepper into thin strips then cut crosswise to mince. Add the pepper to the mashed avocado then immediately wash your hands to remove the caustic oils from your fingers.

Use a fork to mix the mashed avocado and minced hot pepper with the remaining ingredients. Although *guacamole* usually has a coarse texture, use a food processor or a blender to make a smooth purée if you prefer.

Transfer the *guacamole* to a serving bowl. Place a piece of plastic wrap directly on the surface to keep the avocado from discoloring. Stir before serving. Serve as a dip, a salad on a bed of lettuce with tomatoes and olives for garnish, or as a sauce with Mexican meals. *Guacamole* can be kept in the refrigerator for a day or two, but it discolors rapidly when exposed to the air.

GREEN TOMATO SAUCE
Salsa de Tomatillo

Mexico

Makes 1 cup

This sauce may be a challenge because you will need to find *tomatillos,* or Mexican green tomatoes to make it authentically Mexican. If you are lucky, you have access to either a Mexican grocery or a supermarket that features out-of-the-ordinary fresh fruits and vegetables or at least a well-stocked Mexican canned food section. Regular green tomatoes will provide the correct texture and appearance, but they do not have the sweetness or exact flavor of *tomatillos,* which are sweet and tart at once and taste a little like watermelon rind. *Tomatillos* look like green cherry tomatoes wrapped in what masquerades as green tissue paper but turns out to be husks.

It is up to you whether to make this a moderately hot or a searingly hot sauce. Canned green chilies cover a broad range. Either they will be labeled "mild" or "hot" or they will have a thermometer on the label indicating the degree of hotness.

Recipe continues on the following page . . .

Even the mild ones may be hot by American standards, so be careful.

> ¼ **pound fresh or canned tomatillos (about 5)**
> **1 can (4 ounces) peeled green chilies**
> ¼ **cup chopped onion**
> **1 large clove garlic, minced**
> **Salt and freshly ground black pepper**

Remove the husks, then rinse the *tomatillos*, which will be sticky until they are rinsed. Chop the *tomatillos* coarsely. If the chili peppers are hot, remove and discard the seeds. Chop the peppers, then place the *tomatillos*, chilies, onion, and garlic in a blender or food processor and process until you reach the smoothness desired. This does not need to be a smooth purée— bits and pieces of the vegetables give it a nice texture. Transfer to a bowl and add salt and pepper to taste. After a few minutes, drain off the accumulated liquid. Serve uncooked as a relish. Store leftovers in a covered container in the refrigerator, where the sauce will keep for a few days.

For a softer consistency and a slightly different flavor, cook the *tomatillos*, chilies, onion, and garlic over moderate heat for 5 minutes, stirring often until all the liquid evaporates. Add salt and pepper to taste.

UNCOOKED RED SAUCE
Salsa Cruda

Mexico

Makes 1 cup

This sauce starts with a red chili paste made by softening dried hot chili peppers in hot water then puréeing the peppers. Two small fresh hot red peppers can be used in place of the dried peppers. For many South American table sauces the chili paste or fresh peppers are mixed only with a little lemon juice and onion, making a very hot sauce that must be treated with respect. The addition of tomatoes in this recipe makes a pleasingly piquant sauce.

¼ cup dried hontaka or other dried red
  peppers
¼ cup boiling water
1 pound ripe red tomatoes, peeled, seeded,
  and chopped
¼ cup chopped onion
1 large clove garlic, minced
Salt and freshly ground black pepper

Tear the dried peppers open with your fingers and shake out and discard the seeds. Tear the peppers into pieces and place in a small heatproof bowl or cup. Immediately wash your hands to rid them of the caustic pepper oils. Pour the boiling water over the peppers. If the water does not cover the peppers, add hot or boiling water to cover. Allow to soak for 30 minutes, then purée the peppers and water in a blender or food processor.

In a medium-size bowl, mix the pepper purée with the tomatoes, onion, and garlic. Add salt and pepper to taste. Allow the flavors to blend at room temperature for an hour or two, then refrigerate the sauce. The sauce will keep for several days in the refrigerator. Store in a small glass jar instead of a plastic container (the peppers will dye plastic red).

Note: The Indian *cachumbar* on page 208 also makes an appropriate table accompaniment for Mexican meals.

HOT PEPPER AND LEMON-LIME SAUCE
Môlho de Pimenta e Limão

Brazil

Makes ¾ cup

This intriguing sauce is the traditional accompaniment to Brazil's national dish, *feijoada completa.* A small spoonful will enliven a portion of plain black or pinto beans, and it is a unique accompaniment for plain broiled fish.

Recipe continues on the following page . . .

4 jalapeño peppers (2 inches each)
½ cup chopped onion
2 cloves garlic, minced
¼ cup fresh lime juice
¼ cup fresh lemon juice

Cut the peppers in half and remove and discard the seeds and ribs. Slice the peppers into thin strips, then cut crosswise to mince. Wash your hands immediately to remove the caustic oils from your fingers.

Use a mortar and pestle to crush the minced peppers, chopped onion, and minced garlic. Gradually blend in the citrus juices. The sauce will have bits and pieces of the pepper, onion, and garlic. For a smoother purée combine the peppers, onions, and garlic in a blender with just enough lemon or lime juice to process. Gradually add the remaining juice.

Allow the flavors to blend for ½ hour at room temperature before serving. Refrigerate leftovers for a week.

HOT PEPPER-AND-VINEGAR SAUCE
Chimichurri

Argentina

Makes 1 cup

With a quarter cup of ground cayenne pepper mixed with only a cup of liquid you might expect this sauce to be exceedingly hot, but the vinegar tempers the hot pepper, making the sauce palatable. Herbs give the sauce a nice flavor. Argentinians serve this sauce with grilled meats, and it is also very good with *tamales* (page 301) and *empanaditas* (page 281).

¼ cup olive oil
¾ cup red wine vinegar
¼ cup ground cayenne pepper or hot paprika
1 tablespoon minced garlic
1 teaspoon dried oregano
1 large bay leaf

¼ **cup chopped fresh parsley or 4 teaspoons
dried parsley flakes**
½ **teaspoon salt**
¼ **teaspoon freshly ground black pepper**

In a 2-cup jar with a tight lid combine all the ingredients. Close the jar and shake well. Allow the mixture to stand at room temperature for 24 hours, shaking the jar occasionally. Strain and return the liquid to the jar. Shake before serving. The sauce can be served in a bowl and distributed with a spoon, but a small bottle with a shaker top is ideal. (Soy sauce and liquid pepper sauces come in such bottles.) *Chimichurri* can be stored at room temperature for several weeks.

Main Dishes

What could be more tantalizing than the aroma of roast chicken browning in the oven, lamb shoulder roasting with potatoes and onions, brisket of beef simmering on the stove, or a piece of fresh fish rubbed with lemon juice and herbs cooking under the broiler? Many of our most satisfying meat meals center around a large cut of oven-roasted, pot-roasted, or broiled meat supplemented by potatoes, a vegetable, and a salad. Hearty one-dish meals such as chicken-in-the-pot and beef stews are enjoyed as a change of pace, but the basic dinner meal in the United States follows a meat, vegetable, potato pattern. When we become adventurous and look for appealing meals that fall outside of this pattern, we find that some of the regional dishes of the country offer enticing dining, from savory gumbos of Louisiana (page 308) to spicy Texas chilis (page 298).

Some of the most striking combinations of foods are cooked in the Latin American countries, where meat, poultry, or fish is cooked with vegetables, fruit, and varying seasonings to make splendid main dishes. They are not necessarily heavily spiced and may even be sweet (see Argentina's *carbonada en calabaza*, below), but they are never insipid. Unlike the preparations of some European countries, the stews cooked in this part of the world are not merely filling, they are unusually tasty and intriguing.

The main dishes of Latin America are substantial. They are prepared and eaten in an unhurried manner, encouraging relaxation, conversation, and camaraderie. This pleasant association between eating and socializing is especially apparent in the outdoor barbecuing of Argentina and Brazil. Meats are cooked slowly for many hours, making the meal a long, happy social event. Barbecues are popular throughout the Americas, and outdoor barbecuing has become a way of life for many Texans and Californians.

BEEF STEW IN PUMPKIN
Carbonada en Calabaza

Argentina

Serves 4 to 6

Cinderella's pumpkin turned into a coach. Yours will become a dramatic cooking and serving vehicle for this Argentinian meat, vegetable, and fruit stew. Unlike many other South American preparations this stew is sweet rather than spicy.

The West Indian *calabaza* pumpkin (available in Latin American groceries and some supermarkets) is ideal because it will not become too watery or collapse during cooking as a regular pumpkin might, but the strong-shelled Hubbard squash is a good substitute. The specialty South American sweet potatoes called for in the recipe—*batata* or *boniato*—are also available in groceries featuring South American foods. Although beef is the meat of Argentina, veal also goes well with the potatoes, corn, and peaches, and either will work well in this recipe.

The pumpkin and stew are first cooked separately, then to complete the cooking the stew bakes right in the shell. The mingling of the stew with the pumpkin gives added taste to the stew.

> **One 12-pound calabaza pumpkin or Hubbard squash**
> **2 pounds stewing beef or veal**
> **Salt and freshly ground black pepper**
> **2 tablespoons olive oil or vegetable oil**
> **1 cup chopped onion**
> **1 large clove garlic, minced**
> **½ cup chopped green pepper**
> **1 pound ripe red tomatoes, peeled, seeded, and chopped**
> **1 tablespoon granulated sugar**
> **2 cups water, beef broth (for beef), or chicken broth (for veal)**
> **1 pound white potatoes, peeled and cut into 1-inch cubes**
> **1 pound boniato or other South American sweet potato, peeled and cut into 1-inch cubes**
> **2 ears corn, husked and cut into 1-inch slices**
> **1 pound fresh peaches**

Preheat the oven to 375 degrees F. Wash the pumpkin or squash under cold running water, scrubbing with a brush as necessary to remove all dirt. Use a sharp knife to cut off the top of the pumpkin, making a lid that will have a diameter of approximately 7 inches. Make the cut all around on a 45-degree angle so the lid will not slide off. Remove the lid and use a large spoon to scrape the seeds and stringy fibers from the interior of the pumpkin and the lid. Fill a baking pan that has a rack with an inch of hot water. Setting the lid aside, place the pumpkin

Recipe continues on the following page . . .

upside-down on the rack and bake for 15 minutes. Remove the baking pan and transfer the pumpkin right-side-up to an oven-proof shallow casserole or baking dish that will be attractive for serving. Replace the pumpkin lid and bake the pumpkin for 1 to 1½ hours. The interior should be nearly tender when the meat is pierced with a fork. (Do not pierce the pumpkin shell.) If the pumpkin is ready before the stew, remove it from the oven and set aside.

While the pumpkin is baking, prepare the stew as follows. Sprinkle the meat with salt and pepper; set aside. In a 4-quart pot, heat the oil over moderate heat. Sauté the onion, garlic, and green pepper until they are softened but not brown, then add the meat. Cook, stirring often, until the meat is brown all over but not crusty. Stir in the tomatoes, sugar, and the water or broth. Bring to the boil over high heat, reduce the heat to a gentle boil, cover the pot, and cook for 1¾ hours. Now add the white and sweet potatoes and cook for another 15 minutes or until the meat and potatoes are almost tender. The stew can be prepared up to this point and refrigerated overnight. To continue cooking, reheat until the stew is boiling gently. Stir in the corn and cook for an additional 5 minutes. Peel the peaches, discard the peelings and pits, and slice the peaches into 1/2-inch wedges. Add the wedges to the stew, mixing gently.

Transfer the stew to the pumpkin or squash shell. Be sure to spoon in gravy because the liquid is important in the final cooking. (Keep warm any stew that doesn't fit. Add this to the pumpkin shell after the first batch of stew is served.) Replace the lid and bake for an additional 30 minutes. Serve the stew from the pumpkin, scooping out portions of cooked pumpkin from the shell.

CHILI

Texas

Serves 6

Die-hard chili lovers will argue that authentic Texas chili consists only of diced beef, suet, pulverized hot red peppers, and other seasonings. While this may be true, there are other choice versions of chili. Some noted Americans, including an ex-president and a world-famous actress, are known to have enjoyed chili with tomatoes and onions, and in the latter case, pinto beans as well. The chili here is my northeastern version: a thick, tasty mixture of ground beef, pinto beans, tomatoes, onions, and chili powder. Chili powder is made of ground chili peppers, oregano, cumin, and garlic, and you can add any of these ingredients individually to heighten the taste you like best. Additional ground cayenne will make the chili HOT. Canned whole tomatoes add texture, while tomato purée alone adds a stronger tomato taste.

Prepare the chili a day ahead if you can—it is at its best reheated—and serve with rice and warm *tortillas* (page 319).

> **1 pound dried pinto beans or dried pink beans**
> **10 cups (2½ quarts) water**
> **3 dried hot chili peppers**
> **3 pounds ground beef**
> **1 large onion, chopped**
> **1 clove garlic, minced**
> **1 can (28 ounces) whole tomatoes in purée or**
>   **1 can (28 ounces) tomato purée**
> **1 teaspoon salt**
> **¼ teaspoon freshly ground black pepper**
> **2 to 3 tablespoons chili powder, to taste**

Pick through the beans, removing any small pebbles or dirt. Rinse the beans, then place them in a 5- or 6-quart pot. Add the water and chili peppers. Bring to the boil over high heat, reduce the heat to a gentle boil, cover the pot, and cook for 2 hours or until the beans are tender. Stir occasionally. Add water if necessary to keep the beans covered.

When the beans are tender, in a 10- to 12-inch skillet heat the ground beef over moderately high heat. Stir and break up the meat with the side of a spoon so there are no large chunks. When the meat is completely brown, first remove the chili peppers from the beans, then use a slotted spoon to transfer the browned ground beef to the beans. Stir in the onion and garlic, mixing well. Cook uncovered for 30 minutes, stirring occasionally.

Recipe continues on the following page . . .

Now add the tomatoes with their liquid (or the plain purée). Cut the tomatoes into small pieces with the side of a spoon. Cook 15 minutes longer. Stir in the seasonings and cook for an additional 10 to 15 minutes. Taste and correct seasonings. Serve with rice, warm *tortillas* (page 319), and a salad for a complete meal.

GREEN CHILI

New Mexico

Serves 4

Tomatillos and mild green chili peppers give this New Mexican Indian chili its color and very pleasant flavor. The chili is seasoned with some of the spices that are found in prepared chili powder, and the meat is stewing beef (not ground beef) used by southwestern Indians. Even chilis labeled "mild" may be hot to some tastes, therefore the addition of jalapeño peppers is optional. Because this is a thick chili without too much liquid, it makes an ideal filling for *tamales* (page 301). Serve green chili with rice, pinto beans, and warm *tortillas* (page 319).

> **2 pounds lean stewing beef**
> **Salt and freshly ground black pepper**
> **1 pound fresh tomatillos, 1 can (16 ounces)**
>   **tomatillos, or 1 pound green cherry**
>   **tomatoes**
> **2 tablespoons vegetable oil**
> **2 cans (4 ounces each) chopped mild green**
>   **chili peppers**
> **1½ teaspoons ground cumin**
> **1 teaspoon ground coriander**
> **1 teaspoon dried oregano**
> **1 to 2 fresh jalapeño peppers (optional)**

Cut the stewing beef into ½-inch cubes, discarding fat and gristle. Sprinkle with the salt and pepper. Set aside.

Remove the husks from the fresh *tomatillos* and rinse the *tomatillos*. (If using cherry tomatoes, pull off any stems.) Coarsely chop the fresh or canned *tomatillos* or cherry tomatoes.

In a 4-quart pot, heat the oil until moderately hot. Add the stewing beef and cook, stirring often, until the meat is brown but not crusty. Stir in the chopped *tomatillos* or cherry tomatoes, the chili peppers, and the spices, mixing well. Bring to the boil over moderate heat, then reduce the heat so the chili cooks gently. Cover the pot and cook for 30 minutes, adding water as necessary to keep the chili from sticking. Taste the gravy. If the chili is not spicy enough to your taste, cut the jalapeño pepper(s) in half, remove and discard the ribs and seeds, and mince the pepper(s) as fine as possible. Add to the chili, then wash your hands to remove the caustic pepper oils from your fingers.

Cook the chili an additional hour or until the meat is so tender it can be shredded with a fork. Serve at once or refrigerate and reheat. Frozen chili may lose some of its flavor, but additional spices can be added when reheating.

TAMALES

Mexico

Serves 6

    Tamales are filled little corn breads that are wrapped in corn-husks and steamed. The filling may be seasoned meat or poultry, refried beans (page 321), cheese, or a sweet filling to be eaten as a snack or dessert. Mexicans do not bathe *tamales* in a tomato sauce the way they are sometimes served in the United States, but it is appropriate to serve *tamales* with one of the table sauces on pages 290 through 293. Although Mexicans eat *tamales* as snacks and not main dishes (Mexican main dish preparations are more substantial), *tamales* make excellent entrées for casual dining. Serve with rice, refried beans (for meat or cheese *tamales*), and a salad to complete the meal.

    The flour used for making *tamales*, known as *masa harina* (literally, "dough flour"), is available in Mexican groceries and many supermarkets. For the lard used in Mexico, solid white shortening is substituted in this recipe. The cornhusks add a nice corn flavor to the *tamales*, and they make attractive ridges on the dough.

Recipe continues on the following page . . .

How to Prepare Cornhusks for Tamales

Special care must be taken in husking corn if the cornhusks are to be used for *tamales,* because the individual husks should not be split or torn. To husk corn for *tamales* use a sharp knife to cut off the round end of the corn just at the point where the kernels start; discard the silks. Now carefully peel off the individual husks, removing any silks that stick to the husks. A good size husk for *tamales* is 3 x 8 inches. Two smaller husks can be overlapped to make up one larger one.

Fresh cornhusks are soft and easy to work with, but cornhusks can be dried for later use. To dry the husks, spread them out on a large table or work surface and allow them to dry completely at room temperature. Store the dried husks at room temperature in a large brown paper bag that is not tightly closed. Soak dried cornhusks in hot water (130 to 140 degrees F.) for 30 minutes to soften them to use for *tamales.*

 1 cup solid vegetable shortening
 5 cups unsifted masa harina
 1 teaspoon double-acting baking powder
 ½ teaspoon salt (optional)
 2 cups water or chicken or beef broth
30 fresh or softened cornhusks, approximately
    3 x 8 inches each
 2 cups Green Chili (page 300) or other filling
    (see variation)

In the large bowl of a heavy-duty mixer, beat the shortening until it is fluffy. Add 2 cups of the *masa harina* along with the baking powder and optional salt. Beat well, then beat in a cup of the water or broth. Beat in 2 more cups of *masa harina,* the remaining cup of water or broth, and the last cup of flour. Now beat for 5 minutes or until the mixture is light and fluffy.

To assemble the *tamales,* use the back of a spoon to spread 2 to 3 tablespoons of the dough on each cornhusk, starting 1 inch

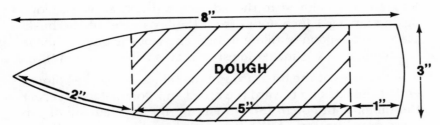

1. Spread a rectangle of dough on the cornhusk.

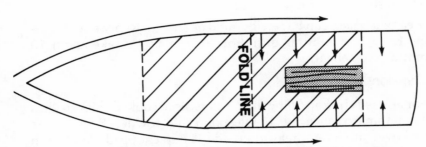

2. Shape the filling into a ½ x 2-inch strip.

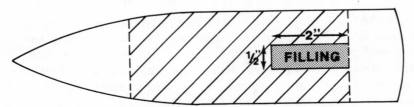

3. Roll the sides of the husk around the filling, then bring the pointed end up toward (and over) the broad end.

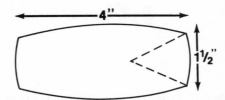

4. The tip of the husk is underneath the packet.

Recipe continues on the following page . . .

down from the broader end. Make a rectangle that is 5 inches long and goes almost to the side edges **(illustration 1).** Now, again starting 1 inch down from the broad end of the husk, place a tablespoon of filling in the center of the dough. Shape the filling into a ½-inch-wide strip that is 2 inches long **(2).**

Roll the sides of the husk around the filling. Bring the pointed end of the husk up toward the broad end, completely covering the filling with dough **(3).** Now bring the pointed end of the husk over the top of the broad end, making a packet that encloses the dough. The tip of the husk will now be underneath the packet **(4).** The packet will be approximately 1½ x 4 inches.

Stack the *tamales* flap side down on one or two steamer trays or in a colander. Place about an inch of water in the bottom of the steaming pot and set the tray(s) or colander in place. (If using more than one tray, you will need to use trays that stack or you will need more than one pot.) The bottom of the colander or tray must be at least an inch above the water. Cover the pot and bring the water to the boil over high heat. Regulate the heat so the water boils constantly but not so rapidly that it boils away. Steam the *tamales* for 45 minutes.

Steamed *tamales* can be refrigerated or frozen. Reheat by steaming for a few minutes until hot. Frozen *tamales* take about 10 minutes to reheat.

Variation:

For an easy chicken filling, mix 2 cups diced cooked chicken with 1 cup tomato sauce and 1 tablespoon chili powder. Bring to the boil over moderate heat, then add ¼ cup chopped olives with pimiento if desired.

FRIED TORTILLAS WITH MEAT
Tostadas con Carne

Mexico

Serves 6

Tostadas are fried *tortillas* (page 319), and when they are covered with meat, beans, shredded lettuce, chopped fresh tomatoes, peppers, onions, and a sauce, they become a meal. Leftovers make tempting snacks, which is appropriate because in Mexico *tostadas* are served as snacks rather than as a meal.

Tacos are rolled or folded *tortillas,* often fried to hold their shape. As a homemade preparation, *tostadas* are easier to shape and they hold more filling, making more of a meal. *Chorizo* (page 79), *empanadita* filling (page 281), leftover diced chicken, turkey, or veal moistened with a seasoned tomato sauce—almost any meat sauce can be used to top a *tostada.* Bowls of cooked pinto beans, refried beans, avocado slices or *guacamole,* and salad ingredients complete the topping selections. Serve *tostadas* buffet style to avoid confusion.

The shells can be prepared a day ahead and served at room temperature or reheated for a few minutes in a 300-degree F. oven, but do not top the *tostadas* until serving time, or they will become soggy.

> Tortillas (page 319)
> Oil for deep-frying
> 2 to 3 pounds Chorizo (page 79) or other
>   cooked meat
> 1 cup (8 ounces) tomato sauce
> Double recipe of Bean Dip (page 280) pre-
>   pared without cheese
> Guacamole (page 290) or sliced avocado
> 2 cups shredded romaine or iceberg lettuce
> 1 pound ripe red tomatoes, chopped
> 1 large onion, chopped fine
> 1 sweet red or green pepper, chopped
> Salad olives, pitted green or ripe olives, sliced
> Green Tomato Sauce (page 291), Uncooked
>   Red Sauce (page 292), or a purchased taco
>   sauce
> Tabasco sauce

To turn *tortillas* into *tostadas,* in a skillet or a pot at least 8 inches in diameter heat an inch of oil. If you are not used to deep-frying in a shallow skillet, use an electric skillet away from the stove to avoid any fire hazard. When the oil just begins to smoke (375 to 400 degrees F.), carefully add a *tortilla* shell. Using tongs or a slotted spoon, push the *tortilla* under the oil. After about half a minute, when it is golden on one side, turn over the *tortilla* and

Recipe continues on the following page . . .

fry it briefly on the second side until it is golden but not darkened. Some of the *tortillas* may puff up and will be a little difficult to turn, but try to do so without puncturing them. Transfer the fried shells to paper towels; allow them to drain well. Serve from a wicker basket lined with clean paper towels.

For the meat, in an electric skillet or a 4-quart pot brown the *chorizo*, stirring often to brown all over. Break up any clumps of meat with the side of a spoon. Spoon off accumulated fat, then mix in the tomato sauce.

Have the meat and beans hot (in separate pots), and arrange all the other ingredients attractively in serving bowls. Transfer the meat and beans to bowls before serving.

CREOLE SAUSAGES

New Orleans

Makes about 1 pound

There is nothing subtle about Creole sausages. They are hot and spicy, full of onions and garlic, seasoned lavishly with red peppers, and tasting of parsley, bay leaves, and allspice. Creole sausages are served as a breakfast sausage and they are used in jambalayas and gumbos. In this recipe, ground beef substitutes for the pork and pork fat used in New Orleans, but the herbs and spices remain the same so you can expect the meat to have the flavor of the authentic sausages.

> **1 pound ground beef, not too lean**
> **⅓ cup chopped onion**
> **1 clove garlic**
> **¼ teaspoon ground cayenne pepper**
> **¼ teaspoon chili powder**
> **¼ teaspoon crushed red pepper**
> **½ teaspoon salt**
> **½ teaspoon freshly ground black pepper**
> **½ teaspoon dried thyme**

2 tablespoons chopped fresh parsley
1 small bay leaf, crushed
Pinch of ground allspice

Combine all the ingredients, mixing very well. If your house is not too warm, allow the mixture to remain at room temperature for an hour or two to blend the flavors. Wrap well and refrigerate until ready to use, up to 2 days. The sausage can be frozen, although you might lose a little of the spiciness during storage.

Use as directed in other recipes, or shape into patties and grill, broil, or fry in a little oil until brown on both sides and cooked through.

JAMBALAYA

New Orleans

Serves 4

Chicken, homemade sausage, vegetables, and rice cook with aromatic herbs and spices in this version of jambalaya. The mixture cooks in chicken broth, and the rice absorbs the broth to become moist, fluffy, and richly seasoned by the meats, vegetables, and seasonings. Creole jambalayas contain ham and pork sausages, but this adaptation is authentic in all other respects.

2 tablespoons vegetable oil
4 chicken thighs with legs, disjointed
3 cups chopped onions
½ cup chopped green pepper
1 cup thinly sliced scallion tops (green part only)
1 tablespoon minced garlic
3 tablespoons chopped fresh parsley
1½ teaspoons freshly ground black pepper
1 to 2 teaspoons salt
½ teaspoon chili powder
¼ teaspoon ground cayenne pepper

Recipe continues on the following page . . .

½ teaspoon crushed bay leaf
¼ teaspoon dried basil
Pinch of mace
1 pound homemade Creole Sausage (previous
  recipe), shaped into 1½-inch balls
1½ cups raw long-grain white rice
3 cups chicken broth

In an 8-quart pot, heat the oil over moderately high heat. Brown the chicken pieces well all over, turning them as necessary. Transfer the browned chicken to a bowl, leaving the drippings in the pot. To the pot add the chopped onions, green pepper, scallion tops, garlic, and parsley. Reduce the heat to medium and cook, stirring often, for 12 to 15 minutes, until the vegetables are beginning to brown. Stir in the seasonings, then add the sausage balls. Cook for about 5 minutes, shaking the pan often to lightly brown the sausage all over. Now sprinkle in the rice, add the chicken broth, stir gently, and return the browned chicken pieces to the pot.

Raise the heat to bring the liquid to the boil, then turn down the heat to low so the broth boils gently. Cover the pot, and cook for 45 minutes, stirring occasionally. The rice should always be covered by liquid, and the chicken pieces should be turned so all sides are in the gravy from time to time.

Taste after 45 minutes. If the rice is not tender and fluffy, continue cooking, covered. When the rice is done, remove the cover and cook for another 10 minutes to dry out the rice a bit. Stir as necessary to keep the rice from sticking.

GUMBO

New Orleans

Serves 4 to 6

If you are the kind of person who can do two things at once, then you might like to try making gumbo. The first 30 to 45 minutes of gumbo preparation consist of preparing a *roux* base. This involves making a flour and oil mixture and stirring the mixture over heat slowly and lovingly to a rich brown. I say lovingly because it takes devotion to sit or stand and stir for this length of time. Which brings me to the point: if you can read, talk, listen to music, or just contemplate the world while you stir the *roux*, you won't feel that you're taking too much time for just one meal.

Gumbo is a rich, thick stew, served over mounds of rice, that can be made of seafood, poultry, sausage, and vegetables in any combination. Cook's choice. There are two essentials: the *roux* base that adds a smoky taste and thickens the mixture; and either okra or filé powder (ground sassafras leaves), used for thickening and flavor. Gumbo actually gets its name from the okra—*gombo* is an African word for okra.

The gumbo presented here is based on the traditional chicken and sausage gumbo served in the South. Homemade Creole beef sausage substitutes for Creole pork sausages. Although this recipe has a number of ingredients in common with the preceding jambalaya, you will see that the *roux*, okra or filé powder, and the separate cooking of the rice make it a very different dish. If you want to spice up the gumbo, experiment with additions of small quantities of allspice, thyme, crushed bay leaves, and cloves.

Before you begin the *roux*, pretend that this is a Chinese recipe and have all your ingredients cut up and at hand.

> 2 tablespoons vegetable oil
> 1 pound homemade Creole Sausage (page 306), shaped into 1½-inch balls
> 1 chicken (3½ to 4 pounds)
> Salt and freshly ground black pepper
> ½ cup vegetable oil
> ½ cup unsifted all-purpose flour
> 2 cups chopped onions
> ½ cup chopped green pepper
> ½ cup thinly sliced scallion tops (green part only)
> ¼ cup chopped fresh parsley
> 1 large clove garlic, minced
> 2 quarts chicken broth
> ½ pound fresh okra, stems and tips removed, sliced into ½-inch rounds
> ¼ teaspoon ground cayenne pepper

Recipe continues on the following page . . .

In a 10-inch skillet, heat the 2 tablespoons of oil until moderately hot. Add the sausage balls, and brown them all over. Using a slotted spoon, transfer the meat from the oil to a bowl.

Rub the chicken with salt and pepper, then cut up the chicken into 10 small pieces (2 wings, 2 legs, 2 thighs, each breast cut in half). In a 6-quart pot, heat the ½ cup oil until it is moderately hot. Brown the chicken pieces in the hot oil, turning often so the chicken browns evenly. Regulate the heat to prevent burning. Remove the chicken from the oil, and set the chicken aside.

Now, gradually stir the flour into the oil, reduce the heat to very low, and cook the *roux*, stirring constantly, until it is a lovely brown, just about the color of pecan shells. The *roux* may be stiff at first but will gradually become smooth. As it becomes smoother, you can raise the heat to moderately low. Get comfortable, because it may take as long as 45 minutes to brown the *roux* properly—it doesn't like to be rushed. Take care not to burn it the slightest bit.

As soon as the *roux* reaches the right color, add the chopped onions, green pepper, scallion tops, parsley, and garlic to the pot, and continue cooking and stirring 10 minutes longer. Gradually add the chicken broth, then the sausage and chicken, the okra, and finally the cayenne pepper. Mix gently. Bring to the boil over moderate heat, reduce the heat to a gentle boil, cover the pot, and cook over low heat for 1 hour. Serve in soup bowls over mountains of hot, fluffy rice.

Variation:

For filé gumbo, omit the okra. Cook everything as directed above. Just before serving, remove the pot from the heat, wait until the liquid completely stops boiling, and stir in 2 tablespoons of filé powder. Serve immediately. A word of caution: if you allow the gumbo to boil after adding the filé powder, you will end up with a very stringy sauce. Note that the filé powder is used more for its thickening power than for its taste, although it does have a flavor faintly reminiscent of okra.

TABLECLOTH STAINER
Mancha Manteles

Mexico

Serves 4

Meats, fruits, and vegetables mingle together in this classic stew. Here, veal is used (in place of pork) because a more strongly flavored meat, such as lamb, would be overpowering. If all you've heard about Mexican food can be summed up in three words—*tacos, tortillas, tamales*—this stew will introduce you to a colorful blend of spicy and sweet that is as authentically Mexican as any preparation. *Mancha manteles* translates literally to "stain tablecloth," no doubt because if that rich and full-bodied red gravy tasting of tomatoes with a subtle nut and spice flavor should splash on a white tablecloth you will have a permanent reminder of this savory stew. This recipe can be prepared almost entirely a day ahead and is even better when the flavors have had a chance to blend overnight.

> 2 tablespoons vegetable oil or chicken fat
> 1 frying chicken (3 pounds), cut into serving
>   pieces, or 2 to 3 pounds chicken parts, cut
>   up
> 1 pound well-trimmed boneless veal
>   shoulder, cut into ¾-inch cubes
> 1 tablespoon chopped blanched almonds
> 1 tablespoon sesame seeds
> ½ cup minced onion
> 1 tablespoon chili powder
> 2 tablespoons granulated sugar
> ½ teaspoon ground cinnamon
> Pinch of ground cloves
> 1 cup (8 ounces) tomato sauce
> 1 quart chicken broth
> 1 tablespoon distilled white vinegar
> 1 large sweet potato or yam (1 pound), peeled
>   and cut into 1-inch cubes
> Salt
> 2 green apples, peeled, cored, and cut into 8
>   wedges each

Recipe continues on the following page . . .

**2 cups pineapple chunks, well drained if
canned
1 large green banana (not a plantain)**

In a 5- or 6-quart pot, heat the oil or fat over moderately high heat. Brown the chicken pieces in the oil or fat, turning as necessary to brown all over. Transfer the chicken to a bowl or plate, then brown the veal cubes on all sides in the same oil or fat. Use a slotted spoon to remove the veal.

Meanwhile, in a food processor or a blender grind the almonds and sesame seeds until they are pulverized but not a paste. Make sure the oil is not too hot—it should not be smoking—and stir the ground almonds and sesame seeds into the same oil in which the chicken and veal have browned. Cook them for a minute, stirring constantly, until they are brown but not burned. Add the minced onion and cook, stirring often, for another minute or two, until the onion is softened but not browned. Reduce the heat to low, then blend in the chili powder, sugar, cinnamon, and cloves. Cook for 2 minutes, stirring constantly. Now stir in the tomato sauce, chicken broth, and vinegar. Raise the heat to bring the liquid to the boil. Carefully add the browned chicken and veal to the pot, and regulate the heat so the meats cook gently, covered, until they are tender, about 30 minutes. Add the sweet potato cubes and raise the heat to moderate. Cook for 15 to 20 minutes, until the potatoes are tender. Add salt to taste. The stew can be prepared up to this point in advance and refrigerated overnight.

To complete the cooking, reheat the stew to the boiling point, add the apples, and cook for 5 minutes, until the apples are softened but not mushy. Stir in the pineapple chunks, and continue cooking just until the pineapple is heated through. Slice the banana (¼-inch slices) directly into the pot. Stir gently and serve immediately or the bananas will soften. Serve *mancha manteles* in soup bowls, with warm *tortillas* on the side.

FISH IN COCONUT MILK
Pescado con Coco

Brazil

Serves 4

The northern Brazilian state of Bahia boasts a fascinating cuisine made up of Indian, African, and Portuguese influences. Although many of of the notable preparations from this area are based on fresh or dried shrimp, a recipe such as this that substitutes a mildly flavored white-fleshed fish allows us to taste the delicious blend that comes from marinating the fish in a lemon-lime mixture then cooking it with ingredients not usually combined—tomatoes, onions, and coconut milk. The result is an unusual preparation that is delicate but tasty. You will want to serve rice to mix with the coconut-flavored gravy.

> **2 pounds fillets of flounder or sole**
> **3 large cloves garlic, minced**
> **¼ cup fresh lemon juice**
> **¼ cup fresh lime juice**
> **¼ cup vegetable oil**
> **1 cup minced onion**
> **4 scallions (white and crisp green parts),**
>   **chopped**
> **1 pound red ripe tomatoes, peeled, seeded,**
>   **and chopped**
> **2 cups Coconut Milk (see page 203)**
> **Salt and freshly ground black pepper**

Cut the fish crosswise into 2-inch pieces. In a medium-size bowl, combine the garlic with the lemon and lime juices. Add the fish and marinate for 30 minutes at room temperature.

In a 10-inch skillet, heat the oil over moderate heat. Sauté the onion and scallions until the onion is softened but not brown. Add the tomatoes and cook for 3 minutes, stirring often. Stir in the coconut milk and the fish with the marinade. Regulate the heat so the liquid boils very gently and cook until the fish turns white, stirring occasionally. Add salt and pepper to taste, cook a minute longer, and serve.

CREOLE DISH FROM CHICLAYO
Causa à la Chiclayana

Peru

Serves 6 as a main dish,
12 as an appetizer

Here, lemony potatoes are mixed with a whole cup of olive oil, topped with vinegared onions and hot peppers, then garnished with enough vegetables, cheese, and fish to make a meal. *Causa à la Chiclayana* is served as an appetizer in Peru, but most of us would consider it a main dish. If the cheese and fish are omitted, it becomes an exciting vegetable side dish.

The potatoes taste predominantly of lemon, olive oil, and vinegar, but because of the fish, corn, and vegetable garnishes, the dish is full of contrasting textures. If you are able to locate any of the exotic South American root vegetables for garnishing, you will be adding some unique tastes as well. *Malanga*, of the *Arum* family, looks like a thick horseradish root, and is starchy but with a slightly sweet, fruity taste; *boniato*, of the sweet potato family, with either a red or white skin, is white-fleshed and subtly flavored; and cassava (yucca), another root vegetable that is not in the potato or sweet potato family but can be boiled or fried like a potato, is more chewy and sweeter than a regular white potato.

This recipe is a lot of work, with many ingredients to prepare and cook (in many different pots). But if you are searching for something with a unique taste that looks very impressive on a buffet table, consider *causa à la Chiclayana*.

> **3 pounds white or yellow-**
> **fleshed potatoes**
> **¼ cup finely chopped onion**
> **½ cup fresh lemon juice**
> **1 cup olive oil**
> **⅛ teaspoon ground turmeric, approximately**
> **Dash of ground cayenne pepper**
> **Salt and freshly ground black pepper**
> **½ pound malanga, peeled and sliced into ½-**
> **inch rounds**

1 pound boniato or other South American
   sweet potato, peeled and sliced into ½-inch
   rounds
1 pound cassava, peeled and sliced into ½-
   inch rounds
2 ears fresh corn, husked and cut into 1-inch
   pieces
Olive oil for frying
2 firm green plantains, peeled and sliced into
   ½-inch pieces
3 jalapeño or other fresh hot peppers (can be
   red or green)
2 medium-size onions, peeled and sliced into
   ⅛-inch rounds
½ cup distilled white vinegar
½ cup olive oil
1½ to 2 pounds sea bass or flounder fillets
   sliced crosswise into 2-inch pieces
Unsifted all-purpose flour for dusting the
   fish
Lettuce leaves
½ pound mozzarella or Muenster cheese, cut
   into wedges
Pitted black olives

Before you even begin peeling the white potatoes, have all the
other ingredients ready and at hand. Read through the recipe
and have ready all the pots and pans that you will need.

Peel the white potatoes, cut them into 2- or 3-inch cubes and
cook them in a pot of boiling water until they are tender.
Meanwhile, in a small bowl combine the chopped onion, lemon
juice, and the cup of olive oil. Set aside. Drain the cooked
potatoes, return them to the pot, and mash them with a fork or
a potato masher, adding the lemon-olive oil mixture and a dash of
turmeric to the potatoes as you mash them. Continue to add just
enough turmeric to turn the potatoes a light yellow—the
turmeric is used only to color the potatoes in place of an herb
(palillo) used by Peruvians as a food color. Season the potatoes
with cayenne, salt, and pepper. Keep the potatoes warm over low
heat or in a 200-degree F. oven.

Recipe continues on the following page . . .

The remaining vegetables should be started while the potatoes are cooking. Fill a 4-quart pot halfway with water and bring to the boil over high heat. Drop in the *malanga* rounds and regulate the heat to a moderate boil. Partially cover the pot and cook the *malanga* for 10 minutes, then add the sweet potato and cassava. Continue to cook until the vegetables are tender (but not falling apart) when pierced with a fork, then add the corn and cook for an additional 3 minutes. Drain the vegetables and return them to the pot. They will keep warm for about 30 minutes if covered.

For the plantains, coat an 8-inch skillet with ⅛ inch of olive oil. Heat the oil over moderately low heat and add the plantain slices. Cook until golden on both sides and tender inside, turning occasionally. The total cooking time for the plantains is about 15 minutes.

For the topping for the potatoes, cut the chili peppers in half lengthwise, remove and discard the ribs and seeds, then slice the peppers into thin strips. Immediately wash your hands to rid them of the caustic pepper oils. In a 2-quart pot, place the sliced hot peppers and the onion rounds with enough water to cover by an inch. Bring to the boil over high heat, drain off the water, then add the vinegar and ½ cup olive oil to the onions and peppers. Bring to a rolling boil then reduce the heat to a gentle boil, cover the pot, and cook for 5 minutes. Allow the mixture to remain in the covered pot until serving time.

Finally, for the fish, in a large skillet heat ¼ inch of olive oil until it is moderately hot, 350 degrees F. Sprinkle the fish with salt and pepper, then dip both sides of the fish in a bowl of flour and shake off the excess flour. Fry the fish until it is golden brown on both sides, turning once after about 3 minutes. Add oil to the pan if the fish is fried in more than 1 batch. Drain the fish on paper towels.

Before assembling the preparation, make sure the potatoes, topping, vegetables and fish are all at serving temperature. To assemble, mound the potatoes in the center of a very large platter (use 2 platters if necessary). Arrange the lettuce leaves around the edges of the potatoes, covering the remainder of the platter. Position the *malanga, boniato,* cassava, corn, plantains, and fish attractively on the lettuce leaves. Pour the onion-and-hot pepper mixture with the vinegar sauce over the mound of potatoes, and garnish the potatoes with the cheese wedges and olives.

FRIED TORTILLAS WITH CHEESE
Tostadas con Queso

Mexico

Serves 6

Cheese-topped *tostadas* make an unusual breakfast or a nice lunch or snack. Top fried *tostadas* lavishly with grated Monterey Jack, Muenster, Cheddar, Swiss, or other cheese, and pop them under the broiler for less than a minute, until the cheese is melted and bubbly.

For a dinner meal follow the recipe for *tostadas con carne* (page 304), omitting the *chorizo* and tomato sauce. Prepare the bean dip with cheese (page 280) and serve a bowl of sour cream along with the other toppings.

Side Dishes

Peru is potato country. Food historians tell us that potatoes originated in the Peruvian Andes and Chile. The Incas did masterful things with potatoes, including the development of a method of preservation related to freeze-drying. Mounds of unusually seasoned yellow potatoes are the focal point of several Peruvian potato dishes (see page 314). Peruvian cuisine features a variety of South American root vegetables that may be baked, boiled, or fried. Some are white and sweet (*boniato*); others are yellow but taste like our white potatoes; some are even a little fruity in taste (*malanga*).

Potatoes found their way from South America to the United States in a roundabout fashion. Spanish explorers brought potatoes back to Spain, the tubers spread through Europe, and when explorations and colonizations began in North America, potatoes were introduced.

Corn and beans are the staples of Mexico, where it is too hot to grow white potatoes. Along with tomatoes, avocados, and peppers, corn and beans sometimes find their way to the table in different forms than we might expect. Beans are served with breakfast (and other meals); peppers are usually the hot peppers used as a seasoning; and corn is most often scraped off the cob, pounded, and treated with lime to make *masa harina*, the flour used for *tortillas* (page 319).

Beans and more beans are the major protein source for many Brazilians, with black beans (page 322) a favorite. The Brazilian counterpart of potatoes is another root vegetable, cassava. A bitter variety of cassava is made into a farina-like meal (manioc meal) that is toasted and served as a table condiment at all meals. A sweet variety of cassava also eaten by

Brazilians makes a fine potato substitute because it is more chewy and has more of a flavor of its own than potatoes.

Dried beans are popular in some areas of the United States, especially New England, where in some households bean pots are standard equipment for baking sweetened navy beans (page 323). While dried beans are eaten as a major protein source in Mexico and Brazil, in the United States baked beans are more likely to round out a meal as a starch in place of potatoes. Pasta or rice are other more popular substitutes for the potato. Wild rice (which is actually not rice at all), the most exotic grain grown in the United States, is a unique alternative to more typical starches. A casserole combining wild rice with vegetables is presented on page 326.

Vegetables and starches are not the only side dishes that appear on American tables. Traditional breakfasts in the South include grits and hash browns potatoes; a breakfast meat and eggs are the breakfast in many American households; and an unusual Pennsylvania Dutch breakfast food that combines meat and corn meal (page 327) is well known in Philadelphia.

TORTILLAS

Mexico

Makes 12

In most parts of Mexico these flat breads are made of moist *masa harina,* but in northern Mexico wheat flour is used for *tortillas.* In addition to their use as plain warm breads, *tortillas* are the basis for *tacos, tostadas, enchiladas, burritos,* and other Mexican-type "sandwiches."

For homemade *tortillas,* flour is easier to work with than corn dough. Flour *tortillas* roll out better, and they don't tear so easily when used in other recipes. Because plain white flour *tortillas* are not as tasty as *tortillas* that use a combination of flours, the recipe below is my own suggested combination of white, whole-wheat, and corn flours. Once the *tortillas* are baked on a griddle, they may be frozen for later use.

Recipe continues on the following page . . .

2 cups unsifted all-purpose flour
1 cup unsifted whole-wheat flour
1 cup cornmeal or masa harina
¼ cup vegetable oil
1¼ cups water, approximately

In a large mixing bowl, combine the flours, sprinkle the oil over the flour mixture, then gradually stir in a cup of water. Add water a tablespoon at a time, until the dough can be rounded up into a ball that holds together but isn't sticky. If you accidentally add too much water, sprinkle in a little white flour to absorb the extra water. Knead the dough on a clean work surface for a minute or two, until it is smooth.

Divide the dough into 12 equal pieces, and shape each piece into a smooth ball. Work with one ball of dough at a time, keeping the remainder covered. Heat an ungreased griddle or an 8-inch skillet over moderate heat. On a clean, smooth work surface, flatten one ball of dough into a small, thick circle. Use a rolling pin to roll the dough into a thin, round *tortilla*, 6 to 8 inches in diameter. Always roll from the center of the circle toward the outside, and turn the dough a quarter-turn to the right or left after each roll to make sure the dough is not sticking.

Pick up the flat *tortilla* with your hands and carefully transfer it to the hot griddle. Bake on one side for 30 seconds to a minute, until it dries out a bit, but do not allow it to brown. Turn the *tortilla* over to bake the other side. Repeat with the remaining balls of dough, stacking the warm *tortillas* as they cook. Wrap in foil, where they will keep warm for an hour. Serve warm.

Tortillas will keep for a day or two at room temperature if wrapped well in foil or a plastic bag, and they freeze well. They can be warmed for a few seconds in a microwave or for a few minutes in a 300-degree F. oven. To be made into *tostadas*, frozen *tortillas* should be thawed, but they do not need to be warmed.

Note: The corn *tortillas* of Mexico are made by mixing *masa harina* with enough water to make a soft but not sticky dough. Mexican Indians are skillful at patting pieces of the dough between their hands to be made into thin flat pancakes that are baked on an ungreased hot griddle. Americans will find it easier to divide the dough into 1- to 2-inch balls and roll each ball between 2 sheets of wax paper (using a rolling pin or in a *tortilla* press), making a 5- to 7-inch *tortilla* that is no thicker than ⅛ inch. One sheet of wax paper is peeled off, the *tortilla* is placed on the grill, and then the other sheet is peeled off. This method will keep the *tortilla* from tearing. The *tortilla* is baked for under a minute, until it darkens slightly but does not brown; then it is turned and baked for 15 to 30 seconds on the other side. The cooked *tortillas* should be firm enough to handle but still pliable. Cooked *tortillas* can be stacked and kept warm in foil.

REFRIED BEANS
Frijoles Refritos

Mexico

Serves 6 to 8

A side dish served with almost all Mexican meals, refried beans aren't really *re*fried. In fact, they aren't actually fried in the first place. They are cooked in water until tender, then mashed into hot fat (lard in Mexico, chicken fat for us) and cooked until they have absorbed as much fat as they can, about half a cup of fat for each pound of dried beans. This makes them stiff and quite dry. Because I think the recipe for Bean Dip (page 280) is tastier and not so dry, I recommend that you double that recipe and serve it as a side dish with your Mexican meals. For nonmeat meals, add the cheese as directed. For meat meals, omit the cheese.

Or, you may simply boil the beans until they are tender, adding salt and a few hot peppers to the water for flavor. When the beans are soft, boil away most of the liquid, remove the hot peppers, and serve the beans whole.

BLACK BEANS WITH TOMATOES
Feijão Preto con Tomate

Brazil

Serves 4 to 6

Black beans, rice, and cassava are standard fare for poorer Brazilians, and from this basic combination comes the meaty, festive Brazilian national dish called *feijoada completa*. However, it is such an elaborate production, made with as many as eight meats and five side dishes, I would have had to simplify it drastically and call it *feijoada* in*completa* and still it would have been imposing. Therefore, I decided to go back to the basics and present a more commonplace black bean dish. While it is commonplace, it is satisfying, and if you have never cooked black beans, here is a fine introduction.

The beans are prepared with tomatoes, onions, garlic, and hot peppers. If you are not Brazilian, add the peppers sparingly. Rice, shredded cooked kale, toasted shredded cassava, orange slices, and a hot pepper sauce are traditional accompaniments for *feijoada completa* and appropriate for any Brazilian black beans.

> 1 pound dried black beans, picked through
>   and rinsed
> 2 quarts water
> 2 tablespoons vegetable oil
> 1 cup chopped onion
> 2 large cloves garlic, minced
> 1 can (1 pound) plum tomatoes, drained and
>   chopped
> Minced tabasco or jalapeño peppers, to taste
> Salt and freshly ground black pepper
> Optional accompaniments: rice, cooked kale,
>   orange slices, Toasted Cassava (page 325),
>   Hot Pepper and Lemon-Lime Sauce (page 293)

In a 4-quart pot, bring the beans and water to the boil over high heat. Boil the beans for 2 minutes, turn off the heat, cover the pot when the water stops boiling, and allow the beans to stand for an hour.

After the beans have soaked, stir them to make sure they are not stuck to the bottom of the pot. Bring the liquid back to the boil, reduce the heat to a gentle boil, cover the pot, and cook the beans for 2 more hours, until they are very tender.

A few minutes before the beans are ready, in an 8-inch skillet heat the oil over moderate heat. Add the onion and garlic, and sauté for a few minutes, until the onion is wilted but not browned. Add the tomatoes, cook for another 2 minutes, stirring often, then sprinkle on a teaspoon of minced hot peppers at a time. This mixture will be added to the beans, so taste after each addition to make sure it is not too hot to be edible.

Drain the beans and return them to the pot. Mix the onion, garlic, tomato, and hot peppers into the beans. Taste for seasoning, and add salt and pepper as necessary. Serve the beans with rice, kale, orange slices, cassava, and the hot pepper sauce to complete the Brazilian touch.

BAKED BEANS

New England

Serves 6 to 8

Baked beans may have evolved as a Sabbath preparation, for Puritans who observed no-work prohibitions on the Sabbath could put a pot of beans over the open fire before the Sabbath began and enjoy them at sunset (reminiscent of *cholent*). Salt pork was used for flavor and to help keep the beans from drying out. A fatty piece of uncooked corned beef is the perfect alternative for us. The beans are sweet, flavored but not overwhelmed by the onion, mustard, and corned beef, and an attractive burnt sienna color. Serve as a side dish, with additional corned beef (cooked separately) as the main dish. For vegetarian baked beans, omit the corned beef.

1 pound dried pea or navy beans
6 cups water
1 medium-size onion, cut in half

Recipe continues on the following page . . .

1 teaspoon salt
1 teaspoon dry mustard
¼ cup molasses
¼ cup firmly packed dark brown sugar
½ to 1 pound chunk of corned beef, taken
   from the thick or point cut (a piece with a
   good layer of fat)

Sort through the beans, removing any small pebbles or dirt. Rinse and drain the beans, then place them in a 4-quart pot with 6 cups of water. Bring to the boil over high heat, reduce the heat to a gentle boil, cover the pot, and cook for 1 hour or until the beans are tender. Stir occasionally. When the beans are tender, drain them, reserving the liquid.

Preheat the oven to 300 degrees F. In a 4- or 5-quart bean pot or a round lidded ovenproof casserole with sides at least 4 inches deep, place the onion halves, cut side down. Add the drained beans to the bean pot or casserole.

In a medium-size mixing bowl, combine the salt, dry mustard, molasses, and brown sugar. Mix in 2 cups of the liquid reserved from the beans (save the remaining liquid), stirring until the ingredients dissolve. Pour the mixture over the beans. Score the fatty side of the corned beef by making ½-inch cuts. Push the corned beef, fatty side up, into the beans, covering it as well as you can. (It will float to the surface somewhat; so will the onions.)

Cover the bean pot or casserole tightly with foil, then put the lid on top. Place on the middle shelf of the 300-degree F. oven. Bake for 6 to 8 hours. Every few hours carefully remove the lid and foil, and check the beans to make sure they are always covered by liquid. If there is not enough liquid saved from cooking the beans, use hot or boiling water. Do not add too much liquid toward the end of the cooking period or the beans will be too soupy.

Half an hour before serving, remove the lid and foil, allowing the beans to brown on top. At this point, the liquid should just barely cover the beans. During the final cooking enough liquid should evaporate so the beans will brown, but there should still be enough liquid so they do not dry out.

TOASTED CASSAVA

Farofa

Brazil

Makes about 2 cups

Cassava, or yucca, may look a little like horseradish, but it is not the least bit sharp. Because fresh cassava is considerably easier to obtain than cassava or manioc meal, this recipe uses shredded fresh cassava in place of the meal that is the common table condiment in Brazil. When fresh cassava is shredded and fried in a little oil, it becomes crisp on the outside, soft but chewy on the inside. (You may be reminded of potato *latkes*.) Serve the cassava as a side dish in place of potatoes.

Crisp deep-fried cassava shreds may be used as a topping for Brazilian black beans (see page 322). Fry a small amount of shredded cassava at a time in an inch of oil until golden brown. Remove with a slotted spoon and drain well on paper towels. For frying, select an oil with a taste you like, because the cassava will pick up the flavor of the oil. Deep-fried cassava can be stored for several days at room temperature in a plastic bag or a covered jar.

½ pound fresh cassava
2 tablespoons vegetable oil

Use a vegetable peeler to peel all the skin off the root, then wash the root. Using a hand grater or a food processor with the grating attachment, shred the cassava.

In an 8-inch skillet, heat the oil over moderate heat until it is hot but not yet smoking, 350 degrees F. Add the shredded cassava and cook, stirring often. Some of the cassava will turn a lovely light brown and become crisp, and some will remain soft and white. Serve immediately.

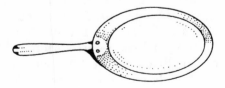

WILD RICE CASSEROLE

Northern United States

Serves 6

The pride of Minnesota and other north-central states is the native North American grain known as wild rice (*zizania aquatica*). It is an aquatic grass (in fact it looks like dark grass seed) unrelated to the cultivated rices grown throughout the world, and tastes more like a wheat grain such as *burghul* than either white or brown rice.

Wild rice was once a staple food of the Indians living in what is now Minnesota, Wisconsin, and parts of Canada. Because it is scarce and expensive to harvest, it is often combined with plain long-grain white or brown rice and sold prepackaged. But you will have a much tastier casserole if you combine a small amount of pure wild rice with vegetables, as in this recipe. The wild rice and vegetable combination can be served as a side dish casserole or used to stuff six Cornish hens for an elegant meal.

> ¼ **pound (scant ¾ cup) wild rice**
> 2 **tablespoons chicken fat or pareve margarine**
> 1 **cup finely chopped onion**
> 2 **cups coarsely chopped fresh mushrooms**
> 1 **cup shredded carrot**
> 2 **cups chicken or beef broth**
> **Salt**
> ½ **cup blanched or unblanched slivered almonds**
> 1 **tablespoon vegetable oil**

Rinse the wild rice carefully so you don't lose any of those precious grains. Set aside.

In a 2-quart pot, heat the chicken fat or margarine over moderate heat until it melts. Add the onion and sauté for a few minutes, stirring occasionally, until wilted but not browned. Add the mushrooms and carrot and continue to cook, stirring occasionally, until the mushrooms are softened. Stir in the wild rice, then the broth. Bring to the boil over high heat, then reduce the heat so the liquid boils gently. Cover the pot and cook for 30 minutes. Taste for seasoning and add salt if desired. The wild rice should be tender enough so it tastes cooked, but it should still be slightly crunchy. If it cooks too long, it will become mushy. If the rice is still hard after 30 minutes, cook 5 minutes longer and taste again. This time the rice should be done, but if you still find it a little hard, cook another few minutes. If there is a lot of broth remaining, cook uncovered for a few minutes to evaporate some of the liquid. The rice should be moist but not soupy.

While the rice is cooking, toast the almonds in a tablespoon of moderately hot vegetable oil. Or place the almonds on a large baking sheet and toast in a 300-degree F. oven for 10 to 15 minutes, stirring once during the baking.

Transfer the rice to a serving casserole, sprinkle with the toasted almonds, and serve.

SCRAPPLE

Pennsylvania Dutch

Serves 6

Anyone who ever lived in the Philadelphia area has heard of scrapple, a breakfast food made of meat scraps, cornmeal, and herbal seasonings. The mixture is cooked, chilled until firm, then sliced and fried. It is crisp on the outside, soft inside, peppery, and distinctly flavored with sage. For the pork products used in scrapple, veal shoulder is substituted here.

> **1 pound boneless veal shoulder, cut into 2-**
> **inch cubes**
> **Salt and freshly ground black pepper**
> **2 cups cold chicken broth, or the broth from**
> **the veal, cooled**
> **1 cup yellow cornmeal**
> **1 teaspoon salt, or to taste**

Recipe continues on the following page . . .

1 teaspoon freshly ground black pepper
½ teaspoon powdered sage
Optional: ¼ teaspoon each dried savory
      and thyme

Sprinkle the veal with salt and pepper. In a 2-quart pot, place the veal with enough water to cover the meat by an inch. Bring to the boil over high heat, then reduce the heat to a gentle boil, cover the pot, and cook for 2 hours, until the meat is very tender. Remove the meat with a slotted spoon. If you intend to use the liquid from the veal later in the recipe, measure 2 cups (add water or chicken broth if necessary to make up the 2 cups), and chill the liquid. Or you may discard the veal liquid and use chicken broth instead. In either case, the broth must be cool or the cornmeal will not blend in smoothly.

Shred the cooked veal by mashing it with a fork, or mince the meat in a food processor, making sure you don't turn it into a paste.

In a clean 2-quart pot, place the 2 cups cold broth, stir in the cornmeal, then mix in the shredded veal. Bring to the boil over moderate heat, stirring constantly so the cornmeal does not become lumpy. Stir in the salt, pepper, and herbs. Cook over low heat, stirring constantly, for about 5 minutes. The mixture will be very thick and difficult to stir.

Line a 4-cup loaf pan (4½ x 7½ inches, approximately) with foil, and grease the foil. Turn the scrapple mixture into the pan, spreading it evenly. Cover the top with foil or plastic wrap, and chill the scrapple thoroughly. To remove the scrapple from the pan, turn the pan upside down and remove the foil and scrapple together, then peel the foil away from the scrapple.

To cook, with a large sharp knife slice the scrapple into ½-inch-thick slices. If the scrapple is crumbly, place it in the freezer until it is firm but not frozen. It will then be easier to slice. Place the slices on a greased griddle, adjust the heat to moderate, and cook for 5 to 8 minutes on each side, until the scrapple is deep brown but not burned. Serve for breakfast with scrambled or fried eggs. Wrap unused scrapple in foil and refrigerate or freeze.

Desserts

Many Americans do not consider a meal complete unless some kind of dessert has been served, which could be as simple as a dish of vanilla ice cream, as hearty as a slice of chocolate-streaked coffeecake, or as elegant as a raspberry mousse. While fruit is sometimes served as dessert, it is not considered the typical conclusion to a meal that it is in Asian cuisines. But when an American cook prepares a fruit-studded pudding (page 334) or a juicy fruit pie (page 337), some of the most luscious dessert preparations are created.

Latin Americans enjoy fruit-based sweets as snacks and desserts. In Brazil, where sugar cane is an important crop, fruit is often coated with sugar before being eaten. Bananas, mangos, even pumpkins find their way into Latin American baked desserts and puddings. Even more popular than fruit desserts are milk puddings, most notably a caramelized custard that comes from the Iberian peninsula (see *flan*, page 104). Sugary cookies and pastries are favored, and a fried pastry common in both Spain and Mexico (*churros*, page 330) is rolled in sugar before it is served. Another fried pastry enjoyed with Mexican meals comes from *New* Mexico, where Mexican-American restaurants serve *sopaipillas* (page 331) with honey for dessert.

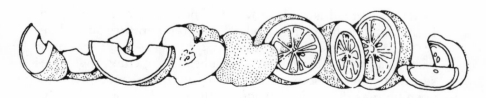

CRULLERS
Churros

Mexico

Makes three dozen
3-inch long pastries

Breakfast crullers, midday snacks, evening pastries—*churros* are eaten morning, noon, and night in both Spain and Mexico. A soft egg dough is squeezed out of a special press into hot oil, then the fried dough is rolled in sugar, to be enjoyed warm with hot coffee or Mexican hot chocolate (Mexican chocolate dissolved in hot milk). If you have a cookie press or a pastry bag or a *churro*-maker, you can make your own *churros*. Mexicans add lemon and fried bread to the oil as it heats, which imparts a subtle flavor. Incidentally, I know for a fact that *churros* will keep as long as 5 minutes—they have never lasted long enough in my house to test for storage qualities.

Oil for deep-frying
1 slice white bread
Half of a lemon
1 cup unsifted all-purpose flour
1 cup boiling water
1 egg (graded large)
¾ cup granulated or sifted confectioners'
sugar

Into an electric skillet or a pot with sides at least 3 inches deep, pour one inch of oil. Add the bread slice and lemon half and place over moderate heat. Meanwhile, in a medium-size mixing bowl place the flour and make a well in the center. Add the boiling water, beating rapidly with a spoon. Add the egg, beating until the mixture is smooth. (Persevere—it *will* become smooth.)

When the bread is dark brown but not burned, remove the bread and lemon from the oil. The oil temperature should be 350 to 375 degrees F. Put the dough into a cookie press or a pastry bag with a large open star tube. The opening *must* have serrated edges or some indentation, because a smooth round opening may cause the outside of the *churro* to cook so quickly that steam pressure builds up inside the dough; if this happens, the inside may suddenly pop out and spatter oil.

Squeeze 3- to 4-inch lengths of dough into the hot oil, and cook until the *churros* are golden all over, turning as necessary. Drain well on paper towels. Repeat until all the oil is used up. Watch the oil temperature, regulating the heat so the oil does not become too hot or cool.

Place the sugar in a shallow bowl or a small brown bag (lunch bag size). While the *churros* are still hot, drop them one at a time into the sugar, and coat completely with the sugar. Serve warm.

SOPAIPILLAS

New Mexico

Serves 4 to 6

Navajo Indians of the Southwest have been making simple fried breads from white flour ever since Spaniards introduced lard and oil for frying. *Sopaipillas* are a Mexican-American variation on Navajo breads. The dough is rolled and cut into triangles or rectangles, fried until golden and puffed, sprinkled with cinnamon and sugar, and eaten with meals as a bread. Or *sopaipillas* may be served with honey and enjoyed for dessert, as they are in this recipe.

> **1 cup unsifted all-purpose flour**
> **1½ teaspoons double-acting baking powder**
> **¼ teaspoon salt**
> **1 tablespoon solid vegetable shortening**
> **⅓ cup water**
> **Oil for deep-frying**
> **Honey**

In a medium-size mixing bowl, mix together the dry ingredients. Using a fork or your fingers, work in the shortening until the particles are small and distributed well. Gradually add the water, stirring with a fork until the dough cleans the side of the bowl and can be formed into a ball.

Recipe continues on the following page . . .

Gather up the dough, shape into a ball, and flatten between 2 sheets of wax paper. Roll the dough into an 8-inch square, ⅛-inch thick. Cut into sixteen 2-inch squares.

In an electric skillet or a 4- or 5-quart pot, heat an inch of oil to 375 degrees F. The oil should be hot but not yet smoking. A drop of water will spatter instantly. Carefully add the *sopaipillas* to the oil, but do not add more than 4 or 5 at once or the oil temperature will be lowered and they may not puff. Using the back of a metal spoon push the *sopaipillas* under the oil to help them puff up. Fry until golden on both sides, turning once. Drain on paper towels. Serve warm in a basket alongside a bowl of honey to be spooned on by the diners.

NORWEGIAN FLAT POTATO BREADS
Lefse

Midwest

Makes 16

A potato-and-flour dough makes up these very thin pliable crepe-like breads, one of the foods prepared by Scandinavians who emigrated to the Midwest in the 1800s. Start this recipe well in advance, because the potatoes must be cooked, mashed, and thoroughly chilled before being mixed with flour and shaped. They are buttered, rolled up, sliced, and eaten as a bread with meals. Or they may be spread with jam and served as dessert, as they are in this recipe. *Lefse* are sweet but not cloying, so you may enjoy serving jam-filled *lefse* as a breakfast treat as well.

2 pounds white potatoes
¼ cup (½ stick) unsalted butter
¼ cup light cream
1 teaspoon granulated sugar
½ teaspoon salt

2 cups unsifted all-purpose flour,
  approximately
Softened butter
1 cup seedless raspberry jam

Peel the potatoes, cut into quarters or cubes, and cook in boiling water until tender. Drain. Place the potatoes in a large mixing bowl, and while they are still hot beat them with an electric mixer until smooth. Beat in the butter, cream, sugar and salt. Cover the bowl or place in a covered container and refrigerate the potatoes until completely cool, a minimum of 3 hours. The potatoes can be cooked and chilled a day in advance.

When ready to make the breads, spread one cup of flour on a clean work surface. Turn out the cooked potatoes onto the flour and sprinkle the top with ½ cup flour. Knead the dough 8 to 10 minutes, sprinkling on more flour as necessary to keep the dough from sticking. At first the dough will be stiff and difficult to knead, but as you continue it will become more like a bread dough. When you finish kneading, the dough should be very smooth, pliable, and not the least bit sticky.

Divide the dough into 16 equal pieces. Roll each piece into a smooth ball. Work with one ball of dough at a time, keeping the remainder covered with a damp but not wet towel. Heat a heavy ungreased 7-inch skillet or a griddle over moderately high heat. A drop of water will skitter and evaporate. On a lightly floured surface roll the dough to a thin 6-inch circle, giving the dough a quarter-turn each time you roll. This will help keep the shape round and will also keep the dough from sticking. Wrap the rolled dough lightly around the rolling pin and transfer to the hot skillet or griddle. Cook for about 45 seconds on one side, until the top bubbles and the bottom browns lightly. Turn with your fingers or a pancake turner and cook the other side for about 15 seconds. The *lefse* will be pliable, not crisp. Remove the cooked *lefse* to a large plate, cover with a clean dry towel and proceed with a second ball of dough. Repeat with all the dough, stacking the cooked breads. Cool to room temperature. The breads are *not* buttered while still warm because a thick layer of butter is considered desirable. The *lefse* can be refrigerated or frozen at this point, but they must be brought back to room temperature before they are served.

Recipe continues on the following page . . .

When ready to serve spread each *lefse* with soft butter and a tablespoon of jam, covering the surface completely. Fold into thirds and slice on the diagonal into 3 or 4 pieces each. Traditionally *lefse* are eaten with the fingers.

Note: For meat meals substitute *pareve* margarine for the butter and water for the cream.

HOT BLUEBERRY PUDDING

New England

Serves 6

   Blueberries grow wild in New England and are cultivated as well, so during blueberry season there is an abundance of this delicate fruit. Although I never tire of munching blueberries out of hand or putting them into pies, when I want to serve a really special dessert, I make this steamed blueberry pudding with a hot blueberry sauce. The pudding itself is more a moist cake with a country kitchen flavor, the sauce a meld of hot cooked blueberries and whole uncooked berries, the latter providing the texture and goodness of the fresh-picked fruit. When topped with hard sauce or vanilla ice cream that melts into the hot pudding, it is superb.
   If you do not have a 6-cup pudding mold, don't worry. I don't either. A 1½-quart round or square Corning casserole is fine. Start this recipe well in advance of serving time, for while it doesn't take too long to mix, the pudding steams for 3 hours.

The Pudding:

   Butter for the mold
   1½ cups cultivated or wild fresh blueberries
   Flour for dusting the blueberries
   ¼ cup (½ stick) unsalted butter, softened
   ¾ cup granulated sugar
   1 egg (graded large)
   1 teaspoon vanilla extract
   2½ cups unsifted all-purpose four

½ teaspoon baking soda
1 cup buttermilk
Boiling water for steaming

First prepare the steaming equipment. You will need a 6-cup pudding mold or a 1½-quart casserole (round or square, 3 inches high, preferably with a lid) that will fit into a pot, probably an 8-quart pot. The steaming mold or casserole should not touch the bottom of the pot, so you will need a rack or a small heatproof bowl to put on the bottom of the pot. Butter the bottom and sides of the pudding mold or casserole and set aside.

Remove any stems from the blueberries, discard soft and underripe berries, wash the blueberries, and dry them on paper towels. Sprinkle the dry berries with about a tablespoon of flour.

In the medium or large bowl of an electric mixer, beat the butter until it is creamy. Beat in the sugar, and continue beating until the mixture is fluffy. Beat in the egg and vanilla extract. Now beat in a cup of flour and the baking soda, then ½ cup of the buttermilk. Add another cup of flour, the remaining ½ cup of buttermilk, finally the remaining ½ cup of flour. Blend well after each addition, scraping down the sides of the mixing bowl as necessary. The batter should be smooth but not overbeaten. Stir in the blueberries.

Pour the mixture into the mold or casserole, leveling the top. Butter a piece of foil and place the foil over the top of the pudding mold or casserole, then put on the lid. If there is no lid, crimp the foil securely around the mold or casserole. Place the mold or casserole on the rack or bowl in the steaming pot, and *carefully* pour enough boiling water into the pot to come to within an inch of the top of the mold or casserole. Cover the pot, bring to the boil over high heat, and adjust the heat so the water boils continuously for 3 hours. Check the pot every hour, and add more boiling water if necessary. When you lift the cover to check the pot, always tilt the cover away from your face so you do not get burned by the steam.

The hard sauce (below) must be chilled until firm, so it should be prepared as soon as the steaming begins. Prepare the hot blueberry sauce (below) about half an hour before the pudding is

Recipe continues on the following page . . .

336 ° T H E   A M E R I C A S

done. The pudding should be served hot. It will remain warm for at least thirty minutes if it is left in the steamer on a turned-off burner. Or it can be prepared a day ahead, refrigerated, and resteamed for a few minutes until it is hot.

To serve, carefully remove the pudding mold or casserole from the pot. Run a knife around the edge of the pudding, place a deep casserole or serving bowl over the top of the pudding mold, rapidly invert the mold so the serving bowl is on the bottom and the pudding on top, and the pudding will come out in one piece into the serving bowl. Pour the hot blueberry sauce over and around the blueberry pudding, and pour any extra sauce into a separate bowl. Serve immediately with any extra blueberry sauce and with hard sauce or ice cream.

The Hard Sauce:

>   ½ cup (1 stick) unsalted butter, softened
>   1 cup sifted confectioners' sugar
>   1 teaspoon vanilla extract

In a small mixing bowl, cream the butter with an electric mixer. Gradually beat in the confectioners' sugar. Beat until light and fluffy, then blend in the vanilla extract. Using an ice cream scoop or a spoon, shape the mixture into a ball and place in a serving bowl. Hard sauce is served chilled and firm.

The Blueberry Sauce:

>   1 quart fresh blueberries
>   1½ cups granulated sugar
>   Pinch of ground cinnamon or nutmeg
>   (optional)

Remove any stems from the blueberries, discard any soft or underripe berries, then wash and drain the blueberries. Measure 3 cups of the blueberries into a 2-quart pot. (The remaining cup of berries is stirred into the sauce later on.) Stir in the sugar. Place the pot over moderately low heat. The blueberries will cook down to form a sauce with the sugar, but you must watch them carefully and stir almost all the time so they do not stick and burn. Bring the sauce to the boil, and cook for an additional 5 to 10 minutes, until the sugar is completely dissolved and the sauce thickened. Stir in the optional cinnamon or nutmeg. Remove from the heat, but leave the sauce in the pot so it will stay warm. Just before serving, stir the remaining uncooked berries into the sauce.

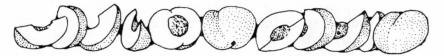

PEACH PIE WITH PECAN CRUNCH TOPPING

Southern United States

Makes one 9-inch pie

When Georgia peaches partner with Texas pecans the result is a peach pie with a difference. A sweet crunchy pecan mixture is used both to line the pie shell and to cover the peaches, making a luscious top "crust."

The Pie Shell:

> **1 cup unsifted all-purpose flour**
> **Dash of salt (optional)**
> **⅓ cup solid vegetable shortening**
> **2 tablespoons water, approximately**

In a small mixing bowl, stir the flour and salt together. Cut in the shortening with a fork or a pastry blender until the particles are small and distributed evenly. Sprinkle the water over the mixture 1 tablespoon at a time, stirring after each addition. The moistened flour should cling together. Sprinkle in a little more water if the dough is crumbly.

With your fingers, gather the dough into a ball. Flatten the ball of dough and place it between 2 sheets of wax paper, each 12 inches square. Roll out the dough to an 11-inch round. Peel off the top sheet of wax paper, replace it, flip over the dough, and peel off what is now the top sheet of wax paper. Ease the dough into a 9-inch pie pan. Fold in any overhanging edges, and shape the dough between your fingers to make a stand-up rim. Flute the edges. Cover the unbaked pie shell with a piece of wax paper until the filling is ready.

Recipe continues on the following page . . .

The Filling and Topping:

⅓ cup unsifted all-purpose flour
½ cup firmly packed light or dark brown
   sugar
⅔ cup coarsely chopped pecans
¼ cup (½ stick) firm unsalted butter or
   margarine
3 pounds fresh peaches
1 teaspoon fresh lemon juice
½ cup granulated sugar
¼ cup unsifted all-purpose flour
¼ teaspoon ground cinnamon

In a small bowl, use a fork to mix the ⅓ cup flour with the brown sugar. Stir in the pecans. Cut the butter into bits and work in the butter with your fingers until the mixture is crumbly. Set aside.

Preheat the oven to 425 degrees F.

Peel the peaches and slice them into ½-inch wedges. There should be about 5 cups of peaches. Place the peaches in a large bowl and sprinkle them with the lemon juice. In a small bowl, combine the granulated sugar and remaining flour with the cinnamon. Mix thoroughly with the peaches.

Sprinkle ½ cup of the pecan mixture on the bottom of the unbaked pie shell. Cover with the peaches, arranging the fruit evenly in the shell. Sprinkle the remaining pecan mixture over the top, covering the peaches completely. Press the topping lightly into the peaches.

Place a 12-inch square of foil on the bottom rack of the oven to catch any spills. Bake the pie on the middle rack for 40 to 45 minutes, until the peaches are bubbly. Check the pie after 30 minutes and cover lightly with a piece of foil if the top is browning too quickly. Serve the pie warm or at room temperature. Do not refrigerate.

CHOCOLATE-FLECKED
WHIPPED CREAM PASTRIES

General United States

Makes 12 pastries

Flecks of melted semisweet chocolate folded into whipped cream makes a heavenly combination atop a chocolate pastry tart. The pastry is easily shaped by pressing the dough into muffin pans lined with paper baking cups. Be prepared for accolades when you serve this dessert.

> **1 cup (6 ounces) semisweet chocolate pieces**
> **⅓ cup solid vegetable shortening**
> **2 tablespoons unsalted butter**
> **1¼ cups unsifted all-purpose flour**
> **1 cup heavy or whipping cream**
> **¼ cup sifted confectioners' sugar**
> **1 teaspoon vanilla extract**

In a small heavy skillet or a 1-quart pot, melt the semisweet chocolate over very low heat. Remove from the heat and set aside.

Preheat the oven to 375 degrees F. In a small or medium-size mixing bowl, cream the shortening and butter with a spoon. Blend in 3 tablespoons of the melted chocolate (the chocolate can be warm but it should not be hot). Stir in the flour, mixing until the dough cleans the sides of the bowl. Using your fingers, gather up the dough into a ball. Divide the dough into 12 equal pieces and shape each piece into a ball. Line twelve 2½-inch (standard size) muffin cups with paper baking cups. Press the dough evenly into the muffin cups, covering the bottom and ½ inch of the sides.

Bake for 12 minutes or until the dough is the consistency of a baked drop cookie. The pastry should hold its shape but be slightly soft, and it should not brown. If underdone the pastry will continue to cook a little after being removed from the oven, but if overdone it will become too hard. Transfer the baked pastry from the muffin cups to a wire rack, leaving them in the paper baking cups until cool.

Recipe continues on the following page . . .

For the filling, chill a small mixing bowl and beaters or a whisk in the freezer for 15 minutes. Or place in the refrigerator for an hour. Pour the cream into the chilled mixing bowl. Add the confectioners' sugar and vanilla extract to the cream and whip until the cream holds stiff peaks. Slowly add the remaining melted chocolate to the whipped cream, gently folding in the chocolate with a spatula so the chocolate hardens into streaks and flecks. The chocolate should not be so thoroughly mixed in with the cream that the mixture becomes chocolate whipped cream. The melted chocolate must still be warm enough so that it pours, but not so warm that it heats the cream. If the chocolate has hardened, reheat over low heat until just barely melted again. Cool as necessary before using.

Remove the baked pastries from the baking cups. Divide the filling among the pastries, mounding the filling attractively. The pastries can be filled 4 hours in advance and refrigerated.

Index

Achiote. *See* Annatto.
Adobo, 228-29
African influences on cuisines of the
    Americas, 270, 273
Allspice, 13
Almonds
    Apricot Cream Parfait, 174-75
    Burghul Pilaf for Meat Meals, 168
    Burghul Pilaf for Vegetarian or
        Dairy Meals, 167
    Cold Chicken With Nut Topping,
        132-34
    Linzertorte, 116-18
    Sole Aux Amandes, 87
    Tablecloth Stainer, 311-12
    Wild Rice Casserole, 326-27
Alu Parathas, 248-49
American Indians, 267, 268, 269,
    272, 274, 318, 326, 331
Americas, 265ff.
Annatto (Achiote), 13
    Deep-fried Vegetable Cakes,
        251-52
    Oxtail Stew, 214-15
Antipasto, 36, 47
Antojito, 276
Appetizers, 47-54, 128-34, 187-96,
    276-86. *See also* Antipasto;
    Mezze; *and* Tapas.
    in Asian cuisines, 187
    Batter-fried Squash Blossoms, 278
    Bean Dip, 280
    Broiled Marinated Chicken, 190-91
    Cheese Triangles, 130-32
    Cold Chicken With Nut Topping,
        132-34
    Creole Dish from Chiclayo, 314-17
    Deviled Tuna, 283-84

    in European cuisines, 47
    Fish Marinated in Lime, 194-95
    Fish With Garlic and Sherry, 54
    Fried Chicken Nuggets, 189-90
    Fried Plantain Chips, 277
    Fried Wontons, 195-96
    Herbed Mushrooms, 50-51
    Herbed Yogurt Cheese, 129
    Lamb "Pies," 143-44
    in Latin American cuisines, 276
    Little Meat-filled Turnovers,
        281-83
    Lomi Lomi Salmon, 193-94
    Marinated Mushrooms, 52-53
    meat-filled triangles, variation, 132
    in Middle Eastern cuisines, 128
    Nachos, 279
    in Pacific Island cuisines, 187
    Pirozhki, 49-50
    Roasted Sweet Red Peppers, 48
    Rumaki, 193
    Salmon With Cream Dressing,
        285-86
    Smoked "Spareribs," 192
    Spanish Sausage Meatballs, 53
    Spicy Vegetable Fritters, 188-89
    in United States cuisines, 276
Apples
    Applesauce, 99-100
    Dried Bean, Fresh Vegetable, and
        Fruit Casserole, 100-101
    Fresh Fruit Chutney, 206-207
    Roasted Fruit-stuffed Chickens,
        155-56
    Tablecloth Stainer, 311-12
    Veal With Apples and Prunes,
        70-71
Applesauce, 99-100

Apricot Cream Parfait, 174-75
Apricots
  Apricot Cream Parfait, 174-75
  Burghul Pilaf for Vegetarian or
    Dairy Meals, 167
  Fresh Fruit Duck Sauce, 207-208
  Roasted Fruit-stuffed Chickens,
    155-56
Aquavit in Swedish cuisine, 45
Argentina, 274-75, 296
  Beef Stew in Pumpkin, 296-98
  Hot Pepper-and-Vinegar Sauce,
    294-95
  Little Meat-filled Turnovers,
    281-83
Armenia, 123-24
  Apricot Cream Parfait, 174-75
  Armenian Thin Bread, 165-67
  Burghul Pilaf for Meat Meals, 168
  Burghul Pilaf for Vegetarian or
    Dairy Meals, 167
  Cheese Triangles, 130-32
  Cucumber-Yogurt Soup, 134-35
  Custard-filled Pastries, 170-72
  Egg-and-Lemon Sauce, 138-39
  Eggplant Purée, 168-69
  Fish Kebobs, 159-60
  Lamb "Pies," 143-44
  Lamb Stew, 142-43
  meat-filled triangles, variation, 132
  Nut Rolls in Honey Syrup, 172-74
  Stuffed Mackerel, 158-59
Armenian Thin Bread, 165-67
Asia and the Pacific Islands, 177ff.
Austria, 41-42, 47
  Applesauce, 99-100
  Boiled Beef, 69-70
  Cottage Cheese "Strudel," 118-20
  Linzertorte, 116-18
  Spätzle, 95-96
Avgolemono sauce. See Egg-and-
    Lemon Sauce.
Avocado
  Guacamole, 290-91

Baked Beans, 323-24
Baked stuffed mackerel, variation,
  159
Baklava, 124, 172
Banana leaves, 13
Bananas. See also Plantains.
  Poe, 260-61
  Tablecloth Stainer, 311-12
Barbecues, 271, 296

Basil, 14
Basque cooking societies, 37
Basted Herb-and-Spice Chicken,
  152-53
Batatas, 297. See also Potatoes.
  Beef Stew in Pumpkin, 296-98
  Creole Dish from Chiclayo, 314-17
Batter-fried Squash Blossoms, 278
Bay leaves, 14
  Fish Kebobs, variation, 160
Bean Dip, 280
Bean paste, Japanese. See Miso.
Bean Paste Soup, 199. See also Miso.
Beans. See also Black beans; Fermented
    black beans; Navy beans; Pink
    beans; and Pinto beans.
  Baked Beans, 323-24
  Bean Dip, 280
  Black Beans With Tomatoes,
    322-23
  in Brazilian cuisine, 273, 318
  Chili, 298-300
  Dried Bean, Fresh Vegetable, and
    Fruit Casserole, 100-101
  Egyptian brown beans, 127, 162
  Fried Tortillas With Meat, 304-306
  in Mexican cuisine, 272, 318
  in New England cuisine, 269, 319
  Refried Beans, 321
Beef
  in Argentinian cuisine, 274
  in Austrian cuisine, 66
  Beef Stew in Pumpkin, 296-98
  beef tongue in Split Pea Soup, 59
  Boiled Beef, 69-70
  Chicken and Beef Stew, 228-29
  Chili, 298-300
  Chorizo, 79-80
  Creole Sausages, 306-307
  Crispy Thai Noodles, 240-42
  Fried Rice, 239-40
  Fried Tortillas With Meat, 304-306
  Fried Wontons, 195-96
  Green Chili, 300-301
  Green Soup, 62-63
  Ground Meat With Peas, 222
  Gumbo, 308-310
  in Indian (Hindu) cuisine, prohibi-
    tion of, 180
  Jambalaya, 307-308
  Korean Barbecue, 212-13
  in Korean cuisine, 185
  Lion's Head, 220-21
  Little Meat-filled Turnovers,
    281-83

meat-filled triangles, variation, 132
Meat With Yellow Split Peas and
    Herbs, 144-45
Mu Shu Beef, 219-20
Oxtail Stew, 214-15
Paella, 80-82
Pepperoni, 76
Pepperoni Pizza, 77-79
Roast Stuffed Chicken, 230
Sauerbraten, 67-68
Spanish Sausage Meatballs, 53
Sukiyaki, 215-17
Swedish Meatballs, 74-75
Tamales, 301-304
variation on Lamb Stew, 224
Wonton Soup, 197
Beef, ground
    Chili, 298-300
    Chorizo, 79-80
    Creole Sausages, 306-307
    Fried Tortillas With Meat, 304-306
    Green Soup, 62-63
    Ground Meat With Peas, 222
    Gumbo, 308-310
    Jambalaya, 307-308
    Lion's Head, 220-21
    Little Meat-filled Turnovers,
        281-83
    Paella, 80-82
    Roast Stuffed Chicken, 230
    Spanish Sausage Meatballs, 53
    Swedish Meatballs, 74-75
Beef, steak
    Korean Barbecue, 212-13
    Sukiyaki, 215-17
Beef, stewing
    Beef Stew in Pumpkin, 296-98
    Chicken and Beef Stew, 228-29
    Green Chili, 300-301
    Meat With Yellow Split Peas and
        Herbs, 144-45
    Oxtail Stew, 214-15
    Pepperoni, 76
    Tamales, 301-304
Beef Stew in Pumpkin, 296-98
Beer in German cuisine, 40
Bell peppers. *See* Green peppers.
Beverages. *See* Aquavit; Beer; Cof-
    fee; Tea; Vodka; Wine; *and*
    Yogurt.
Bigos, 43
Black beans, 14
Black Beans With Tomatoes, 322-23
Black Bread, 90-92
Black pepper, 14
Blanquette de Veau, 71-73

Blindhuhn, 100-101
Blueberry Pudding, Hot, 334-37
Bluefish
    Fish With Garlic and Sherry, 54
    Stuffed Whole Fish, 235-37
Boiled Beef, 69-70
Bok choy. *See* Chinese cabbage.
Boniato, 314, 318. *See also* Batatas *and*
    Potatoes.
Bourekakia, 172-74
Bowl of herbs, 137
Brazil, 273, 276, 277, 296
    Black Beans With Tomatoes,
        322-23
    Fish in Coconut Milk, 313
    Hot Pepper and Lemon-Lime
        Sauce, 293-94
    Little Meat-filled Turnovers,
        281-83
    Toasted Cassava, 325
Breadcrumbs, 14
Breadfruit, 15
Breadfruit Purée (Poi), 258
Breads
    Armenian Thin Bread, 165-67
    Black Bread, 90-92
    in European cuisines, 89
    Flat Whole-wheat Breads, 246-47
    Garlic Croutons, 94-95
    in Indian cuisine, 180, 245
    in Middle Eastern cuisines, 164
    Mu Shu Pancakes, 218-19
    Norwegian Flat Potato Breads,
        332-34
    pita, 126, 164
    Potato-stuffed Whole-wheat
        Breads, 248-49
    Puffed Whole-wheat Breads,
        247-48
    Smörrebröd Bread, 93-94
    Sopaipillas, 331-32
    Tortillas, 319-21
Brisket of beef, fresh
    Boiled Beef, 69-70
    Sauerbraten, 67-68
Broccoli With Garlic Sauce, 98-99
Broiled Marinated Chicken, 190-91
Broth, Vegetarian, 55-56
Bulghur. *See* Burghul.
Bulgur. *See* Burghul.
Burghul (Bulghur, Bulgur), 15, 164
Burghul Pilaf for Meat Meals, 168
Burghul Pilaf for Vegetarian or Dairy
    Meals, 167
Butter, clarified. *See* Clarified butter
    and Ghee.

Cabbage. *See also* Chinese cabbage.
  Dal and Cabbage, 252-53
Cachumbar, 208
Cacik, 134-35
Cajun cuisine, 271
Cannoli, 111-13
Capsicum, 15. *See also* Cayenne pepper; Chilies, peeled green; Chili peppers; Crushed dried red pepper; Green peppers; Peppers; *and* Peppers, sweet red or green.
Cardamom, 15
Carp
  Stuffed Whole Fish, 235-37
Carrots
  Stuffed Whole Fish, 235-37
  Vegetable and Lamb Couscous, 146-48
  Wild Rice Casserole, 326-27
Cassava, 15-16, 314, 318-19
  in Brazilian cuisine, 273, 322
  Creole Dish from Chiclayo, 314-17
  Toasted Cassava, 325
Cauliflower
  Spicy Vegetable Fritters, 188-89
  Tempura, 237-39
Causa à la Chiclayana, 314-17
Cayenne pepper, 16
  Hot Pepper-and-Vinegar Sauce, 294-95
Celery cabbage. *See* Chinese cabbage.
Cellophane noodles, 16
  pho, 187
  Stuffed Whole Fish, 235-37
  Sukiyaki, 215-17
Chapatis, 246-47
Charcoal-grilled Fish in Ti Leaves, 234-35
Charlotte Russe, Simplified, 109-110
Chayote and Squash Blossom Soup, 287-88
Cheddar cheese
  Bean Dip, 280
  Fried Tortillas With Cheese, 317
  Nachos, 279
Cheese. *See also under specific cheeses.*
  Bean Dip (cheese optional), 280
  Cannoli, 111-13
  cheese pizza, variation, 79
  Cheese Triangles, 130-32
  cottae cheese pizza, variation, 79
  Cottage Cheese "Strudel," 118-20
  Creole Dish from Chiclayo, 314-17
  Curd Cheese With Tomatoes and Peas, 253-55

Eggplant Pureé, variation, 169
  Fried Tortillas With Cheese, 317
  Herbed Yogurt Cheese, 129
  in Italian cuisine, 36
  Moussaka, 160-61
  Nachos, 279
  Onion Soup, 57
  panir, 24
  risotto alla milanese, variation, 98
  in Russian cuisine, 44
Cheese pizza, variation, 79
Cherry tomatoes, green. *See* Green Chili.
Cheese Triangles, 130-32
Chicken
  in Asian and Pacific Island cuisines, 211
  Basted Herb-and-Spice Chicken, 152-53
  Broiled Marinated Chicken, 190-91
  Chicken and Beef Stew, 228-29
  Chicken in Green Sauce, 232-33
  chicken in pomegranate sauce, variation, 157
  Chicken Kebobs, 231-32
  Chicken Kiev, 83-84
  Chicken Paprika, 82-83
  chicken tamales, variation, 304
  Chicken With Honey and Lemon, 151-52
  Chicken With Preserved Lemons and Olives, 154-55
  Cold Chicken With Nut Topping, 132-34
  Egyptian Grilled Chicken, 150-51
  Fried Chicken Nuggets, 189-90
  Gumbo, 308-310
  Jambalaya, 307-308
  in Middle Eastern cuisines, 141
  Mogul Chicken, 226-28
  Paella, 80-82
  Roasted Fruit-stuffed Chickens, 155-56
  Roast Stuffed Chicken, 230
  Tablecloth Stainer, 311-12
  Teriyaki, 233-34
  variation on Lamb Stew, 224
Chicken and Beef Stew, 228-29
Chicken in Green Sauce, 232-33
Chicken in pomegranate sauce, variation, 157
Chicken Kebobs, 231-32
Chicken Kiev, 83-84
Chicken livers
  in kosher cooking, 12
  Rumaki, 193

Chicken Paprika, 82-83
Chicken tamales, variation, 304
Chicken With Honey and Lemon, 151-52
Chicken With Preserved Lemons and Olives, 154-55
Chickpea flour, 16
  Spicy Vegetable Fritters, 188-89
Chickpeas
  Felafel, 162-63
  Vegetable and Lamb Couscous, 146-48
Chili, 298-300
Chilies, peeled green, 17
  Green Chili, 300-301
  Green Tomato Sauce, 291-92
Chili, Green, 300-301
Chili peppers, 16
  Black Beans With Tomatoes, 322-23
  Chili, 298-300
  Creole Dish from Chiclayo, 314-17
  Green Chili, 300-301
  Guacamole, 290-91
  Harissa, 148
  Hot Green Curry Paste, 201-203
  Hot Pepper and Lemon-Lime Sauce, 293-94
  Uncooked Red Sauce, 292-93
Chili powder, 16, 299
  Chili, 298-300
  Little Meat-filled Turnovers, 281-83
  Tablecloth Stainer, 311-12
Chimichurri, 294-95
China, 181-82, 187, 211
  Fresh Fruit Duck Sauce, 207-208
  Fried Chicken Nuggets, 189-90
  Fried Wontons, 195-96
  Lion's Head, 220-21
  Mu Shu Beef, 219-20
  Mu Shu Pancakes, 218-19
  Smoked "Spareribs," 192
  "Spareribs" in Black Bean Sauce, 225-26
  Stir-fried Vegetables, 250
  Wonton Soup, 197
Chinese cabbage, 17
  Lion's Head, 220-21
Chinese hot turnip. *See* Hot turnip and hot radish.
Chinese mushrooms, dried. *See* Dried Chinese mushrooms.
Chinese parsley. *See* Coriander.
Chocolate-flecked Whipped Cream

Pastries, 339-40
Chocolate Mousse, 107
Chorizo, 79-80
  Fried Tortillas With Meat, 304-306
  Green Soup, 62-63
  Paella, 80-82
  Roast Stuffed Chicken, 230
  Spanish Sausage Meatballs, 53
Chorizo meatballs, 53
Chupe, 277
Churros, 330-31
Chutney, Fresh Fruit, 206-207
Cilantro. *See* Coriander.
Cinnamon, 17
Clarified butter, 17. *See also* Ghee.
Cocido, 37
  origin as a Jewish preparation, 67
Coconut cream
  Chicken in Green Sauce, 232-33
  Coconut Cream, 205-206
  Coconut Rice Pudding With Mangos, 262-63
  Fish Marinated in Lime, 194-95
  Whipped Coconut Cream, 259-60
Coconut Cream, 205-206
Coconut milk, 179. *See also* Coconuts.
  Chicken and Beef Stew, 228-29
  Coconut Milk (recipe), 203-205
  Coconut Pudding, 261-62
  Coconut Rice Pudding With Mangos, 262-63
  Fish in Coconut Milk, 313
Coconut Milk, 203-205
Coconut oil, 205-206
Coconut Pudding, 261-62
Coconut Rice Pudding With Mangos, 262-63
Coconuts. *See also* Coconut cream *and* Coconut milk.
  in Hawaiian cuisine, 186
  how to open, 204
  how to select, 203
Codfish
  Deviled Tuna, 283-84
  Fish With Garlic and Sherry, 54
  Fresh Fish Stew, 85-86
Coffee
  in Brazilian cuisine, 273
  in French cuisine, 39
  in German cuisine, 40
  in Indonesian cuisine, 184
  in Turkish cuisine, 125
Cold Chicken With Nut Topping, 132-34
Comino. *See* Cumin.

Condiments and Sauces, 63-65, 136-40, 200-210, 289-95. *See also* Sauces *and* Seasonings.
in Asian cuisines, 200
Coconut Cream, 205-206
Coconut Milk, 203-205
Egg-and-Lemon Sauce, 138-39
in European cuisines, 63-65
Fresh Fruit Chutney, 206-207
Fresh Fruit Duck Sauce, 207-208
garlic-and-vinegar sauce, 251
Green Tomato Sauce, 291-92
Guacamole, 290-91
Harissa, 148
Hot Green Curry Paste, 201-203
Hot Pepper and Lemon-Lime Sauce, 293-94
Hot Pepper-and-Vinegar Sauce, 294-95
hot red curry paste, 202
in Indian cuisine, 206
Korean Pickled Vegetables, 209-210
in Latin American cuisines, 289
in Mexican cuisine, 289
in Middle Eastern cuisines, 136-37
Onion and Tomato Relish, 208
in Pacific Island cuisines, 200
in Pennsylvania Dutch cuisine, 289
Preserved Lemons, 139-40
Salmon With Cream Dressing, 285-86
Sauce Base (Sofrito), 65
Spicy Peanut Sauce, 231-32
Tahini, 137-38
Uncooked Red Sauce, 292-93
in the United States, 289
Congee. *See* Soups.
Coriander, 18
Corn. *See also* Cornhusks; Cornmeal; *and* Masa harina.
Beef Stew in Pumpkin, 296-98
Creole Dish from Chiclayo, 314-17
in Italian cuisine, 36
in Mexican cuisine, 272
in New England cuisine, 269
in Southeastern United States cuisine, 271
Corned beef in Baked Beans, 323-24
Corn flour. *See* Masa harina.
Cornhusks, how to prepare for Tamales, 302
Tamales, 301-304
Cornish hen stuffing, 326

Cornmeal
Scrapple, 327-28
Tortillas, 319-21
Corn tortillas, 320-21
Cottage cheese
Cheese Triangles, 130-32
cottage cheese pizza, variation, 77, 79
Cottage Cheese "Strudel," 118-20
in Russian cuisine, 44
Cottage cheese pizza, variation, 77, 79
Cottage Cheese "Strudel," 118-20
Couscous, 18, 126
Vegetable and Lamb Couscous, 146-48
Cream of Mushroom Soup, 58-59
Cream, sour. *See* Sour cream.
Creole, 270
Creole Sausages, 306-307
cuisine, 270-71
Gumbo, 308-310
Jambalaya, 307-308
Creole Dish from Chiclayo, 314-17
Creole Sausages, 306-307
Crispy Thai Noodles, 240-42
Crullers, 330-31
Crushed dried red pepper, 18
Cucumber Pickles, 210
Cucumber-Yogurt Soup, 134-35
Cumin, 18
Curd Cheese With Tomatoes and Peas, 253-55
Curry paste, 18-19
Chicken in Green Sauce, 232-33
Hot Green Curry Paste, 201-203
hot red curry paste, 202
Curry powder, 19. *See also* Masala *and* Garam Masala.
Custard-filled Pastries, 170-72

Dairy dishes
Apricot Cream Parfait, 174-75
Bean Dip (cheese optional), 280
Broccoli With Garlic Sauce (dairy optional), 98-99
Cannoli, 111-13
cheese pizzas, variations, 79
Cheese Triangles, 130-32
Chocolate-flecked Whipped Cream Pastries, 339-40
Cottage Cheese "Strudel," 118-20
Cream of Mushroom Soup, 58-59
Creole Dish from Chiclayo, 314-17

Cucumber-Yogurt Soup, 134-35
Curd Cheese With Tomatoes and
    Peas, 253-55
Custard-filled Pastries, 170-72
Dobostorte, 113-16
Eggplant Purée, variation, 169
Felafel, 162-63
Flan, 104-05
Fried Tortillas With Cheese, 317
Herbed Yogurt Cheese, 129
Hot Blueberry Pudding, 334-37
Linzertorte, 116-18
Moussaka, 160-61
Nachos, 279
New England Fish Chowder,
    286-87
Norwegian Flat Potato Breads,
    332-34
Onion Soup, 57
Pirozhki, 49-50
risotto alla milanese, variation, 98
Salmon With Cream Dressing,
    285-86
Simplified Charlotte Russe,
    109-110
vegetarian lentil soup, 135
Dairy products
in Chinese cuisine, 182
in Danish cuisine, 45
in Dutch cuisine, 46
in European cuisines, 67
in Indian cuisine, 181
Dal, 180
Dal and Cabbage, 252-53
Dashi, 19, 187
    Japanese Soup Stock, 198
    White Noodles, 256-57
Deep-fried Vegetable Cakes,
    251-52
Delicatessen, 40
Denmark, 45-46
    Smörrebröd Bread, 93-94
    Veal With Apples and Prunes,
    70-71
Desserts, 102-120, 170-75, 259-64,
    329-40
in Asian and Pacific Island cui-
    sines, 259, 329
Apricot Cream Parfait, 174-75
Cannoli, 111-13
Chocolate-flecked Whipped Cream
    Pastries, 339-40
Coconut Pudding, 261-62
Coconut Rice Pudding With Man-
    gos, 262-63

Cottage Cheese "Strudel," 118-20
Crullers, 330-31
Custard-filled Pastries, 170-72
Dobostorte, 113-16
in European cuisines, 102
Flan, 104-105
Fresh Strawberry Ices, 102-104
Hot Blueberry Pudding, 334-37
Ladyfingers, 108-109
in Latin American cuisines, 329
Linzertorte, 116-18
Macadamia Nut Pie, 263-64
in Middle Eastern cuisines, 170
Mousse au Chocolat, 107
Norwegian Flat Potato Breads,
    332-34
Nut Rolls in Honey Syrup, 172-74
orange ices, variation, 104
Peach Pie With Pecan Crunch
    Topping, 337-38
Poe, 260-61
Simplified Charlotte Russe, 109-
    110
Sopaipillas, 331-32
Soufflé de Grand Marnier, 105-106
in the United States, 329
Whipped Coconut Cream, 259-60
Deviled Tuna, 283-84
Dill, 19
    Chicken Kiev, 83-84
    Cucumber-Yogurt Soup, 134-35
    Ground Lamb Sandwiches, 149-50
    Lentil Soup, 135-36
    Pirozhki, 49-50
Dim sum, 182
Dobostorte, 113-16
Dolmas, 165
Dried Bean, Fresh Vegetable, and
    Fruit Casserole, 100-101
Dried chili peppers. *See* Chili peppers.
Dried Chinese mushrooms, 19
    Mu Shu Beef, 219-20
    Sukiyaki, 215-17
Dried seaweed. *See* Seaweed, dried.
Duck in Pomegranate Sauce,
    156-57
Duck Sauce, Fresh Fruit, 207-208
Dumplings. *See also* Spätzle *and*
    Wontons.
in Austrian cuisine, 41
in Chinese cuisine, 182
in European cuisines, 89
in German cuisine, 39-40, 89
in Korean cuisine, 185
Dutch cuisine. *See* Netherlands.

Egg-and-Lemon Sauce, 138-39
Eggplant
  Eggplant Purée, 168-69
  Moussaka, 160-61
  Spicy Vegetable Fritters, 188-89
Eggplant Purée, 168-69
Eggs
  Egg-and-Lemon Sauce, 138-39
  egg nets, 240-42
  egg pancake garnish, 240, 244
  in European cuisines, 67
  Flan, 104-105
  Mousse au Chocolat, 107
  Soufflé de Grand Marnier, 105-106
  Spanish Omelet, 87-88
Egypt, 126-27
  Egyptian Grilled Chicken, 150-51
  Felafel, 162-63
Egyptian Grilled Chicken, 150-51
Empanadas. See Empanaditas.
Empanaditas, 281-83
Europe, 33ff.

Fejoada completa, 273, 293, 322
Felafel, 162-63
Fenugreek, 19-20
Fermented black beans, 20
  "Spareribs" in Black Bean Sauce, 225-26
Feta cheese
  Cheese Triangles, 130-32
  in Greek cuisine, 124
Filé gumbo, variation, 310
Filé powder, 20, 309
  Filé gumbo, variation, 310
Filets de Sole à la Meunière, 86-87
Fish. See also Seafood and listings under specific fishes.
  Charcoal-grilled Fish in Ti Leaves, 234-35
  Creole Dish from Chiclayo, 314-17
  Deviled Tuna, 283-84
  Filets de Sole à la Meunière, 86-87
  Fish in Coconut Milk, 313
  Fish Kebobs, 159-60
  Fish Marinated in Lime, 194-95
  Fish With Garlic and Sherry, 54
  Fresh Fish Stew, 85-86
  Japanese Soup Stock, 198
  Lomi Lomi Salmon, 193-94
  New England Fish Chowder, 286-87
  Salmon With Cream Dressing, 285-86

Sole Aux Amandes, variation, 87
  Stuffed Mackerel, 158-59
  Stuffed Whole Fish, 235-37
  Sukiyaki, variation, 217
  Tempura, 237-39
  Teriyaki, 233-34
Fish in Coconut Milk, 313
Fish Kebobs, 159-60
Fish Marinated in Lime, 194-95
Fish With Garlic and Sherry, 54
Flan, 104-105, 329
Flat Whole-wheat Breads, 246-47
Flounder
  Creole Dish from Chiclayo, 314-17
  Filets de Sole à la Meunière, 86-87
  Fish in Coconut Milk, 313
  Fish Marinated in Lime, 194-95
  Fresh Fish Stew, 85-86
  Sukiyaki, variation, 217
  Tempura, 237-39
  Teriyaki, 233-34
Flour tortillas, 319-20
France, 35, 38-39, 64, 89-90, 270
  classical French cuisine, 39
  Filets de Sole à la Meunière, 86-87
  Herbed Mushrooms, 50-51
  Ladyfingers, 108-109
  Mousse au Chocolat, 107
  Onion Soup, 57
  provincial cuisine, 38-39
  Simplified Charlotte Russe, 109-110
  Sole Aux Amandes, variation, 87
  Soufflé de Grand Marnier, 105-106
  Veal Stew, 71-73
Fresh Fish Stew, 85-86
Fresh Fruit Chutney, 206-207
Fresh Fruit Duck Sauce, 207-208
Fresh Strawberry Ices, 102-104
Fried Chicken Nuggets, 189-190
Fried Plantain Chips, 277
Fried Rice, 239-40
Fried Tortillas With Cheese, 317
Fried Tortillas With Meat, 304-306
Fried Wontons, 195-96
Frijoles Refritos, 321
Fruit. See also Fruit sauces; Meat-and-fruit combinations; and listings under specific fruits.
  Apricot Cream Parfait, 174-75
  in Asian and Pacific Island cuisines, 259
  Breadfruit Purée, 258
  Cottage Cheese "Strudel," 118-20
  Dried Bean, Fresh Vegetable, and Fruit Casserole, 100-101

Duck in Pomegranate Sauce, 156-57
Fresh Fruit Chutney, 206-207
Fresh Strawberry Ices, 102-104
Fried Plantain Chips, 277
Guacamole, 290-91
Hot Blueberry Pudding, 334-37
in Iranian cuisine, 126
Linzertorte, 116-18
in Middle Eastern cuisines, 170
Peach Pie With Pecan Crunch Topping, 337-38
in Pennsylvania Dutch cuisine, 269
Poe, 260-61
Roasted Fruit-stuffed Chickens, 155-56
in Scandinavian cuisines, 46
Simplified Charlotte Russe, 109-110
Veal With Apples and Prunes, 70-71
Fruit sauces
Applesauce, 99-100
Fresh Fruit Duck Sauce, 207-208
in German cuisine, 64
in Russian cuisine, 64

Garam Masala, 20, 200-201
Garlic-and-vinegar sauce, 251
Garlic Croutons, 94-95
Gazpacho, 60-61
Germany, 39-41, 66, 89
Applesauce, 99-100
Cottage Cheese "Strudel," 118-20
Dried Bean, Fresh Vegetable, and Fruit Casserole, 100-101
Sauerbraten, 67-68
Spätzle, 95-96
Ghee, 20. See also Clarified butter.
Ginger, ground, 20-21
Ginger root, fresh, 21
Glutinous rice, 21
Coconut Rice Pudding With Mangos, 262-63
Golden needles. See Tiger lily buds.
Granita di Fragole, 102-104
Greece, 124-25
Cheese Triangles, 130-32
Custard-filled Pastries, 170-72
Egg-and-Lemon Sauce, 138-39
Ground Lamb Sandwiches, 149-50
meat-filled triangles, variation, 132
Moussaka, 160-61
Nut Rolls in Honey Syrup, 172-74

Green beans
Dried Bean, Fresh Vegetable, and Fruit Casserole, 100-101
Oxtail Stew, 214-15
Tempura, 237-39
Green Chili, 300-301
Green onions. See Scallions.
Green peppers, 21
Chicken Paprika, 82-83
Spicy Vegetable Fritters, 188-89
Tempura, 237-39
Green Soup, 62-63
Green Tomato Sauce, 291-92
Ground beef. See Beef, ground.
Ground Lamb Sandwiches (Gyros), 149-50
Ground Meat With Peas, 222
Guacamole, 290-91
Gumbo, 308-310
Gyros, 149-50

Haddock
New England Fish Chowder, 286-87
Halibut
Fish Kebobs, 159-60
Fresh Fish Stew, 85-86
Harissa, 148
Hawaii, 186, 187, 211
Breadfruit Purée (Poi), 258
Coconut Cream, 205-206
Coconut Milk, 203-205
Coconut Pudding, 261-62
lamb for a luau, 211
Lomi Lomi Salmon, 193-94
Macadamia Nut Pie, 263-64
Rumaki, 193
Whipped Coconut Cream, 259-60
Herbed Mushrooms, 50-51
Herbed Yogurt Cheese, 129
Herbs. See also listings under specific herbs.
in Armenian cuisine, 124
Basted Herb-and-Spice Chicken, 152-53
bowl of herbs, 137
Creole Sausages, 306-307
Cucumber-Yogurt Soup, 134-35
Felafel, 162-63
Fish Kebobs, variation, 160
Ground Lamb Sandwiches, 149-50
Herbed Yogurt Cheese, 129
in Iranian cuisine, 126, 137
Lamb "Pies," 143-44
Lentil Soup, 135-36
Meat with Yellow Split Peas and

Herbs, 144-45
in Moroccan cuisine, 126
Scrapple, 327-28
Herring
in Danish cuisine, 45
in Swedish cuisine, 45
Hoisin sauce, 21
Mu Shu Beef, 219-20
Holland. *See* Netherlands.
Honey
Chicken With Honey and Lemon,
151-52
Nut Rolls in Honey Syrup, 172-74
Sopaipillas, 331-32
Hot Blueberry Pudding, 334-37
Hot Green Curry Paste, 201-203
Hot Pepper and Lemon-Lime Sauce,
293-94
Hot Pepper-and-Vinegar Sauce,
294-95
Hot red curry paste, 202
Hot turnip and hot radish, 21-22
How to open coconuts, 204
How to prepare cornhusks for
Tamales, 302
Hungary, 42, 64
Chicken Paprika, 82-83
Cottage Cheese "Strudel," 118-20
Cream of Mushroom Soup, 58-59
Dobostorte, 113-16
Spätzle, 95-96

Ices, Fresh Strawberry, 102-104
Ices, orange, variation, 104
Incas. *See* American Indians *and* Peru.
India, 180-81, 187, 211
Broiled Marinated Chicken, 190-91
Coconut Cream, 205-206
Coconut Milk, 203-205
Curd Cheese With Tomatoes and
Peas, 253-55
Dal and Cabbage, 252-53
Flat Whole-wheat Breads, 246-47
Fresh Fruit Chutney, 206-207
Ground Meat With Peas, 222
Indian Spice Blend, 200-201
Lamb Stew, 223-25
Mogul Chicken, 226-28
Onion and Tomato Relish, 208
Potato-stuffed Whole-wheat
Breads, 248-49
Puffed Whole-wheat Breads,
247-48
Spicy Vegetable Fritters, 188-89
Yellow Rice, 256

Indians, American. *See* American
Indians.
Indian Spice Blend, 200-201. *See also*
Garam Masala.
Indonesia, 183-84
Chicken Kebobs, 231-32
Coconut Cream, 205-206
Coconut Milk, 203-205
Fried Rice, 239-40
Ingredients used in international
cooking, 12ff. *See also* International cuisines, general characteristics *and listings under specific ingredients.*
allspice, 13
annatto (achiote), 13
banana leaves, 13
basil, 14
bay leaves, 14
black beans, 14
black pepper, 14
boniatos. *See* Potatoes.
breadcrumbs, 14
breadfruit, 15
burghul (bulghur, bulgur), 15
capsicum, 15
cardamom, 15
cassava, 15-16
cayenne pepper, 16
cellophane noodles, 16
chickpea flour, 16
chilies, peeled green, 17
chili peppers, 16
chili powder, 16
Chinese cabbage, 17
Chinese hot turnip. *See* Hot turnip
and hot radish.
Chinese mushrooms, dried. *See*
Dried Chinese mushrooms.
cinnamon, 17
clarified butter, 17. *See also* Ghee.
coriander, 18
couscous, 18
crushed dried red pepper, 18
cumin (comino), 18
curry paste, 18-19
curry powder, 19. *See also* Masala.
dashi, 19
dill, 19
dried chili peppers. *See* Chili peppers.
dried Chinese mushrooms, 19
fenugreek, 19-20
fermented black beans (salted black
beans), 20
filé powder, 20

garam masala, 20
ghee, 20. *See also* Clarified butter.
ginger, ground, 20-21
ginger root, fresh, 21
glutinous rice, 21
golden needles. *See* Tiger lily buds.
green peppers, 21
hoisin sauce, 21
hot turnip and hot radish, 21-22
laos, 22
leeks, 22
lemon grass, 22
lentils, 22
masa harina, 22-23
masala, 23
mint, 23
mirin, 23. *See also* Rice wine.
miso, 23
mushrooms, dried. *See* Dried Chinese mushrooms.
mustard, 23-24
navy beans, 24
oil, vegetable. *See* Vegetable oils.
okra, 24
olive oil, 24
panir, 24
paprika, 24
parsley, 25
parsley, Chinese. *See* Coriander.
pea beans. *See* Navy beans.
pepper, black. *See* Black pepper.
peppers, chili. *See* Chili peppers.
peppers, sweet red or green, 25
phyllo dough, 25
pilaf, 25
pine nuts, 25
pink beans, 26
pinto beans, 26
potatoes, 26
rice noodles, 26-27
rice wine, 27. *See also* Mirin.
saffron, 27
salted fermented black beans. *See* Fermented black beans.
scallions (green onions, spring onions), 27
seaweed, dried, 27
sesame oil, 28
sesame seeds, 28
shallots, 28
shoyu. *See* Soy sauce.
somen, 28
sour cream, 28
soy sauce, 28-29
squash blossoms, 29
sweet potatoes. *See* Potatoes.

tiger lily buds (golden needles), 29
ti leaves, 29. *See also* Banana leaves.
tofu, 29-30
tomatillo, 30
tree ears (wood ears), 30
turmeric, 30
vegetable oils, 30-31
wasabi paste, 31
water chestnuts, 31
where to buy international ingredients, 12-13
wonton wrappers, 31
yogurt, 31
International cuisines, general characteristics
Argentina, 267-68, 274-75
Armenia, 123-24
Austria, 41-42
Brazil, 268, 273
China, 179, 181-82
Denmark, 45-46
Egypt, 126-27
France, 38-39
Germany, 39-41
Greece, 124-25
Hawaii, 179, 186
Hungary, 42
India, 180-81
Indonesia, 183-84
Iran, 125-26
Israel, 127
Italy, 35-37
Japan, 179, 185
Lebanon, 127
Mexico, 268, 272-73
Morocco, 126
New England, 269-70
New Mexico, 272
New Orleans, 270-71
Peru, 268, 273-74
Philippines, 179, 184
Poland, 42-43, 44
Portugal, 38, 64
Russia, 43-44
Southeastern United States, 271
Spain, 37-38
Sweden, 44-45
Syria, 127
Tahiti, 179, 186
Texas, 271
Thailand, 183, 201
Turkey, 125
Ukraine, 44
United States of America, 268-72
Vietnam, 182-83

International cuisines, geographic and culinary relationships, 11, 35-46, 123-27, 180-86, 269, 271, 273-74
International cuisines, historical influences on, 35, 37, 41, 44, 45, 123-27, 183-84, 267-75
Iran, 125-26
  bowl of herbs, 137
  Duck in Pomegranate Sauce, 156-57
  Meat With Yellow Split Peas and Herbs, 144-45
  Roasted Fruit-stuffed Chickens, 155-56
Israel, 127
Italy, 35-37
  Broccoli With Garlic Sauce, 98-99
  Cannoli, 111-13
  cheese pizza, variations, 79
  Fresh Strawberry Ices, 102-104
  Marinated Mushrooms, 52-53
  orange ices, variation, 104
  Pepperoni, 76
  Pepperoni Pizza, 77-79
  Risotto, 97-98
  risotto alla milanese, variation, 98
  Roasted Sweet Red Peppers, 48

Jambalaya, 307-308
Japan, 179, 185, 187
  Bean Paste Soup (Miso), 199
  Japanese Soup Stock (Dashi), 198
  Sukiyaki, 215-17
  Tempura, 237-39
  Teriyaki, 233-34
  Vegetable Sushi, 243-44
  White Noodles, 256-57
Japanese Soup Stock, 198. *See also* Dashi.

Kale
  Green Soup, 62-63
Kari Kari, 214-15
Kebobs
  Chicken Kebobs, 231-32
  Fish Kebobs, 159-60
  grilled chicken kebobs, variation, 191
  Korean Barbecue as kebobs, 212
  shish kebob, 125
Khoresh, 126
  Meat With Yellow Split Peas and Herbs, 144-45
Kimchee, 185

Cucumber Pickles, 210
Korean Pickled Vegetables, 209-210
Turnip Pickles, 209
Korea, 185
  Korean Barbecue, 212-13
  Korean Pickled Vegetables (Kimchee), 209-210
Korean Barbecue, 212-13
Korean Pickled Vegetables, 179, 209-210. *See also* Kimchee.
Korma, 223-25
Kosher adaptations in international cooking, 11-12. *See also* Modifying recipes for the kosher kitchen.

Ladyfingers, 108-109
Lamb
  in Armenian cuisine, 124
  Burghul Pilaf for Meat Meals, 168
  in Greek cuisine, 124
  Ground Lamb Sandwiches (Gyros), 149-50
  Ground Meat With Peas, 222
  in Indian cuisine, 180
  lamb for a luau, 211
  Lamb "Pies," 143-44
  Lamb Stew (Armenia, Turkey), 142-43
  Lamb Stew (India), 223-25
  meat-filled triangles, variation, 132
  Meat With Yellow Split Peas and Herbs, 144-45
  in Middle Eastern cuisines, 141
  in Middle Eastern soups, 128
  shish kebob, 125
  Smoked "Spareribs," 192
  "Spareribs" in Black Bean Sauce, 225-26
  Vegetable and Lamb Couscous, 146-48
Lamb for a luau, 211
Lamb "Pies," 143-44
Lamb Stew (Armenia, Turkey), 142-43
Lamb Stew (India), 223-25
Laos, 22
  Hot Green Curry Paste, 201-203
Latin America, 267, 276, 296, 329. *See also* Americas; Argentina; Brazil; Mexico; *and* Peru.
  Fried Plantain Chips, 277
Lavash, 165-67
Lebanon, 127

Chicken With Honey and Lemon,
151-52
Herbed Yogurt Cheese, 129
Leeks, 22, 165
Lefse, 332-33
Legumes. *See also* Beans; Chickpeas;
Dal; Lentils; *and* Split peas.
in Indian cuisine, 180
in Middle Eastern cuisines, 127
Lemon grass, 22, 179, 183, 184
Hot Green Curry Paste, 201-203
Lemons
Chicken With Honey and Lemon,
151-52
Chicken With Preserved Lemons
and Olives, 154-55
Creole Dish from Chiclayo, 314-17
Crispy Thai Noodles, 240-42
Crullers, 330-31
Egg-and-Lemon Sauce, 138-39
Egyptian Grilled Chicken, 150-51
Fish in Coconut Milk, 313
Fish Kebobs, 159-60
Hot Pepper and Lemon-Lime
Sauce, 293-94
in Middle Eastern cuisines, 137
Preserved Lemons, 139-40
Tahini, 137-38
Lentils, 22
Dal and Cabbage, 252-53
Lentil Soup, 135-36
Lentil Soup, 135-36
Lima beans, dried
Dried Bean, Fresh Vegetable, and
Fruit Casserole, 100-101
Limes
Charcoal-grilled Fish in Ti Leaves,
234-35
Chicken Kebobs, 231-32
Crispy Thai Noodles, 240-42
Fish in Coconut Milk, 313
Fish Marinated in Lime, 194-95
Guacamole, 290-91
Hot Green Curry Paste, 201-203
Hot Pepper and Lemon-Lime
Sauce, 293-94
Linzertorte, 116-18
Lion's Head, 220-21
Little Meat-filled Turnovers,
281-83
Lomi Lomi Salmon, 193-94
Luau, 259
Breadfruit Purée (Poi), 258
Coconut Pudding, 261-62
lamb for a luau, 211

Macadamia Nut Pie, 263-64
Mackerel, Stuffed, 158-59
Main dishes, 66-88, 141-63,
211-44, 295-317
in Asian and Pacific Island cui-
sines, 211-12
Basted Herb-and-Spice Chicken,
152-53
Beef Stew in Pumpkin, 296-98
Boiled Beef, 69-70
Charcoal-grilled Fish in Ti Leaves,
234-35
cheese pizza, variations, 79
Chicken and Beef Stew, 228-29
Chicken in Green Sauce, 232-33
Chicken Kebobs, 231-32
Chicken Kiev, 83-84
Chicken Paprika, 82-83
Chicken With Honey and Lemon,
151-52
Chicken With Preserved Lemons
and Olives, 154-55
Chili, 298-300
Chorizo, 79-80
Creole Dish from Chiclayo, 314-17
Creole Sausages, 306-307
Crispy Thai Noodles, 240-42
Duck in Pomegranate Sauce,
156-57
Egyptian Grilled Chicken, 150-51
in European cuisines, 66-67
Felafel, 162-63
Filets de Sole à la Meunière, 86-87
Fish in Coconut Milk, 313
Fish Kebobs, 159-60
Fresh Fish Stew, 85-86
fried chicken nuggets with stir-
fried vegetables, 189
Fried Rice, 239-40
Fried Tortillas With Cheese, 317
Fried Tortillas With Meat,
304-306
Green Chili, 300-301
Ground Lamb Sandwiches, 149-50
Ground Meat With Peas, 222
Gumbo, 308-310
Jambalaya, 307-308
Korean Barbecue, 212-13
lamb for a luau, 211
Lamb "Pies," 143-44
Lamb Stew (Armenia, Turkey),
142-43
Lamb Stew (India), 223-25
in Latin American cuisines, 296
Lion's Head, 220-21

Meat With Yellow Split Peas and Herbs, 144-45
in Middle Eastern cuisines, 141-42
Mogul Chicken, 226-28
Moussaka, 160-61
Mu Shu Beef, 219-20
Oxtail Stew, 214-15
Paella, 80-82
Pepperoni, 76
Pepperoni Pizza, 77-79
Roasted Fruit-stuffed Chickens, 155-56
Roast Stuffed Chicken, 230
Sauerbraten, 67-68
Sole Aux Amandes, variation, 87
Spanish Omelet, 87-88
"Spareribs" in Black Bean Sauce, 225-26
Stuffed Mackerel, 158-59
Stuffed Whole Fish, 235-37
Sukiyaki, 215-17
Swedish Meatballs, 74-75
Tablecloth Stainer, 311-12
Tamales, 301-304
Tempura, 237-39
Teriyaki, 233-34
in the United States, 295-96
Veal Stew, 71-73
Veal With Apples and Prunes, 70-71
Vegetable and Lamb Couscous, 146-48
Vegetable Sushi, 243
Malanga, 314, 318
Mancha Manteles, 311-12
Mangos
Coconut Rice Pudding With Mangos, 262-63
Poe, 260-61
Manioc meal, 318, 325
Marinated Mushrooms, 52-53
Masa harina, 22-23, 318
Batter-fried Squash Blossoms, 278
Corn tortillas, 320-321
Tamales, 301-304
Masala, 23, 180, 222. See also Garam masala.
Meal patterns
Armenia, 124
Austria, 41
China, 182, 187, 212
Denmark, 45-46
France, 38-39
Germany, 40
Greece, 124

Hungary, 42
India, 180-81
Indonesia, 184, 212
Italy, 36-37
Japan, 185, 187
Latin American, 296
Lebanon, 129
Mexico, 272-73, 301, 305
Pennsylvania Dutch, 269
Portugal, 47, 66
Russia, 43-44
Spain, 38, 47, 66
Sweden, 47
United States, 295-96, 319
Vietnam, 187
Meat. See also Beef; Chicken; Fish; Lamb; Meatballs; and Veal.
in Asian and Pacific Island cuisines, 211-12
in European cuisines, 66-67
in Latin American cuisines, 296
in Middle Eastern cuisines, 141
in the United States, 295-96
Meat-and-dairy combinations, modifications for the kosher kitchen, 11-12. See also Modifying recipes for the kosher kitchen.
Meat-and-fish combinations, modifications for the kosher kitchen, 11-12. See also Modifying recipes for the kosher kitchen.
Meat-and-fruit combinations
Creole Dish from Chiclayo, 314-17
Duck in Pomegranate Sauce, 156-57
in European cuisines, 70
in Iranian cuisines, 126, 144
in Latin American cuisines, 296
in Moroccan cuisine, 126
Roasted Fruit-stuffed Chickens, 155-56
Tablecloth Stainer, 311-12
Veal With Apples and Prunes, 70-71
Meatballs
Lion's Head, 220-21
Spanish Sausage Meatballs, 53
Swedish Meatballs, 74-75
Meat-filled triangles, variation, 132
Meat With Yellow Split Peas and Herbs, 144-45

Mee Krob, 240-42
Mexico, 272-73, 276, 289, 318
  Bean Dip, 280
  Chayote and Squash Blossom
    Soup, 287-88
  Crullers, 330-31
  "dry soup," 276-77
  Fried Tortillas With Cheese, 317
  Fried Tortillas With Meat, 304-306
  Green Tomato Sauce, 291-92
  Guacamole, 290-91
  Refried Beans, 321
  Tablecloth Stainer, 311-12
  Tamales, 301-304
  Tortillas, 319-21
  Uncooked Red Sauce, 292-93
Mezze, 128
Middle East, 121ff.
Migas, 94
Mint, 23
  Herbed Yogurt Cheese, 129
  Lamb "Pies," 143-44
Mirin, 23. See also Rice wine.
  Sukiyaki, 215-17
  Teriyaki, 233-34
Miso, 23, 187, 199
Modifying recipes for the kosher
    kitchen, 11-12
  chicken livers, 12
  meat-and-dairy combinations, 11-
    12, 57, 74, 77-79, 82, 83, 137,
    141, 149, 152, 160, 169, 181,
    226, 254, 271, 334
  meat-and-fish combinations, 12,
    138, 184, 198, 217, 236
  pork, 12, 40, 59, 70, 100, 182, 183,
    184, 193, 197, 211, 228, 241,
    271, 272, 273, 286, 301, 307,
    309, 311, 321, 323, 327
  shellfish, 12, 50, 54, 159, 182, 183,
    211, 239, 241, 251, 270, 273,
    283, 285, 286, 313
Mogul Chicken, 226-28
Mole, 272
Monterey Jack cheese
  Bean Dip, 280
  Fried Tortillas With Cheese, 317
  in Mexican cooking, 279
  Nachos, 279
Morocco, 126, 164
  Basted Herb-and-Spice Chicken,
    152-53
  Chicken With Preserved Lemons
    and Olives, 154-55
  Preserved Lemons, 139-40

spiced lentil soup, 135-36
  tagine, 148
  Vegetable and Lamb Couscous,
    146-48
Moussaka, 160-61
Mousse au Chocolat, 107
Mozzarella cheese
  cheese pizza, variation, 79
  Creole Dish from Chiclayo, 314-17
  in Italian cuisine, 36
Muenster cheese
  Bean Dip, 280
  Cheese Triangles, 130-32
  Creole Dish from Chiclayo, 314-17
  Fried Tortillas With Cheese, 317
  Nachos, 279
Mushrooms
  Cream of Mushroom Soup, 58-59
  dried Chinese mushrooms, 19
  Herbed Mushrooms, 50-51
  Marinated Mushrooms, 52-53
  Moussaka, 160-61
  Pirozhki, 49-50
  Stir-fried Vegetables, 250
  Tempura, 237-39
  Veal Stew, 71-73
  Wild Rice Casserole, 326-27
Mushrooms, dried. See Dried Chi-
    nese mushrooms.
Mu Shu Beef, 219-20
Mu Shu Pancakes, 218-19
Mustard, 23-24

Nachos, 279
Nappa. See Chinese cabbage.
Nasi Goreng, 239-40
Navy beans, 24
  Baked Beans, 323-24
  Dried Bean, Fresh Vegetable, and
    Fruit Casserole, 100-101
Netherlands, 46
  Split Pea Soup, 59-60
New England, 269-70
  Baked Beans, 323-24
  Hot Blueberry Pudding, 334-37
  New England Fish Chowder,
    286-87
New England Fish Chowder, 286-87
New Mexico, 272
  Batter-fried Squash Blossoms, 278
  Green Chili, 300-301
  Sopaipillas, 331-32
New Orleans, 270-71
  Creole Sausages, 306-307

Gumbo, 308-310
Jambalaya, 307-308
Noodles. *See also* Cellophane noodles;
  Rice noodles; *and* Somen.
  in Asian Cuisines, 245
  in Chinese cuisine, 182
  Crispy Thai Noodles, 240-42
  in Japanese cuisine, 185
  White Noodles, 256-57
Norwegian Flat Potato Breads,
  332-34
Nuoc cham, 183
Nuoc mam, 183
Nut Rolls in Honey Syrup, 172-74
Nuts. *See individual nut listings.*

Oil, vegetable. *See* Vegetable oils.
Okra, 24, 309
  in Egyptian cuisine, 127
  Gumbo, 308-310
Olive oil, 24. *See also* Vegetable oils.
  Creole Dish from Chiclayo, 314-17
  in Middle Eastern cuisines, 137
Olives
  Chicken With Preserved Lemons
    and Olives, 154-55
  in Greek cuisine, 124-25
Onion and Tomato Relish, 208
Onions
  Creole Dish from Chiclayo, 314-17
  in Indian cuisine, 180
  Onion and Tomato Relish, 208,
    293
  Onion Soup, 57
  Spicy Vegetable Fritters, 188-89
  Tempura, 237-39
Onion Soup, 57
Orange ices, variation, 104
Oxtail Stew, 214-15

Pacific Islands. *See* Asia and the Pacific
  Islands; Hawaii; *and* Tahiti.
Paella, 37, 80-82
Palillo, 315
Pakoras, 188-89
Panir, 24
  Curd Cheese With Tomatoes and
    Peas, 253-55
Papayas
  Poe, 260-61
Paprika, 24
  Chicken Paprika, 82-83
  Cream of Mushroom Soup, 58-59

in Hungarian cuisine, 42
in Middle Eastern cuisines, 137
Parathas, 248-49
Parmesan cheese
  cheese pizza, variation, 79
  Eggplant Purée, variation, 169
  in Italian cuisine, 36
  Moussaka, 160-61
  risotto alla milanese, variation, 98
Parsley, 25
  Ground Lamb Sandwiches, 149-50
  Herbed Yogurt Cheese, 129
  Lamb "Pies," 143-44
  Meat With Yellow Split Peas and
    Herbs, 144-45
  Stuffed Mackerel, 158-59
Parsley, Chinese. *See* Coriander.
Pasta
  in Greek cuisine, 124
  in Italian cuisine, 36
Pastrami
  Rumaki, 193
Pastries
  in Austrian cuisine, 41
  Cannoli, 111-13
  Cheese Triangles, 130-32
  Chocolate-flecked Whipped Cream
    Pastries, 339-40
  Cottage Cheese "Strudel," 118-20
  Crullers, 330-31
  Custard-filled Pastries, 170-72
  in Danish cuisine, 45
  Dobostorte, 113-16
  in German cuisine, 40-41
  in Hungarian cuisine, 42
  Linzertorte, 116-18
  meat-filled triangles, variation,
    132
  in Middle Eastern cuisines, 170
  Nut Rolls in Honey Syrup,
    172-74
  Peach Pie With Pecan Crunch
    Topping, 337-38
  Pirozhki, 49-50
Pea beans. *See* Navy beans.
Peaches
  Beef Stew in Pumpkin, 296-98
  Coconut Rice Pudding With Man-
    gos, 262-63
  Fresh Fruit Chutney, 206-207
  Fresh Fruit Duck Sauce, 207-208
  Peach Pie With Pecan Crunch
    Topping, 337-38
Peach Pie With Pecan Crunch Top-
  ping, 337-38

Peanut butter
  Spicy Peanut Sauce, 231-32
Peanuts
  Coconut Rice Pudding With Mangos, 262-63
  Oxtail Stew, 214-15
  peanut soups in the Americas, 277
  Spicy Peanut Sauce, 231-32
Peas, green. See also Split peas.
  Curd Cheese With Tomatoes and Peas, 253-55
  Ground Meat With Peas, 222
  Vegetable Sushi, 243-44
Pea Soup, Split, 59-60
Pecans
  Cottage Cheese "Strudel," 118-20
  Peach Pie With Pecan Crunch Topping, 337-38
Pennsylvania Dutch, 268-69, 289
  Scrapple, 327-28
Peperoni Arrosto, 48
Pepper, black. See Black pepper.
Peppercorns, black, 14, 15
Pepper, crushed dried red. See Crushed dried red pepper.
Pepperoni, 76
Pepperoni Pizza, 77-79
Peppers. See also Capsicum; Cayenne pepper; Chilies, peeled green; Chili peppers; Crushed dried red pepper; Green peppers; and Peppers, sweet red or green.
  in Mexican cuisine, 272
  stuffed, Middle Eastern, 165
Peppers, Roasted Sweet Red, 48
Peppers, Sweet Red or Green, 25
  Roasted Sweet Red Peppers, 48
  Sofrito, 65
Peru, 273-74, 276, 318
  Creole Dish from Chiclayo, 314-17
Philippines, 184
  Chicken and Beef Stew, 228-29
  Coconut Cream, 205-206
  Coconut Milk, 203-205
  Deep-fried Vegetable Cakes, 251-52
  Oxtail Stew, 214-15
  Roast Stuffed Chicken, 230
Phyllo Dough, 25
  Cheese Triangles, 130-32
  Custard-filled Pastries, 170-72
  meat-filled triangles, variation, 132
  Nut Rolls in Honey Syrup, 172-74
Pickles. See also Kimchee.

Korean Pickled Vegetables, 209-210
  in Pennsylvania Dutch cuisine, 269, 289
Pignolia nuts. See Pine nuts.
Pilaf, 25, 164
  Burghul Pilaf for Meat Meals, 168
  Burghul Pilaf for Vegetarian or Dairy Meals, 167
Pimientos Asado, 48
Pineapples
  in Hawaiian cuisine, 186
  Poe, 260-61
  Tablecloth Stainer, 311-12
Pine nuts, 25
  Stuffed Mackerel, 158-59
Pink beans, 26. See also Pinto beans.
Pinto beans, 26
  Bean Dip, 280
  Chili, 298-300
Pirozhki, 49-50
Pita, 126, 162, 164
Pizza
  cheese pizza, variations, 79
  Pepperoni Pizza, 77-79
Plantains
  Creole Dish from Chiclayo, 314-17
  Fried Plantain Chips, 277
Poe, 260-61
Poi, 186
  Breadfruit Purée, 258
Poisson Cru, 194-95
Poland, 42-43, 64
  Pirozhki, 49-50
Pollock
  Fresh Fish Stew, 85-86
  New England Fish Chowder, 286-87
Pomegranate Sauce, Duck in, 156-57
Pork
  in Chinese cuisine, 181
  in German cuisine, 40
  substitutions for, 12, 182. See also Modifying recipes for the kosher kitchen.
Porkolt Csirke, 82-83
Portugal, 38, 47, 66, 273
  Flan, 104-105
  Fresh Fish Stew, 85-86
  Green Soup, 62-63
Potatoes, 26, 267, 274, 314, 318. See also Sweet potatoes, South American and Sweet potatoes, yams.
  Beef Stew in Pumpkin, 296-98
  Creole Dish from Chiclayo, 314-16

Norwegian Flat Potato Breads, 332-34
in Peruvian cuisine, 274, 318
Potato-stuffed Whole-wheat Breads, 248-49
South American sweet potatoes, 26, 297
Spanish Omelet, 87-88
Potato-stuffed Whole-wheat Breads, 248-49
Preserved Lemons, 139-40
Prunes
Roasted Fruit-stuffed Chickens, 155-56
Veal With Apples and Prunes, 70-71
Puffed Whole-wheat Breads, 247-48
Pumpkin. See also Squash.
Beef Stew in Pumpkin, 296-98
Puris, 247-48

Quince
Meat With Yellow Split Peas and Herbs, 144-45

Radish, hot. See Hot turnip and hot radish.
Red peppers. See also Capsicum; Cayenne pepper; Chili peppers; Crushed dried red pepper; and Paprika.
Peppers, Sweet Red or Green, 25
Roasted Sweet Red Peppers, 48
Red Sauce, Uncooked, 292-93
Red snapper
Fresh Fish Stew, 85-86
Refried Beans, 321
Regional cooking
China, 179, 181
Germany, 40
Italy, 36
Spain, 37
Union of Soviet Socialist Republics, 43-44
United States of America, 267-72, 296
Relishes. See Condiments and Sauces.
Rice, glutinous. See Glutinous rice.
Rice. See also Glutinous rice; Rice noodles; and Wild rice.
in Asian cuisines, 212, 245
in Brazilian cuisine, 273
in Chinese cuisine, 182
Fried Rice, 239-40

in Indian cuisine, 180
in Indonesian cuisine, 184
in Iranian cuisine, 126, 164
in Italian cuisine, 36, 97
Jambalaya, 307-308
in Japanese cuisine, 185
in Korean cuisine, 185
Paella, 80-82
Risotto, 97
risotto alla milanese, variation, 98
in Thai cuisine, 183
Vegetable Sushi, 243-44
wine, 27
Yellow Rice, 256
Rice noodles, 26-27
Crispy Thai Noodles, 240-42
Rice wine, 27. See also Mirin.
Ricotta cheese
Cannoli, 111-13
Rijsttafel, 46, 184
Risotto, 97-98
Risotto alla milanese, variation, 98
Roasted Fruit-stuffed Chickens, 155-56
Roasted Sweet Red Peppers, 48
Roast Stuffed Chicken, 230
Roux, 308-309
Rumaki, 193
Russia, 43-44, 64. See also Union of Soviet Socialist Republics.
Applesauce, 99-100
aristocracy, cuisine of, 43-44
Black Bread, 90-92
peasant cuisine, 44
Pirozhki, 49-50

Saffron, 27
Mogul Chicken, 226-28
Salads
Middle Eastern, 164-65
Moroccan, 164
Salmon
Charcoal-grilled Fish in Ti Leaves, 234-35
Lomi Lomi Salmon, 193-94
Salmon With Cream Dressing, 285-86
Salmon With Cream Dressing, 285-86
Salsa Cruda, 292-93
Salsa de Tomatillo, 291-92
Salted black beans. See Fermented black beans.
Salted fermented black beans. See Fermented black beans.

Sashimi, 243
Saté, 231
Sauce Base (Sofrito), 65
Sauces. *See also* Condiments and Sauces; Khoresh; *and* Soy sauce.
  Broccoli With Garlic Sauce, 98-99
  in French cuisine, 39, 64
  garlic-and-vinegar sauce, 251
  in Italian cuisine, 63-64
  in Portuguese cuisine, 64
  Salmon With Cream Dressing, 285-86
  Sofrito, 65
  in Spanish cuisine, 64
  Spicy Peanut Sauce, 231-32
  in Vietnamese cuisine, 183
Sauerbraten, 67-68
Scallions (green onions, spring onions), 27
  Jambalaya, 307-308
  Meat With Yellow Split Peas and Herbs, 144-45
  scallion "flowers," 241
Scrapple, 327-28
Sea bass
  Creole Dish from Chiclayo, 314-17
  Stuffed Whole Fish, 235-37
Seafood. *See also* Fish *and* Shellfish.
  in Asian and Pacific Islands cuisines, 211
  in Brazilian cuisine, 273
  in Chinese cuisine, 182
  in Danish cuisine, 45
  in Greek cuisine, 125
  in Italian cuisine, 36
  in Japanese cuisine, 185
  in Portuguese cuisine, 38
  in Spanish cuisine, 37
  in Swedish cuisine, 45
Seasonings. *See also* Herbs; Ingredients used in international cooking; *and* Spices.
  in Asian cuisines, 200
  Indian Spice Blend, 200-201
  in Vietnamese cuisine, 183
Seaweed, dried, 27
  Japanese Soup Stock, 198
Selecting ingredients, 12
Semolina, 164, 170. *See also* Couscous.
Sesame oil, 28. *See also* Vegetable oils.
Sesame seeds, 28
  Armenian Thin Bread, 165-67
  Korean Barbecue, 212-13
  in Korean cuisine, 185

Tahini, 137-38
  Vegetable Sushi, 243-44
Seviche, 274. *See also* Fish Marinated in Lime.
Shallots, 28
  Hot Green Curry Paste, 201-203
  Stuffed Whole Fish, 235-37
  in Vietnamese cuisine, 183
Shellfish. *See also* Modifying recipes for the kosher kitchen.
  substitutions for, 12, 182
Shish kebob, 125
Shoyu. *See* Soy sauce.
Side dishes, 89-101, 164-69, 245-58, 318-28. *See also* Breads.
  Applesauce, 99-100
  in Asian and Pacific Island cuisines, 245
  Baked Beans, 323-24
  Black Beans With Tomatoes, 322-23
  Breadfruit Purée, 258
  Broccoli With Garlic Sauce, 98-99
  Burghul Pilaf for Meat Meals, 168
  Burghul Pilaf for Vegetarian or Dairy Meals, 167
  Curd Cheese With Tomatoes and Peas, 253-55
  Dal and Cabbage, 252-53
  Deep-fried Vegetable Cakes, 251-52
  Dried Bean, Fresh Vegetable, and Fruit Casserole, 100-101
  Eggplant Purée, 168-69
  in European cuisines, 89-90
  Flat Whole-Wheat Breads, 246-47
  grits, 271
  in Middle Eastern cuisines, 164-65
  Potato-stuffed Whole-wheat Breads, 248-49
  Refried Beans, 321
  Risotto, 97-98
  risotto alla milanese, variation, 98
  Scrapple, 327-28
  Spätzle, 95-96
  Stir-fried Vegetables, 250
  Toasted Cassava, 325
  White Noodles, 256-57
  Wild Rice Casserole, 326-27
  Yellow Rice, 256
Simplified Charlotte Russe, 109-110
Smen, 152
Smoked "Spareribs," 192
Smorgasbord
  Danish (smörrebröd), 45, 93

Swedish, 44-45, 47
Smörrebröd Bread, 93-94
Snow peas
  Stir-fried Vegetables, 250
Sofrito, 64, 65
Sole
  Filets de Sole à la Meunière, 86-87
  Fish in Coconut Milk, 313
  Fish Marinated in Lime, 194-95
  Sole Aux Amandes, variation, 87
  Sukiyaki, variation, 217
  Tempura, 237-39
  Teriyaki, 233-34
Sole Aux Amandes, variation, 87
Somen, 28, 256-57
Sopaipillas, 331-32
Soufflé de Grand Marnier, 105-106
Soups, 47, 55-63, 128, 134-36, 187,
    197-99, 276-77, 286-88
  in Asian cuisines, 187
  Bean Paste Soup (Miso), 199
  Boiled Beef, 69-70
  Chayote and Squash Blossom
    Soup, 287-88
  congee, 187
  Cream of Mushroom Soup, 58-59
  Cucumber-Yogurt Soup, 134-35
  Dashi, 19, 198
  "dry soup," 276-77
  in European cuisines, 47
  Gazpacho, 60-61
  Green Soup, 62-63
  Japanese Soup Stock, 198
  in Latin American cuisines, 276-77
  Lentil Soup, 135-36
  in Middle Eastern cuisines, 128
  New England Fish Chowder,
    286-87
  Onion Soup, 57
  pho, 187
  Spanish sausage meatballs in broth,
    53
  Split Pea Soup, 59-60
  in the United States, 276
  Vegetarian Broth, 55-56
  Wonton Soup, 197
Sour cream, 28
  Cream of Mushroom Soup,
    58-59
  in European cuisines, 64
  Fried Tortillas With Cheese, 317
  Pirozhki, 49-50
South American sweet potatoes. See
    Sweet potatoes, South Amer-
    ican.

Southeastern United States, 271
  Deviled Tuna, 283-84
Soy sauce, 28-29
  Chinese, 29
  Indonesian, 29
  Japanese, 29
Spain, 37-38, 47, 64, 66-67, 270, 272,
    274
  Chorizo, 79-80
  Fish With Garlic and Sherry, 54
  Flan, 104-105
  Garlic Croutons, 94-95
  Gazpacho, 60-61
  Ladyfingers, 108-109
  Paella, 80-82
  Roasted Sweet Red Peppers, 48
  Sauce Base (Sofrito), 65
  Spanish Omelet, 87-88
  Spanish Sausage Meatballs, 53
Spanish Omelet, 87-88
Spanish Sausage Meatballs, 53
"Spareribs"
  Smoked "Spareribs," 192
  "Spareribs" in Black Bean Sauce,
    225-26
"Spareribs" in Black Bean Sauce,
    225-26
Spätzle, 40, 89, 95-96
Spices. See Chili peppers; Chili pow-
    der; Ingredients used in in-
    ternational cooking; Masala;
    and listings under specific spices.
  in Armenian cuisine, 124
  Basted Herb-and-Spice Chicken,
    152-53
  Broiled Marinated Chicken, 190-91
  in Cajun cuisine, 271
  Chicken With Preserved Lemons
    and Olives, 154-55
  in Creole cuisine, 270-71
  Creole Sausages, 306-307
  Curd Cheese With Tomatoes and
    Peas, 253-55
  Felafel, 162-63
  Fresh Fruit Chutney, 206-207
  Green Tomato Sauce, 291-92
  Ground Meat With Peas, 222
  Hot Pepper-and-Vinegar Sauce,
    294-95
  in Indian cuisine, 179, 180
  Indian Spice Blend, 200-201
  in Indonesian cuisine, 184
  Lamb Stew, 223-25
  Mogul Chicken, 226-28
  in Moroccan cuisine, 126

Spicy Vegetable Fritters, 188-89
Stuffed Mackerel, 158-59
Tablecloth Stainer, 311-12
in Thai Cuisine, 179, 183
Vegetable and Lamb Couscous, 146-48
Yellow Rice, 256
Spicy Peanut Sauce, 231-32
Spicy Vegetable Fritters, 188-89
Split Peas
   Meat With Yellow Split Peas and Herbs, 144-45
   Split Pea Soup, 59-60
Split Pea Soup, 59-60
Squash. *See also* Squash blossoms.
   Beef Stew in Pumpkin, 296-98
   Chayote and Squash Blossom Soup, 287-88
   Deep-fried Vegetable Cakes, 251-52
   in New England cuisine, 269
Squash blossoms, 29
   Batter-fried Squash Blossoms, 278
   Chayote and Squash Blossom Soup, 287-88
Stewing beef. *See* Beef, stewing.
Stews
   Beef Stew in Pumpkin, 296-98
   Chicken and Beef Stew, 228-29
   in Chinese cuisine, 181-82
   in European cuisines, 66-67
   Fresh Fish Stew, 85-86
   Gumbo, 308-310
   Lamb Stew, (Armenia, Turkey), 142-43
   Lamb Stew (India), 223-25
   in Latin American cuisines, 296
   Meat With Yellow Split Peas and Herbs, 144-45
   Oxtail Stew, 214-15
   Tablecloth Stainer, 311-12
   Veal Stew, 71-73
   Vegetable and Lamb Couscous, 146-48
Stir-fried Vegetables, 250
Stir-frying, 181, 183, 245
   Stir-fried Vegetables, 250
Strawberry Ices, Fresh, 102-104
"Strudel," Cottage Cheese, 118-20
Stuffed Mackerel, 158-59
Stuffed Whole Fish, 235-37
Sukiyaki, 215-17
Sushi, Vegetable, 243-44
Sweden, 44-45, 66
   Swedish Meatballs, 74-75

Swedish Meatballs, 74-75
Sweet potatoes, South American. *See also* Batatas; Boniato; Malanga; *and* Potatoes.
   Beef Stew in Pumpkin, 296-98
   Creole Dish from Chiclayo, 314-17
Sweet potatoes, yams. *See also* Potatoes.
   Deep-fried Vegetable Cakes, 251-52
   Tablecloth Stainer, 311-12
   Vegetable and Lamb Couscous, 146-48
Swiss cheese
   Cheese Triangles, 130-32
   Fried Tortillas With Cheese, 317
   Nachos, 279
   Onion Soup, 57
Syria, 127
   Lamb "Pies," 143-44
Szechwan radish. *See* Hot turnip and hot radish.
Szechwan turnip. *See* Hot turnip and hot radish.

Tablecloth Stainer, 311-12
Tacos, 305
Tagine, 148
Tahina. *See* Tahini.
Tahini, 137-38
Tahiti, 186, 187, 211, 212
   Charcoal-grilled Fish in Ti Leaves, 234-35
   Coconut Cream, 205-206
   Coconut Milk, 203-205
   Fish Marinated in Lime, 194-95
   Poe, 260-61
   Whipped Coconut Cream, 259-60
Tamales, 301-304
Tapas, 47, 48, 54, 94
Tea
   in Chinese cuisine, 182
   in Indian cuisine, 181
   in Iranian cuisine, 126
   in Moroccan cuisine, 126
   in Russian cuisine, 44
   Smoked "Spareribs," 192
Tempura, 188, 237-39
Teriyaki, 233-34
Texas, 271, 296
   Chili, 298-300
Tex-Mex cuisine, 271
   Nachos, 279

Thailand, 183
  Chicken in Green Sauce, 232-33
  Coconut Cream, 205-206
  Coconut Milk, 203-205
  Coconut Rice Pudding With Mangos, 262-63
  Crispy Thai Noodles, 240-42
  curries, 212, 232
  Hot Green Curry Paste, 201-203
  hot red curry paste, 202
Tiger lily buds (golden needles), 29
  Mu Shu Beef, 219-20
  Stuffed Whole Fish, 235-37
Tikka Murg, 190-91
Ti leaves, 29. See also Banana leaves.
  Charcoal-grilled Fish in Ti Leaves, 234-35
Toasted Cassava, 325
Tofu, 29-30
  Bean Paste Soup, 199
  in Chinese cuisine, 182
  Crispy Thai Noodles, 240-42
  in Japanese cuisine, 185
  Sukiyaki, 215-17
  Vegetable Sushi, 243-44
Tomatillo, 30
  Green Chili, 300-301
  Green Tomato Sauce, 291-92
Tomatoes. See also Tomatillo.
  Beef Stew in Pumpkin, 296-98
  Black Beans With Tomatoes, 322-23
  Chicken Paprika, 82-83
  Chili, 298-300
  Curd Cheese With Tomatoes and Peas, 253-55
  Fish in Coconut Milk, 313
  Fresh Fish Stew, 85-86
  Gazpacho, 60-61
  Green Chili, 300-301
  Ground Lamb Sandwiches, 149-50
  Ground Meat With Peas, 222
  how to peel, 61
  in Italian cuisine, 35-36
  Lamb "Pies," 143-44
  Lamb Stew (Armenia, Turkey), 142-43
  Lamb Stew (India), 223-25
  Lentil Soup, 135-36
  Lomi Lomi Salmon, 193-94
  Moussaka, 160-61
  Onion and Tomato Relish, 208
  Pepperoni Pizza and variations, 77-79
  Sauce Base, 65

Tablecloth Stainer, 311-12
  Uncooked Red Sauce, 292-93
Tomatoes and Peas With Spices, 254
Tongue in Split Pea Soup, 59-60
Tortillas, 319-321. See also Spanish Omelet.
  Fried Tortillas With Cheese, 317
  Fried Tortillas With Meat, 304-306
  Nachos, 279
Tostadas
  Tostadas con Carne, 304-306
  Tostadas con Queso, 317
Tree ears (wood ears), 30
  Mu Shu Beef, 219-20
  Stuffed Whole Fish, 235-37
Tropical fruit. See Mangos; Papayas; Pineapples; and Plantains.
Turkey, 125
  Apricot Cream Parfait, 174-75
  Burghul Pilaf for Meat Meals, 168
  Burghul Pilaf for Vegetarian or Dairy Meals, 167
  Cheese Triangles, 130-32
  Cold Chicken With Nut Topping, 132-34
  Cucumber-Yogurt Soup, 134-35
  Custard-filled Pastries, 170-72
  Egg-and-Lemon Sauce, 138-39
  Eggplant Purée, 168-69
  Fish Kebobs, 159-60
  Ground Lamb Sandwiches, 149-50
  Lamb "Pies," 143-44
  Lamb Stew, 142-43
  meat-filled triangles, variation, 132
  Moussaka, 160-61
  Nut Rolls in Honey Syrup, 172-74
  Stuffed Mackerel, 158-59
Turmeric, 30
Turnip, hot. See Hot turnip and hot radish.
Turnip Pickles, 209
Tyropitta, 130-32

Ukraine, 43, 44. See also Union of Soviet Socialist Republics.
  Black Bread, 90-92
  Chicken Kiev, 83-84
Uncooked Red Sauce, 292-93
Union of Soviet Socialist Republics, 43-44. See also Russia and Ukraine.
United States of America, 267, 268-72, 276, 289, 296, 318, 319,

329. *See also* New England;
New Mexico; New Orleans;
Pennsylvania Dutch; South-
eastern United States; *and*
Texas.
Baked Beans, 323-24
Batter-fried Squash Blossoms, 278
Chili, 298-300
Chocolate-flecked Whipped
Cream Pastries, 339-40
Creole Sausages, 306-307
Deviled Tuna, 283-84
Green Chili, 300-301
Gumbo, 308-310
Hot Blueberry Pudding, 334-37
Jambalaya, 307-308
Nachos, 279
New England Fish Chowder,
286-87
Norwegian Flat Potato Breads,
332-34
Peach Pie With Pecan Crunch
Topping, 337-38
Salmon With Cream Dressing,
285-86
Scrapple, 327-28
Sopaipillas, 331-32
Wild Rice Casserole, 326-27

Veal
Beef Stew in Pumpkin, 296-98
in European cuisines, 66
Ground Meat With Peas, 222
Meat With Yellow Split Peas and
Herbs, 144-45
Scrapple, 327-28
Smoked "Spareribs," 192
"Spareribs" in Black Bean Sauce,
225-26
Swedish Meatballs, 74-75
Tablecloth Strainer, 311-12
Veal Stew, 71-73
Veal With Apples and Prunes,
70-71
Vegetable and Lamb Couscous,
146-48
Veal Stew, 71-73
Veal With Apples and Prunes, 70-71
Vegetable and Lamb Couscous,
146-48
Vegetable oils, 30-31. *See also* Olive
oil *and* Sesame oil.
Vegetables. *See also* Potatoes; Soups;
and listings under specific vegetables.

Baked Beans, 323-24
Batter-fried Squash Blossoms, 278
Bean Dip, 280
Beef Stew in Pumpkin, 296-98
Black Beans With Tomatoes,
322-23
Broccoli With Garlic Sauce, 98-99
Creole Dish from Chiclayo, 314-17
Curd Cheese With Tomatoes and
Peas, 253-55
Dal and Cabbage, 252-53
Deep-fried Vegetable Cakes,
251-52
Dried Bean, Fresh Vegetable, and
Fruit Casserole, 100-101
Eggplant Pureé, 168-69
in European cuisines, 89-90
Felafel, 162-63
Green Tomato Sauce, 291-92
Herbed Mushrooms, 50-51
in Indian cuisine, 245
in Korean cuisine, 209
Korean Pickled Vegetables (Kim-
chee), 209-210
Lion's Head, 220-21
Marinated Mushrooms, 52-53
in Middle Eastern cuisines, 165
Moussaka, 160-61
Onion and Tomato Relish, 208
in Pennsylvania Dutch cuisine, 269
Pirozhki, 49-50
Refried Beans, 321
Roasted Sweet Red Peppers, 48
Spanish Omelet, 87-88
Spicy Vegetable Fritters, 188-89
Stir-fried Vegetables, 250
stuffed vegetables, Middle East-
ern, 165
Sukiyaki, 215-17
taro leaves, 186
Tempura, 237-39
Toasted Cassava, 325
Tomatoes and Peas With Spices,
254
Uncooked Red Sauce, 292-93
Vegetable and Lamb Couscous,
146-48
Vegetable Sushi, 243-44
in Vietnamese cuisine, 183
Wild Rice Casserole, 326-27
Vegetable Sushi, 243-44
Vegetarian Broth, 55-56
Vegetarian burghul pilaf, 167
Vegetarian Indian cuisine, 180
Vegetarian lentil soup, 135-36

Vietnam, 182-83, 187
    Coconut Cream, 205-206
    Coconut Milk, 203-205
    pho, 187
    rice pudding, 262
    Stuffed Whole Fish, 235-37
Vodka in Russian cuisine, 44

Walnuts
    Cottage Cheese "Strudel," 118-20
    Duck in Pomegranate Sauce,
        156-57
    Nut Rolls in Honey Syrup, 172-74
    Stuffed Mackerel, 158-59
Wasabi paste, 31
    White Noodles, 256-57
Water chestnuts, 31
    Lion's Head, 220-21
    Rumaki, 193
Wiener Tafelspitz, 69-70
Whipped Coconut Cream, 259-60
Whitefish
    Japanese Soup Stock, 198
White Noodles (Somen), 256-57
Whiting
    Charcoal-grilled Fish in Ti Leaves,
        234-35
Wild rice, 267, 326
Wild Rice Casserole, 326-27
Wine
    in French cuisine, 38-39
    in German cuisine, 40

    in Italian cuisine, 36
    in Portuguese cuisine, 38
    in Spanish cuisine, 37-38
Wontons
    in Chinese cuisine, 197
    Fried Wontons, 195-96
    Wonton Soup, 197
    wonton wrappers, 31
Wonton Soup, 197
Wonton wrappers, 31
Wood ears. *See* Tree ears.

Yams. *See* Potatoes *and* Sweet pota-
        toes, yams.
Yellow Rice, 256
Yogurt, 31
    as a beverage, 126, 136-37, 181
    Cucumber-Yogurt Soup,
        134-35
    Curd Cheese With Tomatoes and
        Peas, 253-55
    Felafel, 162-63
    Herbed Yogurt Cheese, 129
    in Indian cuisine, 180, 181
    in Middle Eastern cuisines,
        136-37

Zakuska, 43-44

About the Author

Upon graduating from the College of Home Economics at Cornell University in 1961, Betty S. Goldberg's fervent interest in cooking progressed from working casually with cookbook and magazine recipes to extensive entertaining to eventually creating wonderful dishes of her own. She was soon planning and executing banquets for as many as 120 people, and before long she was teaching classes in Jewish, Mexican, and Chinese cooking.

The success of Mrs. Goldberg's classes led to the publication of three books on Chinese cuisine: *Chinese Banquet, Goldberg Style* (1977), *Chinese Cooking, Goldberg Style* (1981), and *Chinese Kosher Cooking* (1984). In *International Cooking for the Kosher Home* she continues the process she initiated with great success in *Chinese Kosher Cooking*, namely, converting authentic nonkosher recipes into splendid kosher dishes.

Betty S. Goldberg resides in Woodbridge, Connecticut, with her husband and four children.

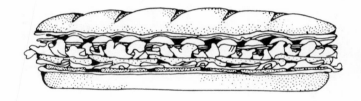